Essential
Social Psychology

SECOND EDITION

Essential Social Psychology

SECOND EDITION

Richard J. Crisp and Rhiannon N. Turner

Los Angeles | London | New Delhi
Singapore | Washington DC

First published 2007 (reprinted 2008, 2009)
Second edition first published 2010

SAGE Publications Ltd
1 Oliver's Yard
55 City Road
London EC1Y 1SP

SAGE Publications Inc.
2455 Teller Road
Thousand Oaks, California 91320

SAGE Publications India Pvt Ltd
B 1/I 1 Mohan Cooperative Industrial Area
Mathura Road
New Delhi 110 044

SAGE Publications Asia-Pacific Pte Ltd
33 Pekin Street #02-01
Far East Square
Singapore 048763

Library of Congress Control Number: 2009934125

British Library Cataloguing in Publication data

A catalogue record for this book is available from
the British Library

ISBN 978-1-84920-385-2
ISBN 978-1-84920-386-9 (pbk)

Typeset by C&M Digitals (P) Ltd, Chennai, India
Printed in Great Britain by TJ International Ltd, Padstow, Cornwall
Printed on paper from sustainable resources

Mixed Sources
Product group from well-managed
forests and other controlled sources
www.fsc.org Cert no. SGS-COC-2482
© 1996 Forest Stewardship Council
FSC

Contents

To Val and John, Lynne and Geoff

Preface to the Second Edition

(OR WHY WE HAD ANOTHER GO)

It's always nice when people say you've done a good job.

We could not have been happier with the reception to the first edition of *Essential Social Psychology*. Loads of you loved the fresh, new textbook feel we tried to create. It seems our idea to present those essential elements of social psychology in short, clear, accessible chapters was just what you were after. So, before we say anything else, thanks for all the positive feedback!

But … we don't just listen to the good stuff. We know a lot of you wanted a little more, a little restructuring, and a few tweaks here and there. We want *Essentials* to be just the way you want it. So here it is, the second edition.

All the good bits from the first edition are still here: short, lively chapters covering the classic and contemporary studies, plenty of illustrations, an extensive glossary and those memory maps to help you remember it all. But we've made it *bigger* (two more chapters), *better* (new debates sections at the end of each chapter) and *bang* up-to-date (even more contemporary stuff). And if you check out the newly designed companion website (**www.uk.sagepub.com/crispandturner2/**) you'll find a bunch of new and extended multiple choice questions, and a lot more beside.

We still think the first edition preface is a pretty good intro to the book, so please take a look at that next. Otherwise that's about it for now. We're really glad so many of you liked the first edition. We hope you'll all *love* this second edition.

Rich and Rhiannon
July 2009
Canterbury and Leeds

Preface to the First Edition

Five years ago in Birmingham one of us first came up with the idea for this book. After many revisions and re-writes, discussion and deliberations (not to mention the fortuitous relocation of the other author to the West Midlands) … here it is. There are loads of social psych textbooks out there though. What's different about this one? Why did we write this book, and, more to the point, why on earth should you read it?

Well, the thing about most social psychology textbooks is that they're quite simply enormous. In our own studies we've worked our way through those huge volumes. So we began to think to ourselves: do you need all this information, especially for your first course in social psychology? Now, don't get us wrong, there are many great social psychology textbooks out there and you'll definitely need them if you choose to study social psychology in more depth later in your studies. But do you need to know all the intricacies and complexities of social psychology at this point in your lives? We think not. What you *really* need is an easy, accessible, enjoyable introduction to the wonderful world of social psychology. Something that'll be interesting and a jolly good read, but will also get you through your exams. So we've stripped down social psychology, got it down to its bones, and laid it bare for you to see. We could have called this *Naked Social Psychology*, but that sounds a bit wrong so we decided to call it *Essentials*.

So what you've got here are short chapters, easily readable in a few hours. Each chapter gives you the basics, what you *really* need to know to pass your first social psychology exam. We've got plenty of figures and illustrations to help you along, and we try to show throughout how social psychology is relevant to everyday life. We're particularly proud of the memory maps. One of us went a bit crazy during our undergraduate finals and wrote out all our revision notes as one big memory map on our college room wall. OK, so that was a bit sad (and we won't mention the 'knowledge mask'), but the point is that they really helped in remembering all those bits and pieces that come together to form each topic. We hope you find them useful too.

Anyway, enough preamble. What follows here is a brief introduction to what social psychology was, and what it is, how it's done, and how all this is covered in the chapters that follow. We'd just like to end with a quick 'thank you' for picking us up in the bookstore to read this first page. Please give us a good home, and we'll try to entertain and inform you during your introduction to social psychology.

Rich and Rhiannon
May 2006
Birmingham

A Guided Tour

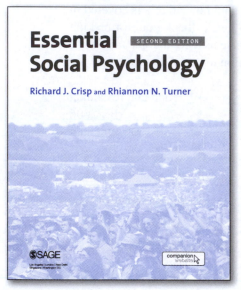

Welcome to the Guided Tour for *Essential Social Psychology, Second Edition*. This short tour will take you through the main sections and special features of the book.

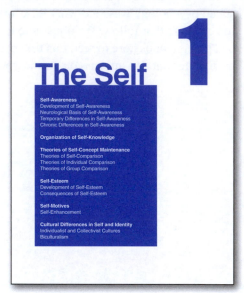

A clear list of contents is provided for each chapter.

Text boxes elaborate on key concepts or discuss cutting edge developments in the field.

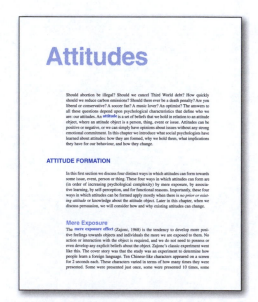

Clear headings and subheadings help structure the topics covered in each chapter. Key words and terms are highlighted throughout and you will find a Glossary at the end of the book.

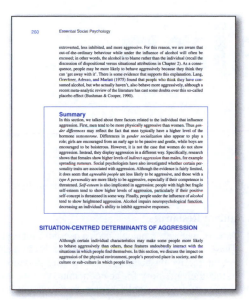

Summary text boxes are provided at key stages throughout chapters to help you consolidate what you have learned.

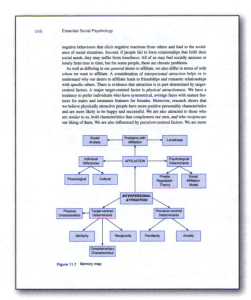

Memory maps provide a graphical summary of each chapter to help revision of key concepts and how they inter-relate.

End of chapter exercises are provided for both individual and class study.

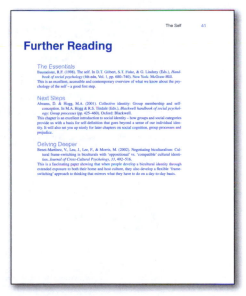

Structured key readings with commentaries help direct further study.

Companion Website

Be sure to visit the companion website at http://www.uk.sagepub.com/crispandturner2/ to find a range of teaching and learning material for both lecturers and students including:

1. Lecturer Resources

(a) A password-protected lecturers' area with a full set of PowerPoint lecture slides to accompany each chapter.

(b) A multiple choice test bank.

(c) Animated memory maps.

2. Student Resources

(a) A set of interactive multiple choice questions for each chapter. These interactive tests provide detailed feedback on answers.

(b) An interactive flashcard glossary, giving students a chance to test their memory for key concepts.

(c) A bank of downloadable chapters from existing Sage books to help students develop their study skills.

(d) Downloadable, blank memory maps to help revision of key concepts and how they inter-relate.

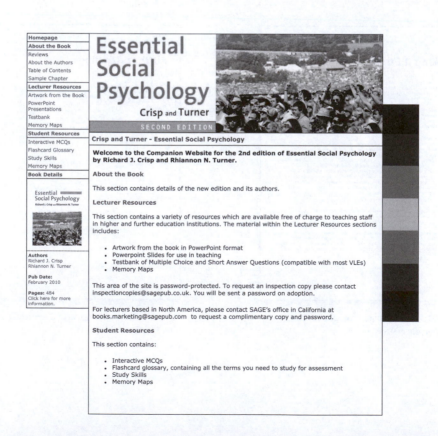

About the Authors

Richard Crisp is Professor of Psychology and Head of the School of Psychology at the University of Kent. He read Experimental Psychology at the University of Oxford and studied for his PhD at Cardiff University. He has over 70 publications on the full range of topics that comprise social psychology: from studies into the formation and reduction of prejudice, to the self and identity processes involved in interpersonal relations; from studies of mere exposure and attitude formation, through to studies of multiple social categorization. For this work he has received prestigious awards from professional bodies including the British Psychology Society's award for Outstanding Doctoral Research Contributions to Psychology (2000), the Society for the Psychological Study of Social Issues Louise Kidder Early Career Award (2003) and the British Psychological Society's Spearman Medal (2006). He is an Associate Editor at the *Journal of Experimental Social Psychology* and in 2009 he was elected an Academician of the Academy of Social Sciences.

Rhiannon Turner is a Lecturer in Social Psychology at the University of Leeds. She did her undergraduate degree at Cardiff University, her MSc at the University of Kent, and her D.Phil. at the University of Oxford. Her primary research interest is intergroup relations, focusing specifically on dimensions, mediators and consequences of intergroup contact. This research has been funded by grants from the Economic and Social Research Council, the Leverhulme Trust, and the British Academy. She is winner of the British Psychological Society's award for Outstanding Doctoral Research Contributions to Psychology (2007), and the Foundation for Personality and Social Psychology's Robert B. Cialdini Award (2007) for contributions to the field of research in social psychological phenomena through the use of field research methods.

Publisher's Acknowledgements

The authors and publishers wish to thank the following for the permission to use copyright material:

We thank the American Psychological Society for granting us permission to use material from the following articles:

Cohn, E.G. & Rotton, J. (1997). Assault as a function of time and temperature: A moderator-variable time-series analysis. *Journal of Personality and Social Psychology*, *72*, 1322–1334. (Figure 9.6). Adapted with permission.

Bushman, B.J. & Baumeister, R.F. (1998). Threatened egotism, narcissism, self-esteem, and direct and displaced aggression: Does self-love or self-hate lead to violence? *Journal of Personality and Social Psychology*, *75*, 219–229. (Figure 1.7). Adapted with permission.

Bargh, J.A., Chen, M., & Burrows, L. (1996). The automaticity of social behavior: Direct effects of trait concept and stereotype activation on action. *Journal of Personality and Social Psychology*, *71*, 230–244. (Text Box 3.2). Adapted with permission.

Isen, A.M., Clark, M., & Schwartz, M. (1976). Duration of the effect of good mood on helping: 'Footprints on the sand of time'. *Journal of Personality and Social Psychology*, *34*, 385–393. Figure 1, p. 387. (Figure 10.6). Adapted with permission.

Milgram, S. (1963). Behavioral study of obedience. *Journal of Abnormal and Social Psychology*, *67*, 371–378. (Figure 6.7). Adapted with permission.

Saegert, S., Swap, W., & Zajonc, R. (1973). Exposure, context and interpersonal attraction. *Journal of Personality and Social Psychology*, *25*, 234–242. (Figure 11.6). Adapted with permission.

Schriesheim, C.A., Tepper, B.J., & Tetrault, L.A. (1994). Least preferred co-worker score, situational control, and leadership effectiveness: A meta-analysis of contingency model performance predictions. *Journal of Applied Psychology*, *79*, 561–573. (Figure 5.7). Adapted with permission.

Zajonc, R.B. (1968). Attitudinal effects of mere exposure. *Journal of Personality and Social Psychology*, *9*, 1–27. (Figure 4.1). Adapted with permission.

We thank Elsevier for granting us permission to use material from the following articles:

Brickman, P., Redfield, J., Harrison, A.A., & Crandall, R. (1972). Drive and predisposition as factors in the attitudinal effects of mere exposure. *Journal of Experimental Social Psychology*, *8*, 31–44. (Text Box 4.1). Adapted with permission from Elsevier.

Schmader, T. (2002). Gender identification moderates stereotype threat effects on women's math performance. *Journal of Experimental Social Psychology*, *38*, 194–201. (Text Box 3.3). Adapted with permission from Elsevier.

We thank Blackwell for granting us permission to use material from Gardner, W. L., Gabriel, S., & Lee, A.Y. (1999). 'I' value freedom but 'we' value relationships: Self-construal priming mirrors cultural differences in judgment. *Psychological Science*, *10*, 321–326. (Figure 1.9). Adapted with permission from Blackwell.

We thank the University of Illinois Press for granting us permission to use material from Heider, F. & Simmel, M. (1944). An experimental study of apparent behavior. *American Journal of Psychology*, *57*, 243–259. (Figure 2.1). Adapted with permission from University of Illinois Press.

We thank the British Psychological Society for granting us permission to use material from Terry, D.J., Hogg, M.A., & White, K.M. (1999). The theory of planned behavior: Self-identity, social identity, and group norms. *British Journal of Social Psychology*, *38*, 225–244. (Text Box 4.2). Adapted with permission from the British *Journal of Social Psychology*, © The British Psychological Society.

We thank Heldref for granting us permission to use material from Hovland, C.I. & Sears, R.R. (1940). Minor studies in aggression: VI. Correlation of lynching with economic indices. *Journal of Psychology*, *9*, 301–310. Figure 1, p. 307. (Figure 9.1). Adapted with permission of the Helen Dwight Reid Educational Foundation. Published by Heldref Publications, 1319 Eighteenth St., NW, Washington, DC 20036–1802. Copyright © (1940).

We thank Sage Publications Ltd for granting us permission to use material from Crisp, R.J., Heuston, S., Farr, M.J., & Turner, R.N. (2007). Seeing red or feeling blue: Differentiated intergroup emotions and ingroup identification in soccer fans. *Group Processes and Intergroup Relations*, *10*, 9–26. (Text Box 9.2). Adapted by permission of Sage Publications Ltd from Author, Title, Copyright (© Sage Publications Ltd., 2006).

A Brief Introduction

This textbook aims to introduce you to the core theories, approaches, and findings that are the necessary foundations for a developing understanding of social psychology. Aimed at those of you who are taking psychology for the first time, whether psychology is your main interest, or if you're taking social psychology as a supplementary course, it covers the essential topics (self and identity, attribution, social cognition, attitudes, group processes, social influence, prejudice, intergroup relations, aggression, pro-social behaviour, affiliation and attraction, friendship and love) in a memorable, readable way. The text focuses on theory and basic level empirical demonstrations of the key phenomena, along with discussion of cutting edge research and application to real-world issues, to ensure that the key concepts are accessible, relevant, and up-to-date. We've tried to be informative without swamping you with too much information.

SO WHAT IS SOCIAL PSYCHOLOGY?

Influential social psychologist Gordon W. Allport defined social psychology as 'an attempt to understand and explain how the thoughts, feelings and behaviour of individuals are influenced by the actual, imagined or implied presence of others' (1985: 3). Put another way, social psychology involves trying to understand the **social behaviour** of individuals in terms of both internal characteristics of the person (e.g. personality, mental processes) and external influences (the effect of the social environment).

HISTORICAL DEVELOPMENT

The idea of studying social processes in a scientific manner emerged in the mid 19th century. French thinker Auguste Comte (1838) helped to lay the foundations for social psychology by arguing that society and social issues should be studied in the same scientific manner as natural science. Although it is difficult to pinpoint an exact starting point, the study of social psychology gathered pace at the turn of the 20th century. In 1895, French writer Gustav LeBon proposed a theory of crowd behaviour, arguing that people behave badly in groups because they are controlled by a *crowd mind*. This work was a precursor to much later work on social influence and aggression, discussed in detail in this book, and was some of the first work to focus on the way in which the behaviour of individuals is influenced by their social context. In 1897, Norman Triplett conducted what was probably the first social psychology experiment, when he systematically compared children who completed a task alone or in the presence of others who were completing the same task. He found that performing in the presence of others led children to complete the task more quickly because it aroused a competitive instinct.

In 1908, the first two textbooks on social psychology were published. English psychologist William McDougall wrote *An Introduction to Social Psychology*, which grounded social behaviour in biology, talking about the role of instincts, which he defined as inherited or innate dispositional characteristics, in producing primary emotions (for example, fear, anger, curiosity, and tenderness) in response to stimuli in the social world. American sociologist Edward Ross wrote *Social Psychology* from a rather different perspective, focusing on more complex social phenomena such as crowd behavior, culture, conformity, and conflict.

The first half of the 20th century saw an explosion in social psychology research. Many of the classic social psychology studies that occurred in this period are discussed in this book. In 1934, in an investigation of behaviour and attitudes of American hotel owners towards a Chinese couple (see Chapter 4 on attitudes), LaPierre found that people's attitudes and behaviour do not always correspond with one another. In 1935, Sherif experimentally demonstrated the role of social norms in influencing people's behaviour when they are in the presence of others (see Chapter 6 on social influence). In 1940, Hovland and Sears proposed and tested a theory that explained why people behaved aggressively, based on how people take out their frustrations about their lives on a scapegoat (see Chapter 9 on aggression).

The Second World War had a profound influence on the direction of social psychological theory and research. At around this time, societies began to realize that prejudice against ethnic minorities (see Chapter 7) was irrational and morally wrong (Harding, Kutner, Proshansky, & Chein, 1954). Psychologists became interested in the idea that bringing together members of different groups would lead to mutual regard and respect. The battlefield in the Second World War also provided a good opportunity to consider the effects of contact. Despite an official policy of segregation between black and white soldiers, combat conditions made it impossible to maintain this, as soldiers relied on one another in battle. Researchers found that white soldiers who had experienced integrated combat had more positive racial attitudes than did those who did not have this experience (Singer, 1948; Stouffer et al., 1949).

Research of this kind resulted in Gordon Allport's classic 1954 text, *The Nature of Prejudice*, in which he proposed the 'contact hypothesis', the idea that bringing different groups together would reduce prejudice, although critically, only under certain conditions (Allport, 1954). At around the same time, a series of classic studies were conducted by Sherif and colleagues looking at group dynamics, at a summer camp for boys (Sherif & Sherif, 1953; Sherif, White, & Harvey, 1955). This research demonstrated two of the key conditions for intergroup contact to reduce prejudice – cooperation and common goals – as well as providing the basis for a classic theory of intergroup conflict: realistic group conflict theory (see Chapter 7 on prejudice).

Events during the Second World War also generated research on conformity, in an attempt to understand events in Nazi Germany. Solomon Asch (1956) experimentally investigated the impact of group members on the individual while, in one of the most famous social psychology experiments, Milgram (1963) explored why people follow orders, even where those orders involve causing harm to other people (see Chapter 6 on social influence). At around the same time, Adorno and colleagues (1950) considered whether people with a certain type of personality were more likely to behave with prejudice towards others, in their research on the authoritarian personality.

In the latter half of the 20th century, through to the present day, research on social psychology has continued to rapidly expand and diversify. The 1960s saw research on a diverse range of topics, including aggression (see Chapter 9), prosocial behaviour (see Chapter 10) and interpersonal relationships (see Chapters 11 and 12), whilst the role of cognition in social psychology came to the fore in the 1970s (see Chapter 3 on social cognition). In this book, we talk about classic theory and research from the first half of the 20th century right through to research that is hot off the press.

RESEARCH METHODS

Social psychology is the scientific study of social behaviour. By this, we mean that the majority of research involves the systematic testing of **hypotheses** that are based on previous observations, research, or theories. As you will see throughout this book, there are a diverse range of methods available to social psychologists in order to test their hypotheses. Here we briefly describe some of these methods, along with their advantages and disadvantages.

Experimental Methods

An experiment involves manipulating one variable, which we call the *independent variable*, and then seeing whether this has an effect on a second variable, which we refer to as the *dependent variable*. We describe many experiments in this book. In Chapter 1, for instance, we describe an experiment conducted by Scheier and Carver (1977) in which the independent variable, self-awareness, was manipulated by having participants either watch themselves in a mirror or not. These two levels of self-awareness (mirror present: high self-awareness, mirror not present: low self-awareness) formed the two experimental conditions. The researchers predicted that people would have more extreme emotional responses in the high self-awareness condition than in the low self-awareness condition, showing that self-awareness leads to more extreme emotional responses. Participants' self-reported emotions were therefore measured to see if this was the case; these emotions provided the dependent variable in the experiment.

Laboratory Experiments

The majority of experiments are conducted in a laboratory, often a designated room in which participants can be tested or observed. In some studies, the laboratory will be equipped with televisions, video cameras, computer monitors, microphones or other experimental apparatus (for example, Berkowitz & LePage's 1967 study on the effect of weapons on aggression, in Chapter 9). In other cases, the laboratory is a simple room with a table and chair in which participants fill out a questionnaire. The benefit of conducting a laboratory experiment is that conditions can be highly controlled. Put another way, within the confines of the laboratory, everything (e.g. environment, temperature, instructions given by the researcher) apart from the independent variable can be held constant. This way, if changes in the independent variable are accompanied by changes in the dependent variable, we can be fairly confident that it *is* the independent variable that *caused* changes in the dependent variable, rather than a *confounding* variable. Experiments can be described as being high on *internal validity*. Another benefit of experiments is that, because they are conducted in such a controlled environment, they can be replicated. If a researcher uses exactly the same method and finds the same results, there can be greater confidence that the effect is a genuine social phenomenon rather than a chance, one-off finding. Outside the laboratory, on the other hand, it is much more difficult to create exactly the same conditions to replicate a study.

As you shall see in this book, laboratory experiments have been used to study a wider range of social phenomena and have formed the basis for a number of highly influential theories. The method does, however, have a number of shortcomings. First, although the high degree of control over conditions allows us to infer causality from the findings, it also makes the experiment rather artificial. In other words, experiments lack *external validity*. Ultimately, social psychologists are interested in why people behave the way they do as a result of the social context in which they exist, and that social context is not present in the laboratory. As a result, it may not be easy to apply something that occurs in very controlled conditions in a laboratory to behaviour that occurs naturally in the 'real world'. Having said that, experiments are the best way to confirm or refute theories about social behaviour. Once an effect has been established in controlled conditions, researchers can then go on to investigate it in a more applied setting.

Experiments are also susceptible to **demand characteristics** (Orne, 1962), information that participants pick up from the experimental context that leads them to guess what the experimenter is predicting will happen. When this happens, they may consciously alter their behaviour to conform to what they believe the researcher is looking for. If this happens a researcher's hypothesis might be inadvertently supported by the results of an experiment even when that hypothesis is incorrect. Social psychological experiments are susceptible to problems of this nature because, unlike in the natural sciences, they involve people. Although almost every aspect of the environment in which the participant finds themselves can be controlled, the internal mental processes of participants cannot. Experimenters themselves may also pose a risk to the validity of an experiment. **Experimenter effects** are subtle cues or signals that are given out by an experimenter who knows the experimental hypotheses. Although it is unlikely that the experimenter realizes that they are doing so, body language (for example, hand gestures, eye movements) and vocal cues like the tone of their voice may inadvertently affect the performance or response of participants in the experiment. The best solution to this problem is to use a *double-blind* procedure, where the person running the experiment does not know what the hypotheses are, or does not know which condition (i.e. which level of the independent variable) the participant is in.

Field Experiments

Experiments are not always confined to the laboratory. They can also be conducted in naturalistic settings. We describe many field experiments in this book. In Chapter 10, for instance, we describe a study conducted by Bryan and Test (1967) which investigated whether we model our behaviour on the behaviour of others. Specifically, they found that people driving down a road were more likely to stop and help a stranded motorist on the side of the road if they had previously observed another stranded motorist being helped by a passer-by than if they had not observed such a situation. Field experiments have greater external validity than laboratory experiments. They are also less likely to be subject to demand characteristics because participants typically have no idea they are taking part in a study.

The drawback to this type of research is that the situation is not nearly as controlled as a laboratory experiment. This makes it difficult to rule out the impact of external influences. In the case of Bryan and Test's (1967) experiment, for example, it may have been that the weather was nicer or the traffic calmer when they were running the 'modelling' condition. If this was the case, the argument could be made that people stopped to help the stranded motorist because they were in a better mood or less stressed at this particular point in time.

Another problem with field experiments is that it is not always possible to randomly assign participants to conditions; in some studies participants may have selected their own condition. In Chapter 12, we discuss a field experiment conducted by Dutton and Aron (1974) in which male participants were stopped by a female experimenter while crossing either a high rope bridge over a canyon or a low bridge over a stream. They found that men crossing the high bridge were more likely to be attracted to the female while on the high bridge than the low bridge, which they explained in terms of a misattribution of physiological arousal experienced by participants. In this study, however, participants selected their own condition; they had chosen to cross either the low or high bridge. As a consequence, any effect of the independent on the dependent variable may be explained by differences between the participants across experimental conditions. Put another way, one might argue that men who chose to cross the low bridge were less adventurous – and therefore less sexually adventurous – than men crossing the high bridge.

Non-Experimental Methods

Although experiments are the best way of determining cause and effect, there are a variety of circumstances where they are not practically feasible. There are many situations in which the independent variable cannot be manipulated. If we are interested in how gender, ethnicity or age affects behaviour, for example, we cannot randomly assign participants to different conditions. Moreover, for social psychologists who are interested in looking at psychological phenomena on a broad societal level (for example, Pettigrew's 1997 investigation of ethnic prejudice across Europe, discussed in Chapter 7), experiments are not particularly useful. There are, however, a number of non-experimental methods available to social psychologists.

A survey is a research method that involves asking participants to respond to a series of questions, through interviews (in which a researcher asks participants questions face-to-face or over the phone, and then records their answers) or questionnaires (in which participants provide written responses to a series of questions on paper). Pettigrew (1997) investigated the relationship between inter-ethnic friendships and prejudice across several European countries using a survey. This research highlights a clear advantage of survey research: surveys can be administered to a very large sample with relative ease and at little expense. Moreover, because they can be administered on a large scale, researchers can be confident that their findings can be generalized rather than being specific to one group of participants. The downside to questionnaires is that if they are not very carefully designed, they can be misinterpreted by participants, and there is no experimenter present to correct these misinterpretations. There are also a number of response biases: participants have a tendency to blindly agree with positively worded questions, and frequently fail to use the full range of possible responses (e.g. sticking to mid-range responses like 'I don't know' or 'sometimes' or alternatively always using the extreme responses on a scale like 'Strongly agree' or 'Strongly disagree').

Another way that social psychologists can observe social phenomena without conducting an experiment is to reanalyse existing data, often data that was collected for a different purpose. This is particularly useful when researchers are interested in the effect of societal events on behaviour, particularly when those events occurred in the past. In Chapter 9, we talk about *archival research* conducted by Hovland and Sears (1940). They analysed existing data to investigate whether the number of lynchings of blacks increased during times of economic crisis in the South of the United States. The main problem with this sort of data is that because it is usually not collected with social psychology in mind, potentially useful information might not be available. There is a whole range of other ways in which social behaviour can be studied, although these are not extensively covered in this book. Other non-experimental methods that are sometimes used by social psychologists include *field studies*, which involve observing and measuring behaviour that occurs in a naturalistic setting, and *case studies*, which involve a detailed, often descriptive, investigation of a particular participant or small group of participants.

In sum, although useful for studying broader social issues in a naturalistic setting, the main drawback of non-experimental methods is that because the independent variable is measured rather than manipulated, it is impossible to confirm that one factor leads to the other. Although Pettigrew (1997), for instance, concluded from his research that people who had friends in other ethnic groups were less prejudiced against minority groups, this relationship was only a correlation. Although inter-ethnic friendship and prejudice co-vary, the relationship could operate in either direction; it may be that people with low levels of prejudice seek out interethnic friendship.

RESEARCH ETHICS

Regardless of the method used to conduct research in social psychology, because it involves people, social psychologists need to be aware of a number of ethical issues. To ensure that research is not physically or psychologically harmful to participants, in 1972 the American Psychological Association put in place a set of principles for ethical conduct to guide psychologists when designing their research.

Participant Welfare: It is essential that the physical and psychological welfare of participants is protected. Although it is not too difficult to determine whether or not a study causes physical harm to a participant, it is less easy to determine the extent of psychological harm. For instance, Milgram's (1963) obedience studies (described in Chapter 6) did not cause physical harm to participants, but participants may have learnt something not very pleasant about themselves (that they would cause physical harm to others if instructed to) which may have had a negative psychological impact. Even in much less controversial studies, it is often necessary to use procedures that could cause some degree of psychological harm. Denigrating participants' performance on a task in order to elicit anger may, for example, lead to temporarily depressed self-esteem (e.g. Carver and Glass, 1978, Chapter 9). Where this is the case, efforts should be made to ensure that the negative psychological impact of the research is inconsequential and short-lived.

Deception: To avoid the problems caused by demand characteristics, it is important that participants are blind to the aims of the study. For this reason, many social psychology studies involve some degree of deception. Milgram (1963), for example, deceived participants by making them believe that they were really administering electric shocks. This was necessary in order to see whether participants would *really* cause harm in order to obey the experimenter. Many experiments also use a *confederate*, someone who is ostensibly a participant in the experiment but who is actually an 'actor', following a script designed by the experimenter in order to test a particular hypothesis. Because so many experiments involve essentially lying to participants, deception is often seen as a controversial aspect of social psychological research. However, most deception is of a trivial nature, participants are told the full purpose of the experiment after completion, and there is no evidence that deception causes long-term harm.

Confidentiality: Participants in social psychology research are often required to disclose information of a personal or intimate nature. To reassure participants that this information will not be used against them in any way, social psychologists need to inform participants that data derived from their participation will be completely confidential. In other words, the researcher will not share this information with anyone else. The anonymity of participants is also usually safeguarded by identifying them with a number rather than a name.

Informed Consent and Debriefing: It is normal practice to obtain informed consent from individuals prior to their participation in a study. That is, participants provide their full and voluntary consent in writing. They are also informed that they can withdraw from the experiment at any time. Following the experiment, participants need to be fully debriefed. This involves telling them the true purpose of the experiment, and so is particularly important where deception was involved. It also gives experimenters the opportunity to demonstrate the importance and relevance of the research, and gives participants the opportunity to learn something about social psychology.

A FINAL WORD BEFORE YOU BEGIN …

So that's a brief outline of how social psychology research is carried out. Empirical studies are central to how social psychologists study thought and behaviour, so we use them quite a bit to illustrate the topics we cover. Now you'll know what we're talking about when we go on about experiments, dependent variables, confederates and correlations in the following chapters. One final thing before you set off: social psychology is not only critically important for understanding the world in which we live; it's also a lot of fun. We hope you find the topics we've written about as fascinating as we do. And remember, in an age where we've mapped the human genome and pretty much worked out everything there is to know about the physical world, the study of people's behaviour is perhaps the final frontier of scientific endeavour. We know quite a lot about social thought and action, but there's a heck of a lot we don't know. Your ideas about social psychology could well be the next big thing …

The Self

1

Self-Awareness
Development of Self-Awareness
Neurological Basis of Self-Awareness
Temporary Differences in Self-Awareness
Chronic Differences in Self-Awareness

Organization of Self-Knowledge

Theories of Self-Concept Maintenance
Theories of Self-Comparison
Theories of Individual Comparison
Theories of Group Comparison

Self-Esteem
Development of Self-Esteem
Consequences of Self-Esteem

Self-Motives
Self-Enhancement

Cultural Differences in Self and Identity
Individualist and Collectivist Cultures
Biculturalism

The Self

One characteristic that distinguishes humans from other animals is our capacity for reflexive thought, the ability to reflect on the way in which we think. Reflexive thought allows us to think about who we are and how we are perceived by others, and we are constantly defining ourselves. Ask any person *who* they are, and they will provide an extensive list of characteristics and identities that represent how they perceive themselves. For instance, one of us writing this book could describe himself as a male, a psychologist, young(ish), British, and liberal (amongst other things). The self is a fundamental part of every human, a symbolic construct which reflects an awareness of our own identity.

In this chapter, we first consider how self-awareness develops and how it affects how we feel and behave. Second, we outline social psychological theories of the self which explain how our perception of the self is formed. These theories can be subdivided into four broad types: those that explain our sense of self based on observations of our *own* behaviour, and those that explain our sense of self in terms of comparisons with personally held standards, other individuals and other groups. Third, we discuss individual differences in self-esteem and how these differences affect the way we deal with life events. Fourth, we consider our motivations where self-perception is concerned, the most powerful of which is the motive for self-enhancement. Finally, although the self is perceived by many to reflect our uniqueness as a human being, there is considerable evidence that it is influenced by culture. We therefore discuss cross-cultural differences in perceptions of the self, and consider how bicultural individuals cope with holding two types of identity simultaneously.

SELF-AWARENESS

Although the self is an essential aspect of every person, we do not think about it all of the time. Instead, our level of self-awareness varies depending on both the situation and our personality. Self-awareness is a psychological state in which people are aware of their traits, feelings and behaviour. Alternatively, it can be defined as the realization of oneself as an individual entity. In this section, we explain how self-awareness develops in humans and discuss the areas of the brain which are responsible for this ability. We then distinguish between two types of self-awareness, private and public, which have diverging consequences for the self. Each form of self-awareness can either be temporary, as a consequence of a particular situation, or chronic, reflecting a personality trait that varies from person to person.

Development of Self-Awareness

Infants are not born with self-awareness. Instead, they develop the ability over time. Lewis and Brooks (1978) put a spot of rouge on the nose of babies and then put them in front of a mirror. Babies aged between 9 and 12 months treated the mirror image as if it was another child and showed no interest in the spot on their nose. Because they lacked self-awareness, they were unable to identify the baby in the mirror as themselves. By around 18 months, however, children would curiously look at themselves in the mirror and touch the spot on their nose; they now recognized that the person they could see was them and that they were looking different from normal.

Neurological Basis of Self-Awareness

Why do children develop self-awareness at around the age of 18 months? Research has shown that at around this time, children show a rapid growth of spindle cells, specialized neurones in the anterior cingulate, an area of the frontal lobe in the cerebral cortex of the brain thought to be responsible for monitoring and controlling intentional behaviour (Allman & Hasenstaub, 1999). There is also evidence among adults that this area of the brain is activated when people are self-aware (Kjaer et al., 2002). In sum, although it is not likely to be the only area of the brain that contributes towards self-awareness, the anterior cingulate appears to play an important role. To read about a study that investigates the role of the anterior cingulate and the prefrontal cortex in how we make inferences about others based on self-reflection, see Text Box 1.1.

Text Box 1.1

Biological Correlates of Self-Perception and Perspective Taking

The prefrontal cortex area of the brain is thought to have a role in a wide range of complex social-cognitive behaviours, including making inferences about what other people are thinking and processing information about the self. At first glance, understanding other people and understanding the self seem to be quite different mental processes, so how can the same area of the brain produce both types of behaviour? One explanation is that we might make

(Continued)

inferences about the thoughts and feelings of other people by imagining what our *own* thoughts and feelings would be if we were in the same situation. Recent research by Mitchell, Banaji, and Macrae (2005) investigated this possibility.

Method

Participants underwent an fMRI (function magnetic resonance imaging) scan, an imaging technique which shows activity in different areas of the brain by recording changes in the blood flow, while making judgements about photographs of a series of faces. Participants either made judgements about the mental state of the target person (how pleased they were to have their photo taken) or a non-mental state task (how symmetrical their face was). After the fMRI scan, participants were shown each photograph again and reported how similar they perceived themselves to be to the person in the photo.

Results

Participants showed mental activity in the prefrontal cortex when they were making inferences about mental state, but not when they were making judgements about the appearance of the individuals in the photographs.

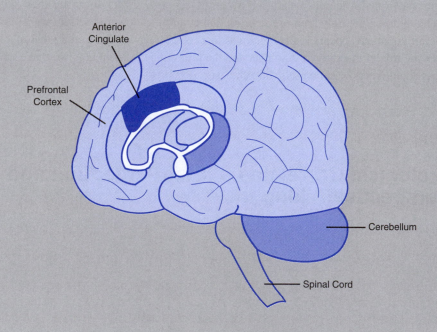

There was also a correlation between the amount of activity in the prefrontal cortex and perceived similarity of the participant to the individuals in the photographs. However, this relationship emerged only when making inferences about mental state, not for the non-mental state task.

Interpreting the Findings

The fact that the prefrontal cortex was activated when making mental inferences about people but not when making judgements about appearance suggests that the prefrontal cortex is specifically used when trying to understand the attributes that other people possess, but not for making more general judgements about others.

In sum, when participants believed they were similar to the individual about whom they were making inferences – and therefore were better able to predict the behaviour of that individual on the basis of how they themselves would feel in the same situation – their prefrontal cortex showed greater activation.

Temporary Differences in Self-Awareness

Social psychologists have distinguished between private and public self-awareness. **Private self-awareness** refers to when an individual temporarily becomes aware of private, personal aspects of the self. People become privately self-aware when they see their face in a mirror, or experience physiological arousal which may lead them to reflect on their emotional state, for example whether they are happy, excited, or angry. Private self-awareness has three important consequences for how people act. First, it results in an intensified emotional response. If an individual already feels positive, reflecting on those feelings of happiness will lead them to feel even happier. In contrast, a sad individual who is privately self-aware may come to feel worse because they dwell on their negative state of mind. Scheier and Carver (1977) had participants read aloud a series of positive statements (e.g. 'I feel light-hearted') or a series of negative statements (e.g. 'Everything seems empty and futile'), tasks previously shown to elicit elation and depression. They found that participants who looked at themselves in a mirror during the task – and were thus made privately self-aware – become more extreme in their emotional responses than participants who had not been looking in a mirror during the task (see Figure 1.1).

Second, privately self-aware people are likely to experience clarification of knowledge; by focusing on internal events individuals are able to report them with greater accuracy. Gibbons, Carver, Scheier, and Hormuth (1979) gave participants a placebo which they were told was a drug that would induce arousal and a number of other side-effects. Participants with mirror-induced self-awareness reported less

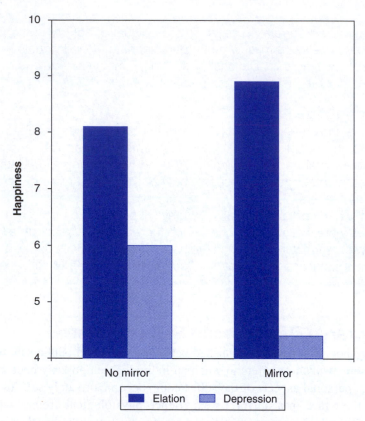

Figure 1.1 The effect of self-awareness on emotional response following a mood manipulation task. Data from Scheier and Carver (1977)

arousal and fewer side-effects than participants in a control condition who could not see themselves in a mirror. While people who were not self-aware based their self-knowledge on their perceptions of the drug they believed they had taken, self-aware individuals ignored the placebo and focused on how they were really feeling, resulting in more accurate self-perceptions.

Third, people who are privately self-aware are more likely to adhere to personal standards of behaviour. As they are more aware of their true beliefs, they will act in line with those beliefs rather than being influenced by normative pressures (see Chapter 6). Scheier and Carver (1980) had participants write a counter-attitudinal essay. According to the theory of cognitive dissonance (see Chapter 4), people feel negative arousal if their attitudes and behaviour are inconsistent, and often deal with this by changing their attitudes in line with their behaviour. However, participants who wrote the essay in front of a mirror showed less attitude change than participants who wrote the essay without the presence of a mirror.

Public self-awareness arises when a person is aware of public aspects of themselves that can be seen and evaluated by others. People are publicly self-aware when they are being watched by others, for example giving a presentation, talking in a seminar, being photographed or being filmed. Public self-awareness is associated with evaluation apprehension. When people are the focus of others' attention, they realize they are being appraised by those observers (see also Chapter 5). The fear of a negative evaluation can lead to nervousness and a loss of self-esteem, particularly if a person's perceived actual public image does not match their desired public image. Finally, in contrast to the effects of private self-awareness, public self-awareness leads to adherence to social standards of behaviour; people who are aware of the perceptions of others, for example their social group, are more likely to conform to group norms, even if this does not match their private point of view (see Chapter 6).

Chronic Differences in Self-Awareness

In addition to temporary heightening of self-awareness that people experience from time to time as a result of the situation, some people are chronically more likely to experience self-awareness. Such individuals can be described as possessing the personality trait of self-consciousness. Mirroring temporary differences in self-awareness, people can be either publicly or privately self-conscious. A simple way to think about self-consciousness is that it is the same as public or private self-awareness, but refers to chronic (i.e. general tendencies) to be one or the other. Public and private self-consciousness are not mutually exclusive; an individual can be high in one of these traits, both of these traits, or neither.

People who are high in **private self-consciousness** experience chronically heightened private self-awareness; they therefore experience more intense emotions, are more likely to remain true to their personal beliefs and have more accurate self-perceptions. Being privately self-conscious has both positive and negative implications for the individual. On the plus side, such individuals are less likely to suffer from ill health as a result of stress because they pay more attention to their physiological state and so notice earlier if there is a problem (Mullen & Suls, 1982). However, the down side of being high in private self-consciousness is a greater tendency to suffer from depression and neuroticism; such individuals are more likely to pay attention to and ruminate about any feelings of unhappiness or discomfort they are experiencing.

People who are high in **public self-consciousness** are particularly concerned with how they are perceived by those around them. As a result they are more likely to adhere to group norms, more likely to avoid embarrassing situations (Froming et al., 1990), more concerned with their own physical appearance and more likely to judge others based on their physical appearance.

Summary

Self-awareness is a psychological state in which people are aware of their traits, feelings and behaviour. The ability to be self-aware develops during early childhood, as the *anterior cingulate*, an area of the frontal lobe in the cerebral cortex of the brain develops. In adulthood, this area of the brain is only activated when people are self-aware. We have both temporary and chronic differences in self-awareness. Individuals who are temporarily *privately self-aware* experience intensified emotional response and clarification of knowledge, and are more likely to adhere to personal standards of behaviour. When an individual is temporarily *publicly self-aware*, on the other hand, they may experience evaluation apprehension and a loss of self-esteem, and they are more likely to adhere to social standards of behaviour. The effects of private and public self-consciousness, or chronic self-awareness, parallel the impact of being temporarily privately or publicly self-aware.

ORGANIZATION OF SELF-KNOWLEDGE

When we are self-aware, we access the information we have about ourselves. But how is this information organized in our minds? The knowledge that we have about the world is stored as schemas, cognitive structures that represent the knowledge we have about a particular concept or type of stimulus (see also Chapter 3). Each schema is developed through our experiences with a stimulus, and holds all the information we have about it. A **self-schema** reflects how we expect ourselves to think, feel and behave in a particular situation. Each self-schema consists of our perception of our self (for example, 'shy') and incorporates our experience on this dimension (for example, we know that we are likely to be shy when at a party, or when asked to talk about our opinions during a seminar).

For each of us, some self-schemas are particularly important whilst others are less important or even irrelevant. Markus (1977) argued that if a particular aspect of the self is perceived as particularly important, if the person thinks they are *extreme* on that dimension (high or low on it), and if they are certain that the *opposite* is not true for them, then an individual can be described as **self-schematic** on that dimension. If, for example, you are a student, you are likely to be self-schematic on that dimension if being a student is very important to you, you think you are a highly typical example of a student, and you think you are very different from someone who is not a student. In contrast, you would be *self-aschematic* on a particular dimension if it is not important to you and does not reflect who you are.

Each of us holds a complex self-concept made up of a number of discrete self-schemas. Our self-schemas are likely to be more complex and varied than

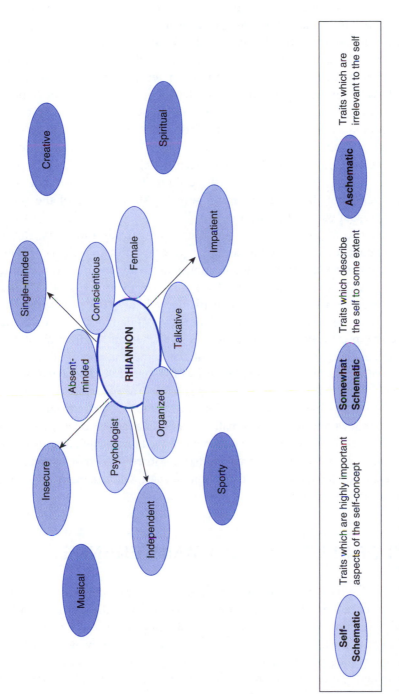

Figure 1.2 An example of self-schemas

other schemas represented in memory, given that we acquire more information about the self than about anything else. Markus and Sentis (1982) proposed that as well as current self-schema, we also hold possible future self-schema, for example self-schemas that reflect how we would like to be in the future, and self-schemas that reflect how we think (or fear) we will actually turn out (we will look at this distinction between how we perceive ourselves to be, and how we would ideally like to be, later on in this chapter). Having complex and varied self-schemas is beneficial for us, buffering us from negative events or failures in our life. This is because if one self-schema is having a negative impact on us, there will be other self-schemas from which we derive satisfaction, or that allow us to see ourselves in a positive light. To give you an example of how self-schemas might be organized, Figure 1.2 shows some of the self-schemas that represent one of the authors.

We now know how our self-knowledge is organized in memory. But how does the organization of self-schemas affect how we think, feel and behave? Self-schemas become active in relevant situations and provide us with information regarding how – based on our beliefs of who we are – we should respond. Dimensions on which we are self-schematic are particularly likely to be activated in relevant domains, as a study conducted by Markus (1977) demonstrated. Participants who had either previously rated themselves as self-schematic on the trait of dependence or independence, or aschematic on both, completed a reaction-time task. Participants were presented on a screen with words that were associated with independence (for example, assertive) and dependence (for example, obliging) and were asked to press a 'me' button if this described them or a 'not me' button if it did not. Participants who were self-schematic on independence or dependence were much faster at identifying whether a word characterized them than participants who were aschematic on either of these characteristics. Moreover, self-schematic participants also had better memory for incidents from the past which demonstrated their dependence or independence.

THEORIES OF SELF-CONCEPT MAINTENANCE

Having identified when and why we are likely to become self-aware, the consequences of self-awareness, and how knowledge about the self is organized in our minds, we now turn to how self-schemas develop. What is the content of our self-schemas, and why do we come to view ourselves in the way that we do? In this section, we discuss six theories that explain how our self-concept is managed and maintained. These are control theory of self-regulation, self-discrepancy theory, social comparison theory, self-evaluation maintenance, social identity theory and self-categorization theory. All of these theories propose that how we define the self and how it subsequently affects our behaviour depend largely upon how the self *compares* to a particular point of comparison. There are three types of comparative theory which each focus on a different target of comparison. The self can be compared to perceptions of how the self *should* be, to other individuals, or to other groups. We discuss each of these types of theory below.

Theories of Self-Comparison

Many social psychologists believe that people form a sense of self from a comparison process. The first class of these comparison theories focuses on comparing the self with … the self. This is not as strange as it might first appear. As we discussed above, people have different versions of the self. They can, for instance, know how they actually are, but also have an idea of how they would like to be. Two theories fall into this category: control theory of self-regulation and self-discrepancy theory. Both theories argue that when people are self-aware, they can think about whether they are the sort of person they want to be or whether there are ways in which they would like to change.

Control Theory of Self-Regulation

Carver and Scheier (1981, 1998) proposed that through self-awareness we are able to assess whether or not we are meeting our goals. The central element of the **control theory of self-regulation** is a cognitive feedback loop which illustrates four steps involved in self-regulation: *Test, Operate, Test,* and *Exit* (see Figure 1.3). In the first *test* phase, people compare the self against one of two standards. People who are privately self-aware compare themselves against a private standard, such as the values we believe to be important. In contrast, people who are publicly self-aware compare themselves against a public standard, for example the values held by our friends and family (see the discussion of private versus public self-awareness earlier in the chapter). If someone believes they are failing to meet the relevant standard, they put into *operation* a change in behaviour in order to meet this standard. When they next self-reflect on that issue, they re-*test* themselves, comparing their self to their values or the values of others for a second time. If the self still falls short of the standard, the feedback loop will repeat itself. If, however, the self and the standard are now in line with one another, the individual will *exit* the feedback loop.

The control theory of self-regulation is, on first glance, an optimistic theory, illustrating how we can improve the self through a combination of self-awareness and self-regulation. However, an intriguing study conducted by Baumeister, Bratslavsky, Muraven, and Tice (1998) showed that self-regulating one aspect of the self makes it subsequently more difficult to self-regulate other aspects of the self. Participants who had signed up to take part in a study which they were led to believe was about taste perception were

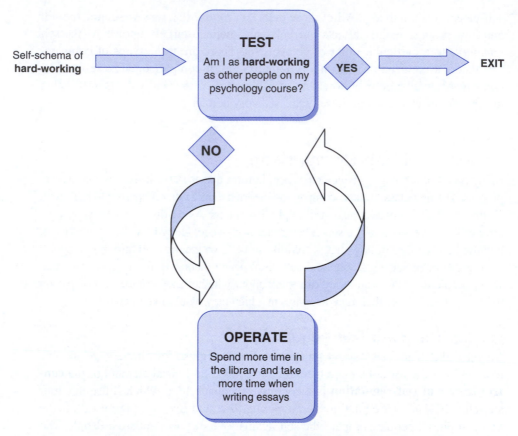

Figure 1.3 Carver and Scheier's (1981, 1998) control theory of self-regulation.
Illustration of TEST-OPERATE-TEST-EXIT feedback loop

instructed to make sure they had not eaten for at least three hours when they came to the laboratory. On arrival, participants entered a room with a small oven in which chocolate chip cookies had just been baked, ensuring that the delicious aroma of chocolate and baking filled the room. They were then seated at a table which had a stack of chocolate chip cookies on one side and a bowl of radishes on the other. In the *radishes* condition, participants were asked to eat at least two or three radishes while in the *chocolate* condition, participants were asked to eat at least two or three cookies. In both conditions, participants were reminded that they should only eat the food assigned to them. They were left for five minutes and observed through a one-way mirror to ensure that they had followed the instructions given to them by the experimenter.

After completing this task, participants were asked if they minded helping out the experimenter by taking part in an unrelated experiment on problem-solving. In actual fact, this was part of the same study. Participants were instructed to complete a problem-solving task, taking as much time as they wanted, and were told that they would not be judged on how long they took, only on whether or not they managed to solve the puzzle. In reality, the task had actually been prepared so that it was impossible to solve. The dependent measure in the study was how long participants kept working on the task before giving up. Participants gave up on the problem-solving task much more quickly in the *radishes* condition, after an average of just 8 minutes, than in the *chocolate* condition, where participants spent on average 19 minutes on the task. In sum, participants who had previously had to exert self-control – by eating the radishes and ignoring the chocolate – were less able to persist on the difficult and frustrating puzzle task. On the basis of these and similar findings, Baumeister and colleagues argued that we have limited cognitive resources at our disposal to self-regulate. As a result, when we self-regulate in one domain, the resources we have left to self-regulate in another domain are temporarily depleted.

Self-Discrepancy Theory

Higgins (1987) proposed a theory which also argues that people compare the self to a relevant standard. However, **self-discrepancy theory** focuses not only on the awareness of discrepancies between actual and ideal identity, but also on people's *emotional* response to such discrepancies. Higgins argued that people possess three types of self-schema. The *actual self* reflects how we are at present. The *ideal self* is a point of reference which reflects how we would really like to be (this ideal self is made up of the traits, characteristics and qualities that an individual wishes or hopes they could possess). The *ought self*, in contrast, represents the traits or characteristics that an individual believes they *should* possess, based on a sense of duty, responsibility or obligation. According to the theory, people are motivated to ensure that their actual self matches their ideal and ought self; the greater the discrepancy between the actual self and a self-guide (either ideal or ought), the greater the psychological discomfort that will be experienced. To give a specific example of this, imagine that you work in a supermarket, but you are an aspiring artist. Your parents, however, are keen for you to pursue a medical career. In this case, your actual self (supermarket employee) differs from both your ideal self (artist) and your ought self (doctor).

The two types of self-discrepancy are thought to be related to unique emotional responses. An actual-ideal discrepancy is associated with the absence of positive outcomes, which results in dejection-related emotions like disappointment and sadness. Thus, if you are doing a painting on your day off from work, causing you to think about the fact that although you are a checkout assistant you would rather be a professional artist, you may feel somewhat depressed. Actual-ought discrepancies, on the other hand, are associated with the presence of negative outcomes, which

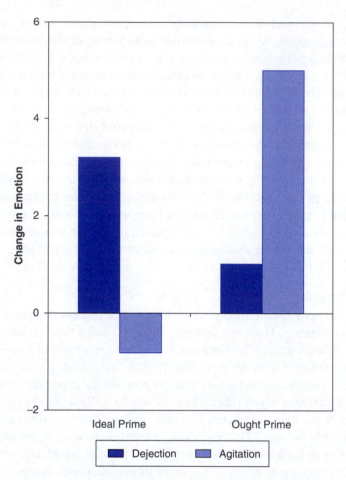

Figure 1.4 Evidence for self-discrepancy theory. Data from Higgins, Bond, Klein, and Strauman (1986)

results in agitation-related emotions like anger, fear, and nervousness. So, if you visit your parents on your day off from work, this may remind you that you are failing to meet their high expectations for you to become a doctor, making you feel anxious or annoyed. Higgins, Bond, Klein, and Strauman (1986) identified participants who had previously reported either a low or a high discrepancy between their ideal and their actual and ought selves. Several weeks later, these participants completed a task in which they either had to focus on and describe the difference between their ideal or ought self, and their actual self. Their findings are reported in Figure 1.4. Participants with a high level of discrepancy showed an increase in dejection-related emotions after thinking about their actual-ideal discrepancies, and an increase in agitation-related emotions after thinking about their actual-ought discrepancies. In contrast, participants with low discrepancies showed no significant changes in either emotion.

Self-discrepancy theory implies that by generating negative arousal, discrepancies will motivate people to reduce the discomfort they are experiencing by making changes that reduce discrepancies (see the discussion of cognitive dissonance in Chapter 4 for a similar idea). However, this may not always be the case. Negative emotions often hinder successful self-regulation because if people feel upset they are more likely to give in to their immediate impulses to make themselves feel better rather than working towards a more distant goal. For instance, if we ideally want to be slimmer than we actually are, we may reduce our calorie intake in an attempt to reduce this actual-ideal discrepancy. However, if we look in the mirror one day and are reminded of the difference that still remains between our actual self and our ideal self, we may give in to our impulses, providing ourselves with instant comfort by eating a large piece of cake. This will reduce unhappiness and discomfort in the short term, but makes our overall goal a more distant prospect.

Theories of Individual Comparison

In the previous section we saw how people can develop a sense of who they are from observing their own behaviour and from comparing themselves to 'better' versions of the *self*. Social comparison theory and self-evaluation maintenance theory argue, in contrast, that we learn about the self by comparing ourselves with *other* individuals.

Social Comparison Theory

According to **social comparison theory** (Festinger, 1954), we learn how to define the self by comparing ourselves with those around us. Although comparing ourselves with different ideal and ought version of ourselves, and comparing ourselves with other people, are not mutually exclusive processes, there is one crucial difference. Social comparison theory argues that beliefs, feelings, and behaviours are *subjective*; they are, in isolation, simply the product of our own ruminations. In other words, there is no *objective* benchmark against which we can compare them. As such, while comparing ourselves with notions of how we should be or how we would like to be can lead to changes in the self-concept, the resulting self-definition remains subjectively defined: that is, without any feeling of external validation. In contrast, comparing ourselves with others provides an external, objective benchmark against which to compare our thoughts, feelings and behaviours – providing people with a sense of validation for the way they are.

Where behaviour is concerned (e.g. academic performance), rather than always comparing the self to someone who is very similar, people may sometimes make *upward comparisons* (comparing themselves to someone who they believe to be better than them) or *downward comparisons* (comparing themselves to someone who they believe to be worse than them. People who are motivated by a desire for an *accurate* self-evaluation may make both upward and downward comparisons as both types of comparison are useful for deriving the most precise estimate of, for instance, academic ability. However, as we discuss in more detail in the later section in this chapter on self-motives, people are typically motivated to see themselves in a positive light. The self-evaluation maintenance model tries to explain how we maintain a positive self-esteem when comparing ourselves to others.

Self-Evaluation Maintenance Model

Imagine an acquaintance on your psychology course who always seems to get a higher grade than you on essays and projects. How would you deal with this situation? Tesser's (1988) **self-evaluation maintenance model** explains what we do when we are faced with someone whose success has implications for our own self-esteem. People respond to the success of someone else in one of two ways. **Social reflection** is when we derive our self-esteem from the accomplishments of those who are close to us, without considering our own achievement in that domain. This may help to explain why parents are often so proud of their children's achievements. However, knowing someone who is successful can also evoke an upward social comparison, comparing our *own* achievements with the achievements of the target person. When someone we know is doing very well in a particular domain, what determines whether we engage in social reflection or social comparison?

We are only likely to engage in social reflection with the successful individual under two conditions. First, the domain on which the individual is successful must be *irrelevant* to us. When this is the case, the success of someone else does not threaten our self-concept in any way. As such, we can enjoy their success because it *adds* to our abilities rather than challenging them. Second, we must be *certain* about our abilities in that particular domain. If we are confident that we are also very successful, the success of someone else should pose no threat to us. Instead, their success should actually add to our perception of success. If, for example, you are certain that you are excellent at psychology, the success of another student is unlikely to concern you. Instead, knowing that someone else is also very good should lead you to reflect on the fact that you are on a top psychology course where the students tend to be excellent, enhancing rather than threatening your self-concept.

	Strategy	Example
1	Exaggerate the ability of successful target	'They're just a genius so how can you compare them to normal people?'
2	Change the target of comparison	'Yeah, anyway, forget about her, I did better than Briony, Phillipa, and Tasmin'.'
3	Distance the self from successful target	'She's a bit weird – we've got nothing in common at all! I think I'm going to avoid sitting near her in class …'
4	Devalue the dimension of comparison	'She may get better grades than me, but I have a much better social life – and being popular is much more important!'

Figure 1.5 Strategies used to maintain self-esteem in the face of upward comparison

When the domain on which another person is successful is *relevant*, however, this evokes an upward comparison. If the success of the other person is on a dimension that is important to how we see the self, this will challenge our view of the self as being successful on this domain and will have a negative impact on our self-esteem. *Uncertainty* about our own abilities will also evoke an upward comparison. If we are uncertain about our own abilities and we are then confronted by someone who is very able on a particular domain, this is likely to further increase our uncertainty in our own abilities. Again, this is likely to have a negative impact on our self-esteem. In sum, when we compare ourselves to a successful person on a domain that is relevant to our self-concept but on which we are uncertain about our own abilities, we are making an upward comparison which can have a detrimental effect on our self-esteem. But how can we maintain a positive self-concept in such circumstances?

According to the self-evaluation maintenance model, we have *four* strategies at our disposal (see Figure 1.5). First, we can exaggerate the ability of the person who is outperforming us. In the case of the clever psychology student, if you reclassify that student as 'a genius', the comparison is no longer relevant – the student is essentially in a different league from you – and you can still classify yourself as above average in psychology ability. Second, we can switch the target of comparison to someone who we know to be less successful than us, creating a downward comparison that is good for self-esteem. So, you might compare yourself to someone else on your psychology course who generally does less well on essays and exams than you do. By making this new and different comparison, it is now *you* who is the success. Third, we can downplay our similarity to the target of comparison or physically and emotionally distance ourselves from them. You might, for example, stop sitting with or talking to the clever student. Fourth and finally, we can maintain positive self-esteem by devaluing the dimension of comparison. You might, for example, argue that academic success is not important to you, but that having a good social life is much more important.

Theories of Group Comparison

Although early researchers investigating the self (e.g. Freud, 1921) perceived the self to be a unique identity which we share with no-one else, social psychologists now have a more flexible notion of the self. The self-concept is thought to be made up of many self-schemas, some of which reflect individual aspects of the self, such as personality, but others which reflect our *relationships* with family, friends, and social groups. Although in combination these self-schemas make us unique because no other person is likely to have exactly the same configuration, we certainly share aspects of our identity with others. 'Social psychologist', for example, is an important self-schema held by *both* authors of this book, and many thousands of other people (believe it or not). More broadly, being either female or male is part of all of our self-concepts, but it is a part that we share with millions of other people. Brewer and Gardner (1996) proposed three types of self that reflect these shared and non-shared aspects. The *individual self* consists of attributes and personality traits that differentiate us from other individuals (for example, 'introverted'). The *relational self* is defined by our relationships with significant others (for example, 'sister'). Finally, the *collective self* reflects our membership in social groups (for example, 'British'). In this section we focus on the collective self, and how our membership in social groups contributes towards the definition of our self-concept.

Social Identity Approach

Aspects of the self, according to **social identity theory** (Hogg & Abrams, 1988; Tajfel & Turner, 1979), can be divided into those that reflect our personal identity and those that reflect our social identity. Personal identities are those that reflect idiosyncratic aspects of the self, such as personality traits. In contrast, our social identity reflects the broader social groups to which we belong. The organization of our self-schemas means that each identity we hold is associated with a range of associated concepts that guide our thoughts, feelings and behaviour. However, given that we hold many different identities it would be impossible, and indeed impractical, for us to use every identity to guide our behaviour. Instead, our sense of self at any particular point in time depends upon *which* of our many personal or social identities is psychologically salient (i.e. which identity we are most aware of).

Which identity is salient at any given time depends on the *context*. Imagine, for example, that you are chatting to a close friend on your college campus. At this point in time, it is your personal identity that is likely to be salient, as you talk about your personal experiences with another individual. Imagine now that you arrive at the college soccer pitch to watch a match between your college and a rival college. Because you are here to support *your* college team, your social identity as a member of that college will now be salient. Each social identity is associated with a range of attributes that characterize the prototypical group member. They are also associated with a set of group norms, a collection of shared beliefs about how group members should think and behave.

Self-categorization theory (Turner, Hogg, Oakes, Reicher, & Wetherell, 1987) is an extension of social identity theory that focuses on the set of group norms that define collective identities. According to this theory, when an individual's social identity becomes salient, their perceptions of themselves and others become depersonalized. In other words, rather than seeing themselves as a unique individual, they will perceive themselves more in terms of the shared features that define group membership, thinking and behaving more in line with the norms of that group. Group members also obey what is referred to as the **meta-contrast principle**, which means that they exaggerate similarities within the group and differences with other groups.

Jetten, Spears, and Manstead (1996) illustrated the effect of social identity on adherence to group norms. Participants first had their social identity made salient by being told they were being assigned to one of two groups, based on the technique they had used during an initial task in which they were required to estimate the number of dots on a computer screen. To increase identification with their group, they then took part in what they believed was a 'group task', although in actual fact there were no other group members (see Chapter 8 to learn more about this type of 'minimal group' paradigm). In this task, they estimated the number of black squares appearing on a screen and were given false feedback about the estimates of three other group members. They were then asked to distribute money between members of their own group and members of another group. To manipulate the group norm, participants learned that 10 out of 15 members of their group who had already taken part in the study had either distributed money equally between the two groups (a 'fairness' strategy), or had given more money to their own group (a 'discrimination' strategy). The norm of the other group was also manipulated, so that participants believed that the other group tended to distribute money equally or fairly. As Figure 1.6 illustrates, participants were strongly influenced by the norms of their own group, giving a greater proportion of money to members of their own group when there was a norm of discrimination but distributing money more equally between the two groups when there was a group norm of fairness. In contrast, they paid somewhat less attention to the norms of the other group.

There are many real-life examples of how group norms can affect our attitudes and behaviour. People who are normally perfectly reasonable and non-violent sometimes become aggressive and anti-social when they act as a group member rather than as an individual. A clear example of this is the fights and riots that sometimes erupt at football matches between the supporters of different teams (see our discussion of collective aggression in Chapter 9). Similarly, research has shown that women perform more poorly on maths tests than men when their gender identity is made salient because they conform to the negative stereotypes associated with their group membership (Steele, 1997; see the discussion of stereotype threat in Chapter 3).

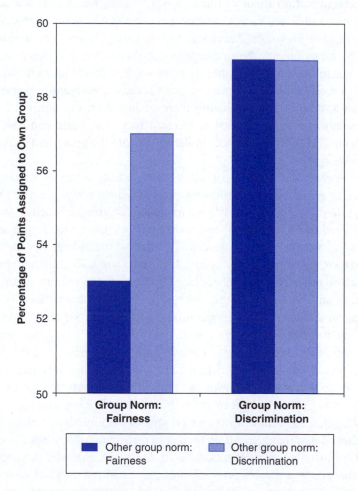

Figure 1.6   The effect of group norms on behaviour when social identity is salient. Data from Jetten, Spears, and Manstead (1996)

Finally, it is important to note that adherence to group norms does not always mean that people define themselves as group members; in fact, being part of a group can be a way of asserting one's sense of individuality. Bengry-Howell and Griffin (2007) used ethnographic methods to examine how young male 'car modifiers' from the midlands of England and North Wales constructed their identity from their cultural context. The study illustrates how discourse relating to people's identities can sometimes reveal conscious motivations that might be less readily identifiable from a purely quantitative analysis. Analysis of interviews with participants in this study showed that, on the whole, they resisted categorizing themselves as a collective ('car modifiers'), despite their apparent conformity to the norms of this culture, instead repeatedly proclaiming their (modified) cars as a source of their individuality. Their discourse emphasized the way that these young working-class men distanced themselves from 'typical' car owners, thus making them unique individuals. This study illustrates the complex processes involved in the construal of social identity, and how group membership can, perhaps ironically, sometimes be a source of individuality.

Summary

Three types of theory explain how our self-concept is formed, differing on the basis of whether the self is compared to a self-standard, to other individuals, or to other groups. Two theories propose that the self is often compared to an ideal version of the self. The *control theory of self-regulation* argues that, depending on whether we are privately or publicly self-aware, we compare the self against a private or a public self-standard, and when there is a mismatch between the self and the self-standard, we are motivated to change our behaviour to eliminate this mismatch. Similarly, *self-discrepancy theory* proposes that the actual self is compared to one of two self-guides, the ideal self and the ought self. A discrepancy between the actual and ideal self generates dejection-related emotions, whereas a discrepancy between the actual-ought self generates agitation-related emotions. In both cases, the psychological discomfort motivates a change to reduce the discrepancy.

Social comparison theory and the *self-evaluation maintenance* model both propose that our self-concept can be derived from comparisons with other individuals. According to social comparison theory, because there is no objectively 'correct' self, we compare ourselves to similar others to validate our attitudes and behaviour. The self-evaluation maintenance model proposes that we

(Continued)

maintain a positive self-image through two processes: social reflection (deriving self-esteem from the accomplishments of others) and social comparison (comparing our achievements with the achievements of others). Finally, according to the *social identity* approach, we can also derive a sense of self from the social groups to which we belong. When a particular group membership is salient, we define ourselves in terms of our social identity rather than our personal identity, and think and behave in accordance with the set of social norms associated with that particular group.

SELF-ESTEEM

It is clear from the theories described above that we devote much time to working out *who* exactly we are, often by making comparisons with self-standards, other individuals and other groups. Given the amount of time we spend thinking about the self and comparing it to others, it is not surprising that the self has an important *evaluative* component. We touched on this briefly above in our discussion of self-evaluative maintenance theory; we not only think about what our self-concept is, but also whether aspects of our self-concept are positive or negative. An individual's **self-esteem** is their subjective appraisal of themselves as intrinsically positive or negative (Sedikides & Gregg, 2002), and can have significant implications for psychological functioning.

Our level of self-esteem inevitably varies from time to time, depending on the context we find ourselves in. Getting a good mark for your psychology coursework is likely to elevate your self-esteem; getting a poor mark is likely to depress it. However, it is quite easy to bring to mind some people who always seem to be self-confident and others who display more self-doubt and pessimism about their lives. In this section, we talk about such *chronic* individual differences in self-esteem, how they develop and what consequences they have.

Development of Self-Esteem

How positive our self-concept is in later life appears to depend, at least to some extent, on the *parenting style* of our primary caregivers (Baumrind, 1991). There are three parenting styles which differ on two dimensions: how *demanding* (controlling, imposing rules and punishments) and how *responsive* (warm and supportive) the parent is towards the child. Children with the highest self-esteem are typically brought up by *authoritative parents*. This type of parent has a style high on both of these dimensions. They place a lot of demands on their child, imposing rules on them and disciplining them for disobedience. However, they are also responsive, supportive and warm. Children with lower self-esteem and less confidence in their abilities are often brought up with one of two less effective styles of parenting. *Authoritarian parents* are overly strict and demanding, failing to be responsive to the child's needs (see also Chapter 7, on the authoritarian personality). At the opposite end of the spectrum, *permissive parents* are responsive, but not strict enough, indulging their child's every desire.

Although the levels of chronic self-esteem people have may be determined during childhood, a meta-analysis of 50 self-esteem studies conducted by Robins and colleagues (2002) showed that over the course of people's lifespan general tendencies to have either high or low self-esteem can vary. They found that self-esteem among children aged between 6 and 11 was relatively unstable. This may be because young children are still in the process of developing their self-concept. Self-esteem was most stable among people in their 20s and remained relatively stable until mid-adulthood, probably because by this point in time, people have a fully developed sense of self and are less affected by temporary life changes. By the age of 60, however, self-esteem stability declines. Robins and colleagues explained that this might reflect the life changes that occur later in life, for example retirement, declining health and the death of others from their generation.

Consequences of Self-Esteem

Many researchers have investigated the consequences of having low or high self-esteem. However, before we go any further, it is important to note that a review by Baumeister and colleagues (1989) showed that the 'low self-esteem' individuals in most studies do not have low levels of self-esteem in *absolute* terms. Instead, they simply have low*er* self-esteem, in *relative* terms, compared to high self-esteem individuals. Nevertheless, as we shall see, there is evidence that people with low*er* self-esteem deal with life events quite differently from individuals with higher self-esteem.

Mood Regulation

There is a general assumption that everyone wants to feel positive about themselves and their lives and, to this end, do everything possible to maintain a positive outlook. However, recent research by Joanne Wood and her colleague indicates that people with lower self-esteem are less likely to make the *effort* to feel good than people with higher self-esteem. Two studies succinctly demonstrate how people with higher and lower self-esteem differ in their reactions to positive and negative life events. Wood, Heimpel, and Michela (2003) recorded participants' memories of positive events. They found that people with lower self-esteem were more likely to 'dampen' the good feelings they experienced, by distracting themselves, trying to make themselves feel less good, and trying to calm themselves, than were people with higher self-esteem. Heimpel, Wood, Marshall, and Brown (2002) got participants who had reported a failure in their everyday life to list their immediate plans and reasons for those plans. Participants with lower self-esteem were less likely to express goals to improve their mood than were participants higher in self-esteem. Heimpel and colleagues also found that having a goal to improve one's mood was associated with a greater improvement in mood the following day.

Together, these findings indicate that people with lower self-esteem make less effort to regulate their mood; they do not try and maintain a good mood after a positive life event, neither are they motivated to elevate their mood after a negative life event. These findings demonstrate that having lower self-esteem can be maladaptive, and explain why people with lower self-esteem tend to feel worse than those with higher self-esteem after a negative event (e.g. Brown & Dutton, 1995).

Narcissism

One of the major criticisms of the study of self-esteem has been the over-emphasis on the negative consequences of lower self-esteem. Clearly, having lower self-esteem can be maladaptive for that individual, as the findings of Wood and colleagues discussed above show. However, lower self-esteem is also frequently cited as an antecedent of anti-social behaviour, including the violent behaviour of youth gangs (Anderson, 1994), perpetrators of domestic violence (Renzetti, 1992), armed robbers (MacDonald, 1975), murderers (Kirschner, 1992) and terrorists (Long, 1990). Despite these claims, there is actually very little supportive evidence for this.

Baumeister, Smart, and Boden (1996) put forward the alternative argument that it is in fact higher self-esteem that is associated with higher levels of aggression and violence (see Chapter 9 for a more detailed discussion of the antecedents of aggression), although only under certain circumstances. Specifically, they proposed that people with higher self-esteem who have their ego threatened in some way, for example someone contradicting their viewpoint or their positive self-appraisal, will react aggressively to defend their higher self-esteem. Clearly, not all people with higher self-esteem behave aggressively when they feel threatened, so what determines *who* becomes aggressive? It seems that individuals who respond with aggression to an ego-threat are **narcissistic**. In other words, they tend to have *extremely* high self-esteem, believing that they are somehow special and superior to others, but at the same time, their self-esteem is *unstable*. As a result, they are

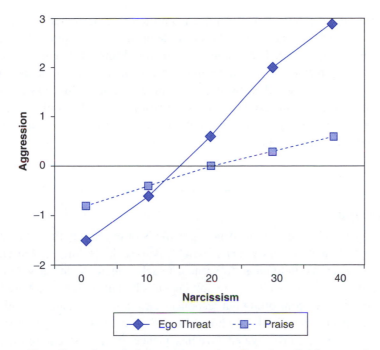

Figure 1.7 The effect of narcissism on aggression. Data from Bushman and Baumeister (1998)

reliant on validation from others in order to maintain their fragile positive self-concept (Kernis & Paradise, 2002). This may explain why criticism may generate such an explosive response from these individuals. In contrast, people with normal, *stable* higher levels of self-esteem are typically no more aggressive than individuals with lower self-esteem.

Bushman and Baumeister (1998) illustrated the relationship between narcissism and the tendency to be aggressive. Participants were told they were taking part in a study on how people respond to feedback from others and that they would be working with another participant. They then wrote a one paragraph essay which was subsequently taken away to be shown to the other participant (although there was, in fact, no second participant). Participants marked and gave feedback on the essay of the 'other participant' and were then given feedback on their own essay, supposedly from that other participant. In the *praise* condition, participants were given positive ratings and the comment 'Great essay!', whilst in the *threat* condition, they were given negative ratings and the comment 'This is one of the worst essays I have read!' Finally, participants were told that they would take part in a competitive reaction time task with the other participant, in which they would have to press a button as fast as possible on each trial. Whoever failed the trial would then receive a blast of noise from the other participant, which could be varied in intensity, and which therefore determined how much discomfort it would cause the recipient. The results are shown in Figure 1.7. There was a positive relationship between narcissism and aggression (measured by the intensity of noise delivered to the other participant), but this relationship was particularly strong when there was an ego threat. In other words, individuals higher in narcissism were even more aggressive than individuals lower in narcissism when they felt their ego was threatened.

Summary

An individual's self-esteem reflects how positively or negatively they evaluate their self-concept. Although *self-esteem* inevitably varies depending on the situation, there are also chronic individual differences in self-esteem. Whether we view ourselves positively or negatively as an adult depends in part on how we were brought up; people who have controlling but responsive, *authoritarian* parents tend to have higher self-esteem than children whose parents were authoritarian or permissive. Many researchers have investigated the consequences of self-esteem for the individual. People with high self-esteem are better at *mood regulation*, and therefore better able to react constructively to life events, than people with low self-esteem, who tend to dampen positive feelings but dwell on the negative feelings that they experience. Having high self-esteem can have negative consequences, however; research has shown that *narcissistic* individuals, who have a high but fragile self-esteem, are more likely to be aggressive than people with lower self-esteem, particularly if their self-esteem is threatened in some way.

SELF-MOTIVES

Given that the self-concept is central to every individual, guiding attitudes and behaviour and determining whether people feel positive or negative about themselves, we might expect it to be a key guiding principle in motivating our behaviour. In this next section, we discuss three of these motivations.

First, we hold a motive for **self-assessment**, a desire to know who we truly are, regardless of whether the truth is positive or negative. We are motivated to have an accurate self-perception to reduce uncertainty about our abilities or personal characteristics. For this reason, people like to complete *diagnostic* tests, which evaluate the performance of an individual and distinguish their performance from the performance of others, when evaluating the self (Trope, 1983).

Second, we are motivated to seek information that enables **self-verification** (Swann, 1997). Put another way, we want to confirm what we already believe to be true about our self-concept, even if we see ourselves in a negative light. If our search for information confirms what we already believe, this reassures us that we have an accurate self-perception and provides us with a sense of security and stability. To demonstrate the self-verification motivation, Swann, Stein-Seroussi, and Giesler (1992) asked people who had either a positive or a negative self-concept whether they would prefer to interact with evaluators who had a favourable impression of them, or an unfavourable impression of them. They found that people with a positive self-concept were more likely to choose the evaluator who viewed them positively, but people with a negative self-concept tended to choose the evaluator who viewed them negatively.

Third, we have a motivation for **self-enhancement**, a desire to seek out information about ourselves that allows us to see the self in a positive light. We discuss self-enhancement in more detail in the following section, but before we do that it is important to think about which of these three motives are the most important for guiding people's behaviour. This is not such an easy question, because the three can be somewhat contradictory, particularly for people with lower self-esteem. Self-enhancement would involve looking for positive self-knowledge whereas self-verification would involve seeking out negative self-knowledge. However, some research has suggested that individuals with lower self-esteem seek a compromise between these two motives, seeking out individuals who make them feel better about themselves without completely disconfirming their existing negative self-concept (Morling & Epstein, 1997).

Despite some inventive compromises to enable people to satisfy all three motives, ultimately one appears to come out on top. Sedikides (1993) conducted a series of studies in which the motives of self-assessment, self-verification and self-enhancement were pitted against each other. Participants completed a self-reflection task in which they could pick questions to ask themselves in order to learn what sort of person they were. Participants' strongest tendency was to ask themselves questions that focused on positive rather than negative aspects of the self. They were much less likely to ask themselves questions that focused on core aspects of themselves that they already know a lot about (self-verification) or peripheral aspects of themselves that they didn't know much about (self-assessment). In sum, self-enhancement appears to be the most powerful self-motive. As such, it has received most of the attention of researchers seeking to understand how self-motives shape our behaviours. It is this research we turn to in the next section.

Self-Enhancement

Why is self-enhancement so important to us? It is clear from the work on self-esteem discussed earlier that it is adaptive to have high self-esteem, provided it is not *too* high, and is stable rather than extreme and unstable. As we explained in the previous section, we self-regulate more effectively, and therefore cope with negative and positive life events in a more constructive way, when we have high self-esteem. But, given its usefulness, how can we maintain positive self-esteem? The types of strategies employed can be divided into two broad classes, depending on whether they involve deriving a positive self-concept from *personal* or *social* aspects of the self.

Strategies to Enhance the Personal Self

According to **self-affirmation theory** (Steele, 1975), when self-esteem has been damaged or threatened in some way, people often compensate by focusing on and publicly affirming positive aspects of themselves, thereby allowing them to maintain a positive self-concept. Steele demonstrated this effect in a study conducted among Mormon women, for whom community cooperation is an important ethic. These participants were first rung by a researcher who claimed she was conducting a poll. In the *self-concept threat condition*, the researcher commented that Mormons were typically uncooperative with community projects, whilst in the *self-concept irrelevant threat condition* they were told that Mormons were typically unconcerned with driver safety and care. Finally, in a *self-concept affirmation condition* participants were told that Mormons were typically cooperative with community projects. Two days later, participants received an apparently unrelated phone call from a researcher posing as a member of the local community asking them if they would be willing to list the contents of their kitchen as part of some research to help develop a community food cooperative. Steele found that compared to 65 per cent who agreed to help in the self-concept affirmation condition, approximately 95 per cent of participants in both threat conditions agreed to help. Presumably participants who felt threatened (even on an unrelated domain) wanted to reaffirm a positive aspect of their self-concept, and did so by publicly demonstrating their community spirit.

Another phenomenon that highlights people's tendency to self-enhance is the **self-serving attribution bias** (see also Chapter 2). There is considerable evidence that when people are making attributions about themselves on the basis of their behaviour, they show self-serving biases. When we are successful, we tend to show a self-enhancing bias, attributing our success to internal characteristics; for example, we might think 'I got an A grade in the examination because I am clever'. When we fail, however, we tend to show a self-protecting bias, attributing our failure to external characteristics. We might, for example, think 'I got a D grade because

I wasn't feeling well on the day of the examination'. People also have a memory bias in favour of self-enhancing information. Mischel, Ebbesen, and Zeiss (1976) exposed participants to an equal amount of positive and negative information about their personality and then tested their memory of that information. They found that participants had better memory for the positive information than for the negative information. Other research suggests that people are more critical of information that criticizes them than information that praises them. Wyer and Frey (1983) had participants complete an intelligence test and then gave them either positive or negative feedback. Participants were then given the opportunity to read a report on the validity of intelligence tests which contained a mix of supportive and critical information. Participants who had been told they had performed poorly subsequently judged intelligence tests to be less valid than did participants who had received positive feedback.

Strategies to Enhance the Social Self

In addition to these individual self-enhancement strategies, people also derive a positive self-image from their group memberships. According to the social identity approach (Tajfel & Turner, 1979), when people's social self is salient, they incorporate in their self-concept any traits that are thought to be part of the group, regardless of whether those traits are positive or negative. It is therefore understandably important to group members that their group is evaluated positively. In the same way that people try to maintain a positive personal identity by comparing themselves favourably to other individuals (see the discussion of social comparison theory earlier in this chapter), group members are also motivated to hold a positive social or *collective* identity. They do so by comparing themselves favourably with members of other groups.

The desire to maintain a positive social identity can explain why group members show ingroup bias, a preference for their own group over outgroups, groups to which they do not belong (see Chapter 8 for more on the role of social identity in intergroup relations). By expressing how good your group is compared to others, by implication, the self as a group member reaps the benefits of this positive intergroup comparison (Hogg & Abrams, 1988). Given the importance of the link between the self and the ingroup, but not the outgroup, in promoting disharmony between groups, some researchers have focused on the self as a way of improving intergroup relations. In particular, if it is the absence of a link between the self and outgroup that is partly responsible for intergroup bias (including prejudice and discrimination), then perhaps forging such links can reduce such bias. We describe one of these approaches in more detail in Text Box 1.2.

Text Box 1.2

Reducing Prejudice by Including the Other in the Self

People are generally motivated to see themselves in a positive light; for example, we take pride in our success and attribute it to personal characteristics, while blaming failures on external characteristics beyond our control. Although these self-serving tendencies sound selfish and biased, they actually have benefits for our relationships with other individuals and other social groups. Research in the past decade has shown that our self-concept cognitively overlaps with the self-concept of close friends and romantic partners, a process which Aron and colleagues (1992) refer to as *including other in the self*. This has a number of benefits for interpersonal relationships because the positive feelings and treatment we usually reserve for the self can then be extended to others. Indeed, Agnew et al. (1998) found that greater inclusion of other in the self among dating couples was associated with greater satisfaction, commitment and investment in the relationship.

Wright, Aron, McLaughlin-Volpe, and Ropp (1997) investigated the role of inclusion of other in the self in the *extended contact effect*, the finding that just knowing members of the ingroup (the group to which you belong) who have friends in an outgroup (a group to which you do not belong) reduces prejudice. Wright and colleagues argued that we spontaneously incorporate close others in the self, including ingroup members (Smith & Henry, 1996). Moreover, we have a tendency to group together people who we perceive to be friends; for example, partners in a close relationship are treated by observers as a single cognitive unit (Sedikides, Olsen, & Reis, 1993). Thus, when participants observe an ingroup member in a close relationship with an outgroup member, they will perceive there to be a considerable overlap between the two. Consequently, they come to see the outgroup member, and eventually the outgroup in general, as part of the self as well. In this situation, the outgroup will enjoy the same benefits bestowed upon ingroup members, including showing positive biases in attribution, feeling pain at their trouble, generously sharing resources and taking pride in their successes.

Method

Wright and colleagues (1997) led participants to believe they had been assigned to one of two groups based on their performance on an initial task. Participants then observed an ingroup and an outgroup member (actually two confederates) interact on a problem-solving task. The relationship between the individuals was either one of close friends, strangers, or disliked acquaintances.

Results and Discussion

The outgroup was evaluated more positively when the observed interaction was friendly than when it was neutral or hostile. This is because the participant only perceived there to be self-other overlap when the observed ingroup and outgroup member were friends; only friends are perceived to have overlapping self-concepts.

So the groups to which we belong can provide an important source of self-esteem, and we are motivated to create a positive image of them because this then reflects well on us. But our ingroups can sometimes be seen as either positive *or* negative, depending upon factors beyond our control. Under these circumstances, group members use a number of strategies to both maintain a positive social identity *and* buffer themselves from the potentially damaging self-esteem implications of being a member of a low status group. It is easy for high status groups to maintain a positive social identity because they can compare themselves favourably with low status groups (see our earlier discussion of intergroup social comparisons). However, low status group members have to resort to other strategies, particularly if they are not willing or able to leave their group to join a higher status group (Tajfel & Turner, 1979). They may attempt a *social change strategy*, where they compete with the high status group to improve their status relative to that group. Alternatively, they may attempt a *social creativity strategy*, finding new dimensions on which they compare more favourably. Members of a college that is academically poor, for example, may maintain a positive social identity when being compared to a top academic college by saying that they are better at sport, or throw better parties. Finally, members of low status groups may simply dis-identify with the group, disregarding that membership as an important part of their identity.

Robert Cialdini and colleagues (1976) illustrated this dis-identification strategy when they investigated the behaviour of fans of college American football teams. During the 1973 collegiate football season, students at seven universities were covertly monitored every Monday during an introductory psychology class. The proportion of students at the class wearing apparel that identified their university name, insignia or emblem (for example, jackets, sweatshirts, scarfs and caps) was recorded. Researchers then considered whether students' apparel differed depending on whether their university's football team had won or not won at the weekend. Figure 1.8 demonstrates what they found. Students wore

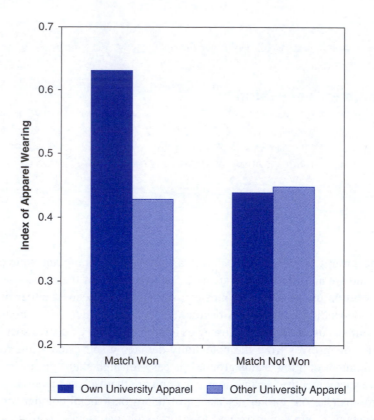

Figure 1.8 Basking in reflected glory. Data from Cialdini and colleagues (1976)

more apparel that displayed the name or insignia of their university when their university football team had been recently successful than when their team had not been successful.

Cialdini et al. (1976) called this phenomenon **basking in reflected glory**. Essentially, people derive a positive self-concept from the achievements of other group members even if they were not personally instrumental in those achievements. When one's group is performing poorly, however, group members often use a very different strategy, which is illustrated by the lack of apparel seen in Cialdini's study when the team had lost. Illustrating this in more detail, Snyder, Lassegard, and Ford (1986) found that compared to groups of college students who performed adequately on a group task, groups who failed on the task were more likely to distance themselves from other members of their group. They reported a desire to avoid the group, and took off and discarded their group name badges. This tendency is referred to as **cutting off reflected failure**.

Summary

Given how central it is to us, we do not perceive the self in a passive way. Instead, we are influenced by three key motives. First, we hold a motive for *self-assessment*, to hold an accurate self-perception in order to reduce uncertainty about the self. Second, we have a motive for *self-verification*; we want to confirm what we already believe to be true about the self. However, the most powerful self-motive we hold is for *self-enhancement*. We hold several strategies that enable us to maintain positive self-esteem. First, according to *self-affirmation theory*, when self-esteem has been damaged or threatened in some way, people maintain a positive self-concept by focusing on and publicly affirming positive aspects of themselves. Second, people have a self-serving attribution bias, attributing successes to internal characteristics and failures to factors outside their control.

According to the social identity approach we also derive a positive self-image from our group memberships, which explains why we often show ingroup favourit-ism. Although it can be difficult for low status groups to maintain a positive social identity, they do so by competing with the high status group to improve their social standing, comparing themselves on different dimensions, or by dis-identifying with a group. People also maintain a positive social identity by *basking in reflected glory* when their group has been successful but cutting off reflected failure when their group has not done so well.

CULTURAL DIFFERENCES IN SELF AND IDENTITY

Although everyone has a unique sense of self, there are also some broad cultural differences in people's self-concept, depending on the society in which they were brought up. A growing number of people also belong to more than one culture and therefore have two quite different self-concepts that exist alongside one another. In this section, we discuss some of the effects that culture can have on the self.

Individualist and Collectivist Cultures

As we have discussed earlier, social psychologists recognize that there are both individual aspects of the self, including traits, states and personal behaviours, and collective aspects of the self, which reflect our relationships with other individuals and groups (Triandis, 1989). Although it is highly likely that most people, regard-less of their culture, have both individual and collective self-schemas, there are some broad cultural trends. In **individualist cultures** such as the United States and Europe, from an early age children are encouraged to think of themselves as unique individuals. In **collectivist cultures**, on the other hand, children are encouraged to be obedient and respectful of their family and to conform to societal norms. Given these differences in emphasis, you will probably not be surprised to learn that people in collectivist societies have a more collective sense of self, whereas people in an individualist culture have a more individual sense of self.

To illustrate this difference, Trafimow, Triandis, and Goto (1991) had North American and Chinese participants write down 20 self-descriptions. They found that North American students wrote down a significantly greater proportion of individual self descriptions than Chinese students, for example 'I am intelligent'. In contrast, Chinese students wrote down significantly more collective self-descriptions, for example 'I am a Roman Catholic', than North American students.

These cultural differences in self-conception help to explain the different values held by people from individualist and collectivist cultures. Gardner, Gabriel, and Lee (1999) demonstrated the relationship between self-construal and values by priming American students to temporarily have either a more individualist or a more collectivist self-concept. Participants read a story about a trip to the city. The story either used independent pronouns (e.g. I, mine) or interdependent pronouns (e.g. we, ours), a technique which has previously been shown to prime the personal and cultural self-concept respectively. Participants then wrote down 20 self-descriptions and completed a questionnaire in which they reported the values which were most important to them. The findings to this study are illustrated in Figure 1.9. Participants primed to hold a personal self-concept wrote more individual self-descriptions and more strongly endorsed individualist values, such as freedom and independence, whereas participants primed to hold a collective self-concept wrote more collective self-descriptions and more strongly endorsed collectivist values, such as friendship and family safety.

Biculturalism

Many countries are now multicultural, made up of not only the original inhabitants of a country but of a diverse body of immigrants from all over the world, generated by increasing geographic mobility, wars and humanitarian crises. In the US in 2000, for example, 26.4 million people – approximately 10 per cent of the population – were born overseas. Immigrants often find themselves in a position where they have to deal with multiple identities, derived from their original culture and that of the majority or 'host' society (Phinney, Lochner, & Murphy, 1990). Given the diversity of different cultures, this may mean incorporating into the self-concept two cultures that are likely to differ in terms of values, attitudes, customs and styles of interaction (Berry & Annis, 1974). Some individuals struggle to deal with the presence of two different identities, either assimilating to the identity of the host society *or* retaining

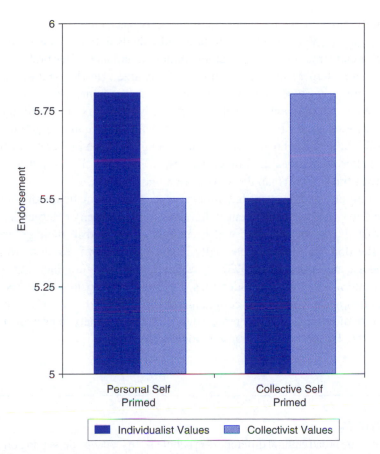

Figure 1.9 The effect of priming the personal versus the collective self on endorsement of individualistic and collectivist values. Data from Gardner, Gabriel and Lee (1999)

their original immigrant identity, but others maintain their original sense of identity while also sharing an identity with the host society. People who are adept at dealing with both cultures are known as *bicultural* (Ramirez, 1983).

The **alternation model** suggests that it is possible for an individual to deal with multiple identities by understanding the cultural assumptions that guide behaviour and using this knowledge to think and behave appropriately in each (Yamada & Singelis, 1999). The model argues that by alternating one's cultural orientation depending on the situation, it is possible for an individual to have a sense of belonging in two cultures without compromising his or her sense of cultural identity. Hong, Morris, Chiu and Benet-Martinez (2000), for example, found that Chinese American bicultural individuals primed with Western or East Asian cues changed their behaviour in line with the cued culture.

The ability to hold two identities simultaneously has a number of benefits. Buriel and colleagues (1998) found that bicultural individuals felt more at ease interacting with individuals from outside their ethnic minority, and had better problem-solving strategies and interpersonal skills. Similarly, Schwarzer, Bowler, and Rauch (1985) found that minority students who were proficient at communicating with the majority culture had not only higher levels of self-esteem than less bicultural individuals but also reported having less experience with racial tension and interethnic conflict. Bicultural individuals who alternate are also thought to have higher cognitive functioning, better mental health (Rogler, Cortes, & Malgady, 1991) and higher self-esteem (Martinez, 1987) than those who are monocultural.

It is worth noting, however, that not everyone is so optimistic about people who simultaneously hold two different cultural identities. Lorenzo-Hernandez (1998) argued that those who alternate will be neither committed to their group of origin nor the dominant group, potentially leading to negative reactions from both. LaFromboise and colleagues (1993) suggested that for bicultural individuals to successfully alternate between two identities, they must hold positive attitudes towards both cultures and the ability to communicate effectively. It is also important that their culture of origin is strongly represented in the host society to provide a support system and to buffer the bicultural individual from stress.

Summary

There are some broad cultural differences in people's self-concept, depending on whether someone has been brought up in an *individualist* or a *collectivist* culture. In individualist cultures, people tend to hold a stronger individual self, thinking of themselves in terms of uniquely personal traits, and holding values of freedom and independence, whereas in collectivist cultures, people tend to see themselves in terms of a collective self, describing themselves in terms of group memberships and their relations with others and strongly endorsing values like friendship and family safety.

A growing number of people, particularly immigrants, now have to juggle two identities, one derived from their original culture and another from their host society. Some individuals struggle to deal with two very different identities and their associated norms and values, but other individuals are *bicultural*, adept at dealing with both cultures. According to the *alternation* model, bicultural individuals are able to alternate their cultural orientation when the situation calls for it and derive a number of benefits from this ability, including better problem-solving and interpersonal skills.

CHAPTER SUMMARY

The way in which we can look inwards, to think about who we are and why we think, act, and behave as we do, is a uniquely human ability, and something that affects every aspect of our lives. Research on the self has largely focused on how our self-perceptions affect our thoughts, feelings, and actions. These effects only occur when we are *self-aware*. We are not born with self-awareness, but develop the ability to be introspective during early childhood. Self-awareness appears to be connected to a particular area of the brain, the *anterior cingulate* in the frontal lobe. Self-awareness varies depending on the situation and our personality, and can be public or private in nature. When we are *privately self-aware*, we tend to experience intensified emotional reactions, behave in accordance with our true beliefs, and have a more accurate self-perception. In contrast, when we are *publicly self-aware*, we are more likely to suffer from *evaluation apprehension* and behave in accordance with *social norms* regardless of our true beliefs. The information about the self that we access when we are self-aware is stored in *self-schemas*, cognitive structures that hold knowledge about different aspects of the self. Self-schemas vary on a continuum, from self-schematic schemas that are central to our self-concept, to aschematic schemas that are irrelevant to us.

Numerous theories have been offered to explain how we perceive the self and how this perception affects our thoughts, feelings, and behaviour. Two theories propose that the self is often compared to an ideal version of the self and that discrepancies have certain consequences for the individual. The *control theory of self-regulation* argues that depending on whether we are privately or publicly self-aware, we compare the self against a private or a public self-standard. When there is a mismatch between the two, we attempt to change our behaviour to increase their congruence. According to *self-discrepancy theory*, the actual self is compared to one of two self-guides, the ideal self and the ought self. A discrepancy between the self and a self-guide causes psychological discomfort which motivates change to reduce the discrepancy. However, the two types of self-discrepancy are thought to be related to unique responses: actual-ideal discrepancy with dejection related emotions and actual-ought discrepancy with agitation related emotions.

Social comparison theory and the *self-evaluation maintenance* model both propose that our self-concept can be derived from comparisons with other individuals. According to social comparison theory, because there is no objectively 'correct' self, we compare ourselves to similar others to validate our attitudes and behaviour. The self-evaluation maintenance model proposes that we maintain a positive self-image through two processes: social reflection and social comparison. Finally, according to the *social identity* approach, we can also derive a sense of self from the social groups to which we belong.

It is clear from these theories that we do not think about the self in a detached way. Instead, we are keen to determine whether we should evaluate the many aspects of the self in a positive or a negative light. Although our level of *self-esteem* inevitably varies depending on the situation, there are also chronic differences in self-esteem which may in part reflect the way in which we were brought up. Self-esteem has far-reaching consequences for how we deal with life events. In contrast to people with lower self-esteem, those with higher self-esteem are better able to regulate their moods, buffering themselves from the negative impact of unpleasant events and deriving pleasure from positive events. It is worth noting, however, that high self-esteem is not always a good thing; *narcissistic* individuals with very high but unstable self-esteem tend to have aggressive tendencies, particularly if their ego has been threatened.

Given the importance of a positive self-esteem, it is unsurprising that we have a strong motivation for self-*enhancement*, which appears to override our motives for *self-assessment* and *self-verification*. We use a number of strategies to enhance our personal and social self. According to *self-affirmation theory*, if our self-esteem has been threatened on one dimension, we maintain a positive self-concept by publicly affirming an aspect of ourselves that we know to be positive. We also maintain a positive self-concept through self-serving attribution biases, by paying more attention to positive information about the self than negative information, and by being more critical of negative information about the self than positive information. When our group membership is salient, we use group-based strategies to maintain a positive social identity, for example *basking in the reflected glory* of successful group members, but cutting off the reflected failure of unsuccessful group members.

Finally, there are some broad cultural differences in people's self-concept, depending on the society in which they were brought up. People from individualist cultures like Europe and the United States have a stronger individual sense of self, whereas people from collectivist cultures like China and India are more likely to see themselves in terms of their relationships with family members and social groups. There is also a growing minority of *bicultural* individuals who have two sets of cultural identities because they have been brought up in one culture and have then migrated to a country with a sharply diverging culture. Although it can be difficult to juggle two different self-concepts, people that successfully *alternate* between the values and attitudes of two cultures develop excellent problem-solving strategies and interpersonal skills, and have higher cognitive functioning, better mental health and higher self-esteem than monocultural individuals.

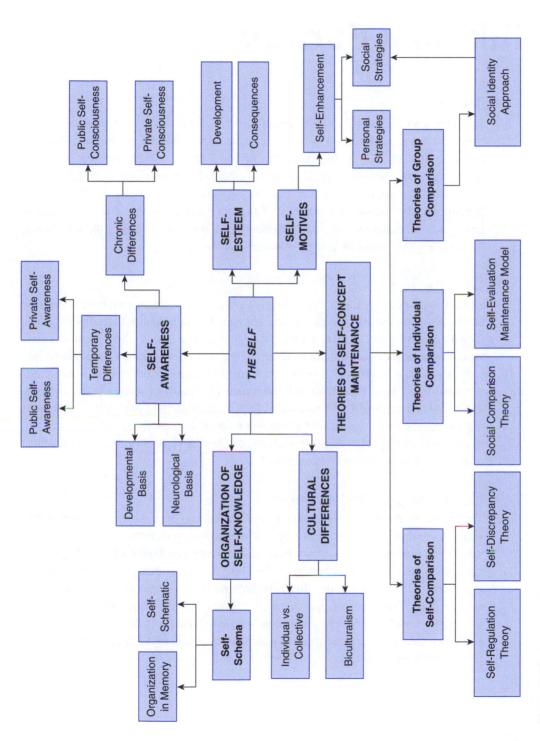

Figure 1.10 Memory map

Taking it Further

Try This

Look back to Figure 1.2 and the organization of Rhiannon's self-schema. With a friend do two self-schemas. First do a self-schema for yourself, positioning the traits closer or further away from the centre of the diagram to illustrate the extent to which they describe you. Second, do a self-schema for your friend. Does the schema you created for your friend match the one they created for themselves? Does their schema for you match your schema? If there are any traits that differ, or differ in terms of how central they are, can you identify reasons why? (maybe think about the difference between public and private views of the self).

Debate This

Does the apparent dominance of self-enhancement mean that we all have inherently fragile egos, preferring to seek out and engage only in behaviours that will furnish us with a positive self-image, avoiding or ignoring unwelcome 'home truths'? How would we ever grow as individuals if we never acknowledge things we could do better? In what situations might we be encouraged to focus on self-assessment or self-verification motives rather than self-enhancement? Are there some situations where self-enhancement might be better for us (e.g. in the wake of a particularly bad set of events, or when we are already feeling down for other reasons). Could you develop a 'self-help' strategy that engineers a focus on the different self-motives that is most adaptive following different life events?

Something for the Weekend

Think back to the last time that someone annoyed you because they did better than you at something. If you were annoyed it was probably something that was important to you (maybe they beat you in a test, or maybe you both ended up buying the same dress and *she* looked better in it!). Did you use a strategy of self-evaluation maintenance? Perhaps you devalued the dimension of comparison ('well, you know what, I think I've gone off that dress …') or maybe you distanced yourself from the target ('who? her? Sorry, don't know who you mean …'). What other strategies could you have used, and are there any factors that might make some of these strategies more likely to be used over others?

Further Reading

The Essentials

Baumeister, R.F. (1998). The self. In D.T. Gilbert, S.T. Fiske, & G. Lindzey (Eds.), *Handbook of social psychology* (4th edn, Vol. 1, pp. 680–740). New York: McGraw-Hill.

This is an excellent, accessible and contemporary overview of what we know about the psychology of the self – a good first step.

Next Steps

Abrams, D. & Hogg, M.A. (2001). Collective identity: Group membership and self-conception. In M.A. Hogg & R.S. Tindale (Eds.), *Blackwell handbook of social psychology: Group processes* (pp. 425–460). Oxford: Blackwell.

This chapter is an excellent introduction to social identity – how groups and social categories provide us with a basis for self-definition that goes beyond a sense of our individual identity. It will also set you up nicely for later chapters on social cognition, group processes and prejudice.

Delving Deeper

Benet-Martínez, V., Leu, J., Lee, F., & Morris, M. (2002). Negotiating biculturalism: Cultural frame-switching in biculturals with 'oppositional' vs. 'compatible' cultural identities. *Journal of Cross-Cultural Psychology, 33*, 492–516.

This is a fascinating paper showing that when people develop a bicultural identity through extended exposure to both their home and host culture, they also develop a flexible 'frame-switching' approach to thinking that mirrors what they have to do on a day-to-day basis.

Attribution 2

Attribution

So you're queuing up in the campus supermarket. 'Hello' you chirp as you cheerfully place your shopping down in front of you at the checkout. The shop assistant, Dorothy (who you've seen many times on your visits to the shop, but don't really know), looks at you as if you've just hurled the world's worst insult at her. She slams your purchases through without barely another word and you leave the shop wondering what on earth just happened.

When things like this happen to us, we naturally wonder why. What was wrong with Dorothy? Was it something you'd said? Did she just get some bad news? Is she having some sort of breakdown? Any or all of these thoughts might pass through your head as you leave the shop. These questions, and the psychological processes they trigger, are the focus of this chapter. Explaining other people's behaviour (or *attributing* causality to actions we observe) is the bedrock of research into social inference, and more generally, social cognition – how we think about people. We'll get on to social cognition more generally in Chapter 3, but we start, in this chapter, by explaining the essentials of *attribution theory*. Year after year students have told us that they find attribution the hardest topic in their introduction to social psychology. So we've done two things: 1. We've done everything we can to explain the concepts involved in a jargon-free way (with many references to how the processes might work in the real world). 2. We've made this the shortest chapter in the book. Attribution is less about facts and more about understanding how to apply the models' rules to everyday social behaviour (and this is what exam questions on attribution often ask you to do). We'd like you to have more time to practise applying the principles rather than reading about them (and to try out the suggested exercises at the end of the chapter). Anyway, before we get on to how people make attributions, we need to know *why* they make them, so that's where we'll start …

THE NAÏVE SCIENTIST

Let us begin with common sense. Humans are rationale creatures, right? (okay, we're going to come back to that one later on, but let's go with this assumption for now). We are able to solve complex mathematical problems, use sophisticated logic to construct arguments: we are cogent, balanced, and analytical. It should therefore follow that we apply these principles to everyday social thought and action. This was the view of social inference that characterized early theorizing. This highly influential view was presented by Heider (1958), who argued that people are motivated by two primary needs: (1) the need to form a coherent view of the world and (2) the need to gain control over the environment. Heider believed that this desire for consistency and stability, the ability to predict and control, makes us behave like **naïve scientists**, rationally and logically testing our hypotheses about the behaviour of others. In particular, this need to attribute causes to effects (for example, observed behaviours and events) and to create a meaningful, stable world where things make sense was the basis for a theoretical approach that became highly influential in how social psychologists viewed social inference processes. This set of ideas and models can be referred to as **attribution theory**.

ATTRIBUTION THEORY

Heider (1958) believed that we have a basic need to attribute causality because this ascribes meaning to our world, making it clear, definable, and predictable, thereby reducing uncertainty. This need, Heider argued, is a major driving force in human social inference. A clever experiment illustrated this basic need. Heider and Simmel (1944) asked participants to simply describe the movement of abstract geometric shapes. They found a general tendency to describe the movement in ways indicative of human intentions and motives (see Figure 2.1). This readiness to ascribe human intentionality to things that we know have little or no capacity for such intention is a common characteristic of how we think (just think about how people sometimes talk to their pets as if they can understand them).

Types of Attribution

This apparent desire to attribute causality was the basis for a great deal of work that attempted to model the ways in which humans try to explain the actions of themselves and others. To understand these models we first need to define different types of attribution. We can refer to this as defining the *locus of causality*.

The main distinction that can be made between types of attribution is internal-external. An **internal attribution** is any explanation that locates the cause as being internal to the person, such as personality, mood, abilities, attitudes, and effort (also known as a personal attribution). An **external attribution** is any explanation that locates the cause as being external to the person, such as the actions of others, the nature of the situation, social pressures, or luck (also know as a situational

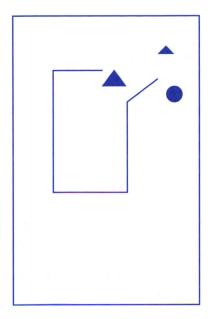

– Participants were asked to interpret a moving picture-film in which three geometric figures (a large triangle, a small triangle, and a disc) were shown moving in various directions and at various speeds in and around a rectangle which could be opened or closed with a 'door'.

– Out of 34 participants, only one participant described the film in geometrical terms (e.g. 'A large triangle enters a rectangle and moves around.').

– All other participants described the movements as actions of animate beings, mostly humans, but in two cases as birds.

– Example response: 'A man has planned to meet a girl and the girl comes along with another man. The first man tells the second to go. The second man shakes his head. Then the two men have a fight.'

Figure 2.1 An illustration of the picture-film used in the Heider and Simmel (1944) study

attribution). Take Dorothy, our shop assistant. How do you explain her rude and aggressive behaviour? Given that you do not really know her or, to be more precise, you don't have direct access to her inner thoughts and feelings, you can only infer a cause from her behaviour. You might come to the conclusion that she is basically just a rude and unpleasant person and her behaviour was this underlying tendency coming though (a dispositional, internal attribution). Alternatively, you might think she is just having a bad day – maybe she had just had an argument with her husband (a situational attribution). Ok, let's leave Dorothy for a while – what about your professor? Lets say she's in a particularly good mood in class one day – joking, humming happily to herself (behaviour that is perhaps different from the norm). Do you think her personality might have suddenly changed (a dispositional attribution), or would you infer some other cause (perhaps she has just got a paper accepted to a leading journal – a situational cause). We'll discuss how people arrive at either of these different types of attribution later on (in other words, the *process* of attribution), but for now it is just important to note that there are fundamentally two different ways that behaviour can be explained: by internal or by external causes.

As well as this fundamental distinction between internal and external attributions, it is possible to further subdivide types of inference along two other independent dimensions: stability and controllability (Weiner, 1982; 1986). Stability refers to the extent to which causes are relatively stable and permanent (e.g. natural ability) versus temporary and fluctuating (e.g. being drunk). Controllability refers to the extent to which causes can be influenced by others (e.g. effort) versus the extent to which they are random (e.g. luck). Together, these three dimensions appear to be the typical ways in which people explain events (Meyer & Koebl, 1982) in both individualist and collectivist countries (Hau & Salili, 1991). However, for our purposes, we only need to focus on the most common and clearest distinction: internal versus external causes. How people arrive at either an internal or external attribution is the focus of the next section.

MAKING ATTRIBUTIONS

In the previous section we classified the types of attribution people can make, the conclusions that we can arrive at when trying to explain someone else's behaviour. But how do people reach that conclusion, what are the thought processes involved? In this section we discuss the two main models of attribution process that emerged from research in the 1970s: *correspondent inference theory* and the *co-variation model*.

Correspondent Inference Theory

According to Jones and Davis's (1965) **correspondent inference theory**, when making social inferences people *try* to infer that the action of an actor corresponds to, or is indicative of, a stable personality characteristic. The idea is that people prefer internal, dispositional attributions over external, situational attributions because the former type of knowledge is more valuable with regard to making predictions about behaviour. A dispositional attribution such as 'rude' is a judgement that the person in question has a particular set of personality attributes, which are assumed to be stable and do not change over time. In contrast a situation attribution – such as explaining behaviour as being down to a transitory mood – is by definition a variable and changeable cause. The former, being stable and unchanging, is a much more valuable conclusion (if valid) for predicting future behaviour. For example, attributing a shop assistant's rudeness to an internal cause – his grumpy personality – is useful because we can then assume he will always be grumpy when we visit the shop, and so we should avoid his till. If we can find dispositional causes for behaviour these help us to fulfil what Heider (1958) argued is our basic drive towards coherence and clarity, stability and a predictable world.

According to Jones and Davis (1965) we assess whether there is a correspondence between behaviour and personality (i.e. arrive at a correspondent inference or, in other words, a dispositional attribution) by processing three key types of information: *social desirability*, *choice*, and *non-common effects*.

Social desirability information refers to whether the behaviour observed is consistent with, or counter to, social norms. An internal, dispositional attribution is more likely when socially undesirable behaviours are observed. People have a tendency to go along with social norms – to adhere to the majority viewpoint – because they wish to avoid exclusion and ridicule for standing out and being different from the crowd (we discuss this normative social influence in detail in Chapter 6). As such, behaviour that is socially desirable does not tell us much about people's personalities because they may simply be going along with the group norm, which may or may not coincide with their own personal point of view. In contrast, someone who exhibits socially undesirable behaviour – who goes against the social norm – is much more likely to be displaying behaviour that corresponds to an underlying personality trait, because the behaviour cannot be attributed to the person simply conforming to the majority.

According to Jones and Davis, another type of information that social perceivers seek in order to make a correspondent inference is whether the behaviour in question was freely chosen or not. An internal, dispositional attribution is more likely when the person being observed has *freely chosen* the given behaviour. Again, this makes a lot of sense; if behaviour has been freely chosen then it is much more likely to be the result of an underlying personality characteristic or attitude, rather than a result of coercion, threat, or inducements.

When a behaviour has a unique consequence, rather than having a range of possible other consequences, we can refer to it as having non-common effects. An internal, dispositional attribution is more likely when the outcome of a behaviour has a unique (or non-common) effect. For instance, a punch has really only one possible outcome so it is more likely to be attributed to an internal, dispositional cause.

Although there is some evidence to support the idea that people use these three types of information outlined above to attribute causality to others' behaviour (e.g. Jones & Harris, 1967), ultimately the theory has declined in popularity due to some clear limitations. In particular, the model is limited to *single instances* of behaviour and focuses on *internal attributions*. The latter point is especially important. It is very easy to think of the many times that we have put someone's behaviour down to bad luck, or them having a bad day. People clearly and consistently make external attributions as well as internal. The model we turn to next directly addresses these limitations and is arguably the most influential of the attribution theories.

The Co-variation Model

Kelley's (1967) **co-variation model** accounts for *multiple* behaviours. Importantly, it also details the processes that result in *external* as well as internal attributions. According to Kelley, causality is attributed using the **co-variation principle**. This principle states that for something to be the cause of a particular behaviour it must be *present* when the behaviour is *present* and *absent* when the behaviour is *absent* (i.e. it must co-vary). From multiple potential causes we ascribe causality to the one that *co-varies* with the behaviour to the greatest extent – acting, as Heider (1958) would say, exactly like naïve scientists.

The co-variation model states that three types of information are crucial for arriving at an internal or external attribution: *consensus*, *consistency*, and *distinctiveness* information. When observing someone's behaviour in a particular social context, the combined impact of these three types of information will determine what type of attribution is made. Consensus information is the extent to which other people in the scene react in the same way as the target person. Consistency information is the extent to which the target person reacts in the same way on different occasions. Distinctiveness information is the extent to which the target person reacts in the same way in other social contexts (see Figure 2.2).

TYPE OF INFORMATION	EXAMPLE	IMPLICATION
Consensus information	**High:** Everyone is wearing a dodgy sweater	**Situation**
The extent to which the target and and audience behave in the same way	**Low:** Only our professor is wearing a dodgy sweater	**Disposition**
Consistency information	**High:** Your professor is wearing the dodgy sweater in every lecturer	**Disposition**
The extent to which the target behaves in the same way on different occasions	**Low:** Your professor wears the dodgy sweater today	**Situation**
Distinctiveness information	**High:** Your professor only wears the dodgy sweater in this lecture	**Situation**
The extent to which the target behaves in the same way in other situations	**Low:** Your professor wears the dodgy sweater around campus	**Disposition**

Note:

Dispositional attribution

Any explanation that locates the cause as being internal to the person *(personality, mood, attitudes, abilities, effort)*

Situational attribution

Any explanation that locates the cause as being external to the person *(actions of others, the nature of the situation, luck)*

Figure 2.2   Kelley's co-variation model: Using consensus, consistency and distinctiveness information to explain why your professor is wearing a dodgy sweater

Independently, the presence or absence of each of these types of information has implications for whether a dispositional or situational attribution will be more likely. The presence of consensus information (if everyone else is behaving in the same way as the target person) implies a situational cause, whereas the *absence* of consensus information implies a dispositional cause. The presence of consistency information (the target person behaves in the same way over and over again) implies a dispositional cause, while the *absence* of consistency information implies a situational cause. The presence of distinctiveness information (the target person acts in the same way in many different contexts) implies a dispositional cause, but the *absence* of distinctiveness information implies a situational cause.

Here's an example to illustrate. Imagine you are sitting in class one day and your professor walks in wearing an unusual and particularly garish multi-coloured sweater, sporting on its front a picture of a large happy badger. As naïve scientists we like to have a stable and predictable world, so you would be compelled to try to figure out why your professor has chosen to wear such a strange garment. According to the co-variation model, you would assess whether the three types of information outlined above are present or absent.

First: consensus. Is everyone wearing the same type of sweater or is it only your professor? If it is only your professor you're likely to begin to make an internal, dispositional attribution: no-one else is behaving in the same way (i.e. wearing a strange sweater), so the cause of this strange behaviour is likely to be something uniquely to do with your professor, and not the situation (otherwise other people would also be affected by whatever the cause might be – such as a new fashion – and would also be wearing a dodgy sweater).

Second: consistency. Is this the first time your professor has worn this sweater, or does he do it every week? If he wears this weird sweater every week, then you're going to be even more inclined to make a dispositional attribution. If he is only wearing it this week then you might think he's having only a temporary fashion crisis – perhaps his washing machine has broken (a situational attribution) and the peculiar sweater is the only one he has left that is clean.

Third: distinctiveness. Does your professor wear this sweater in different classes? Do you see him around campus sporting similarly ill-advised sweaters? If you do, again you're going to be more inclined to make a dispositional attribution (i.e. your professor has chronic fashion problems, or perhaps an enduring badger fixation). This is because the behaviour is not distinctive to the current situation (which would make it likely that it is something in the immediate context that is making your professor wear the sweater).

In sum, if your professor wears bad badger sweaters consistently over time and in different contexts, and he is the only person to be doing so, then you're going to make a dispositional attribution and conclude that he has terrible fashion sense (or a badger fixation). But anyway, enough of the authors' fashion dilemmas, back to attribution theory …

It is important to note that the pattern of presence or absence across the three types of information is not always as clear-cut as in the above illustration. The way the information is combined is not simply additive, but depends on an interaction of the different elements. The important point here is that people really are acting like *naïve scientists* if they attribute causality in this way: seeking out and assessing these three types of information, then weighing them all up to conclude either an internal or external attribution.

There is evidence that, when given all the relevant information, and the time within which to make a judgement, people can make attributional decisions in the way outlined by Kelley's co-variation model (Kassin, 1979; McArthur, 1972). However, the model appears to be far from being universally applicable. For instance, while people do use all three types of information, they are not equally attended to (Chen, Yates, & McGinnies, 1988); people pay more attention to the target person information (consistency and distinctiveness information) than to information relating to the other people in the context (consensus information; Windschild & Wells, 1997). Perhaps more importantly, although people follow these rules and deduce causality logically in some circumstances, these appear to only be in circumstances where *all* the information is laid out for participants to clearly see and when participants have the *time* to work out a likely cause in the complex way described above. However, when some information is missing (e.g. there is no distinctiveness information available), people can *still* make attributions. This implies that there are *alternative* ways in which people can make these sorts of judgements.

Summary

So far in this chapter we have seen how people can act like *naïve scientists*. We like a stable and predictable world, and explaining other people's behaviour as being down to internal, *dispositional* causes or external, *situational* causes is one way of achieving this. The *correspondent inference model* proposes that people try to infer a dispositional cause for behaviour because such attributions are most valuable for making predictions. Three types of information are relevant here: whether the behaviour in question is socially *desirable*, *chosen* or *non-chosen*, and has a *unique* effect. However, this model is limited in focusing only on dispositional attributions. The *co-variation model* is more flexible, able to account for both internal and external attributions. According to Kelley's co-variation model, people combine *consensus*, *consistency* and *distinctiveness* information to arrive at an internal or external attribution.

ATTRIBUTIONAL BIASES

Kelley's model is an *idealized* account of how people make causality judgements. People can, but often do not, look for and combine the three types of information outlined above. Can any of us say we routinely perform the sorts of complex, attention-demanding calculations that are required by the co-variation model? Rather than being such logical and rational creatures, it feels more like we often make assessments about other people by things like 'gut feeling' and 'intuition'. Certainly, we don't always spend much time or effort arriving at many of the impressions we form about people we meet on a daily basis.

The idea that we take shortcuts in social judgement, rather than always going through complex processes like that outlined above, began to gain weight when attribution researchers started to observe a number of systematic 'errors' people were making when asked to make assessments of causality in psychology experiments. These errors or biases were not random, but appeared to be made with such regularity as to suggest the existence of alternative psychological strategies being engaged. In the next section we'll document some of these biases. This will lead us to an important shift in theorizing that arose from dealing with the shortcomings of the naïve scientist account.

Attributional biases describe the tendency in particular contexts to make one type of attribution – internal or external – over another. The attributions made in this way are not necessarily wrong, but they are made in a much quicker and less careful way than the elaborate processes detailed by the models discussed in the previous section. We will here consider three of the most documented biases: *the fundamental attribution error*, *the actor-observer bias*, and *self-serving attributions*.

The Fundamental Attribution Error

All other things being equal, people have a general tendency to make *internal* rather than external attributions, even when there are clear potential situational causes (Ross, 1977). The error is illustrated in a study by Jones and Harris (1967). Participants were instructed to read essays that had been written by fellow students and that were either for or against Fidel Castro's rule in Cuba. Participants were told that the writers had either chosen the essay topic themselves, or had been told which one (pro- or anti-Castro) to write by the experimenter. Participants were subsequently asked to guess what attitude the person who had written the essay had towards Castro. In the choice condition participants reasonably assumed the writer had written an essay that reflected their own opinions. However, participants *also* thought the essay reflected the writer's true opinion in the no-choice condition. In other words, even though there was a clear contextual cause for the behaviour observed

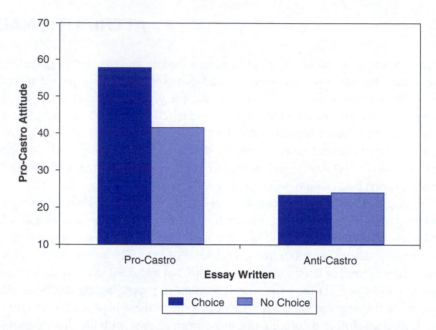

Figure 2.3   The fundamental attribution error. Data from Jones and Harris (1967)

(the experimenter's instruction to write one essay or another), which should logically reduce the probability that the essay reflected the writer's own attitude, participants still made an internal attribution. They paid no attention to the possible discounting information and assumed the essay reflected the writer's opinion (see Figure 2.3).

The reason why this **fundamental attribution error** occurs appears to be perceptual salience. The person being observed is the most perceptually salient aspect of the situation (i.e. moving, talking, etc.) and so an internal (personal) attribution becomes much more accessible (Taylor & Fiske, 1975). What is important to note here is that something much simpler (i.e. what appears to capture attention the most) determines the social judgement, not a complex naïve scientist-like thought process. The idea that people use simple rules of thumb such as perceptual salience to arrive at social judgements is reinforced by the observation of another attribution bias, the actor-observer bias.

Although it was originally thought to be a universal tendency, it has become apparent that the fundamental attribution error might not be quite as pervasive as early work suggested. Most of the original research was carried out in countries such as the USA and the UK. Subsequently, cross-cultural researchers began to realize that in non-Western cultures the tendency to make internal attributions was not quite so fundamental (e.g. Miller, 1984; Morris and Peng, 1994). This makes sense based on what we know about some basic differences in self-focus between individualist and collectivist cultures (see the discussion of some of these differences in Chapter 1). In particular, if individualist cultures tend to focus on the individual rather than the collective, it seems consistent that explanations for people's behaviour tends also to focus on the individual (i.e. internal, dispositional attributions). In contrast, if collectivist cultures tend to focus on the broader collective (others in one's social world), then the tendency to attribute behaviour to internal causes should indeed be lower (and external attributions, including the influence of others in the social context, should become more likely).

However, culture is not the only thing that can alter the fundamental attribution error. As we discuss below, there are some more basic cognitive and motivational factors that can also change the focus of our attributional efforts.

The Actor-Observer Bias

Let's get back to our irritable shop assistant. In this scenario, in line with the fundamental attribution error, we would be likely to conclude a dispositional attribution, and decide that Dorothy was simply not a nice person. But imagine a time before when you have been rude to someone. On this basis do you consider yourself a rude and unpleasant person? Probably not. You probably consider yourself to be a nice person who was rude because of a specific (external) – and justifiable – reason, for example stress from work pressures. This tendency to attribute other people's behaviour to *internal* causes and our own behaviours to *external* causes is called the actor-observer effect (Jones & Nisbett, 1972).

Storms (1973) carried out an experiment that neatly illustrated this bias. In an apparent 'conversation task' two participants were allocated to observer roles and two as actors who would simply have a five-minute conversation with each other. In a subsequent phase participants were required to attribute causality (that is, judge whether the opinions expressed reflected the speakers' stable personality or some other contextual determinant). Storms found that observers emphasized *dispositional* factors when explaining the actors' behaviours, while actors emphasized *situational* factors when explaining their *own* behaviour. The explanation for this is again *perceptual salience*. The actors' attention was directed away from themselves; they were looking at the situation. Correspondingly, this made a situation attribution more salient or accessible to them. Observers' attention was focused on the actor, making an explanation focused on the actor – an internal, dispositional attribution – more salient or accessible. Further support for the idea that it was simply perceptual salience that was driving these effects comes from the observation that the actor-observer bias was reversed when the actors were shown videotapes of their *opposite perspective* before making attributions. When the actors saw their own faces during the task, their attention shifted to be focused on themselves and not the situation, which led to them making an internal attribution.

Self-Serving Attributions

As well as cognitive-perceptual processes providing an inferential shortcut in attribution judgements, motivations can also bias attributions. Imagine you do well in your social psychology exam. Are you likely to attribute your success to luck, a fluke, or are you likely to feel quite proud, and attribute your success to the effort you put in? According to the self-serving attribution bias it's the latter. Olson and Ross (1988) argue that we are more likely to make internal attributions for our successes (e.g. 'I'm intelligent') and external attributions for failures (e.g. 'it was a particularly hard exam') because making attributions in this way protects and maintains our self-esteem. Internally attributing success and externally attributing failure both boosts our feelings of self-worth and protects us from feeling bad when we don't do well. This type of bias can also work at a group level; we tend to attribute our group's successes to internal factors and other group's successes to external factors (Hewstone, 1990). Such group-serving attributions help to bolster the positive view we hold of the groups we belong to (relative to other groups), and therefore help us to feel good by association. In Chapter 7 we'll see how such own-group bias can contribute to prejudice and discrimination between groups.

Intergroup Attributions

In Chapter 8 we'll be discussing intergroup processes – how we can (and often do) divide the world into 'us' and 'them'. Ingroups 'us' versus outgroups 'them' can be anything from Brits vs. Italians, Women vs. Men, Christian vs. Muslims, to Young vs. Old. In the same way as we are sometimes motivated to make self-serving attributions, we can also make 'group'-serving attributions. For instance, supporters of soccer teams may often attribute their team's winning performance to skill and ability, but when their team loses they might be more likely to attribute this loss to bad luck ('We were robbed by the referee!'). These group-focused explanations are called *intergroup attributions* (Hewstone & Jaspars, 1982). Intergroup attributions can serve to propagate prejudice and discrimination against minority groups in society. If a minority group's positive behaviours are consistently attributed to external causes, but their negative behaviours to internal causes, then it is easy to see how this will lead to a persistently held negative stereotype of such groups. We'll be discussing the causes of intergroup biases, as well as social psychological solutions to the problem of prejudice, in more depth in Chapters 7 and 8.

Text Box 2.1

Attributional Mindsets

Whether we make internal or external attributions can sometimes be determined by the state of mind we are in. Roland Neumann (2000) carried out an ingenious experiment in which he tested whether guilt (that presupposes the cause of a negative event is located within the individual – an internal attribution) could be elicited experimentally in contrast to anger (that presupposes the cause of a negative event is located outside the individual – a external attribution).

Method

Using a procedural priming technique, participants had to repeatedly ascribe neutral actions to either themselves (internal attribution) or to another person (external attribution). The cover story was that the experimenters were interested in the relationship between memory performance and visual perception. Consistent with this they were asked to pair 20 symbols depicting everyday activities with 20 phrases describing these activities (e.g. wait for the bus, brush teeth, etc.). They then had to come up with either *self* or *other* referent sentences (depending on the condition to which they had been assigned) on the basis of these phrases (e.g. *I* wait for the bus; *he* waits for the bus). Following this, participants were instructed to go to a second laboratory down the hall. When they entered the laboratory, however, a confederate of the experimenter, who was ostensibly running a visual perception experiment, shouted. 'Get out! Didn't you read the sign on the door? You disturbed our experiment. Wait outside the door.' Participants' verbal reactions were then coded unobtrusively by two observers who were blind to the experimental hypotheses. Responses were coded for guilt (e.g. 'I'm sorry') versus anger ('It was not my fault!').

Results

As expected, participants who had been put into a self-referent mindset were more likely to react with guilt than anger – an internal attribution. In contrast, participants who had been put into an other-referent mindset were more likely to react with anger – and external attribution.

Interpreting the Findings

The findings support Weiner's (1986) idea that anger emerges from external attributions for negative events while guilt from the internal attribution for

(Continued)

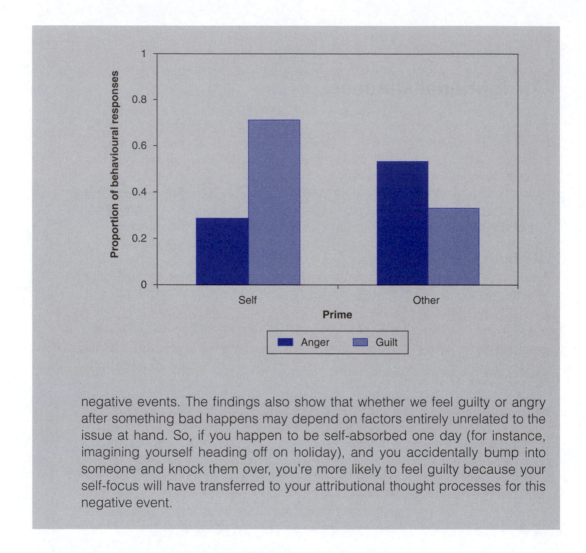

negative events. The findings also show that whether we feel guilty or angry after something bad happens may depend on factors entirely unrelated to the issue at hand. So, if you happen to be self-absorbed one day (for instance, imagining yourself heading off on holiday), and you accidentally bump into someone and knock them over, you're more likely to feel guilty because your self-focus will have transferred to your attributional thought processes for this negative event.

ATTRIBUTION AND SOCIAL PROCESSES

At the start of this chapter we said that it was important to cover attribution early on, because it is central to some of the key social psychological theories and processes that we'll discuss later on. We've already touched on this in the section above on intergroup attributions. Before we leave attribution and go on to talk about social cognitive processes more generally, here's a brief introduction to just some of the other areas where it'll pop up again.

1) Attitude Formation. In Chapter 4 we'll discuss all the ways in which attitudes can be formed. One of the ways is through self-perception (that is, reviewing one's own behaviour and then coming to a conclusion about one's own attitudes). For example, imagine you wake up the morning after the end-of-term party with a bit of a headache, a telephone number written on the back of your hand, and several traffic cones residing at the foot of your bed. Later that morning your friends pop in and ask you whether you had a good time last night. Although you can't quite remember you figure you must have (given the evidence laying around your room and written on your body). Your affirmative answer in this case would be an example of a self-perception process. You've constructed an attitude (a positive one about your night out) from an analysis of your apparent behaviour. We'll discuss self-perception processes later on in Chapter 4, but for now the thing to note is that an important element of the process involves *attribution* (i.e. your attitude about last night was based on a dispositional attribution arising from an analysis of the behavioural evidence).

2) Social Influence. In Chapter 6 we are going to be talking about social influence – how others have an impact on our attitudes and behaviour. We'll talk about how we often fall into line with the majority point of view, but also how sometimes we can be affected by smaller minority groups (who are vastly outnumbered by the majority). One of the reasons we sometimes believe minorities is that we *attribute* credibility to them, so long as they stick to their guns. It can be difficult for minorities to resist the urge to conform (it can be hard being the only vegetarian when all your mates want to head off to the local steak house). But if minorities consistently resist conforming one has to start thinking that they really believe what they're saying (and so they might just be on to something …).

3) Romantic Love. In Chapter 12 we'll talk about the psychology of romantic love and some interesting studies showing that we can be 'fooled' into thinking we are in love because of a heightened state of physiological arousal … arising from an entirely unrelated cause. It's a great study so we won't give it away here – suffice it to say the whole thing rests upon a *mis-attribution* of arousal.

SOCIAL REPRESENTATIONS

Although much of the research on attribution that we have discussed in this chapter has arisen from quantitatively focused research, there are other perspectives based on a more qualitative analysis of social explanations which also provide a means by which people can construct a sense of reality without the need for complex attributional rules. Moscovici's (1961) theory of *social representations* is one such approach. Social representations refer to shared beliefs and understandings between broad groups of people, and these can include culturally held and transmitted knowledge about causal relations. According to this theory understanding about causality is transformed and communicated through informal discussion to form a common-place, consensually held belief (a 'social representation'). Social representations are shared beliefs about issues ranging from health to politics; they can be derived from formal theories that are then transformed into the popular consciousness through discussions between individuals, or the news, media or literature. A good example is Freud's theory of psychoanalysis. Although most people would not have read Freud's original work, it is common to hear psychoanalytic explanations or concepts used to account for people's behaviour (e.g. they're 'anal'). Social representations, perhaps by their fluid and dynamic nature, tend to be studied using qualitative methodologies, involving analysis of interviews and archival materials. As such, this research illustrates how diverse methodologies can help us achieve a more rounded understanding of social explanations. In particular, they help us understand how beliefs about causality can be consensually shared and transmitted at a broader societal level, providing the common-sense theories that help us all make sense of our social worlds. This returns us neatly to where we started, with Heider's (1958) assertion that we are all naïve scientists, attempting to make sense of the world around us – whether this be through the individual-focused and fine-grained reasoned analysis outlined by attribution theory, or the cognitive shortcuts we sometimes take to arrive at such judgements, or the collective social representations that form through the everyday discussion and transmission of causal beliefs.

Summary

Although people can use the sort of complex, time-consuming attributional rules that we described at the start of this chapter, in many cases people instead use a number of attributional shortcuts, such as the *fundamental attribution error*, the *actor-observer bias*, and *self-serving* attributions. The fundamental attribution error describes how we are inclined to make internal, dispositional attributions much of the time when describing others' behaviours, and this is due to other people being the most *perceptually salient* thing in our field of vision (and so the most *accessible* source of information). For our own behaviour, however, we tend to make external, situation attributions (the actor-observer bias), which can also be explained by perceptual salience (our attention is most of the time directed away from ourselves, so the context, or situation in which we find ourselves, is the most accessible source of information). Our motivations toward self-enhancement (see Chapter 1) can also direct attributions, notably by inclining us to make internal attributions for success, and external attributions for failure. (Inter)group serving attributions can be biased in the same way (see Chapter 8). Using simple cues like perception salience are simpler, easier, and quicker than more complex processes outlined by correspondent inference theory and the co-variation model.

CHAPTER SUMMARY

In this chapter we have seen how people can be *naïve scientists*, with a basic desire to make sense of the world, to understand it and to be able to predict what will happen. To do so they engage in complex attribution calculations based on combining information relating to *consensus*, *consistency* and *distinctiveness*, and they can combine these sources of information in complex ways and can arrive at an internal or external attribution. But we have also seen how in many cases people do not use these complex rules, and do not go through an elaborate process when forming an impression of others. Instead a number of attribution 'errors' are apparent, such as the *fundamental attribution error, the actor-observer bias*, and *self-serving* attributions. The fundamental attribution error shows how we are typically inclined towards making an internal, dispositional attribution, at least with respect to others' behaviours. For our own behaviour, however, we tend to make external, situational attributions (the actor-observer bias). The explanation for these biases is that people

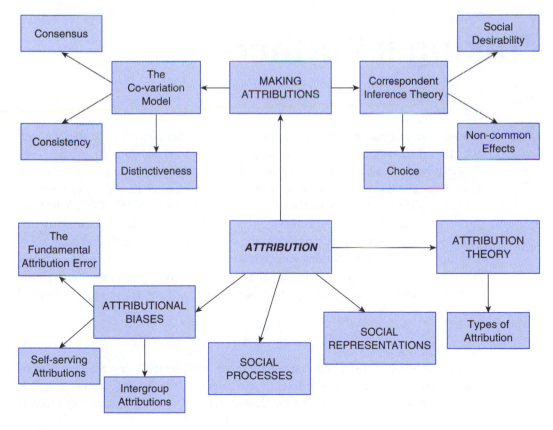

Figure 2.4   Memory map

sometimes tend to rely on simpler cues for making attributions, like *perceptual salience*. Motivations to enhance the self or the group can also bias attributions such that positive things like successes are internally attributed, while negative things like failures are externally attributed. Finally, the tendency to make sense of the world through logical, thought out analysis, or through cognitive shortcuts, can also be satisfied through consensual, shared attribution of causality in the form of social representations. These fluid and dynamic forms of shared knowledge provide a further basis upon which to construct a sense of reality without the need for complex attributional rules. The more general observation of attributional bias is critical to how psychologists' understanding of social inference built upon the early work on attribution theory. It became clear that people are not *always* naïve scientists, but that sometimes they just do not want (or cannot) engage in the long, time-consuming, complex processes that were specified by early attribution models. Sometimes people can form a coherent and clear view of their worlds through much simpler means. It appeared that a new perspective was needed to understand the cognition of the social perceiver, and it is this perspective to which we turn in the next chapter.

Taking it Further

Try This

Do we *really* spend this much time thinking about other people, what they do, and why they do the things they do? The early attribution theorists think so, at least some of the time, but can anyone really come up with examples of times when they've gone through these processes? Well, we may do it more often than you think – when we read celebrity gossip mags ('why on earth did Britney do THAT?!'), when our favourite sports team loses that all important match ('we were SO unlucky with that penalty'), or even when walking down the street ('why is he staring at me?'). Try writing down all the attributions you've made just up until this point today. It might be surprising how many you can come up with – illustrating just how much of the time we spend each day making attributions (and how central this psychological process is in our lives).

Debate This

Olson and Ross (1988) argue that we are more likely to make internal attributions for our successes (e.g., 'I'm intelligent') and external attributions for failures (e.g. 'it was an unexpectedly hard exam') because making attributions in this way protects and maintains our self-esteem. This idea rests on the assumption that we are always motivated to see the world in a way that makes us look good. But if we always did this, how would we ever get better at anything (we would be always denying any flaws we might have)? Surely it's good to be self-critical, at least sometimes? What might determine whether we make biased self-serving attributions rather than recognizing more accurate (but perhaps painful) self-truths? Well, if you recall all of the different self and social comparison motives we discussed in Chapter 1, this might provide some answers …

Something for the Weekend

Think back to the last time you felt angry, upset or annoyed with someone. Can you give an account of the thoughts that ran through your mind afterwards, and then organize them using Kelley's co-variation model framework? Can you identify the consensus, consistency and distinctiveness information and discuss how they could have been used to account for the judgement you finally made? Once you have done this, think about whether there were other salient cues in the environment that could have explained your attribution – were they particularly animated? Did the argument have any consequences for your self-esteem, or how you felt about your self-worth, or the worth of a group to which you belong? Was your conclusion based on principles or causal beliefs that are widely held in society?

Further Reading

The Essentials

Kelley, H.H. & Michela, J.L. (1980). Attribution theory and research. *Annual Review of Psychology*, *31*, 457–501.

Everything you ever wanted to know about attribution theory, straight from the horse's mouth. There've been advances since this original paper, of course, but it remains a classic account of the fundamental principles of attribution.

Next Steps

Sutton, R.M. and McClure, J.L. (2001). Covariational influences on goal-based explanation: An integrative model. *Journal of Personality and Social Psychology*, *80*, 222–236.

Attribution theory is one of the building blocks of social cognition, but that's not to mean it's not still evolving. This great paper is a more recent exploration of the processes underlying causal judgements, and shows that strategies of social inference are as important to a complete understanding of social behaviour today as in the 1970s when attribution theory first emerged.

Delving Deeper

Hewstone, M. (1989). *Causal attribution: From cognitive processes to collective beliefs*. Oxford: Blackwell.

If you've been bitten by the attribution bug, then it's time to graduate to the serious stuff. This whole book on attribution is a modern classic, and will tell you in depth what you need to know from … well, cognitive processes to collective beliefs.

Social Cognition

3

Social Cognition

This chapter is about how people think about other people. **Social cognition** is a broad term that describes the way people encode, process, remember, and use information in social contexts in order to make sense of others' behaviour (where a social context is defined as any real or imagined scenario including reference to self or others). Social cognition will be an important element to many of the topics we cover later on in the book. The way that we organize and use social information is essential for our understanding of intergroup and interpersonal processes, social identity and prejudice, attitudes and conformity. Below we will examine strategies of social inference, the way in which we categorize others and use cognitive 'short-cuts' to clarify and understand all of the information that constantly bombards our senses. We will see how an understanding of social thought has developed from seeing people as just cold, logical and rational information processors, to a recognition that we are often inclined to go on 'gut feeling' and 'intuition' when making judgements about others.

THE COGNITIVE MISER VS. THE NAÏVE SCIENTIST

In the previous chapter on attribution we saw how people have a basic desire to make sense of the world, to understand it and to be able to predict what will happen. Making attributions is one way that people can try to do this – they can try to work out cause and effect, operating like what Heider referred to as *naïve scientists*. Naïve scientists are rationale and logical in making social inferences. They can look for consensus, consistency and distinctiveness information and combine these sources of information in a systematic way to arrive at an internal or external attribution. However, we also saw how people do not always engage in such systematic, effortful – and time-consuming – processes when making social judgements and that sometimes people can take mental shortcuts. The fundamental attribution error shows how we are typically inclined towards making dispositional attributions when thinking about other people's behaviour. For our own behaviour, however, we tend to make external, situational attributions (the actor-observer bias). The explanation for these biases is that people sometimes tend to rely on simpler cues for making attributions like perceptual salience. The observation of these biases is critical to how psychologists' understanding of social inference built upon the early work on attribution theory. It became clear that people are not *always* naïve scientists, but that sometimes just do not want (or cannot) engage in the long, time-consuming systematic processes that were specified by early attribution models. A new perspective was needed to understand social inference, and it is this perspective that is the focus of this chapter.

Far from being naïve scientists, rationally and logically devoting our time and cognitive effort to analysing our social worlds, Fiske and Taylor (1991) argued that we are **cognitive misers**. As cognitive misers we are reluctant to expend cognitive resources and we look for any opportunity to avoid engaging in the sort of effortful thought that the attribution models of Jones and Davis (1965) and Kelley (1967) proposed (resulting in the attributional biases we discussed in the last chapter). According to Fiske and Taylor our mental processing resources are highly valued (and inherently limited), so we find ways of saving time and effort when trying to understand the social world. In this next section we will discuss some of the ways in which we do this and illustrate how people can be remarkably adept at making reasonably accurate inferences without having to engage in a great deal of cognitive processing.

HEURISTICS

People save time and effort in making judgements by using **heuristics** (Tversky & Kahneman, 1974). Heuristics are timesaving mental shortcuts that reduce complex judgements to simple rules of thumb. They are quick and easy, but can result in biased information processing (Ajzen, 1996). Detecting these biases is one of the ways that we know they have been used instead of more time-consuming, but more accurate, strategies of systematic cognitive processing. Below we outline two of the most commonly used types of heuristics: *representativeness* and *availability*.

The Representativeness Heuristic

The **representativeness heuristic** is the tendency to allocate a set of attributes to someone if they match the prototype of a given category (Kahneman & Tversky, 1973). In other words, it is a quick-and-easy way of putting people into categories. For instance, if you arrive at a hospital in need of help, you'll look for the person wearing a white coat and stethoscope, because these specific attributes indicate that the person is (representative of) a doctor. Similarly, when you enter your lecture class you may very quickly identify your professor as being the one with the interesting fashion sense and slightly unkempt looking hair. Later on we will talk at greater length about the use of representativeness information in the context of *social categorization*, but for now it is important to note one important drawback of using this mental shortcut. While assessing representativeness to a category prototype may often be a good way of making inferences about someone, like any heuristic it is prone to error. In particular, there is the *base rate fallacy*, which is the tendency to ignore statistical information (base rates) in favour of representativeness information. For example, relying on your stereotype of professors (scruffy, a bit eccentric) might mean you fail to correctly identify your new psychology tutor if they are, in fact, impossibly cool and trendy (well, you never know …). More seriously, the representativeness heuristic can propagate problems like gender stereotyping and discrimination. For instance, some occupations are viewed as more representative of some genders than others (e.g. caring professions such as nursing and teaching are seen as more representative of women while other professions such as engineering or mathematics are seen as more representative of men). Use of the representativeness heuristic in these situations can make it difficult for women to progress in 'male' occupations, and difficult for men to progress in 'female' occupations, a phenomenon called 'stereotype threat'. We'll talk about these negative effects of representativeness later on in this chapter.

The Availability Heuristic

The **availability heuristic** is the tendency to judge the frequency or probability of an event in terms of how easy it is to think of examples of that event (Tversky & Kahneman, 1973). It is related to the concept of accessibility, which is the extent to which a concept is readily brought to mind (see Chapter 4 on attitudes). The difference is that availability can refer to one's subjective experience of accessibility – the awareness that something is accessible – whereas accessibility is typically regarded as an objective measure of how quickly something can be brought to mind, without explicit awareness being a necessary component.

The availability heuristic can be illustrated with varied examples from everyday life. For instance, you might feel more trepidation about taking a flight if you have just heard about a horrific plane crash. In this example, your assessment of how likely it is that the plane journey will be a safe one will be influenced by the availability of information to the contrary. A neat experiment illustrates this heuristic. Schwarz and colleagues (1991) asked participants to recall 12 or six examples of when they had been either assertive or unassertive. After having completed this task participants were then asked to rate their own assertiveness. Counter to what one

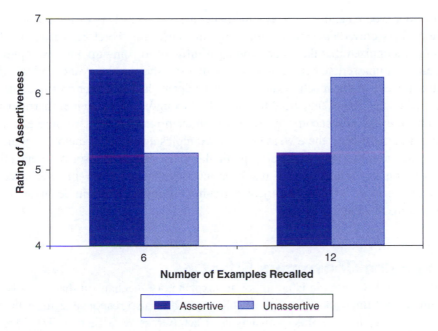

Figure 3.1   Evidence for the availability heuristic. Data from Schwarz et al. (1991)

might logically expect, participants who recalled six examples of their own assertive behaviour subsequently rated themselves as *more* assertive than people who had recalled 12 examples of their own assertive behaviour. The same effect occurred for people who recalled examples of unassertive behaviour: those who recalled six examples of unassertive behaviour rated themselves less assertive (more unassertive) than those who recalled 12 examples of unassertive behaviour (see Figure 3.1).

These findings are really quite different from what one might expect. Surely someone who can recall more examples of assertive behaviour should regard themselves as *more* assertive than someone who can only recall a few examples. Similarly, someone who can recall more examples of when they have been unassertive should logically then rate themselves as *more* unassertive. In contrast, the more examples of assertive or unassertive behaviour people were asked to generate, the less assertive or unassertive respectively they perceived themselves to be.

The explanation for this effect lies with the availability heuristic. The key is in thinking about how easy or difficult the task might be to people. On average, people don't normally spend much time listing the number of times they are assertive or unassertive in their lives. As such, being asked to list assertive or unassertive behaviours might be something they are not used to and, one imagines, is a task that gets more difficult after the first two or three examples that come to mind. We can assume that being asked to recall 12 examples of assertive or unassertive

behaviour would be more *difficult* that being asked to recall six examples of assertive or unassertive behaviour. While doing this task, it is therefore reasonable that
people recognized that they were finding it difficult to come up with examples of
assertive or unassertive behaviour after the first few that came to mind, and that this
realization should be much greater when participants had to labour on and come up
with 12 examples. As they tried to think of 12 examples of behaviour, participants
will have eventually become aware that such examples were not coming easily to
mind. In other words, there were no more examples *available* to them. They therefore concluded that they must not be particularly assertive or unassertive (depending
on what type of behaviour they had been instructed to generate). In sum, it seems
that people attend to the *difficulty* of retrieving instances of certain behaviours and
not just the content.

The False Consensus Effect

The availability heuristic is an important explanatory mechanism that we will see
again several times in the course of this book. It is also responsible for a highly
robust bias called the **false consensus effect** (Gross & Miller, 1997). This is
the tendency to exaggerate how common one's own opinions are in the general
population.

   Ross, Greene, and House (1977) illustrated this effect by asking participants
whether they would walk around campus for 30 minutes wearing a sandwich board
advertising a cafeteria. Whether they agreed or not, the experimenter then asked
them how many other students asked would make the same choice as they did.
Ross et al. found that whatever choice the participant made, they estimated that the
majority of other people would agree with them and make the same choice. Clearly,
this consensus estimate is not objectively possible. If, for example, 70 per cent of
people support one political party, then 30 per cent must not – you cannot have 50
per cent of people *not* supporting this party. There must therefore be a *false consensus*, whereby people believe that everybody usually agrees with them. The *availability heuristic* provides the explanation for the false consensus effect. Our own
self-beliefs are easily recalled from memory, making them most available when we
are asked to judge whether others agree with us. This makes it likely that our judgements of others' attitudes and opinions will, at least to some extent, be influenced
by our own.

The Anchoring Heuristic

It is often the case that a distinction is made between the availability heuristic and
another called the **anchoring heuristic.** Anchoring is the tendency to be biased
towards the starting value (or anchor) in making quantitative judgements (Wyer,

1976). There have been a number of illustrations of this effect. Plous (1989) carried out a survey during the Cold War in which he asked the same question in two slightly different ways. For half of the participants he asked whether they thought there was a greater than 1 per cent chance of a nuclear war occurring soon, and for the other half he asked whether they thought there was a less than 90 per cent chance of a nuclear war occurring soon. Both questions asked for a quantitative estimate of probability, so one imagines how the question asked should not have an impact on the judgements made. In fact, there is quite a considerable effect of the anchor provided in the question. Participants who received the 1 per cent question anchor estimated a 10 per cent chance of a nuclear war occurring, while those who received the 90 per cent anchor estimated a 25 per cent chance of a nuclear war occurring. A similar effect was observed by Greenberg et al. (1986), who found in a mock jury study that participants asked first to consider a harsh verdict were subsequently harsher in their final decision than participants asked first to consider a lenient verdict.

In sum, it appears that our judgements on a range of issues are significantly influenced by the point at which we start our deliberations. While the anchoring heuristic has often been considered to be distinct from the availability heuristic, in essence it comes down to the same psychological mechanism. The starting point or anchor exerts an impact on judgement because it is the most available source of information relevant to the issue at hand. Either way, this bias has some clearly important implications for a range of social contexts from the way in which lawyers structure questions in the courtroom (to elicit particular answers), to the way that opinion pollsters gauge attitudes.

THE MOTIVATED TACTICIAN

So far in this chapter we have seen how heuristics are sometimes used in social judgement over and above more rational, logical, but time-consuming ways of thinking. In other words, people can sometime be *cognitive misers* rather than *naïve scientists*, preferring ease and speed over accuracy.

As we noted above in our discussion of attribution theory, participants can and do use the complex systems outlined by models proposed by Jones and Davis (1965) and Kelley (1967), but this only appears to be the case under certain conditions. Other times people seem to revert to making quick and easy judgements using mental shortcuts like availability or representativeness, or relying on simple cues like perceptual salience (which can also be considered a type of availability). These heuristic shortcuts are much less accurate than using more rational, logical modes of thought, but they do approximate a response that is often within acceptable parameters. So what determines whether people will adopt one of these strategies over the other? When are people naïve scientists and when are they cognitive misers?

According to Kruglanski (1996) people are *flexible* social thinkers who choose between multiple cognitive strategies (i.e. speed/ease vs. accuracy/logic) based on their current *goals*, *motives*, and *needs*. Kruglanski argued that people are neither exclusively cognitive misers nor naïve scientists, but in fact **motivated tacticians**. Put another way, people are strategic in their allocation of cognitive resources and as such can decide to be a cognitive miser or a naïve scientist depending on a number of factors. Macrae, Hewstone, and Griffiths (1993) outline a number of factors that determine whether people will adopt logical, rationale, and time-consuming processing strategies in social inference, or whether they will go for a quick and easy, but quite possibly adequate, solution (see Figure 3.2).

First, people will be more likely to be a cognitive miser when they are short of *time* than when they have plenty of it. This makes sense. Heuristics are quick and easy – they save time, therefore, when we have to make a quick decision. So although it is less accurate, heuristics may be the best option open to use in order to make a judgement that at least approximates an adequate response. Second is *cogni-*

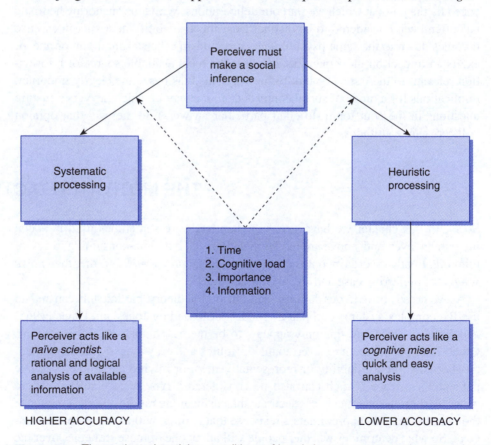

Figure 3.2 The motivated-tactician: conditions of heuristic versus systematic processing

tive load. Heuristics do not require much thought – they can be made off the cuff, simply made from a 'gut instinct' or intuition (or, what we would *now* call, availability). In contrast, the naïve scientist approach requires a lot of thought, analysis, and contemplation. If we are busy with lots on our mind, we're unlikely to devote much time to social perception, and are much more likely to use heuristics because, again, they approximate a right answer without having to give the issue at hand much thought. Third is *importance*. Heuristics are useful for providing estimates, but they cannot match more logical, rational, and detailed analyses. If a decision we have to make is important to us (e.g. whether to go for that new job) then we are much less likely to use a heuristic and much more likely to be a naïve scientist. Fourth, and final, is *information* level. As we noted in our discussion of attribution theory, people can and do make use of complex attribution rules in forming impressions, combining consensus, consistency, and distinctiveness information in elaborate ways, but *only* when they have all the necessary pieces of information. If we don't have all the facts then sometimes it is simply impossible for us to be naïve scientists; we may simply not have enough information to be able to rationally and logically make a detailed analysis of the issue at hand. In such situations the only recourse is to use a heuristic shortcut to approximate the correct response.

Summary

What do we know so far about social cognition? We have seen how people can be *naïve scientists* and engage in complex attribution calculations based on combining information relating to consensus, consistency and distinctiveness. But we have also seen how in many cases people do not use these complex rules, and do not go through an elaborate process when forming an impression of others. Instead a number of attribution 'errors' are apparent, such as the *fundamental attribution error*, the *actor-observer bias*, and *self-serving attributions*, all of which indicate a reliance on more basic information, for example external cues like *perceptual salience*, and internal motivations like *self-esteem maintenance*. This reliance on simple cues to make quick and easy judgements is indicative of a different approach to social inference, the *cognitive miser* perspective. Cognitive misers use a number of *heuristics* to shortcut long and elaborate mental processes. These include the *representativeness* and *availability* heuristics, which can lead to biases like the *false consensus effect* and the *anchoring* of quantitative judgements. There are a number of factors that determine whether we use these *heuristic* or *systematic* strategies of social inference, whether we act like naïve scientists or cognitive misers. In fact we are more like *motivated tacticians*, choosing between ease and speed and accuracy, depending upon things like *time*, *cognitive load*, *importance* and the amount of *information* available.

(Continued)

From what we have discussed so far it is clear that we use heuristics routinely and consistently. Just think for a moment. In your daily life how often do you have plenty of time, have nothing else to think about, regard every issue as important and self-relevant, and have all the information needed to make a detailed analysis? Not that often. Heuristic thought is used a great deal in social perception. We now move on to consider a unique heuristic that has received considerable attention from social psychologists because it is particularly important for understanding how people think, feel, and behave. It is a heuristic that defines attitudes and social behaviour, and a heuristic that we will see time and again throughout this book: *social categorization*.

SOCIAL CATEGORIZATION

Basic Principles

Categorization is 'the process of understanding what something is by knowing what other things it is equivalent to, and what other things it is different from' (McGarty, 1999: 1). This definition captures the key qualities of categorization that will be important in this chapter and others in the book. Categorization is a way of classifying some collection of objects, events, opinions, attitudes, concepts or people. It is a way of labelling some group of things as being all related to each other in some way, all linked and interconnected to a greater or lesser extent (e.g. 'dogs', 'furniture', 'weather', 'women', 'World War 2', 'vegetables', 'Manchester United'), and a way of comparing one thing to another (e.g. 'British' versus 'French', 'dogs versus 'cats', 'rock' versus 'pop').

The way that researchers have conceptualized categorization has evolved over time. The view used to be that there was a precise definition of category boundaries (Smith & Medin, 1981). Bruner, Goodnow, and Austin (1956), for instance, postulated that category membership was determined via defined features (i.e. an animal with three body divisions, six legs, an external skeleton, and a rapid reproductive system is therefore an insect). If just one of these attributes was missing the animal was quite simply something else.

It soon became clear, however, that a rigid system of all-or-nothing categorization does not capture the flexibility and fluidity of human perception. Many categories have uncertain or 'fuzzy' boundaries (Rosch, 1978) and do not fit in with a strict classification system (e.g. a dog is more 'pet-like' than an iguana, despite having the same 'pet' attributes). A more flexible view of categorization argues that it is not defined attributes that determine category membership, but members can be more or less *typical* of a category (Labov, 1973). Importantly, typicality is variable; group members can be highly typical or highly atypical of a category. What defines typicality is the prototype of the category. **Prototypes** are the most representative members of a category (Barsalou, 1991); categorization of less typical members may be slower or prone to error because they are less *available*. In other words, we can conceptualize the extent to which a category member is prototypical of that category to the extent that it is easy to bring to mind. Think for a moment about an item of fruit. We bet you thought of an apple or an orange (for 99 per cent of you at least). We're pretty certain you did not think of a kiwi fruit, and almost certainly not a tomato. Apples and oranges are highly prototypical of the category 'fruit', and are easy to bring to mind. In contrast, kiwi fruit and tomatoes, while still members of the fruit category, are quite atypical, and so are brought to mind far less easily. The high probability of people bringing prototypical group members to mind when categorizing others can lead to errors. The prototype of the category 'engineers', for instance, is a male, which may lead to errors in categorization when encountering a female engineer.

Category content

So categories are defined by prototypes. When we are dealing with social categories, we can refer to prototypes as **stereotypes**. But how do prototypes and stereotypes form in the first place? Why do we come to perceive some characteristics as typical of certain categories and some not? Social learning and exposure clearly play a role (we discuss these in more detail below). But there is another way in which specifically *negative* stereotypes can come to be associated with *minority* groups. This is something called the **illusory correlation**. Illusory correlation describes the belief that two variables are associated with one another when in fact there is little or no actual association (Hamilton & Gifford, 1976). In their classic experiment, Hamilton and Gifford asked participants to read information about people from two made-up groups, group A and group B. Twice as much information was provided about Group A (the majority) than Group B (the minority). In addition, twice as much of the information provided for both groups involved desirable behaviours rather than undesirable behaviours.

Despite there being no *actual* correlation between group membership and the proportion of positive or negative information provided, in a subsequent phase where participants were asked to attribute the behaviours they had seen to the two groups, more of the undesirable negative behaviours were attributed to Group B, the minority group, than Group A, the majority group. Participants therefore perceived an illusory correlation – they believed that negative behaviours were more characteristic of the smaller group than the bigger group.

Hamilton and Gifford explained this effect with reference to the notion of shared distinctiveness. Half as many total behaviours were used to describe the minority group compared to the majority group. There were, overall, half as many negative behaviours as positive behaviours. Because both the minority group characteristics and negative characteristics were relatively *infrequent*, both were distinctive and stood out. Consistent with the use of the *representativeness* heuristic, the low number of negative behaviours came to be seen to be representative of the smaller group. These findings show how heuristics can, in some part, account for the development of negative stereotypes that come to be regarded as stereotypical of minority groups.

Category structure

As we discussed above, categories are defined by prototypes. Prototypes are a representation of the most typical member of the category – the easiest example to bring to mind or the most available. However, as Rosch (1978) noted, categories have fuzzy boundaries, and if categorizing someone depends upon assessing their *representativeness* to the prototype then category structure needs to reflect this variability in typicality. Categories do indeed vary not only in content, but also in *structure* – in terms of the degree of intra-category variability. When the category is *heterogeneous* it is perceived to be made up of many different sorts of people. When it is *homogeneous* it is perceived to be made up of only a few types of people who are all very similar to each other.

In Chapter 6 we will discuss how categorizing people into ingroups and outgroups leads to an attenuation of intra-category variability, but here it is just important to note that on average this tendency to perceive group members as all similar to each other in intergroup contexts appears to be more apparent in the way we think about outgroups, compared to the way we think about ingroups, a tendency referred to as the outgroup homogeneity effect (OHE; Jones, Wood, & Quattrone, 1981). This effect is not only revealed in simple variability judgements (e.g. Park & Judd, 1990) but also perceptual judgements. Shapiro and Penrod (1986), for instance, found that white people found it difficult to tell Japanese faces apart, and Japanese people found it difficult to tell white faces apart. The outgroup homogeneity effect is also apparent in terms of how people structure their memory for groups. People simply remember more about someone they encounter from their own group than from another group (Park & Rothbart, 1982; see Figure 3.3).

There are several explanations for the OHE. The first, and most obvious, is that we have a more detailed and varied impression of our own social category compared to others because, quite simply, we have more experience of people within our own category – we are more familiar with them (Linville, Fischer, & Salovey, 1989). For example, you are probably able to think about more different types of people who attend your social psychology class than people who attend the engineering class down the hall. Although this seems reasonable it cannot, however, be the whole story. First, the OHE is observed for groups that people should have equal levels of exposure to, such as gender (Crisp & Hewstone, 2001; Park & Rothbart, 1982). Second, the OHE is observed even for artificial groups created in the laboratory (Wilder, 1984), where there is no prior contact, and even when group membership is totally anonymous. Finally, with increasing ingroup familiarity the OHE should increase, but often it does not (Brown & Wootton-Millward, 1993).

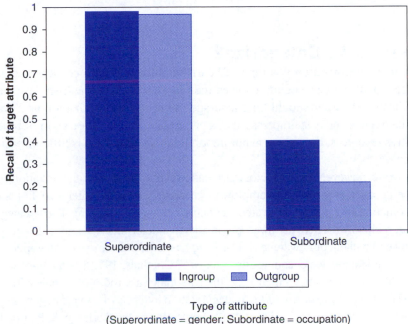

Figure 3.3 Memory for category labels and more detailed information as a function of ingroup or outgroup membership. Data from Park and Rothbart (1982)

Why Do We Categorize?

So we know what categories are, what they contain, and how they are structured. But why would we want to use them? Categories are in some ways the ultimate heuristic. They can be applied to all aspects of our lives, from the food we buy in supermarkets, through to whether we like pubs or clubs, cafés or restaurants, what careers we choose, where we live and what we wear. In all of these cases categorization does two things. First, it saves us time and cognitive processing; it allows us to be a cognitive miser (Fiske & Taylor, 1991). Stereotyping is fast and provides a lot of information about people we do not know (Gilbert & Hixon, 1991), thereby *freeing up* cognitive resources for other tasks (Macrae, Milne, & Bodenhausen, 1994). Expending cognitive resources as cheaply as possible enables more pressing concerns to be dealt with (Gilbert, 1989). Second, categorization clarifies and refines our perception of the world. Once a category is activated we tend to see members as possessing all the traits associated with the stereotype (Wyer, 1988). As such, categorization provides *meaning* (Turner, Hogg, Oakes, Reicher, & Wetherell, 1987), it reduces uncertainty (Hogg, 2000), and helps us to predict social behaviour (Heider, 1958), providing prescriptive norms for understand ourselves in relation to others (Hogg, 2002).

When Do We Categorize?

Given that categorization is a type of heuristic, allowing us to conserve cognitive resources and act like a cognitive miser, the four conditions of heuristic use that we have discussed earlier should all encourage the use of categorization as a way of forming a quick and easy impression of a person (i.e. when we are short of time and cognitive resources, the person is not important to *us*, and there is little information available).

There are, however, several factors that tend to evoke the use of categorization even if we don't consciously *choose* to employ it as a strategy of social inference. Put another way, sometimes we are not motivated tacticians, but we will be compelled to categorize without realizing it. There are three key factors that determine whether a category will be activated without our awareness. These are *temporal primacy* (we categorize on the basis of the features we encounter first; Jones & Goethals, 1972), *perceptual salience* (when difference becomes salient, e.g. the sole male in a room of females; Taylor et al., 1977), and *chronic accessibility* (categorization in terms of some categories – race, age, gender – is so common that it can become automatized; Bargh & Pratto, 1986; Fiske & Neuberg, 1990). Interestingly, even when we are trying our hardest not to use categories to think about other people, ironically, this can lead us to use them even more without knowing it. This is because the very act of trying to suppress a category stereotype means we have to first, on some level, think about it. We discuss evidence for this stereotype suppression and rebound effect in Text Box 3.1.

Text Box 3.1

When Stereotypes Rebound

We are always thinking of things that we probably shouldn't be thinking about. We might, for example, have the desire to tell a disliked work colleague what we *really* think of them or be tempted to eat fried bacon and eggs for break- fast even though we are trying to lead a healthy lifestyle. We often deal with these types of situations by actively pushing unwanted thoughts out of our mind. However, a series of studies (e.g. Wegner, 1994) showed that trying to suppress such thoughts can, ironically, increase the extent that those thoughts spring to mind once we stop actively trying to suppress them. Macrae, Bodenhausen, Milne, and Jetten (1994) investigated the use of suppression as a strategy to avoid using stereotypes.

Study 1: The effect of stereotype suppression on stereotyping

Undergraduate students were shown a photograph of a male skinhead and were asked to spend 5 minutes writing a paragraph about a typical day in the life of that individual. In the *suppression* condition, participants were asked to actively avoid trying to think about the person in the photo in a stereotypical manner, whereas in the *control* condition, participants were given no such instructions. After this initial task, participants were then asked to write a second paragraph about a different male skinhead, but this time without being given any explicit instructions.

In the first passage, participants who had been asked to suppress stereotypes appeared to do so effectively, writing significantly less stereotyped paragraphs than participants in the control condition. However, suppressors showed significantly *more* stereotyping than control participants when writing the second paragraph.

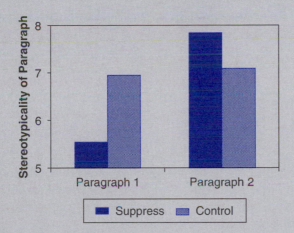

Study 2: The effect of stereotype suppression on behaviour

Study 1 revealed that suppressors show more stereotyping than non-suppressors once they were no longer actively trying to suppress their stereotypes. But does this have implications for *behaviour* towards members of stereotyped groups? In a second study, participants were once again instructed to either

(Continued)

suppress stereotypes or not while writing a paragraph about a skinhead. This time, after writing the paragraph, they were taken into a different room, ostensibly to actually meet the skinhead in the photograph (although this was not, in fact, going to happen). In the room, there was a row of eight chairs, and on the first chair, there was a bag and jacket. The researcher remarked that they belonged to the person in the photograph, who would return in a moment, and that the participant should sit down and wait for his return.

Participants who had suppressed their stereotypes in the paragraph showed more discriminatory behaviour, sitting further away from the skinhead's chair than those who had not suppressed their initial stereotypes.

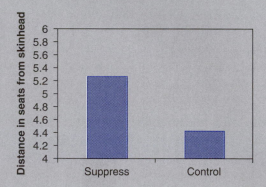

Interpreting the Findings

To suppress a stereotype, it is necessary to conduct a monitoring process, scanning consciousness for any trace of the stereotype. This has the unfortunate consequence of actually *increasing its accessibility*. As a result, when an individual is no longer actively trying to suppress their stereotype, encounters with someone who is a member of the stereotyped category will result in greater stereotyping and stereotype-consistent behaviour than if no attempt had been made to suppress the stereotype.

Most people know that stereotypes – particularly negative ones – are socially unacceptable and attempt to avoid using them. In sum, the important thing to note here is that we do not always choose to employ a heuristic over a systematic strategy. Instead, something like perceptual salience (which we also discussed earlier) can sometimes mean categories affect our judgements of others without us even realizing it. We discuss these implicit effects on impression formation in more detail in Chapter 7.

Consequences of Categorization

Categorization typically leads to heightened accessibility of *stereotype consistent* information and selective encoding of subsequently acquired target information. Cohen (1981), for instance, showed participants a videotape of a woman having a birthday dinner. Participants were told that she was either a waitress or a librarian. In the former case, participants subsequently had better recall for seeing the woman on the videotape drinking beer (behaviour associated more with the category waitress). In the latter case participants subsequently had better recall of the woman wearing *glasses* (behaviour associated more with the category *librarian*). This illustrates how stereotypes can influence our attention and what we remember from any social scene. For both groups of participants the videotape was the same, but simply being told that the person they were about to see was either a librarian or waitress led participants to remember what they saw in a completely different way. The categorization information made them evaluate the scene through two alternative lenses.

Categorization and Prejudice

These stereotype-consistent biases do not only apply to relatively neutral categories like 'librarian' but also to more important social distinctions, such as those formed on the basis of race or ethnicity. Gaertner and McLaughlin (1983) found that white participants were faster to name positive words ('smart', 'ambitious') after they had seen the racial category 'white' compared to 'black'. People also recall more positive than negative information about someone in their own group, but more negative than positive information about someone in another group (Howard & Rothbart, 1980). These positive versus negative stereotypes associated with different social groups are therefore highly divisive, and can contribute to continuing problems of racial prejudice and discrimination, a topic we discuss in depth in Chapter 7.

Despite the power of stereotypes to bias perception towards stereotype-consistent interpretations, there are some exceptions to this rule, and sometimes stereotype-inconsistent information is better remembered (Hastie & Kumar, 1979). Inconsistent information is salient and attention-grabbing, so for this reason it is sometimes well remembered. However, the process of recognizing and remembering inconsistent information requires *cognitive effort*. Cognitive overload – a condition that encourages the use of heuristics – leads people to use categories and associated stereotypes, thereby reducing memory for inconsistent information (Srull, 1981). Even if stereotype-inconsistent information is remembered, it will often be remembered as an *exception* to the rule, a '**subtype**' (Hewstone, Macrae, Griffiths, Milne, & Brown, 1994) of the overall stereotype (e.g. the one librarian who *does* drink beer). Subtyping can actually preserve and perpetuate the overall stereotype by negating the impact of stereotype-disconfirming information (it does not have to challenge the existing stereotype if it is placed in a new subcategory). Having said this, if enough stereotype-inconsistent information is subtyped, the number of exceptions will eventually be too great for the overall stereotype to remain insulated, leading to a re-definition of the category prototype. We discuss how these processes lead to stereotype change in more depth in Chapter 8.

Categorization and Unconscious Behaviour

When people think about categories they can unconsciously begin to act in line with the stereotype associated with those categories, a phenomenon known as **behavioural assimilation** (Bargh et al., 1996). Bargh and colleagues conducted several studies that established the behavioural assimilation effect. In a classic experiment they observed that priming stereotypes of 'elderly people' made participants subsequently walk more slowly; in other words, it made them *act* like an elderly person. Full details of this study can be found in Text Box 3.2. In another experiment participants were judged to have behaved in a more hostile manner when a computer error occurred during a study after they had been subliminally primed with photographs of African Americans (for whom there is an associated stereotype of 'hostile') than if they had been subliminally primed with photographs of Caucasian faces. In none of these studies did participants express any knowledge that they had been primed by the category in question, nor had any awareness of its influence on their subsequent behaviour.

Text Box 3.2

Thinking About Old People Can Make you Walk More Slowly

In a classic study, Bargh, Chen, and Burrows (1996) investigated whether priming participants with a social category (elderly) would lead participants to behave in line with the traits stereotypically associated with that category.

Method

Undergraduate students completed a 'scrambled sentence' task, making grammatically correct sentences out of a series of randomly ordered words, supposedly as a test of language proficiency. In the *elderly* condition, words related to the elderly stereotype were embedded in the task, such as 'old', 'lonely', 'grey', 'sentimental' and 'wise', whereas in the *control* condition, neutral words, such as 'thirsty', 'clean', and 'private', were embedded in the task. After completing this task, participants were told that the experiment was over and were directed to the elevator down the hall. A confederate sitting in a chair in the hall used a hidden stopwatch to time how long the participant took to walk from the experimental room to the elevator.

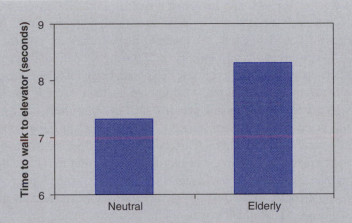

Results

Participants who had been primed with the elderly stereotype walked significantly more slowly from the experimental room to the elevator than participants in the control condition.

Interpreting the Findings

Priming participants with a social category (elderly) that is associated with a particular stereotypical trait (slowness) increases the extent to which participants behave in line with that trait, a phenomenon known as *behavioural assimilation*. Critically, these findings emerged despite the fact that the words associated with elderly did not include any reference to slowness. It appears that the category 'elderly' increased accessibility of stereotypes associated with the category, including slowness. But why does activating a particular stereotype lead people to behave in line with that stereotype? Psychologists have argued that stereotypical behavioural responses are mentally represented in a similar way to other social information like trait concepts, stereotypes and attitudes. Supporting this idea, the same area of the premotor cortex is active when humans perceive an action and when they perform that action themselves (Buccino et al., 2001).

Activating category information may influence behaviour as well as impression formation because behavioural responses are mentally represented in a similar way to other social information like trait concepts, stereotypes and attitudes (Chartrand & Bargh, 1999; Dijksterhuis & Van Knippenberg, 1998). Indeed, there is neuropsychological evidence for this link; the same area of the pre-motor cortex is active when humans perceive an action and when they perform that action themselves (Buccino et al., 2001).

Subsequent research by Dijksterhuis and Van Knippenberg (1998) demonstrated that the behavioural assimilation effect can occur also on more complex social behaviours.

They found that participants who imagined a typical *professor* (associated with the stereotype 'intelligent') subsequently outperformed those who imagined a typical *secretary*, on a general knowledge task. In explaining how priming can influence complex behaviours, Dijksterhuis and Van Knippenberg (1998) argued that although intelligence is an abstract concept rather than a concrete behaviour, behavioural representations are likely to be hierarchically structured, whereby the abstract concept 'intelligence' is associated with a series of behavioural patterns, such as *concentration*, *careful consideration* of information and *systematic thinking*. Thus, although priming would not have changed participants' actual level of intelligence or knowledge, it may have temporarily induced participants to behave differently in their reaction to the multiple choice task. Priming participants with 'intelligent' may have, for example, subconsciously induced concentration, led to the use of more varied strategies and additional cues, and increased confidence, all of which may have affected performance.

Categorization and Self-efficacy

The type of behavioural assimilation effects outlined above can adversely impact on our academic performance, when negative performance stereotypes define our own groups. **Stereotype threat** is defined as the predicament felt by people in situations where they could conform to negative stereotypes associated with their own group membership (Steele, 1997). The result of this fear of conforming to threatening stereotypes is that individuals may underperform on a task associated with the threatened domain. For example, women may underperform on a maths test or African Americans may underperform on an intelligence test because they are aware that there is a stereotype that their category is not supposed to be as good as a comparison category on such tasks (e.g. mathematics ability is a dimension upon which men and women are stereotypically expected to differ). Steele and Aronson (1995), for example, found that African Americans underperformed on a test when they were told it was indicative of intelligence, but they also found that simply asking African Americans to state their race before taking a test reduced the students' subsequent performance. More details of these effects can be found in Text Box 3.3.

Text Box 3.3

Stereotype Threat and Gender Identification

Numerous studies have demonstrated the *stereotype threat* effect. This is where individuals who are made aware of a negative stereotype associated with a group to which they belong suffer from impaired performance on relevant tasks. Schmader (2002) extended research on stereotype threat by investigating one factor that might make people more or less susceptible to stereotype threat effects: the extent to which an individual identifies with a particular group.

Method

At the beginning of the semester, female and male participants indicated how important their gender identity was to them. At a later date, they came to the laboratory to undertake a difficult maths test. A male researcher informed participants that he was developing a maths exam, and was interested in each individual's performance on the test, which he would be comparing with the performance of other students. Participants were then assigned to one of two conditions. In the *gender identity relevant* condition, the researcher went on to inform participants that he was interested in how women performed on the test compared to men, and that he would be using their score as an indication of their gender's general maths ability. In the *gender identity not relevant* condition, participants received no further instructions.

Results

Where gender identity was not made relevant to performance, there were no significant differences between men and women's performance on the maths

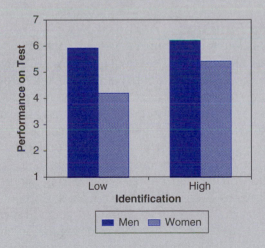

Gender Identity Not Relevant

(Continued)

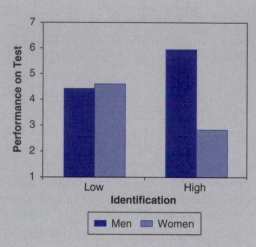

Gender Identity Relevant

test, regardless of whether gender was an important part of participants' identity. In contrast, when gender identity was made relevant to performance, a stereotype threat effect occurred: women performed significantly worse than men on the maths test. However, this effect *only* occurred if participants highly identified with their gender group.

Interpreting the Findings

According to social identity theorizing, individuals conform more to their group's norms when (a) that group identity is salient and (b) when they are accustomed to thinking about themselves as a group member (i.e. they are a high identifier). In this study, women for whom gender identity was not particularly important did not feel threatened by having a negative stereotype about their group made salient, so their performance on the maths test did not suffer. In contrast, when gender identity was a central part of their self-concept there was a stereotype threat effect: they performed worse on the maths test. This finding makes sense according to what we know about group norms and social identity. The female participants were aware of the stereotype that women were not as good as men on maths tests. The threat (a state comparison between women and men) primed their female identity, especially for female participants who were used to thinking about their female identity (high identifiers). This led these participants to act in line with their group norm: they actually performed worse than normal on the maths test.

DUAL PROCESS THEORIES

In this last section we discuss models that have attempted to provide an integrative framework within which to understand all of the impression formation processes that we have discussed above. Brewer's (1988) **dual process theory** and Fiske and Neuberg's (1990) continuum model both consider impression formation to comprise two distinct processes: *categorization* and *individuation*. Brewer argues that either a heuristic (category) or a systematic (individuated) approach is used when forming impressions of others, and this distinction maps directly on to the cognitive miser versus naïve scientist approaches we have discussed in this chapter. Fiske and Neuberg's model is similar and conceptualized as a *continuum* where one extremity is category-based (heuristic) processing and the other is attribute-based (systematic) processing. On this continuum people can be perceived as a representative of a group, or as an individual separate from any category membership (see Figure 3.4).

Fiske and Neuberg argue that people begin the process of impression formation by adopting a cognitive miser mode of processing: they try to fit the target person to a category (for instance, using the *representativeness* heuristic). If, however, there is not a good fit between the category and target then perceivers will shift towards an individuated mode of perception, moving along the continuum, and invoking an attribute-based approach. Similarly, Brewer argues that the mode of perception will change from the use of category-based heuristics to a systematic, individuated mode of perception under conditions that either favour, or do not favour, one over the other.

This switch in processing from using categorization to individuation can be termed **decategorization**. If decategorization has occurred the target person should be primarily defined as an individual rather than as a group member, which should remove category-based bias. Previous research has found decategorization to be associated with less stereotyping and less unfair attribution of negative characteristics because the judgement is made on an appreciation of individual, personal merit, rather than pre-conceived stereotypic expectancies (e.g. Brewer & Miller, 1984; Krueger & Rothbart, 1988). Decategorization also allows the perceiver to develop a more personalized and less homogeneous perception of ingroup and outgroup members (Ensari & Miller, 2001; Fiske & Neuberg, 1989), reducing outgroup homogeneity and de-biasing social perception. We discuss ways in which social

Figure 3.4   A continuum of impression formation

psychologists have capitalized on the idea of this continuum model, developing ways of encouraging decategorization and reductions in stereotyping and bias, in Chapter 8.

Summary

In this section we have discussed social categorization, an extremely well-used heuristic. Categories are ways of putting people and things into different boxes, and come with expectations, *prototypes*, or stereotypes about what the typical member of that category will be like. *Stereotypes* can form when people perceive an *illusory correlation* between negative attributes and group size. Category structures can also be biased, as illustrated by the *outgroup homogeneity effect*, the tendency to perceive outgroup members as all similar to each other. People use categories and stereotypes because, as heuristics, they are fast and provide a lot of information about people we do not know. Categories can become salient for reasons of *temporal primacy*, *perceptual salience* or *chronic accessibility*. Categorization, while cognitively useful, can have a damaging effect on societies due to their tendency to be biased and lead to prejudice. This is because category activation can lead to heightened accessibility of stereotype-consistent information and *selective encoding* of negative information (especially of minority group members). Thinking about categories can also lead us to behave in line with stereotypes associated with those categories, without any awareness we are doing this. This type of *behavioural assimilation* can occur when thinking about either categories we are members of or categories we are not members of. Finally, if we are members of a category that possesses a negative performance stereotype, in contexts where our category membership is salient, we may be adversely affected by this stereotype. This tendency is called *stereotype threat*. *Dual-process models* bring together the cognitive miser and naïve scientist approaches, showing how impression formation can rely on heuristic, categorical processing, or more systematic individuated processing, and how encouraging decategorization may be a means of countering all of the negative impacts of categorization that we have discussed in this chapter.

CHAPTER SUMMARY

When we are not being *naïve scientists*, we are being *cognitive misers*. Cognitive misers use a number of *heuristics* to avoid long and elaborate mental processes. Two of the most common heuristics are the *representativeness* and *availability* heuristics, which can lead to biases like the *false consensus effect* and the *anchoring* of quantitative judgements. There are a number of factors that determine whether we

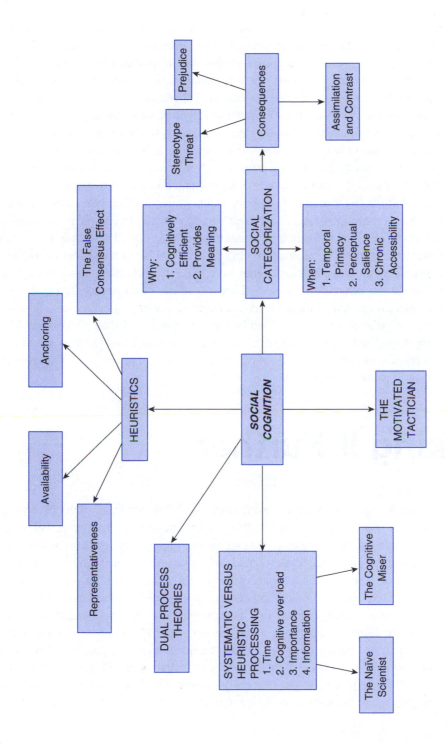

Figure 3.5 Memory map

use these *heuristic* or *systematic* strategies of social inference such as *time*, *cognitive load*, *importance* and the amount of *information* available. Rather than being either naïve scientists or cognitive misers we are perhaps better characterized as *motivated tacticians* – choosing between heuristic or systematic strategies depending on whether we are aiming for ease and speed or accuracy. We also discussed the use of *social categorization* as one of the most wide-ranging heuristics used in social perception. In addition, we have discussed how the representativeness heuristic can explain how *illusory correlations* develop, biasing the category content used to define minority groups. We have seen how categories vary around *prototypes*, and how prototypicality – *stereotypicality* – can be defined by the availability heuristic. Familiarity can cause *outgroup homogeneity*, which compounds the extent to which outgroup members are seen to conform to stereotypical characteristics. We discussed how activation of categories leads to biased processing in favour of stereotype-consistent information (and how stereotype-inconsistent information is *subtyped* so as to insulate the overall stereotype from change), how stereotypes can influence our behaviour, and how awareness of the negative stereotypes that define our own groups can sometimes have a negative impact on even our academic performance (*stereotype threat*). Finally, we have discussed *dual-process models* that bring together the cognitive miser and naïve scientist approaches, showing how impression formation can rely on heuristic, categorical processing, or more systematic individuated processing.

Taking it Further

Try This

Are you a cognitive miser or a naïve scientist? Think about all of the psychological processes that we've discussed in this chapter and list (a) three judgements you've made when you have engaged in a systematic, logical time-consuming process and then (b) three judgements you've made when you have gone with your 'gut feeling' or 'instinct'. For instance, you probably thought quite a bit about your choice of college or university. The thought processes you engaged in here are classic examples of systematic, naïve scientist-like thought. For instance, you might have listed a number of factors – quality of course, distance from home, cost – and assigned an importance weighting to each of them (an attribution-like process). On the other hand, perhaps you visited the university you ended up at and just had that gut feeling 'this is the place for me' (there's no reason why both systematic and heuristic thought cannot contribute to the same decision-making process). Other examples of judgements you could recall might be less life-changing – like choosing what to wear or what to have for breakfast – but you can apply the same heuristic-systematic distinction to them all when analysing the thought processes you went through. Finally, go back through each of the examples you generated and say why you think you chose a heuristic or systematic mode of thought in each case, in line with the principles outlined by the idea of the motivated tactician. So, you might have been in a rush to leave the house one day – or nervous about an upcoming exam – so you simply went with a breakfast you fancied, while on another day (with more time and motivation) your breakfast might be a more considered, healthy, option.

Debate This

Is social categorization a good or a bad thing? Your immediate response might be that it's obviously a bad thing – it can lead to negative stereotyping, prejudice, academic under-performance, and incorrect judgements. But where would we be without it? If we did not categorize we would be unable to generalize our knowledge from one class of objects to another, and we'd have to re-learn everything about each new experience we encounter. For example, you don't need to learn how to hold every new knife and fork you come across; you know you like orange juice better than grapefruit juice without having to try every new brand. So is categorization good for non-social objects but bad when applied to social perception? Well, some stereotypes of people are useful – in a medical emergency you know a doctor will be able to help more than a plumber (and *any* doctor will do, you don't need to know the individual, or get to know them). Can we determine when categorization is good or bad, and if we can, if categorization is so fundamental to psychological functioning, how can we counteract it when it is negative? (If you take a look forward to Chapter 8, this might provide some answers…)

Something for the Weekend

Stereotype threat – the impact that stereotypes have on our own behaviour – has been the focus of a great deal of research recently (see Text Box 3.3). This research shows how society's stereotypic expectations can stifle individual aspirations and lead to disengagement by large segments of society in occupational domains defined by one gender group (e.g. women and maths/engineering subjects). Try an internet search for any issue to do with gender differences in choice of academic subjects at school, college or university – you'll find some marked disparities. The literature on stereotype threat offers an explanation for these disparities, as well as some potential solutions. If you were asked to devise a programme for school children to help them resist the negative impacts of stereotype threat, how would you go about it?

Further Reading

The Essentials

Fiske, S.T. & Taylor, S.E. (1991). *Social cognition* (2nd ed.). New York: McGraw-Hill.
This is a classic – Fiske and Taylor's panoramic view of social cognition centred around the theoretical core of the cognitive miser. Although now a little dated, it's a wonderfully simple and clear account of the fundamental tenants of social cognition, and an excellent first step to developing a deeper understanding of how we process information in our social worlds.

Next Steps

Hamilton, D.L. (2004). *Social cognition: Essential readings.* Philadelphia: Psychology Press.
This is a collection of classic and key papers in social cognition, and an excellent way to read about many of the phenomena and experiments that we've talked about in this chapter in their original published form. This is a particularly good way to develop your understanding of the methodologies used in social cognition.

Delving Deeper

Nosek, B.A., Banaji, M.R., & Greenwald, A.G. (2002). Math = male, me = female, therefore math ≠ me. *Journal of Personality and Social Psychology*, *83*, 44–59.
Cunningham, W.A., Johnson, M.K., Raye, C.L., Gatenby, J.C., Gore, J.C., & Banaji, M.R. (2004). Separable neural components in the processing of black and white faces. *Psychological Science*, *15,* 806–813.
Recent research on social cognition has taken the idea of effortless, heuristic thought to new levels by using millisecond response times to assess so-called implicit associations. If stereotypes are sometimes heuristics, then such methodologies should (and do) provide reliable windows into how they operate and influence judgement. The first paper listed above uses something called the Implicit Association Test (IAT) to measure the kind of stereotypical associations between gender and academic subject (and occupation) that we were discussing earlier. We've listed a second paper here as well, because it shows how far sophisticated methodologies have now progressed in the study of social cognition. Again, this paper uses the IAT computerized technique, but this time in conjunction with functional magnetic resonance imaging (fMRI) in an attempt to isolate the biological correlates of social cognitive processes.

Attitudes 4

Attitudes

Should abortion be illegal? Should we cancel Third World debt? How quickly should we reduce carbon emissions? Should there ever be a death penalty? Are you liberal or conservative? A soccer fan? A music lover? An optimist? The answers to all these questions depend upon psychological characteristics that define who we are: our attitudes. An **attitude** is a set of beliefs that we hold in relation to an attitude object, where an attitude object is a person, thing, event or issue. Attitudes can be positive or negative, or we can simply have opinions about issues without any strong emotional commitment. In this chapter we introduce what social psychologists have learned about attitudes: how they are formed, why we hold them, what implications they have for our behaviour, and how they change.

ATTITUDE FORMATION

In this first section we discuss four distinct ways in which attitudes can form towards some issue, event, person or thing. These four ways in which attitudes can form are (in order of increasing psychological complexity) by mere exposure, by associative learning, by self-perception, and for functional reasons. Importantly, these four ways in which attitudes can be formed apply mostly when there is *no prior or existing attitude* or knowledge about the attitude object. Later in this chapter, when we discuss persuasion, we will consider how and why existing attitudes can change.

Mere Exposure

The **mere exposure effect** (Zajonc, 1968) is the tendency to develop more positive feelings towards objects and individuals the more we are exposed to them. No action or interaction with the object is required, and we do not need to possess or even develop any explicit beliefs about the object. Zajonc's classic experiment went like this. The cover story was that the study was an experiment to determine how people learn a foreign language. Ten Chinese-like characters appeared on a screen for 2 seconds each. These characters varied in terms of how many times they were presented. Some were presented just once, some were presented 10 times, some

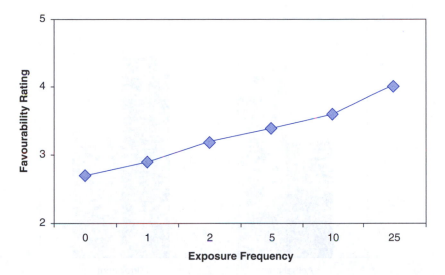

Figure 4.1 The relationship between exposure and liking. Data from Zajonc (1968)

25 times, etc. Following this, in phase 2 participants were told that the characters were adjectives and that the experimenter would like them to guess whether they were positive or negative in connotation. The adjectives were then presented one more time to the participants who rated the favourability of each one (i.e. whether they thought the symbol represented an adjective indicative of something positive or negative).

Zajonc found a positive linear correlation between exposure frequency and liking (see Figure 4.1). In other words, the more the symbol had been presented to participants in phase 1, the more positive were their feelings towards it in phase 2. Controlling for all other variables (the symbols were completely new to participants), mere exposure had a significant impact on attitudes. The implications of this finding were considerable and wide-ranging. It suggested that familiarity does not, as the old adage says, breed contempt, nor does absence make the heart grow fonder. On the contrary – it appears that, quite simply, the more we see something, the more we like it.

There have been many replications of the mere exposure effect, and recent meta-analyses have confirmed that it is a very robust phenomenon. Some interesting studies subsequent to Zajonc's include one by Mita, Dermer, and Knight (1977). In their experiment, participants were shown two photographs of themselves (taken prior to the experiment). One was a normal photograph, but the other was the mirror image of this original image. In other words, the first image was analogous to the perspective other people normally have of us (like we normally see in a photograph of ourselves) while the second was the perspective we are used to seeing (our mirror image, which we see every day). The prints were taken so that they would be

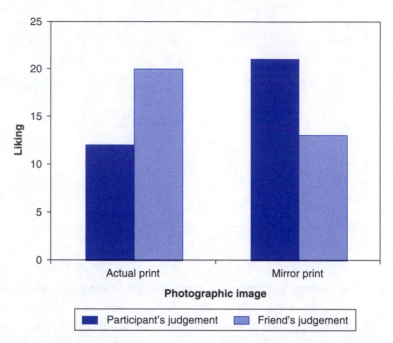

Figure 4.2 Preference for actual print and mirror image of own photographic image. Data from Mita, Dermer, and Knight (1977)

effectively (at least on a conscious level) indistinguishable from each other. Participants were then asked to rate which of the two prints they liked better. Mita et al. found that participants had a significant tendency to favour the mirror image print over the normal photo print (see Figure 4.2).

The findings observed by Mita et al. (1977) can be explained by the mere exposure effect. We prefer the mirror print because this is the view of ourselves we most often see. Supporting this idea, when friends of the original participants rated the same prints, they preferred the 'actual' photo view. In both cases, preference was higher for the perspective that was most commonly experienced by the person rating the photo. In other words, mere exposure to one view compared to another had a significant impact on likeability ratings. Mita et al.'s findings may finally help us to explain why we never like photos of ourselves!

There have been over 200 investigations of this 'mere exposure' effect, and reviews of the literature suggest that it is a highly pervasive and robust phenomenon (Bornstein, 1989). The effect is not limited to visual stimuli (as used in Zajonc's original demonstration), but has also been observed with auditory (Heingartner & Hall, 1974) and even food stimuli (Crandall, 1970), and it has been applied to varied domains (e.g. to advertising, Sawyer, 1981; to food preference, Pilner, 1982; and even liking for rock-and-roll music, see Text Box 4.1). In sum, the mere exposure effect appears to be an important way in which attitudes can form.

Text Box 4.1

Rock … and Rock around the Clock: Mere Exposure and Music Preference

Brickman, Redfield, Harrison, and Crandall (1972) investigated whether repeated exposure to rock-and-roll music would lead to a more positive attitude towards that type of music.

Method

Undergraduate students listened to 90 second segments of five rock-and-roll songs from the B-sides of popular records from the 1960s. They either listened to each song 0, 1, 2, 5, or 10 times. Finally, participants listened to a 3 to 5-second segment from the chorus of each song and were asked to rate how much they liked the song.

Results

Brickman and his colleagues expected to observe the mere exposure effect: a greater preference for the songs they had heard more frequently. However, what they actually found was a *decrease* in liking with increased exposure. This was particularly surprising given that prior to the study participants had reported that they liked rock-and-roll music. So why did increased exposure make attitudes less positive in this case?

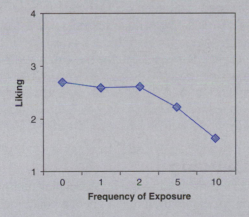

(Continued)

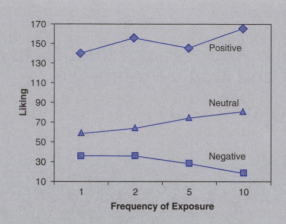

Interpreting the Findings

The researchers noticed after the experiment that many of the participants indicated that although they usually liked rock-and-roll music, they did not like the antiquated style of music used in this experiment. The mere exposure effect assumes that stimuli are novel and neutral in connotation. If participants began with an initially *negative* attitude towards the music, however, repeated exposure may strengthen these negative affective reactions. To test this hypothesis, Brickman and colleagues conducted a further study in which participants were exposed to abstract paintings that they had previously rated very positively, very negatively, or neutrally. The figure shows what they found.

As expected, people with an initially neutral impression of the paintings liked them more with repeated exposure, as did people with an initially positive impression of the paintings. However, participants with an initially negative attitude liked the paintings less with repeated exposure. This confirmed a boundary condition on the effectiveness of mere exposure for improving attitudes: the initial attitude must be neutral or positive. This is consistent with the idea that mere exposure is most applicable when little is initially known about the attitude object.

Associative Learning

There are two ways in which we can learn by association, either implicitly through classical conditioning, or explicitly through operant conditioning. **Classical conditioning** refers to a learning process that occurs when a neutral stimulus is paired with a stimulus that naturally evokes an emotional response (i.e. learning through implicit association; Pavlov, 1906). Consequently, the previously neutral stimulus, after enough pairings with the positive or negative object, will acquire a positivity or negativity of its own. The question is, does this effect occur with social groups?

In a classic study, Staats and Staats (1958) found just this. They paired the national social category label 'Dutch' with negative words and the national category label 'Swedish' with positive words; or they paired the 'Swedish' with negative words and 'Dutch' with positive words. They found that in the former case, the subsequent evaluation of Dutch people was more negative than the evaluation of Swedish people. However, when Dutch was paired with positive traits and Swedish with negative then the opposite occurred – the evaluation of Dutch was more positive. In other words, it appeared that the repeated association of Dutch with positive led to a more positive evaluation of this group – a case of associative learning.

This is a different effect from that observed in Zajonc's mere exposure study described above because it was not simply that exposure led to positive feelings about the attitude object: pairing with a positive or negative stimulus was required, and the nature of the pairing determined the subsequent attitude (i.e. the attitude could also become more *negative* when the category was paired with negative words; see also Zanna, Kiesler, & Pilkonis, 1970). Also important to note was that the magnitude of the conditioned effect was not great (that is, the impact of pairing positive or negative words was quite small: attitudes only changed slightly in the direction of the paired stimulus). This suggests that while associative learning may represent one way in which our attitudes can form, it cannot be the whole answer.

Interestingly, a stronger effect is found when aversive stimuli are paired with *nonsense* words (Cacioppo, Marshall-Goodell, Tassinary, & Petty, 1992), rather than familiar words like nationality labels. This suggests that associative learning may be a more powerful determinant of attitude formation when little *knowledge* is available about the attitude object (i.e. people are unfamiliar and have no preconceived attitudes towards nonsense words, but they presumably have some existing opinions about different national groups). This seems to make a lot of sense – if our mind is a 'blank slate' with respect to any particular issue, then we are going to be more influenced by exposure to attitude-relevant information. This could be one of the reasons why racial prejudice develops – there is a lack of knowledge about other groups because of low inter-racial contact, therefore encountering people expressing prejudiced views (i.e. using negative adjectives to describe the group) might lead to conditioned associations (see sections on implicit prejudice in Chapter 7). We will see how knowledge is also an important factor later on with respect to other processes associated with attitude formation.

The second way in which people can learn by association is **operant conditioning**. This is where behaviour is strengthened following rewards and weakened following punishments (Skinner, 1938; Thorndike, 1911). It is different from classical conditioning in that the former occurs implicitly – no action is required on behalf of the participant for associations to form. In contrast, operant conditioning is behavioural in nature:

participants must carry out some action that is either rewarded or punished. For example, when learning a new skill, such as a sporting activity, we may be more likely to continue with it if our early attempts are met with praise, rather than negative reinforcements such as laughter and ridicule. We discuss how operant conditioning might offer an explanation for the link observed between childhood exposure to violence and later adult aggressive attitudes and behaviour in Chapter 9.

Self-Perception

The idea behind **self-perception theory** (Bem, 1965) is that we form attitudes not due to exposure or associative learning, but from observations of our *own* behaviour. According to Bem, attitudes are formed from observing our own behaviours (e.g. the opinions we openly express on particular issues) and then attributing them to either internal or external causes, with internal attributions (inference that the behaviour is indicative of an attitude) more likely when the behaviour was freely chosen. This is an attributional process exactly like that discussed in Chapter 2.

Importantly, inference of one's attitudes from behaviour is more likely to occur when someone has little or no existing knowledge about the issue at hand, or does not hold a strong prior attitude towards it (this is similarly the case with mere exposure and classical conditioning). A neat study that illustrated exactly the conditions under which behaviour will be used to infer attitudes was carried out by Chaiken and Baldwin (1981). In this study participants were first pre-screened to assess their attitude towards pro-environment practices – whether the attitudes possessed by each participant were either strong and coherent or weak and inconsistent. This was to test the idea that self-perception of one's attitudes from behaviours would only occur when people had little prior knowledge or opinions on the subject at hand. Participants were then allocated to one of two conditions. By asking questions relating to pro- or anti-environmental behaviours in specific ways, the experimenters were able to elicit answers from the participants that either emphasized the pro-environmental practices they engaged in (e.g. recycling) or the anti-environmental practices they engaged in (e.g. driving a car). After this, participants were asked to indicate their own attitude towards environmental practices. Chaiken and Baldwin's findings can be seen in Figure 4.3.

As you can see, consistent with self-perception theory participants who were induced into reporting behaviours they carried out that were pro-environmental in nature were more likely to subsequently rate themselves as having pro-environmental attitudes, while participants who were induced into reporting behaviours they carried out that were anti-environmental in nature were more likely to subsequently rate themselves as having anti-environmental attitudes … but only when they had a weak prior attitude. When participants were identified from the pre-screening as having strong pro- or anti-environmental attitudes, the experimental manipulation had no effect on their final reported attitude.

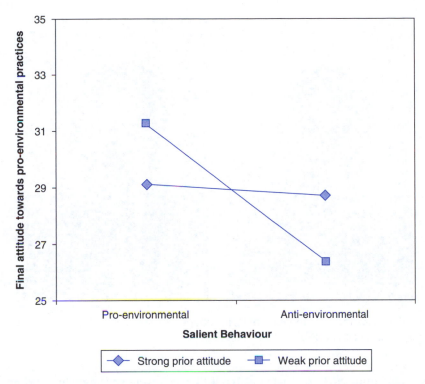

Figure 4.3 Self-perception processes for participants with weak or strong prior attitudes. Data from Chaiken and Baldwin (1981)

A specific example of self-perception of attitudes from behaviour – facial feedback – was demonstrated by Strack, Martin, and Stepper (1988). In this experiment participants were asked to evaluate a series of humorous cartoon images (i.e. they were asked how funny they thought each was). Half of the participants were asked to do this while they were holding a pen in their teeth and half were asked to do this while holding a pen in their lips (an illustration of how this looks can be found in Figure 4.4).

The results were rather interesting – Strack et al. (1988) found that participants who were asked to form an attitude about how amusing the cartoons were when they were holding the pen in their teeth formed a more positive impression than participants who did the same while holding the pen in their lips. An explanation for this effect can be found in self-perception theory. The idea is that people attend to their own behaviour – even to their own facial expression – an idea referred to as the **facial feedback hypothesis**. Holding a pen in your teeth creates a facial expression that *feels* like you're smiling, whereas holding a pen in your lips creates a facial expression that *feels* like you're frowning. The results from this study seem to suggest that these facial 'behaviours', just like any other behaviour, can inform

Figure 4.4   Illustration of the type of facial feedback manipulation used by Strack et al. (1988)

subsequent attitudes. Participants who felt like they were smiling while forming an impression of the cartoon misattributed their facial expression as being indicative of their opinion towards it. People who felt like they were frowning did the same and formed a negative opinion (see Chapter 12 for how such misattributions can also lead to romantic attraction).

Although self-perception theory provides a neat explanation for Strack et al.'s (1988) findings, there is an alternative. Zajonc (1993) argued for a physiological explanation for the effect – the **vascular theory of emotion**. Zajonc argued that smiling (or any behaviour that *feels* like smiling) causes the facial muscles to increase the flow of blood to the brain, which then creates a positive mood by lowering brain temperature. In contrast, frowning constricts facial muscles, lowering blood flow to the brain, and increasing brain temperature, causing a negative mood. Supporting this idea, Zajonc et al. (1989) found that making vowel sounds that mimicked frowning (e.g. 'u' or 'o') lowered forehead temperature and lowered mood, whereas vowel sounds that mimicked smiling (e.g. 'a' or 'e') decreased forehead temperature and elevated mood.

Functional Approach

The three ways in which attitudes can form discussed so far – exposure, learning and self-perception – all operate apparently outside of people's awareness. Typically people are not aware of mere exposure effects (indeed, these effects are stronger when people do not realize they have seen something many times; Bornstein, Leone, & Galley, 1987), nor conditioning, nor the fact that their behaviours can sometimes influence their attitudes. All of these theories argue that attitude formation is a passive process. In other words, it does not require any introspection, or conscious consideration of issues. Instead, attitudes are formed via observation or association. However, it seems self-evident that not all attitudes are formed outside of our awareness – sometimes we engage in deliberate thought about an issue with the aim of forming an opinion. This last way in which attitudes can form is psychologically the most complex, and we can draw the distinction here between naïve scientist and cognitive miser approaches (see Chapter 3). The previous three ways in which attitudes can form might be those that apply to the cognitive miser; but the naïve scientist thinks deliberately about things, processes information carefully, weighs it all up, and comes to a judgement. This is the type of process that goes on when attitudes are formed for *functional* reasons (see Figure 4.5).

According to the **functional approach** attitudes are sometimes formed based on the degree to which they satisfy different psychological needs, so this is an *active* rather than passive attitude theory. There are four basic psychological needs that adopting different attitudes can address: utilitarian, knowledge, ego-defensive and value-expression (Katz, 1960; Smith, 1956; for more recent research on the impacts of attitudes functions on racial attitudes, see Watt & Maio, 2007).

Utilitarian Function

Attitudes are sometimes formed because they help us to gain approval from others. This function creates what can be referred to as instrumental attitudes. These attitudes help us get along and make our lives better. For example, it makes sense for us to develop a positive attitude towards our parents because in childhood we are completely dependent upon them. One can also make a link here with work on conformity (see Chapter 6) where it is in our interests sometimes to go along with a

Psychological need	Example
Utilitarian	Liking your psychology degree because it will help you get a job in the future
Knowledge	Liking your psychology degree because it provides you with useful information in dealing with people
Ego defensive	Liking your psychology degree because you really wanted to become a vet but weren't good enough
Value-expressive	Liking your psychology degree because it illustrates your commitment to helping people

Figure 4.5 Four psychological needs that can influence attitude formation

majority, even though we may disagree with them; our public attitude, may be different from our privately held attitude, but this might serve to prevent us from being ridiculed and excluded from a group to which we belong (especially if we value that group membership, see Chapter 5).

Knowledge Function

Holding particular attitudes can also help us to organize and predict our social worlds, providing a sense of meaning and coherence to our lives. This idea is very similar to that expressed in Chapter 2 (Heider, 1958). Attitudes can be thought of as cognitive schemes. Stereotypes, for instance, can be thought of as attitudes that define our expectations about different social groups. As we saw in Chapter 3, these types of attitudes are simplifying mechanisms (Fiske & Taylor, 1991) that help us to prescribe meaning and structure to our worlds (Turner et al., 1987).

Ego-Defensive Function

Attitudes formed to satisfy ego-defensive psychological needs help people protect themselves from acknowledging threatening self-truths, enabling them to maintain a positive view of themselves. For instance, we may develop an unfavourable attitude towards a co-worker who is enjoying more success than us. Such an attitude serves to protect us from acknowledging a potentially damaging social comparison; as 1980s indie-saviours The Smiths front-man Morrissey proclaimed, 'We hate it when our friends become successful!'.

Value-Expressive Function

Finally, sometimes we may develop an attitude that expresses values that are important to us. For example, we may develop a taste for coffee that we know to have been grown under conditions that ensure fair treatment of Third World workers. We might therefore come to like the taste of this coffee due, in part, to the fact that liking it helps us to express more general beliefs and values that we hold.

Summary

In this first section we have discussed all the ways in which attitudes can be formed: via *exposure*, *learning*, *self-perception*, and because they fulfil certain psychological needs or *functions*. We discussed how simply being exposed to something a number of times can lead to us developing a positive view of it. We also learned how something that consistently elicits positive feelings can promote liking, while something that consistently elicits negative feelings can promote disliking. We saw how rewards such as praise can lead to liking whereas punishments can lead to disliking.

Attitudes can also be inferred from observation of our own behaviours, even at the level of detecting our own facial expressions. Finally, attitudes can form because they serve important psychological functions, like helping us to express values or ideals that are important to us.

So we know how attitudes are formed, but why is it important for us to know this anyway? Why are attitudes important? The simple answer is that if we want to understand how people behave, we need to know *why* they behave in such ways and, since attitudes form the core of our self-concepts, our beliefs about ourselves, about others, about politics, our jobs, our hobbies, and everything else that we do, it seems logical that they are what we need to look at if we are to predict behaviour. If we can understand the attitudes people hold, and why they hold them, then we should be able to predict when people will help others, when they will be aggressive, when they will be prejudiced, when they will engage in healthy behaviours and when they will buy some products but not others. Attitudes are at the core of social psychology because they should be the one thing that enables us to predict how others will behave. In the next section we examine the nature of the relationship between attitudes and behaviours and see that things are not quite as simple as we might imagine. There are a number of conditions that determine if, when and how the attitudes we hold will be reflected in our behaviour.

ATTITUDES AND BEHAVIOUR

One classic study sparked a debate over the nature of the relationship between attitudes and behaviour. In 1934 sociologist Richard LaPierre travelled round the United States with a Chinese couple for three months. His aim was to examine intergroup attitudes, and to see whether those attitudes would predict behaviour. Intuitively, we should indeed expect this to be the case – of course people's attitudes should determine how they behave. If someone doesn't like coffee, for example, then why on earth would they drink it? LaPierre's findings, however, showed us that what seems intuitively to make sense does not always apply to human social perception.

LaPierre was specifically interested in racial prejudice. In the US in the 1930s there was widespread prejudice again Asians, and LaPierre wanted to understand the nature of this negative attitude and whether it predicted discrimination (see Chapter 7 for a discussion specifically relating to prejudiced attitudes and discriminatory behaviour). In the first phase of the study LaPierre travelled around the US visiting restaurants and hotels to see how many would refuse to serve the Chinese couple (such blatant discrimination would not be unusual around this time).

Only 1 out of 250 hotels and restaurants refused to serve the Chinese couple – apparently showing low levels of discrimination (the negative behaviour supposedly associated with prejudiced attitudes). This pattern of data, however, was inconsistent with widespread and frequent reports of racial prejudice that were apparent around this time. To assess these attitudes objectively, after the trip LaPierre sent a letter asking the same restaurant and hotel managers whether they would serve a Chinese couple in their establishment. Of the 128 replies 90 per cent said they would *refuse* to serve Chinese people. It was therefore quite apparent from LaPierre's findings that, contrary to common intuition, attitudes did not predict behaviour at all.

Determinants of the Attitude-Behaviour Relationship

Is it the case that our attitudes bear no relation at all to our behaviour? This would perhaps be a little strange. Well, subsequent research has identified several reasons why LaPierre observed a discrepancy between expressed attitudes and observed behaviour. We discuss each of these factors below.

Specificity

In order for attitudes to predict behaviour the two have to refer to the same level of specificity (Fishbein & Ajzen, 1975). In LaPierre's study the behaviour that was assessed was specific (i.e. would you serve *this* Chinese couple), but the attitude subsequently assessed was broader (i.e. would you serve Chinese people *in general*). It might therefore not be surprising that such general attitudes are not linked to specific behaviours. Think about your attitude towards *psychology*: if you feel like you are good at psychology in general, does this mean you would predict a high mark in all of your psychology exams (e.g. social psychology, neuropsychology, vision)? It is more likely that you're better at some *specific* topic within psychology than others – for instance, you may be better at social psychology than visual perception, while still having a general opinion that you're good at psychology. Your general attitude concerning your ability at psychology would therefore not necessarily predict your performance in a specific aspect of psychology, such as visual perception.

We'll return to this issue later in the book when we discuss prejudice, and how people can develop positive attitudes towards a specific member of a racial group, but this does not necessarily lead to more general attitudes towards all members of that racial group (see Chapter 7). For now, however, it is just important to note that in order to observe a relationship between attitudes and behaviour, then they both need to be assessed at the same level of specificity.

Time

Quite simply, the longer the time between attitude measurement and the measurement of behaviour, the more likely it is that the attitude will change, and so the two will become mismatched. A study by Fishbein and Coombs (1974) is illustrative: they observed that the correlation between attitudes and voting behaviour was stronger one week before voting in an election compared to one *month* before voting.

Self-Awareness

People can experience different kinds of self-awareness prior to carrying out a behaviour, and this can impact on the strength of the relationship between attitudes and behaviour (Echabe & Garate, 1994). Essentially, people who are privately self-aware behave in line with their own attitude whereas people who are publicly self-aware behave in line with the attitude they perceive the majority of other people to hold, especially when there is an audience physically present (see Chapter 1 for an in-depth discussion of self-awareness). You may, for example, privately hold the belief that people should not litter in public places. When you are on your own (and you are more privately self-aware) you might then act in line with this private attitude, making sure you make use of litter bins and do not throw litter on the ground. In other words, your private attitude will predict your behaviour. You may, however, act differently when you are with a group of friends, especially if the norm of the group is that it is not cool to conform to societal norms, like ensuring you don't litter. Here, then, due to conformity pressure you might be more publicly self-aware and act in line with a public attitude (i.e. the group norm) and throw litter on the streets, counter to your private attitude. Later in this book we will see how people sometimes conform to the view of the majority of people present, even though they might not privately agree with this view (see Chapter 6). But for now it is sufficient to know that attitude-behaviour consistency is dependent upon social context: whether your private or public attitudes are more accessible.

Attitude Accessibility

Private or public self-awareness can be thought of as the extent to which either private or public attitudes are more or less *accessible*, a concept we first discussed in Chapter 3 on social cognition. If you recall, people's judgements and behaviours are influenced by the availability heuristic. According to this heuristic, the easier it is for something to come to mind, the more likely it is that it will affect our behaviour (Fazio, 1995). This idea is closely linked to the concept of automatic behaviour that we discussed in Chapter 3. As we saw, priming with a specific type of attitude – a stereotype – can exert a significant impact on people's behaviour (for instance, people walk slower down a corridor when they have been primed with a stereotype of the elderly; Bargh et al., 1996). The accessibility of attitudes can be measured using response times to answering questions relating to the attitude object: the speed of these responses predicts later behaviour (see Fazio and Williams, 1986, for an illustration again with respect to voting behaviour).

Attitude Strength

Related to the concept of attitude accessibility is attitude strength. As you might expect, the stronger one's attitudes are, the more likely they are to have an influence on behaviour. While one might expect strong attitudes to be also *accessible* (they will be the attitudes people more frequently bring to mind), this is not necessarily the case. Attitudes can be held either with strong conviction or be weakly held, irrespective of whether they can be brought easily to mind (that is to say, while related, attitude accessibility and attitude strength are independent concepts). For instance, a case on the news may suddenly bring issues of euthanasia to the fore, sparking public debates not only in the media but between groups of friends. Attitudes related to this issue have therefore become contextually accessible, but people can still vary in the extent to which they either have strong opinions on the subject or have little interest or particular opinion one way or another.

Three things can affect attitude strength and attitude-behaviour consistency: information, personal involvement and direct experience with the attitude object. Possessing more information about an attitude object leads to greater attitude strength and behavioural consistency (Chaiken et al., 1995). The more personally involved someone is with a particular issue, the more likely it will be that they will act in line with their attitudes (Lieberman & Chaiken, 1996). Finally, people who have formed attitudes via direct experience are more likely to have a stronger attitude and show greater consistency with behaviour.

Above we have discussed five factors that can all determine when and whether attitudes will predict behaviour. However, as well as these factors that specifically affect whether *attitudes* affect behaviour, it is important to acknowledge that there are other determinants of behaviour, and that to fully understand when and why we behave in certain ways we need to look at how attitudes affect behaviour *in conjunction with* these other factors. We turn next to an integrative model for predicting behaviour that does just this.

The Theory of Planned Behaviour

Ajzen (1989; see also Ajzen & Fishbein, 1980; Fishbein & Ajzen, 1974) addressed the issue of whether, when, and how attitudes, in conjunction with several other key determinants, predict behaviour. The **theory of planned behaviour** was developed to account for the processes by which people consciously decide to engage in specific actions. It states that behavioural intentions are the most proximal determinant of behaviour, and that three factors converge to predict behavioural intentions (see Figure 4.6).

The first factor is attitudes. Attitudes are determined by one's beliefs about the consequences of performing the behaviour and one's evaluation of the possible consequences of performing the behaviour. The second factor is **subjective norms**.

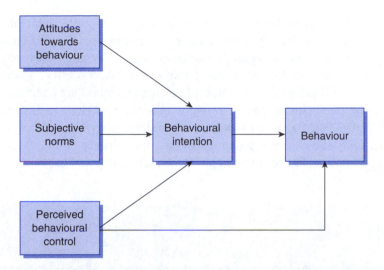

Figure 4.6   The theory of planned behaviour

Subjective norms are determined by the perceived expectations of significant others and one's motivation to conform to these expectations. The third factor is **perceived control** which is determined by one's perception of how easy or difficult it is to perform the behaviour. According to the model these three factors combine in an interactive (not additive) way to determine **behavioural intention,** which in turn determines behaviour (although perceived behavioural control can also directly influence behaviour). We need behavioural intention in the model because an important underlying component of the theory is that neither attitudes nor norms can on their own determine behaviour. It is the *interaction* of these factors with perceived control that predicts attitudes. Any link between these three factors and actual behaviour would imply that the particular antecedent could exert some effect on behaviour independent of the other factors, but this isn't the case. This is why both attitudes and norms only feed into behavioural intention, and only via this concept that takes account of the interaction between all three antecedents can we predict actual behaviour. Perceived control is the only factor that can feed directly into actual behaviour because although knowing how possible it is for you to perform a behaviour or not affects intention, it could ultimately reduce the likelihood of actually performing a behaviour, even if intention is strong.

To illustrate, imagine someone who wants to try to quit smoking. The attitude may be positive (I want to stop smoking); the subjective norms may also be positive ('my family wants me to stop smoking'), but perceived control may be low ('I'm addicted and don't know whether I can stop'). All three factors feed into behavioural intention, even perceived control, because the extent to which the person feels they can overcome their addiction and withdrawal effects will determine their *intention* to carry out the behaviour (i.e. trying to quit). However, while there may be strong intention, ultimately the behaviour may not be carried out because when the person comes to try to engage the behaviour (stop smoking) they may find it too difficult because of low behavioural control (withdrawal effects) which feed directly into actual behaviour. The effect of the three factors is not additive, because if one of the three components is strongly anti- the behaviour (e.g. behavioural control: 'I'm addicted'), intention will be low and the behaviour will not be carried out. For a study showing how *group* norms (see also Chapters 1 and 5) rather than *subjective* norms predict behavioural intentions, see Text Box 4.2.

Text Box 4.2

Group Norms and Behavioural Intentions

According to the theory of planned behaviour, whether or not people perform a particular behaviour is determined by their *intention* to perform that behaviour which, in turn, is influenced by three independent components: attitudes towards the behaviour, perceived behavioural control, and subjective norms. Terry, Hogg, and White (1999), however, suggested that in some cases subjective norms could be better conceptualized as *group* norms – the set of shared beliefs about how group members should think and behave They investigated the possibility that when people define themselves in terms of a particular group membership – when they are high group *identifiers* – *group* norms may influence people's behavioural intentions.

Method

One hundred and forty-three participants from households that had access to recycling bins were asked to report how likely it was that they would engage in household recycling during the following fortnight. Perceived *group norms* were measured by asking participants to report how many of their friends and peers they thought would engage in household recycling and how much they thought their friends and peers would approve of them engaging in household recycling. *Identification* with the group was measured by asking participants how much they identified with and fit in with their group of friends and peers.

Results

The graph shows what Terry and her colleagues found. Participants who strongly identified with their peer group had stronger behavioural intentions if they believed their group had strong norms concerning recycling.

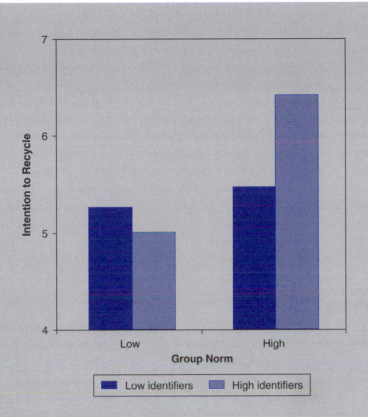

In contrast, participants who did not strongly identify with their peer group were not influenced by the perceived strength of group norms.

Interpreting the Findings

According to the social identity approach, when people categorize themselves as members of a social group they become depersonalized, seeing themselves in terms of the shared features that define that group membership rather than as a unique individual. When this is the case, people think and behave in line with the norms of that group. Adopting the group norm on an issue is beneficial for group members as it provides an attitude with subjective validity. This is because it is based on a group consensus. In line with social identity theory, only individuals for whom group membership was important (i.e. those who highly identified with the group) were influenced by group norms in forming behavioural intentions.

Reasoned Action versus Spontaneity

While the theory of planned behaviour accounts well for thought-out rational deci-sion-making, it appears less useful in predicting spontaneous, unintentional and habitual types of behaviour. This is linked to the idea of attitude accessibility that we discussed earlier in this chapter, and more generally to the notion that there are many social behaviours that we carry out that are automatic, not open to conscious control (see Chapter 3), and which certainly do not entail much deliberative thought. For instance, most people now habitually wear seat belts but they do not engage in a long internal dialogue or debate with themselves as to whether it is a good or bad thing to do. In many ways we can therefore think of the theory of planned behav-iour as a model of behavioural prediction for the *naïve scientist*, with spontaneous behaviours carried out due to habit or 'gut feeling' more associated with the *cogni-tive miser* (see Chapter 3). We will return shortly to the idea of dual processing in discussing attitude change.

Summary

In this section we have looked at whether, when and how attitudes predict behaviour. From early studies like that of LaPierre it was apparent that there is not a clear link between the attitudes and opinions that people hold and the way they behave. Subse-quent research has identified five key factors that determine whether attitudes will corre-late with behaviours: *specificity*, *time*, *self-awareness*, *attitude accessibility* and *attitude strength*. However, attitudes do not predict behaviour on their own, and for a complete understanding of how they impact on behaviour we need to see how they interact with other antecedents. The theory of planned behaviour specifies three factors that interact to determine behavioural intention, which in turn determines behaviour: *attitudes*, *subjec-tive norms* and perceived *behavioural control*. This theory accounts well for reasoned, rational, logical decision-making (and is a good example of how people can be naïve scientists), but it does not account well for habitual or spontaneous behaviours. The latter are accounted for much better by cognitive miser explanations, such as the way accessibility affects the attitude-behaviour relationship.

So far in this chapter we have examined how attitudes are formed, and when and how they determine behaviour. We therefore have an emerging picture of how people's thoughts, opinions and judgements determine how they behave, and thus determine the shape of our social worlds. But, once formed, do attitudes stay the same? Of course, we know they don't – we change many of our own opinions over time. Since attitudes appear to be so crucial for determining behaviour, it is not enough to know how they are formed; we also need to know how they change. This is the focus of the final section of this chapter.

ATTITUDE CHANGE

In this section we will examine what factors cause attitudes to change. Later on we will consider persuasion, attempts from others to change how we perceive particular issues, whether in terms of the political party we vote for, or the coffee brand we buy. First, however, we will look at attitude change resulting from people's own introspection and analysis: a process called *cognitive dissonance*.

Cognitive Dissonance

When we discussed attitude formation, one of the ways in which attitudes could form was from observations of our own behaviour. Bem's (1965) *self-perception theory* argues that when we have no (or a very weak) prior existing attitude on a particular issue we can infer our attitudes from observing our own behaviours. Thus, while there is much work that focuses on whether attitudes predict behaviour, in some cases the causal direction is reversed and attitudes can be created from observations of our own behaviour. When we discussed self-perception theory we noted that this process of attributing attitudes to oneself from observations of our behaviours is likely only when there is initially a very weak attitude relating to the particular attitude object. Well, while this may be true with respect to the attributional processes that underlie self-perception theory, under some conditions even existing attitudes can change as a result of observations of our own behaviour. This is particular likely when the behaviour concerned is clearly *counter* to an existing belief.

Cognitive dissonance theory (Festinger, 1957) argues that behaving in a way that contradicts existing attitudes creates a feeling of discomfort. Put another way, people feel bad when they perform an action that is inconsistent with their attitudes. For example, an animal lover may feel upset if they accidentally run over a hedgehog; a pro-environmentalist may feel bad if they drink a little too much and throw their chips on the ground at the end of a night out.

Despite its name, at the heart of this theory is the motivation to avoid the types of dissonance or discrepancy described above. According to Festinger, when people carry out an action that is incongruous to their attitudes, this knowledge creates an internal imbalance, or dissonance. A little like Heider's (1958) argument that people prefer consistency and stability (see Chapter 2), Festinger suggested that people will be motivated to try to resolve this dissonance. People will look for ways to try to explain it and, if none are apparent, they will resort to the only means left to them to resolve the discrepancy: they will change their attitude so that it matches the behaviour they have performed. Like self-perception theory, cognitive dissonance theory predicts that behaviours cause attitudes rather than the other way around, but unlike self-perception theory, a weak prior attitude is not a prerequisite for the effect. In fact, dissonance will not occur unless there is a prior attitude that is fairly strong; otherwise there will be no discrepancy, and no strong feelings of discomfort.

In a clever experiment, Festinger and Carlsmith (1959) demonstrated the conditions under which cognitive dissonance will change attitudes. In this experiment participants had to complete two boring tasks – emptying and re-filling a tray with spools and then repeatedly turning 48 wooden pegs on a board. Following the hour-long task the experimenter explained that the study was really about the effects of prior knowledge on perceptions of a task. Participants were told that they had been allocated to the control condition, where participants are told nothing at all prior to the start of the task. However, they were also told that in a different condition, participants were being told that the task was very enjoyable.

After this, the experimenter said that their assistant could not help them with the next participant, who will be put into the 'favourable' condition, so would they mind helping out? The participant was required to tell the next participant they had just taken part in the experiment, and that it was fun and enjoyable; in other words, a lie. This was the crucial part of the experiment; the participants were asked to behave in a way that was counter to their attitudes (i.e. to tell someone that the task is enjoyable, when in fact it is clearly boring).

Three manipulations took place at this stage in the experiment. Some of the participants were asked to lie about the task being enjoyable but were offered different amounts of money for doing so. Some were offered $1 while others were offered $20. Some other participants were not instructed to lie and were offered no money; they simply completed the boring task. After having completed the task, or after having completed the task and having told the next participant that the task is enjoyable, all participants were asked to give their true attitude regarding how fun and interesting they really found the task to be. These final ratings of task favourability can be found in Figure 4.7.

As you can see, the results significantly varied as a function of lie-instruction and payment. First of all, participants in the control condition rated the task least favourably. This is unsurprising given the nature of the task, and confirms that it really was boring. What is interesting is what happened when people were asked to lie to the next participant and say that the task really was quite fun. Participants who received $1 to lie to the next participant subsequently rated the task as being significantly more enjoyable than participants in the control condition, while participants who received $20 did not; in fact this latter group of participants did not rate the task as any more enjoyable than participants in the control condition. Why should Festinger and Carlsmith have observed this pattern of attitude change?

It is important to note that the pattern of findings observed is counter to what would have been predicted from *operant conditioning* theory. If we recall from earlier in this chapter, people can develop favourable attitudes towards some behaviour because they are consistently rewarded for carrying it out (e.g. developing a love of mathematics after having been praised for it many times at school). According to these principles, the people in this experiment who would be most likely to develop

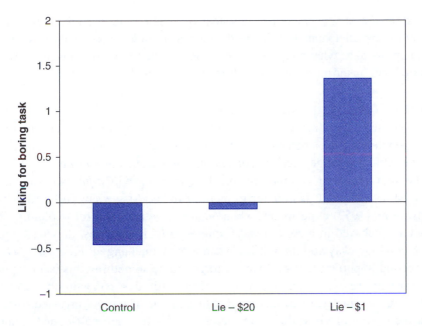

Figure 4.7   The effects of cognitive dissonance on attitude change. Data from Festinger and Carlsmith (1959)

a favourable attitude towards the task would be those rewarded for saying it was enjoyable (and the greater the reward, the stronger the positive feelings that develop). Participants who received $20 for saying that the task was enjoyable should have had that attitude reinforced, and so should have developed the most positive attitude towards the task. This, however, was the opposite of what happened: it was the group of participants who received only $1 who, at the end, reported most favourable attitudes. The pattern *can* be explained by cognitive dissonance theory.

According to Festinger and Carlsmith (1959) the awareness of having carried out a behaviour that is inconsistent with one's attitudes causes an uncomfortable internal state which people are motivated to resolve. If possible, people will use any number of cognitions to explain and thus resolve the discrepancy, but if no other explanation is available, participants will have no choice but to change their attitude so that it fits in with the behaviour they have performed. In the above experiment, $1 and $20 represent different levels of justification for carrying out the behaviour. In the $20 condition, Festinger and Carlsmith argued that participants had sufficient justification to explain away the fact that they had lied to the next participant. The addition of this third cognition resolves the discrepancy between an existing attitude and the awareness that a behaviour has been carried out that contradicts that attitude. In contrast, participants who only received $1 following the experiment may have begun to ask themselves why exactly they had lied to the next participant (and therefore condemning them to one hour of tedium) – $1 is insufficient justification for having carried out a behaviour inconsistent with their attitude, so the only recourse left for these participants is to change their actual attitude to resolve the discrepancy. This appears to be what happened; participants in the $1 condition were those who reported feeling most positive towards the task they had carried out.

Factors Affecting Dissonance

There are three key factors that determine whether cognitive dissonance occurs when people carry out a behaviour that is inconsistent with their attitudes, and hence whether attitude change occurs: *justification*, *choice*, and *investment*.

The first refers to whether people feel they have *justification* for having behaved in a way that is counter to their attitudes. As we saw in Festinger and Carlsmith's (1959) experiment, when people have a reason for explaining why they have behaved in a certain way, counter to their attitudes, they can explain this behaviour away and their attitude can remain unchanged. *Freedom of choice* is a second important factor. If we are forced to do something this is an explanation for why we did it in contravention of our attitudes, so again no dissonance should occur. Finally, *investment* is the third factor. The more invested someone is in their point of view, the more important it is for their self-concept, and so the *stronger* will be any effects of dissonance. In sum, when there is no justification, we freely choose a behaviour, and the relevant attitude is one that is important to us, cognitive dissonance is likely to occur, and we are more likely to change our attitudes to fit in with our behaviours.

Dissonance or Self-perception

We noted earlier how both cognitive dissonance and self-perception theories argue that attitudes are inferred from behaviours. But which of these accounts is correct? It is likely that both are, but apply in different situations. Aronson (1969) argues that cognitive dissonance will occur when discrepancies are clear and distinct, the attitude in question is important for the self-concept, and when it is not possible to explain away the discrepancy (i.e. the conditions outlined in the previous section). When discrepancies are mild, and/or the attitude is not particularly important to someone, then self-perception processes are likely to operate. This is, of course, consistent with our previous discussion of how self-perception theory is most likely to operate when people do not have strong existing attitudes (which presumably co-varies with attitudes being less important to the self-concept, and reduces the extent to which any discrepancy is sharp and distinct).

Persuasion

While cognitive dissonance is attitude change via an *internal* discrepancy, **persuasion** refers to attitude change via an *external* message. How do people think about, and incorporate, information they receive that is counter to their current point of view? What determines whether they are persuaded by arguments or not? This is a question of obvious relevance to our understanding of how people think, feel, and behave. Do TV adverts work? When do people change their brand of toothpaste? What changes people's vote in political election campaigns? What makes people decide to adopt a healthier diet? How people react to messages intended to make them change their mind is the focus of this final section.

Dual Process Models of Persuasion

Understanding how people react to persuasive messages takes us back to thinking about *naïve scientists* and *cognitive misers*, the dual route models of social information processing that we discussed in Chapter 3. It is a dual route approach that has proved most successful in explaining how, when and why people are or are not persuaded by others. Two models characterize this approach, the **elaboration-likelihood model** (Petty & Cacioppo, 1986a) and the **heuristic-systematic model** (Chaiken, 1980). Although slightly different in emphasis both argue that there are two ways that a persuasive message can cause attitude change, each differing in the amount of cognitive effort or elaboration they require: the central (systematic) route and the peripheral (heuristic) route (see Figure 4.8).

The **central route** is taken when people are motivated and able to think carefully about the content of a message (referred to as high elaboration conditions). Here people are influenced by the strength and quality of the arguments. In contrast, the **peripheral route** is taken when people are unwilling or unable to analyse message content. Here people pay attention to cues that are irrelevant to the content or quality of the communication (referred to as low elaboration conditions), such as the attractiveness of the communicator or the amount of information presented. It is important to note that attitudes can change via both routes, but that the resulting attitudes may be qualitatively different as a result. Attitudes formed via the peripheral route do not require comprehension of the message, are weaker, less resistant to counter argument, and less predictive of behaviour than central route attitudes (Petty, Haugtvedt, & Smith, 1995). The two routes capture the definition of the dual process approach to social information processing that we discussed in Chapter 3 and, as such, which route is taken is a function of contextual factors which we discuss next.

Processing Route Determinants

As well as the general conditions for heuristic use that we described in Chapter 3 (i.e. cognitive overload, little information about the issue, low self-relevance, time pressure), there are a number of factors that specifically affect which route might

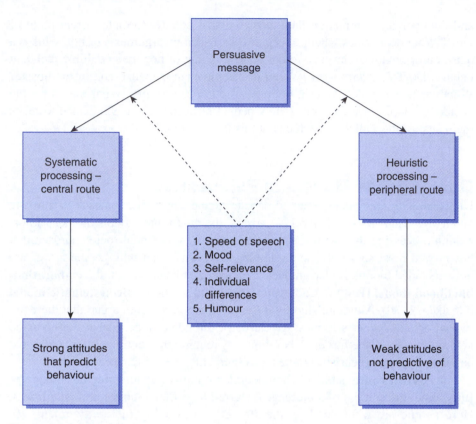

Figure 4.8 Systematic versus heuristic processing of attitude-relevant persuasive messages

be taken when people process persuasive messages. Here we outline five of them: speed of speech, mood, involvement, individual differences, and humour.

Rapid speech makes it hard to process the content of a persuasive message, so people abandon the central route in favour of the peripheral route, relying on just the *number of arguments* as a heuristic for deciding whether to accept the message.

Mood can also have an impact on what route is taken. In general, happy people use the peripheral route, while unhappy people tend to use the central route. The explanation for this is that negative moods can signal that something is 'wrong', which triggers an increase in attention to identify the problem (Bohner, Crow, Erb, & Schwartz, 1992). The implication is that happy people are therefore more susceptible to weak cues like source attractiveness.

The extent to which the issue is important to the self has an impact on which route is taken. If the outcome of the argument or the issue at hand directly affects, and has important implications for, the self then it is more likely that the perceiver will pay more attention and the central route will be taken. Martin and Hewstone (2003a) carried out a study which investigated how issue importance to the self, combined with whether the message comes from a numerical minority or majority, has an impact on whether the central or peripheral route is taken. This study is described in Text Box 4.3.

Text Box 4.3

Minorities and Majorities Change Attitudes in Different Ways

A persuasive message may have different effects depending on whether it comes from a numerical minority or majority source. Martin and Hewstone (2003a) were interested in whether the source of a message influences how carefully it is processed. They also considered whether the type of processing that occurs was affected by whether or not the message argues for a negative personal outcome for the participant.

Method

Participants who were in favour of voluntary euthanasia and against the introduction of a single currency in Europe (the Euro) read a counter-attitudinal argument which pilot studies showed was high in personal interest and would have a very negative personal outcome for them (pro-Euro) or an argument which was of moderate personal interest and would have less of a negative personal outcome for them (anti-voluntary Euthanasia). Participants either received the message from a minority source ('18% of students at your college think this') or from a majority source ('82% of students at your college think this'). Participants in each condition also read either strong evidence-based messages on the topic or weak messages on the topic.

Results

When the message did *not* have a very negative personal outcome for participants (anti-euthanasia), people receiving information from a *minority* source were more persuaded by *strong* messages than by weak messages, whereas people receiving information from a majority source were equally influenced by strong and weak messages. In contrast, when the message concerned was perceived as having a *very negative* personal outcome for participants

(Continued)

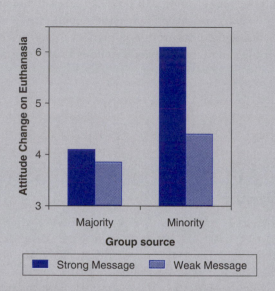

Negative Personal Outcome: Low

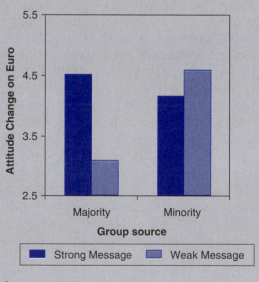

Negative Personal Outcome: High

(pro-Euro), people receiving information from a *majority* source were more persuaded by *strong* messages than by weak messages, whereas people receiving information from a minority source were equally persuaded by strong and weak messages.

Interpreting the Findings

When the message did not have a negative personal outcome, participants who received their message from a minority source were only influenced by high quality messages, indicating that they took the central route to persuasion. In contrast, participants who received their message from a majority source were equally influenced by strong and weak messages, indicating that they disregarded message content and took the peripheral route to persuasion. According to conversion theory (Moscovici, 1980), when an argument is made by the majority, people focus on their relationship with the source of the message rather than the content of the message, because they feel social pressure to conform to the majority viewpoint. In contrast, when an argument is made by the minority, people are more likely to focus on the message content to try to understand why the minority is taking this divergent standpoint. This leads to more central processing.

When the message had a negative personal outcome for participants, however, the opposite pattern emerged; only a message from a majority source led to central processing. Martin and Hewstone argued that when a majority endorses a position which is against their self-interests, it leads to curiosity and therefore a closer examination of the message. In contrast, when a minority source argues for a negative personal outcome it is ignored to protect one's self-interests.

In line with conversion theory, thus, a majority source is likely to lead to *heuristic* processing whereas a minority source is more likely to lead to *systematic* processing.

There are also *individual differences* that make some people more likely than others to take one route over another. Need for cognition (Haugtvedt & Petty, 1992) is the degree to which someone is oriented to engaging in effortful thought. People who are higher in need for cognition are therefore more likely to take the central route while people who are lower in need for cognition are more likely to take the peripheral route. Similar effects have been found using related tendencies, such as need for closure (Kruglanski et al., 1993) and need to evaluate (Jarvis & Petty, 1995). Differences in self-monitoring (Snyder & DeBono, 1985) can also have an impact. This is the degree to which someone is concerned with what other people think of them. People who are higher in self-monitoring will be more likely to take the central route while people who are lower in self-monitoring will be more likely to take the peripheral route.

Finally the use of *humour* can influence which route is taken. Relevant humour leads to the central route being taken while irrelevant humour leads to the peripheral route being taken (Smith, Haugtvedt, & Petty, 1994).

Peripheral Cues

Once a route is taken, it may prove persuasive or not depending upon the characteristics of the context. If the central route is taken the key determinant of persuasion will be the argument quality (is it convincing or not?). If the peripheral route is taken, then several characteristics of the message source will be critical. First, peripheral route processing is more likely to lead to attitude change if the source has physical attractiveness. Chaiken (1979), for instance, found that experimenters trying to persuade undergraduates to sign a petition to stop the university serving meat were more successful if they were attractive than if they were unattractive. Second, as we will see when we discuss affiliation and attraction in Chapter 11, similarity to self is an important determinant of attraction. Similarity in terms of shared attitudes, appearance, or social categories can all enhance the persuasiveness of a message (Simons et al., 1970). Finally, source credibility is a key peripheral cue that increases the likelihood of attitude change. A source is perceived as credible if they are seen to be an expert, unbiased, and trustworthy. In the 1950s Hovland and Weiss (1951) found that US college students who read an article arguing that nuclear submarines were safe were more persuaded when the author was Robert Oppenheimer (the scientist who was in charge of developing the atomic bomb) compared to when the same article was attributed to the Soviet news agency, *Pravda*. This study was carried out during the Cold War, so these two sources represented clear differences in credibility. What is interesting is that differences in persuasion caused by differences in credibility tend to diminish over time, something called the 'sleeper effect'. Four weeks after the initial test phase in Hovland and Weiss's experiment, participants' attitudes towards nuclear submarines were again tested. The change can be seen in Figure 4.9.

As you can see, the effects of source credibility had disappeared when the participants were re-tested four weeks after receiving the persuasive message. The implication is that even non-credible people can persuade us … over time. The explanation for this effect is something called *source memory*. The idea is that we do not only encode information about the argument, but also about who is the source of the argument (hence the initial impact of source variables like attractiveness, and here, credibility). Over time, however, source memory decays and so any influence of source credibility – whether facilitating or inhibitory – is diminished. This explains the increase in low credibility source persuasion as well as the decrease in high credibility persuasion. Further supporting this idea, Kelman and Hovland (1953)

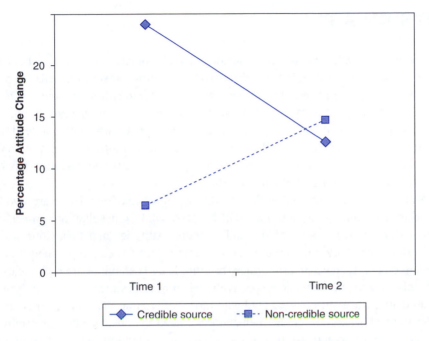

Figure 4.9   The sleeper effect. Data from Hovland and Weiss (1951)

replicated the original experiment but reminded participants of the source before their attitudes were reassessed. This eliminated the sleeper effect.

Summary

In this section we have looked at attitude change. Attitudes can change via *self-perception* if the attitude is initially very weak, or it is less important for our self-concept, or via *cognitive dissonance* processes when we have a clear opinion of the issue at hand or it is important to us. While self-perception and dissonance-reduction lead to attitude change from internal processes, there can also be external pressures to change our attitudes, such as from the media, advertising, political parties, etc. We can process persuasive messages in either of two ways: systematically via the *central route*, or heuristically via the *peripheral route*. A number of factors influence which route is taken: *speed of speech, mood, self-relevance, individual differences* in processing tendencies and *humour*. If the peripheral route is taken then surface characteristics like *attractiveness, similarity* and perceived *credibility* will determine whether attitude change occurs.

CHAPTER SUMMARY

In this chapter we have explored what social psychologists have learned about attitudes and attitude change. We first discussed how attitudes were formed. There are four ways: *mere exposure*, *associative learning*, *self-perception* and the *functional approach*. Merely being exposed to something many times can increase liking of it. Consistent pairings of something with pleasant or unpleasant stimuli can lead to an association being developed. Sometimes we can infer our attitudes from observing our own behaviours, and sometimes we adopt particular attitudes because they help us address important psychological needs.

We then examined the link between attitudes and behaviour. There are five factors that determine when attitudes will be correlated with behaviour: *specificity*, *time*, *self-awareness*, *accessibility* and *strength*. Attitudes and behaviour will be correlated when they are measured at the same level of specificity, when they are measured close together in time, when the attitude and behaviour are both measured privately or with an audience respectively, when attitudes are more easily brought to mind, and when attitudes are held with more conviction. We also saw here that in order to most accurately predict behaviour we need to consider other determinants that combined interactively to form a behavioural intention, which then predicts actual behaviour. Attitudes, subjective norms and perceived behavioural control all need to be taken into account to predict behavioural intention.

Finally, we looked at how attitudes can change. Attitudes can sometimes change from observations of our own behaviours. This can be via *self-perception* if the attitude is initially very weak, or it is less important for our self-concepts, or it can be via *cognitive dissonance* processes when we have a clear opinion of the issue at hand or it is important to us. Cognitive dissonance describes the discrepancy that we feel when we have acted in a way that is clearly counter to our attitudes and we have no way of justifying why we did so. This is an unpleasant state and we will be motivated to resolve it – if there is no way to explain our behaviour the only option left is to change our attitude to be in line with the behaviour and therefore resolve the discrepancy.

Aside from attitudes resulting from internal conflict, which characterizes self-perception and dissonance theories, often we are faced with external pressures to change our attitudes, such as from the media, advertising, political parties, etc. We can process persuasive messages in either of two ways: *systematically*, as naïve scientists, via the central route, or *heuristically*, as cognitive misers, via the peripheral route. Apart from more general tendencies that determine use of heuristic over systematic processing strategies discussed in Chapter 3, which route is taken is influenced by *speed of speech*, *mood*, *self-relevance*, *individual differences* in processing tendencies and *humour*.

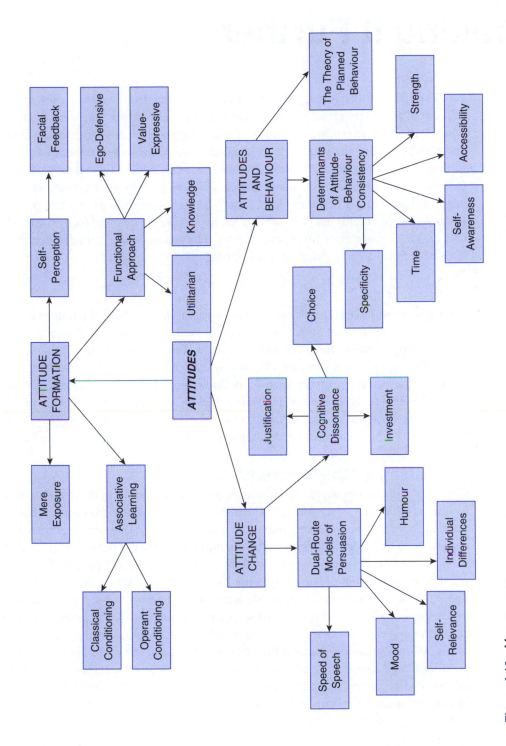

Figure 4.10 Memory map

Taking it Further

Try This

Pick five attitudes that you hold. They can be on anything from your favourite cereal to your political party preference. For each, can you identify how they were formed? Was it through mere repeated exposure? Does the attitude serve an important value-expressive function for you? Is there a pattern: are some attitudes more likely to form via routes like exposure and associative learning while others through a reasoned process associated with what function they hold? For example, your preferred brand of cereal might be more likely formed by exposure (maybe you had it a lot when you were a child) but your political preference might be more likely the result of a reasoned analysis of functional benefits. Do you have any attitudes that may have been formed via a combination of routes?

Debate This

In Chapter 3 we talked about how the way in which people think about their social world can be determined by factors such as amount of available information, time pressure, importance of the issue, and motivation. Think about all the ways attitudes can form, the ways they can affect behaviour, and the ways in which attitudes can change – can you apply the same analysis here? In some cases this is explicitly the case – the elaboration likelihood model is a dual process theory, but what about the theory of planned behaviour, or the different ways in which attitudes can form – can these fit into a dual process framework, and if so, how?

Something for the Weekend

Come up with an intervention to encourage positive changes in behaviour that uses techniques based on what you've learned in this chapter. For example, you might want to encourage people to recycle more. First, you could develop an advertising campaign to help people form a positive attitude towards the behaviour (repeated exposure to this campaign, pairings with positive outcomes, and appeals to values might help here). Some people might not have a positive view of recycling in the first place, so you will need to persuade them, perhaps using two-sided approaches to increase credibility (should you use peripheral cues – like a famous person endorsing recycling – or more central cues – like well-researched and justified arguments?). Finally, having changed the attitude you'll need to ensure that it is translated into behaviour, taking account of factors such as time, specificity, and other influences like norms and past behaviour (how could you also ensure these other factors are optimal for behaviour change?).

Further Reading

The Essentials

Eagly, A.H. & Chaiken, S. (1993). *The psychology of attitudes*. Fort Worth: Harcourt, Brace, Jovanovich.

Petty, R.E. & Cacioppo, J.T. (1986). *Communication and persuasion: Central and peripheral routes to attitude change*. New York: Springer.

These are two classic books that discuss everything we've covered in this chapter in depth. They both helped shaped the field of attitudes as we see it today, and will give you a comprehensive historical perspective from which to approach more contemporary work on attitudes.

Next Steps

Fishbein, M. & Ajzen, I. (1974). Attitudes towards objects as predictors of single and multiple behavioural criteria. *Psychological Review*, *81*, 59–75.

A classic paper that was the starting point for a sustained and extensive programme of work on the theory of planned behaviour. Read this, and you'll be ready to dive into a huge amount of applied research, including some of the best illustrations of applied social psychological theory, notably in terms of promoting more healthly behaviours,

Delving Deeper

Webb, T. L. & Sheeran, P. (2008). Mechanisms of implementation intention effects: The role of goal intentions, self-efficacy, and accessibility of plan components. *British Journal of Social Psychology*, *47*, 373–395.

If you want to read about some cutting edge research on the link between attitudes and behaviour, take a look at this. The theory of planned behaviour argues that attitudes (amongst other things) influence behaviour via intentions. This research explores specifically how intentions influence behaviour, outlining the form that interventions should take in order for intentions to be implemented, and the psychological mechanisms that such 'implementation intentions' invoke (there are some nice links back to social cognitive mechanisms here – like accessibility – that we discussed in Chapter 3).

Group Processes

5

Group Processes

Social psychology is all about how other people affect how we think, feel and behave. So far in this textbook we have looked at mental representations of the self, how we process information, form attitudes about ourselves and others; but we have not yet looked at what happens when people are physically in a group, interacting with others. We have already discussed a broad type of group – social categories – in Chapter 3. Here the focus is on the effects of physically interacting (for instance in a tutorial group, a sports team or at work). We will focus on how groups affect productivity and decision-making in the first half of the chapter, and in the second half on how leaders emerge.

GROUPS

What is a Group?

What do we mean by a group? We all kind-of know what we mean when we talk about groups, but for the purposes of this chapter we need a more concrete definition. Previously, social psychologists have talked about how groups can be defined in a number of ways. **Cohesiveness** is one way of thinking about groups. Social cohesion increases as individuals start to think and act more in line with a collection of other people (Fine & Holyfield, 1996). Cohesive groups tend to exert more social influence (see Chapter 6) and their members are typically more committed to the group. There is an inverse correlation between group size and cohesiveness; as more and more members join a group, it becomes more difficult to maintain cohesion.

We can also think about groups in terms of similarity and interconnectedness. We discussed in Chapter 3 how category formation tends to emphasize similarities

	Type of group	Examples
1	Intimacy groups (most group-like)	Family, Partners in a romantic relationship, Friends
2	Task groups	Colleagues, Committees, Work groups
3	Social categories	Women, Muslim, British
4	Loose associations (least group-like)	People who live on the same street, people who like rock music

Figure 5.1 Four types of group of increasing entitativity, from Lickel et al. (2000)

and de-emphasize differences within categories, and the same is true within physical groups (Jackson et al., 1991). In a physical group this makes sense; groups usually come together because they have a common goal, which is a *de facto* basis for similarity.

Entitativity

One way of defining groups that encompasses all of the qualities outlined above is in terms of **entitativity**. Entitativity refers to the extent to which any collection of individuals can be perceived as 'groupy'. Although definitions vary, it is generally agreed that entitativity encompasses concepts like *cohesiveness, interconnectedness, similarity* and *common goals* as well as *importance* of the group and the tendency for group members to physically *interact* with one another. The more a collection of individuals exhibits these characteristics, the more they can be described as a group. Lickel et al. (2000) found that it was possible to divide a wide range of groups into four types of increasing entitativity: loose collections of people (e.g. people standing at a bus stop, people who listen to thrash-metal), social categories (e.g. nationality, race), task groups (e.g. colleagues), and finally intimacy groups (e.g. friends) – see Figure 5.1.

Lickel et al.'s taxonomy provides the perfect way to think about the types of group we will discuss in this chapter. We are going to discuss the effects of the presence of others where there is no prior relationship or interconnectedness between the people involved, but we are also going to talk about task groups, such as work groups that have specific goals. We will not be talking here about social categories (we did this in Chapter 3) or high intimacy groups (we discuss the inter-individual processes involved in friendships groups and romantic partners in Chapter 12).

GROUP PRODUCTIVITY

Social Facilitation and Social Inhibition

In this section we focus on groups of low entitativity. In fact, these groups are in some ways not groups at all. Rather, in this section we will examine the impact of the *presence* of other people on an individual's performance. Do we perform better or worse in the presence of others? We can all think of examples where we've had to perform in front of someone else, whether a student project presentation or a sporting event at school. Do audiences help or hinder us?

Floyd Allport (1920) coined the term **social facilitation** to describe the tendency for people to perform better when in front of an audience (an effect originally observed by Triplett, 1897). Social facilitation was one of the most researched effects in the early days of social psychology, with demonstrations not only with people but with a wide variety of animals (from cockroaches to chickens) performing a wide variety of behaviours (from running faster to eating more; e.g. Chen, 1937). Importantly, however, the *type* of task is an essential determinant of whether social facilitation will occur. Indeed, sometimes the opposite effect is observed: a detriment in performance when an audience is present, something we can refer to as **social inhibition**.

It became apparent that while the presence of others increases performance on simple tasks (e.g. running, eating, shouting), it inhibits performance on more complex tasks (e.g. solving maths problems, answering questions on a presentation you have just given; Allport, 1920; Bond & Titus, 1983; Travis, 1925). Just think for a moment about tasks you have had to carry out in the past. At school, it is likely that you ran faster on the sports track when there were other people running with you: a simple task and a well-learned response. In contrast, completing those maths questions in an examination room, with lots of people around you, probably seemed more difficult than when you were revising them at home on your own; this is a complex task and one that is difficult to make a well-learned response. The key question that emerged from this research was *why* the presence of others had these opposite effects depending upon *task complexity*. We discuss below three theories that attempt to provide some answers.

Explanations of Facilitation and Inhibition

In this section we discuss the three key theories that have been offered as explanations for why the presence of others apparently facilitates performance on easy tasks but inhibits performance on more complex or difficult tasks: *drive theory*, *evaluation apprehension*, and *distraction conflict*.

Drive Theory

We first met Zajonc in our discussion of attitude formation in Chapter 4. In 1965 he also offered an explanation of social facilitation and inhibition effects. According to Zajonc both facilitation and inhibition effects can be explained by physiological arousal. The theory goes like this. First, the mere presence of others increases physiological arousal. This is an evolutionary idea; it makes sense for all organisms to experience a heightened sense of physiological readiness when other organisms are present, because these other organisms could represent either a threat to survival, or an opportunity to reproduce. A state of physiological arousal is therefore useful in both scenarios. The second part of the model rests upon the assumption that physiological arousal enhances the performance of dominant, or well-learned, response tendencies (Hull, 1943). This second component also makes sense. We know that some types of arousal (e.g. anxiety) narrow the focus of attention (Kahneman, 1973) and reduce processing capacity (Mueller & Thompson, 1984). This lends support to the idea that arousal activates the autonomic nervous system such that internal cues compete with task demands for processing capacity (Mandler, 1975). Arousal can therefore lead to increased reliance on automatic processing (Ingram & Kendall, 1987) or, in other words, increased dependence on dominant and well-learned responses (see Chapters 3 and 7 for discussion of *automaticity*).

Whether social facilitation or inhibition occurs, therefore, all depends on whether the dominant response that is evoked by physiological arousal is correct or incorrect for the task at hand. For instance, if the task is running – a well-practised activity – then drive theory predicts that we should run faster in the presence of an audience, because the audience will increase physiological arousal and improve that well-learned, dominant response. If, however, the task is to solve a maths problem – something that for most of us may not be particularly well learned – then the physiological arousal (and restriction of cognitive resources) that comes with the presence of an audience may inhibit our ability to solve the problem.

What is important about drive theory is that it is not whether the task at hand is simple or complex that determines whether social facilitation or inhibition occurs, but the match between the dominant response and the task requirements. In most cases, however, these two things will co-vary; dominant and well-learned responses will be more likely on simple tasks (like riding a bike) but not on more complex tasks (like solving maths questions). A good test of drive theory will therefore involve participants who have *dominant* responses on *complex* tasks. If facilitation or inhibition effects are dependent not on task complexity *per se* but determined instead by whether the person has a fitting dominant response for the task at hand, then experts should show facilitation, not inhibition, on complex tasks. This is because experts should have well-learned responses to the relevant

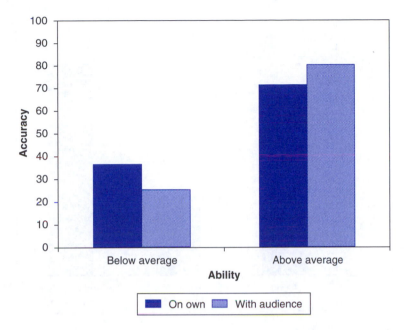

Figure 5.2   Pool players' accuracy as a function of audience presence and ability. Data from Michaels et al. (1982)

complex problems. For instance, we would expect, on the basis of drive theory, that most of us may show social inhibition in the presence of others when carrying out a maths test. But what about maths experts? Think about maths professors at a university. It's likely that these individuals are so well-versed in solving maths problems that for them such tasks are well learned. They should therefore perform better with an audience (e.g. when giving a lecture).

Michaels et al. (1982) provided empirical evidence for the idea that experts *do* perform better with an audience. After first assessing the ability of a selection of pool players at a college student union, their shooting accuracy was assessed with and without an audience present. Michaels and colleagues found that, in line with drive theory, while below average players' performance decreased with an audience present (a typical audience inhibition effect for a complex task), above average players' performance *increased* with an audience present (see Figure 5.2).

Evaluation Apprehension

This second explanation for social facilitation and inhibition effects does not dispute that it is physiological arousal that increases the tendency to make well-learned responses (typically the correct response on simple tasks and the incorrect response

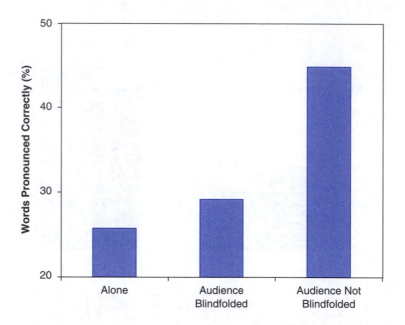

Figure 5.3   The effect of mere presence versus an audience on performance.
Data from Cottrell et al. (1968)

on complex tasks), but it does argue against the idea that it is the *mere presence* of others that causes this arousal. Instead, some theorists have argued that it is *evaluation apprehension* that causes physiological arousal in the presence of others. **Evaluation apprehension** is concern about being evaluated by others (Cottrell, 1972). In the presence of others, this evaluation apprehension can translate into being concerned that you will look stupid in front of the people watching you – you'll be apprehensive about being evaluated (negatively) by them.

Cottrell and colleagues (1968) carried out a clever experiment that distinguished between the mere presence and evaluation apprehension explanations of social facilitation. In this experiment participants had to complete a simple task (pronounce out loud nonsense words that appeared every four seconds on a screen) either on their own or in the presence of an audience. The key manipulation here was that some of the participants carried out the task in front of a blindfolded audience, while some carried out the task in front of an audience who could see them. The non-blindfolded participants showed the typical social facilitation effect on the easy task: they performed better in the presence of an audience. According to Zajonc's (1968) drive theory, the same effect should be observed when the audience is blindfolded – the mere *presence* of others should lead to physiological arousal that should then lead to dominant response facilitation on this simple task. According to Cottrell and colleagues, however, it is not mere presence but evaluation apprehension that causes heightened arousal and better performance. A blindfolded audience is prevented from evaluating your performance. As such, if evaluation apprehension, and not mere presence, causes physiological arousal and subsequent response facilitation, then preventing this evaluation by blindfolding the audience should wipe out the facilitation effect. This is exactly what Cottrell and colleagues found. Social facilitation only occurred when the audience could see (and evaluate) the participant, but no facilitation occurred (no difference in audience present and audience absent conditions) when the audience was blindfolded (see Figure 5.3).

Distraction Conflict

Cottrell et al.'s (1968) findings appear to contradict the mere presence assumption of drive theory, suggesting that it is instead evaluation apprehension that causes physiological arousal and subsequent social facilitation and inhibition effects. However, evaluation apprehension cannot explain all social facilitation and inhibition effects. In particular, it has considerable difficulty in explaining social facilitation effects that have been observed in animals (Chen, 1937; Gates & Allee, 1933). Chickens are probably not laying lots of eggs because they are worried about what other chickens think of them! So, while evaluation apprehension offers a good explanation for social facilitation effects with people, only drive theory can account for animal findings. A third theory attempts to reconcile the findings from human and animal studies with an alternative explanation: **distraction conflict** (Baron, 1986).

According to distraction conflict theory it is neither mere presence nor evaluation apprehension that causes the physiological arousal that leads to facilitation or inhibition effects, but conflict experienced between the task at hand and attending to others in the immediate surroundings. The appeal of this explanation is that it can explain the heightened arousal caused by an audience in both animals and humans. Conflict between attending to different things in one's immediate surroundings is well-established as a source of arousal for both animal and humans. Moreover, that conflict does not even have to be other people or animals, but can be any conflict-inducing stimulus (e.g. loud noises, flashing lights; Sanders & Baron, 1975).

Should we therefore conclude that distraction conflict is the only explanation for social facilitation and inhibition effects? Although it can explain a wide variety of these phenomena, what is important is that there is yet to be any conclusive evidence that argues in favour of distraction conflict at the expense of mere presence or evaluation apprehension. As such, the most sensible conclusion is that in any particular situation any combination of these three explanations may be applicable, or even all three simultaneously. They are not necessarily mutually exclusive. In sum, it seems that the mere presence of others, the ability of others to evaluate your performance, and the distraction caused by others being present all contribute to social facilitation and inhibition effects.

Social Loafing

So far, we know that individuals appear to work harder when others are present because of physiological arousal caused by their presence, attentional conflict and, for humans at least, evaluation apprehension. Concern over how other people will evaluate you appears to make people work harder on simple tasks. All of this research focuses on what happens to an individual's performance when in front of an audience. But what happens when we are working as a *team*? Does the presence of others make us work harder? Research suggests that this is, in fact, not the case; in teamwork people appear to put in *less* effort. This phenomenon is called **social loafing** (Karau & Williams, 1995).

The key difference between work on social facilitation and work on social loafing is the unit of assessment. In contrast to social facilitation and inhibition effects, which apply when the individual's *own* specific performance is evaluated by others, social loafing applies when the unit of assessment is the *group* product. In other words, social loafing occurs when each person's individual contribution to the output is pooled.

A classic study of social loafing was provided by Latané et al. (1979). In this study six blindfolded participants had to sit in a semicircle wearing headphones that played a recording of people shouting into their ears. Participants were asked to shout as loudly as possible while listening to the shouts coming through into their headphones. In one condition participants were told that they were shouting alone. In a second condition they were told that they were shouting with five other people. In fact, only the participant was shouting on any one trial. The intensity of their shouts was the dependent measure. The findings can be seen in Figure 5.4.

These findings illustrate the social loafing effect. Participants who believed they were shouting in a group shouted with less intensity than participants who believed they were shouting alone. Importantly, this difference in intensity can only be attributed to the different information participants were given about the number of people who were joining in with them during the task. In both conditions participants were blindfolded, so could not see who else was taking part, and in both conditions the same shouting noises were being played through their earphones. The only difference was whether participants thought they were solely responsible for the shouting task, or whether other people were also responsible.

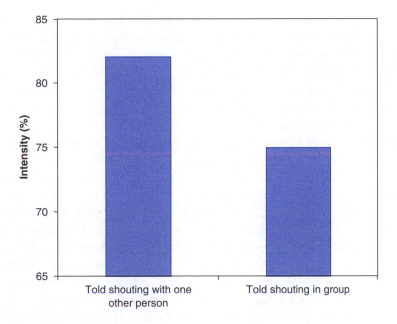

Figure 5.4 Social loafing. Data from Latané et al. (1979)

How can we explain this social loafing effect? What appears to be happening in these situations is that participants experience a **diffusion of responsibility** (Comer, 1995). This term describes how people in a group feel individually less personally responsible for any task at hand – their contribution is literally 'lost in the crowd'. This same process can inhibit people from helping others in emergency situations (see Chapter 10 on prosocial behaviour) and has resulted in collective acts of aggression (see Chapter 9 on aggression).

Diffusion of Responsibility

Recall our discussion of social facilitation and inhibition effects above. The impact of an audience on individuals' productivity appeared to depend on the type of task: simple or complex (assuming people's dominant response was usually only helpful on simple tasks). Interestingly, the work on social loafing that we have just discussed focuses on simple tasks – such as shouting loudly. Would social loafing occur even on complex tasks? On such tasks when people's performance is being individually judged there is an inhibitory effect – they perform worse than if they would carry out the same task on their own. Does working on a complex task in a group also lead to poorer performance?

Jackson and Williams (1985) carried out a task to investigate this possibility. The task was complex, involving navigation of a computer maze with one other person.

There were two conditions. In one condition participants were told that each co-worker's performance would be assessed at the end of the experiment. In the other, participants were told that their performance would be pooled with their co-worker and that their individual contributions would not be identifiable. Interestingly, in this study the exact opposite of typical social loafing effects was observed: participants performed *better* when their contribution was pooled, rather than when their efforts were individually identified. Why might this be?

In the previous section we discussed how diffusion of responsibility explains why social loafing occurs on simple tasks. Recall also from our discussion of work on social facilitation that the reason why people may not perform well on complex tasks is because of evaluation apprehension (fear of getting it wrong and therefore being evaluated negatively by others). What is interesting is that these two processes, diffusion of responsibility and evaluation apprehension, appear to cancel each other out when people are carrying out a complex task, but in a team where their individual contribution cannot be assessed. The evaluation apprehension that normally causes the detriment to performance when people are being individually assessed on a complex task is removed when they are just one of a team working on the problem because this diffusion of responsibility makes them less responsible for the outcome – reducing any anxiety they might feel about 'being in the spotlight'.

Summary

In this section we have looked at the impact of others on individual and group productivity. We have seen how when an individual's productivity is individually judged in front of an audience then they tend to perform better on *simple* tasks (such as clapping), but not so well on *complex* tasks (such as maths problems). These tendencies can be referred to as *social facilitation* and *social inhibition* respectively.

Three theories try to account for whether social facilitation or social inhibition will be observed. All of these theories argue that *physiological arousal* is the key process, but differ in what they specify causes such arousal. Zajonc's *drive theory* argues that the mere presence of others causes physiological arousal, which is consistent with an evolutionary explanation and can account for both *animal* and *human* social facilitation effects. The idea here is that physiological arousal increases tendencies to make a dominant response, which is usually the response that enables better performance on simple tasks, and accounts for why people don't do well with an audience on complex tasks (unless they are an expert, in which case complex responses are the *dominant, well-learned* response).

However, the mere presence explanation cannot account for why people do not show social facilitation effects when audiences are blindfolded. Here, *evaluation apprehension* is a better explanation: blindfolds remove the ability for an audience to evaluate the performance of an individual, so they remove the physiological arousal that facilitates simple task performance, but they disrupt performance on complex tasks. Evaluation apprehension cannot, however, explain the observation of social facilitation in animals. *Distraction conflict* offers an explanation that can account for both animal and human findings. According to this theory, any stimulus – social or non-social – that divides attention can increase physiological arousal. However, because there is no evidence that distraction conflict rules out either alternative explanation it is likely that all three apply to a greater or lesser extent in different situations. While social facilitation and inhibition effects apply when an individual's performance is judged in the presence of others, *social loafing* applies when individual efforts are pooled and a group product is the unit of assessment. In this situation each individual's performance declines because of a *diffusion of responsibility*. However, this same diffusion of responsibility can prevent evaluation apprehension that can occur when individuals are being judged in front of an audience on a difficult (complex) task. An integration of these ideas regarding the impact of task complexity and unit of assessment can be seen in Figure 5.5.

Having examined the impact of others on individual performance, and the performance of groups on simple and complex tasks, we now turn to another important determinant of group productivity: the characteristics of the group's *leader*.

LEADERSHIP

If you were asked to think of a public figure who you particularly admire, what would you say? Maybe you would suggest Nelson Mandela, or Martin Luther King. Or maybe you would say that Mahatma Gandhi is the person you admire the most. These people are admirable for different reasons, but they all share one thing in common: they can all be described as leaders. A leader is the most influential or powerful individual in a group, the person who is primarily responsible for determining a group's direction and goals. As we shall discuss in this section, leadership can take many different forms. There may be one leader who takes complete control, or multiple leaders who are responsible for controlling different aspects of the group. There are also many different styles of leadership, from relaxed and person-oriented to strict and task-oriented. But regardless of the form

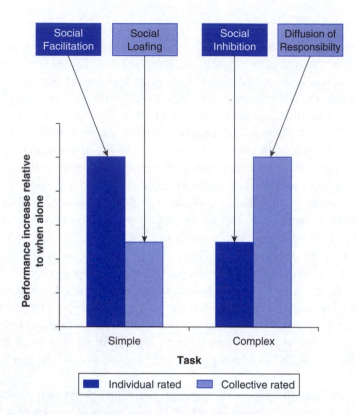

Figure 5.5 Illustration of the combined effects of task complexity and individual versus group unit of assessment of performance (compared to when alone)

leadership takes – and as the above examples of famous leaders illustrate – leaders exert a powerful influence on many aspects of our lives, whether inspiring us from afar, making the important decisions in the country in which we live, or directing us on a day-to-day basis in the workplace.

In this section, we first introduce the two broad factors that determine *who* becomes a leader, personality and situational characteristics. We then explore in detail research that has taken either one of these perspectives, or an integration of the two. We consider how the behaviour or *style* of leadership determines leader effectiveness. We will see how varied leadership styles can be classified along two independent dimensions: task-focus or socio-emotional. Finally, we discuss theories of leadership effectiveness that propose that an individual's leadership style *interacts* with external factors. These theories can be broadly divided into those which focus on the interaction between leadership style and the requirements of the situation, and those which focus on the interaction between leadership style and characteristics of the group members or followers.

What Makes a Leader?

What determines whether an individual becomes a leader? Traditionally, leaders were considered to be individuals who stood out from the rest of the group, holding unique personality traits that made them ideally suited to direct the rest of us. However, groups – and their leaders – do not exist in a social vacuum. Instead they are influenced by the social context. Increasingly, the role of the situation is being taken into account. In this section, we first introduce how individual differences in personality characteristics seem to determine leader effectiveness, and then discuss the role of situational determinants. This section will set the scene for a more in-depth examination of personality and situational determinants later in this chapter.

Personality Determinants

There is a general perception that leaders have distinctive *personality* traits that enable them to have a powerful influence over others. This is particularly the case for famous (and infamous) leaders, whose personalities are often scrutinized by the media and the general public. Margaret Thatcher, British Prime Minister between 1979 and 1990, earned the nickname 'the Iron Lady' as a result of her forceful personality, and was described by one journalist as 'a cross between a B2 bomber and a sabre-toothed tiger'. Undoubtedly, these formidable characteristics were perceived to have enabled Thatcher to gain – and maintain – her position as leader.

There is also some empirical evidence for a relationship between personality and leadership. Chemers, Watson, and May (2000) found that military cadets at university who were *confident* in their leadership skills were rated as having the greatest leadership potential by their professors; group members are more likely to follow a leader who seems certain of their abilities and is confident about the direction in which they are taking the group. Mullen, Salas, and Driskell (1989) showed that group members who made the greatest verbal contribution were most likely to be chosen to be group leader, presumably because *talkative* individuals attract more attention and are therefore better recognized by the rest of the group. Leaders also tend to have above average *intelligence* (Mann, 1959), a necessary characteristic if they are to respond quickly and effectively to the problems and issues that the group faces. A recent meta-analysis of 73 studies looking at the relationship between personality and leadership found that extraversion, openness to experience, and conscientiousness are positively correlated with leadership, whilst neuroticism is negatively correlated with leadership (Judge, Bono, Ilies, & Gerhardt, 2002). Physical characteristics have been found to be associated with leadership; leaders tend to be slightly taller (Judge and Cable, 2004) and more physically attractive (Weisfeld, Bloch, & Ivers, 1984) than followers (for a detailed discussion of the relationship between physical attributes and attraction, see Chapter 11).

Despite this evidence, the idea that leaders have a unique personality and characteristics has been increasingly criticized for two main reasons. First, many other studies have failed to find a reliable relationship between leadership and personality (Northouse, 2001; Stogdill, 1974; Yukl, 2002). Second, few leaders retain their leadership position indefinitely; British Prime Minister Tony Blair was extremely popular and considered to be very charismatic when he came to power in 1997, but by 2006 his popularity was waning and his leadership skills being called into question. If personality was the key determinant of leadership, leaders would remain popular and powerful rather than being criticized and eventually replaced. Clearly, personality is only part of the story. In the case of Tony Blair, the terrorist attacks of 11 September 2001 and the subsequent wars in Afghanistan and Iraq affected his popularity: these were situational factors. In the next section, we discuss how such situational factors can influence leadership.

Situational Determinants

Most social psychologists now believe that characteristics of the leader and the situation *interact* to determine leadership success. Simonton (1980) looked at archival data from 300 military battles and found that characteristics of army generals, such as how experienced they were and how successful they had been in previous battles, predicted victory on the battlefield. However, situational characteristics were also found to be influential. Specifically, the *size* and the *command structure* of the army were correlated with the number of casualties inflicted on the opposing army.

There is also some evidence that the personality characteristics of an individual may make them suitable to lead their group in some situations but not in others. Carter and Nixon (1949) had pairs of high school students perform three different tasks: an intellectual task, a clerical task, and a mechanical task. They found that the students who took the lead in the intellectual and clerical tasks rarely went on to take the lead in the mechanical task. It is easy to identify real-life examples of this; Winston Churchill's argumentative and stubborn personality made him an ideal leader during the Second World War, but as the war came to an end he was replaced by Clement Attlee, presumably because Churchill's personal qualities did not make him so ideally suited to leading a country during a time of peace.

The characteristics necessary to be an effective leader may also differ depending on whether the culture of the society is *collectivist* or *individualist*. In collectivist cultures, the best leaders are seen as those who foster positive relationships between group members and encourage a cooperative, cohesive working atmosphere (Ayman & Chemers, 1983). In contrast, in individualist cultures, the best leaders are seen as those who focus directly on reaching the goal of the group rather than on the group dynamics, and who reward the achievements of individuals (Sanchez-Burks et al., 2000).

Summary

Characteristics of the individual and the situation interact to determine how successful a leader will be. Traditionally, the *personality* of the leader was thought to be the most important factor in explaining why someone becomes a successful leader. Indeed, there is some evidence that *confident*, *talkative*, *attractive* and *extroverted* individuals are most likely to gain positions of leadership. But most social psychologists now believe that personality interacts with *situational factors* to determine the success of leadership, such as the match between leadership style and the requirements of the task at hand. This explains why leaders whose personality is particularly suited to a particular type of task or a particular time in history do not remain in a position of leadership once the circumstances changes. There are also *cultural* differences in leader preference; *collectivist* cultures tend to endorse leaders who nurture group relations whereas *individualist* cultures prefer leaders who focus on the achievement of goals.

Leadership Style

In the section above we introduced the two broad perspectives on what makes a good leader: personality and situational determinants. In the last part of this chapter we will look at this distinction in more detail and outline the theories that have taken either a personality approach or a personality-situation interaction approach. First, we will focus on personality determinants, and in particular research into different leadership styles.

Autocratic, Democratic and Laissez-Faire Leadership

A classic study that has generated much subsequent research on leadership style was conducted by Lippitt and White (1943). The researchers trained confederates in three different leadership styles – autocratic, democratic, and laissez-faire – before establishing them as the leaders of after-school activity clubs for school boys. **Autocratic leaders** remained aloof and focused on organizing the activities of the club and giving out orders to group members. **Democratic leaders** were very hands-on, discussing their plans with group members and making them feel a part of any decisions that were made. **Laissez-faire leaders** showed little interest in the activities of the group and generally left it to organize and carry out activities on its own, only intervening when absolutely necessary. Each club was assigned to one leadership style but the confederates swapped around every seven weeks so that they led in all three styles. This was done to ensure that leadership style was not confounded by the individual characteristics of the confederate. The researchers then considered the effect of leadership style on how much the leader was *liked*, the *atmosphere* of the group, and the *productivity* of the group.

Unsurprisingly, Lippitt and White found that democratic leaders were the most popular with group members. Such leaders fostered a friendly, cooperative, task-oriented atmosphere that was associated with high group productivity, regardless of whether the group leader was present. Autocratic and laissez-faire leaders were both less popular with group members, but for quite different reasons. Autocratic leaders created an aggressive atmosphere which was only productive when the leader was present to guide activities. Laissez-faire leaders, on the other hand, created a more pleasant and cooperative group atmosphere but had low productivity, although productivity increased if the leader was absent.

Task-focused versus Socio-Emotional Leadership

On the basis of a later series of studies, Bales (1950) proposed that there were two types of leadership: task-focused and socio-emotional. **Task-focused leaders** are primarily concerned with achieving the aims and goals of the group, and ensure this happens by focusing on the tasks needed to reach those goals. They are knowledgeable, directive, and efficient, but tend to distance themselves from other members of the group. An example of an individual with this type of leadership style is entrepreneur Sir Alan Sugar. He might be familiar to readers from his appearance on the reality BBC TV show *The Apprentice*, in which contestants compete on various business tasks for a position in his company. Sugar is famous for his 'no-nonsense', confrontational leadership style, and believes in single-mindedly focusing on overall goals rather than fostering close interpersonal relations with his employees. He has, however, been frequently criticized in the media for being too blunt and failing to give contestants constructive guidance.

Socio-emotional leaders pay more attention to the group dynamics, ensuring that group members form a cohesive and friendly group. Individuals with a socio-emotional leadership style are friendly, empathic, and adept at sorting out disagreements. Sir Richard Branson, entrepreneur and CEO of the Virgin group, is an example of someone who has a socio-emotional leadership style. In contrast to Sugar, Branson believes in creating a fun working environment and pays close attention to his employees. Bales argued that people could be either a task-focused leader or a socio-emotional leader but could not be *both* simultaneously. Thus, a group would ideally need two leaders: one task-focused to ensure that the

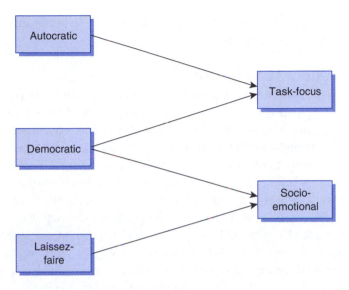

Figure 5.6   Leadership style defined by task focus and socio-emotional focus

group has direction and is productive, and one socio-emotional to ensure that the group is friendly and cohesive.

It is easy to see how these two leadership styles apply to the earlier research conducted by Lippitt and White (1943). *Autocratic* leaders are high in task-focus but low on the socio-emotional dimension, whereas *laissez-faire* leaders are low in task-focus but high in socio-emotional focus. Although Bales argued that people cannot have both styles, Lippitt and White have argued that *democratic* leaders can be defined in precisely this way, being both task-focused *and* socio-emotional (see Figure 5.6). Subsequent research has echoed the idea that task-focused and socio-emotional leadership styles cannot be rigidly separated from one another.

Sorrentino and Field (1986) had groups of four people take part in a series of problem-solving tasks. They found that group members who were success-oriented (focused on achieving the goals of the group) *and* affiliation-oriented (focused on gaining approval and establishing friendly relations with group members) were rated by others as being the most competent, confident, influential and motivated group members, making the biggest contribution to the group. Moreover, these individuals were nominated to be leader by 94 per cent of other group members. In sum, it appears that the most effective leaders are those who can combine the best of both worlds – an ability to focus on the task at hand to achieve the goals of the group, but also a friendly, interactive style that generates a positive group atmosphere and pleasant leader-follower relations.

Transformational Leadership

Some leaders stand out as being particularly influential, managing to not only effectively lead their group but also dramatically changing the direction of the group, influencing the attitudes and behaviour of group members. Such individuals can be described as **transformational leaders**. It is important to note here that either task-focused or socio-emotional leaders can *also* be transformational leaders – the two dimensions of definition are independent of one another. What makes leaders with a transformational style exceptional is their ability to motivate group members to abandon self-interest in order to achieve the goals of the group. An example of a transformational leader in recent history is Nelson Mandela. Mandela was a prominent anti-apartheid activist in South Africa who spent 27 years in prison for his cause. Following his release from prison in 1990, he became leader of the African National Congress and, in 1994, President of South Africa, playing an instrumental role in the transition from apartheid to democracy.

What characteristics do transformational leaders like Nelson Mandela have that enable them to have such influence over their group? Three characteristics have been found to be associated with transformational leaders (Bass, 1985; Bass, Avolio, & Goodheim, 1987). They are usually *charismatic*, having the type of personality that inspires and motivates followers to commit to the goals of the group. They are able to captivate their followers when they communicate with them, using eye contact and non-verbal cues in addition to eloquent verbal skills. Second, they show *individualized consideration*. This is when a leader treats each individual group member with respect, giving them the opportunity to learn new skills by delegating important tasks to them. Third, they endorse *intellectual stimulation*, encouraging group members to think in novel ways in order to solve problems and issues faced by the group.

Yammarino and Bass (1990) demonstrated the positive consequences of having a transformational leader. They asked members of the Navy about their senior officers and found that the subordinates of transformational leaders put in more effort at work, were more satisfied with their officers and perceived their commanders to be more effective than subordinates whose leaders had a democratic or laissez-faire leadership style. Bass (1990) cautioned, however, that transformational leadership is not appropriate in all situations. He proposed that it would be particularly useful during turbulent times when the future of the group is uncertain, but that more democratic leadership styles may be more appropriate when a group is stable. Although research into this unique leadership style is interesting, there are few genuinely transformational leaders. As a result, it is difficult to draw broad conclusions about the effects of different leadership styles from this research alone.

Summary

Research on leadership style reveals that there are two broad styles: *task-focused* leadership and *socio-emotional* leadership. Bales (1950) believed that these styles were mutually exclusive, that a leader could not be adept at both, so to be optimally effective a group would need two leaders with different but complementary leadership styles. In contrast, however, Lippitt and White (1943) found that *democratic* leaders, who are both task-focused and group-focused, were the most popular and productive, whereas task-focused *autocratic* leaders and group-focused laissez-faire leaders were less popular and productive. Similarly, Sorrentino and Field (1986) found that leaders who were both success- and affiliation-oriented were the most popular leaders. Research on leadership style has also found evidence for the *transformational* leader. Individuals with this style of leadership tend to be *charismatic*, engender *commitment* among group members and often take the group in a dramatic *new direction*. They are, however, relatively rare.

To summarize, it is clear that individual differences in leadership style are an important determinant of group success. However, as we mentioned earlier, *situational* factors can also influence the success of leadership. A number of theories have focused on the *interaction* between leadership style and external factors unrelated to the characteristics of the leader, and how they contribute to the effectiveness of a leader. We discuss these theories in the following section.

Theories of Situation and Style

In this last section, we bring together all of the research we have discussed so far on leadership. Above we have looked in detail at how individual differences in leaders' style can impact on leader effectiveness. However, as we indicated earlier, situational determinants also have a key role to play. In this section we outline theories of leadership effectiveness that specify an interaction between leadership style (personality) and elements of the situation. These theories of leadership effectiveness can be broadly divided into two types. Contingency theory explains how an individual's leadership style interacts with the situation to determine how successful their leadership will be. *Leader-member exchange theory* and the *social identity* approach to leadership instead focus on the interaction between leadership style and the group members that they lead.

Leader-Situation Interaction

Fiedler (1965) argued that the effectiveness of a leader is contingent upon how well leadership style matches the situation in which a group finds itself. According to

contingency theory, leaders have a chronic tendency to be either *socio-emotional* or *task-oriented*. In line with the distinction proposed by Bales (1950), task-oriented leaders are driven by the overall goals of a group and are focused on the implementation of tasks that help to achieve those goals, whereas socio-emotional leaders work towards creating a sociable, harmonious group. Fiedler developed the *least preferred co-worker (LPC) scale* to determine which type of leadership style people are oriented towards. The scale involves participants rating all the people they have worked with on a number of dimensions. Their ratings are then scored to determine how negatively they rated the co-worker they liked the *least*. Individuals who rated even their least preferred co-worker fairly positively were classified as being *high-LPC*, socio-emotional or relationship-oriented leaders who can cope with even difficult employees. Individuals who rated their least preferred co-worker negatively were classified as being *low-LPC*, task-oriented leaders who believe that the goals of the group are more important than their relationships with individual group members.

Whether a socio-emotional or a task-oriented style will be most effective depends upon the amount of situational control a leader has. Situational control is determined by three factors: whether *leader-member relations* are harmonious, whether the *structure of group tasks* is clear and goals are well-defined, and whether the leader has *legitimate authority* over group members. There is high situational control if leader-member relations are good, group tasks are clearly structured and the leader has legitimate power. In these circumstances it is relatively easy to lead the group effectively. Conversely, there is low situational control, making it difficult to lead the group, if leader-member relations are poor, group tasks are poorly structured and the leader does not have legitimate power.

Fiedler (1965) argued that different styles of leadership would be effective depending on whether situational control was high, moderate, or low. When situational control is low, the group needs strong guidance in order to achieve their goals. In this situation, a task-focused leadership style is likely to be most effective; being nice to group members is, for example, unlikely to help the group reach their goals if tasks are poorly defined. Instead it is necessary for someone to take charge and ensure that goals are clear and the roles of group members *are* clearly defined. When situational control is high, leader-member relations are already harmonious. For this reason, it is not necessary for the leader to waste time fostering positive relations with group members. Instead, to improve group performance they are better off taking control and focusing on achieving the goals of the group. Only where there is moderate situational control is the socio-emotional leadership style most effective. Where tasks are somewhat unclear and the leader does not have total control over the group, an interactive approach is most likely to re-establish power to the leader and generate creative solutions to problems faced by the group.

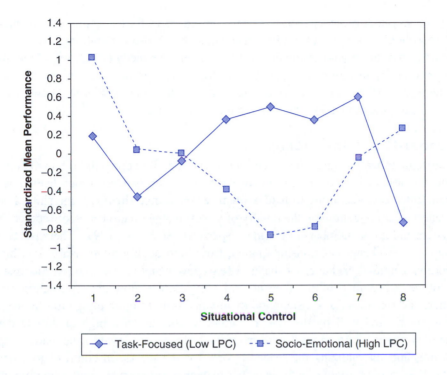

Figure 5.7 Group performance as a function of situational control and leadership style. Data from Schriesheim, Tepper, and Tetrault (1994)

There is considerable empirical support for the contingency model. Schriesheim, Tepper, and Tetrault (1994), for example, conducted a meta-analysis of studies testing contingency theory and found broad support for the model. As Figure 5.7 shows, high-LPC leaders elicited better group performance at moderate levels than at low or high levels of situational control whereas low-LPC leaders elicited better group performance at low and high levels than at moderate levels of situational control. Contingency theory's major contribution to our understanding of leadership is to show that there is no *ideal* style of leadership; instead, different leaders may be more or less effective depending on the situation.

Despite its utility in explaining when certain leadership styles will be most effective, the theory has been criticized for two main reasons. First, the theory assumes that leaders have a chronic tendency to behave in accordance with *either* a task-oriented *or* a socio-emotional leadership style. But, as we described earlier, there is evidence that this is not the case. Indeed, the best leaders appear to be those that are high on *both* task-focused and socio-emotional orientations (Sorrentino & Field,

1986). Second, the theory focuses on the consequences for leadership effectiveness of scoring high or low on the LPC scale, neglecting those who fall in between – in other words, those who are moderate-LPC leaders. Kennedy (1982) found that the large minority of individuals who fell in this middle ground were more effective leaders, regardless of the degree of situational control, than low or high-LPC leaders. In sum, the model does not explain the behaviour of *all* leaders.

Leader-Group Interaction

Leader-member exchange theory and the social identity approach both explain the effectiveness of leadership in terms of the relationship *between* group leaders and their followers. According to **leader-member exchange theory**, leadership effectiveness is contingent upon the quality of the exchange relationship between group leaders and group members (e.g. Liden, Sparrowe, & Wayne, 1997). There is a continuum of exchange relationship quality, from high quality relationships in which there is a mutual exchange of material (e.g. power and status) and psychological resources (e.g. trust, liking, respect, and obligation) to low quality relationships where the relationship is distant and maintained only through obligation. Because they are treated well by the leader, members who are in a high quality leader-member exchange relationship are more likely to remain loyal to the leader, supporting and internalizing the leader's goals for the group. In contrast, members who have a poor quality leader-member exchange relationship may comply with the goals of the group in order to fulfil their role as a group member, but they are unlikely to internalize them.

Unsurprisingly, the theory predicts that leaders who have high quality exchange relationships with their members will be more effective leaders. Indeed, research has shown that subordinates who are in a high quality exchange relationship with their leader are more motivated, perform better, have greater psychological wellbeing, and are less likely to leave their job than subordinates in low quality relationships with their leader (Liden et al., 1997). In a recent survey of private sector workers, Kacmar et al. (2003) found that workers who reported a high quality exchange relationship with their supervisor received high job-performance ratings, although this trend only emerged for workers who communicated with their supervisor on a frequent basis.

An alternative explanation of leadership effectiveness was recently proposed by Hogg and Van Knippenberg (2003), who applied the social identity approach (e.g. Tajfel & Turner, 1979) to our understanding of leadership (see Chapters 1 and 7 for a more detailed explanation of social identity theory). According to this approach, when an individual's membership in a particular group is salient, they come to think of themselves in terms of their *social identity* rather than as a unique individual. Each social identity is associated with a range of attributes that characterize the *prototypical* group member and a set of group norms, a collection of shared beliefs about how group members should think and behave. When an individual's social identity is salient, their perceptions of themselves and other group members become *deperson-alized.* In other words, rather than seeing themselves as a unique individual, group members perceive themselves more in terms of the shared features that define group membership, thinking and behaving more in line with the norms of that group.

According to this approach, when the social identity of group members is salient and people see their group as prototypical, comprising members who exemplify the norms of the group, prototypical group members will be perceived as being the most effective leaders. Prototypical individuals are those who strongly identify with the group and adhere to its attitudes and values. As such, they will be perceived by other group members as being particularly likely to act in the best interests of the group as a whole.

Fielding and Hogg (1997) illustrated the social identity approach to leadership in a field study carried out among participants on an Outward Bound course, who worked cooperatively together in groups over a two or three week period. The more prototypical the leader of the group was, the more effective participants rated them as being. This relationship was particularly pronounced for people who highly iden-tified with their Outward Bound group, for whom prototypicality was particularly important (see Figure 5.8).

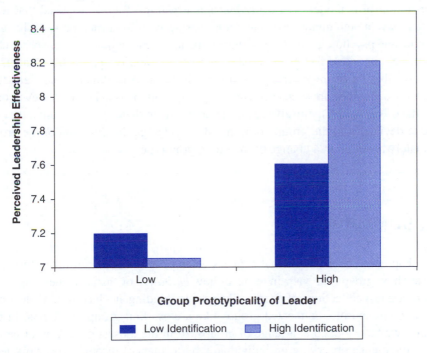

Figure 5.8 The effect of group leader prototypicality on perceived leadership effectiveness. Data from Fielding and Hogg (1997)

Interestingly, the social identity approach to leadership notes that although a leader needs to be seen as prototypical to consolidate their position of power, once they are established and have the support and trust of their members, they no longer need to be prototypical. Indeed, in order to move the group forward, it is necessary for them to be innovative and to actually deviate from the group norm. In doing so, they may eventually *change* the group norms and create a new prototype for the group.

Summary

There are two types of theory that consider leadership effectiveness. Both consider the interaction between leadership style and external factors, but one type considers the interaction between the leader style and the *situation* and the other considers the inter-action between the leader style and the group of followers. According to *contingency theory* the effectiveness of leaders depends upon an interaction of their leadership style (task-focused or socio-emotional) and the degree of *situational* control they have. Research shows that task-focused leaders are most effective when situational control is low or high, but that socio-emotional leaders are most effective when situational control is moderate. *Leader-member exchange theory* proposed that leaders that have a high quality exchange relationship with their members, exchanging material and psychological benefits with them, have better adjusted, more productive and more committed followers. Finally, the *social identity* approach to leadership proposes that *prototypical* group members will be perceived as the most effective leaders because they are seen as having the group's interests at heart. However, once they have established themselves as leader and proven their prototypicality, they are able to deviate from the group norm in order to change the direction of the group, ultimately resulting in a change of the group prototype.

CHAPTER SUMMARY

This chapter has been about what happens when people work in groups. At the start we saw how groups can vary in terms of how *entitative* or 'groupy' they are. Some groups are just collections of people, like people standing at a bus stop, while others are coherent and interconnected groups like a close-knit group of friends. In this chapter we have looked at a range of groups, from the loosest collection of people (i.e. an audience observing an individual's performance) through to a work team with a specific productivity goal, and have also looked at the impact of group leaders on performance and productivity.

We first examined what happens to an individual's performance on any task when they are in the presence of others (e.g. an audience). This work has revealed a robust tendency for people to show *social facilitation*, improved performance when in the presence of others. However, this effect only occurs on simple tasks; on complex tasks *social inhibition* is observed, a reduction in productivity (or the likelihood that a task will be completed successfully). Social facilitation and social inhibition effect can be explained in three ways: *drive theory*, *evaluation apprehension*, and *distraction conflict* explanations. Social facilitation and social inhibition occur when the individual is assessed in the presence of others. When the unit of assessment is the group, not the individuals that make up that group, *social loafing* occurs. This is a reduction in performance on simple tasks when the group is judged, due to a *diffusion of responsibility*. However, this same diffusion of responsibility prevents social inhibition on complex tasks, because it prevents *evaluation apprehension*.

After examining the impact of others on individual performance, and then the performance of groups on simple and complex tasks, we turned to another key determinant of group productivity, leadership. What makes a successful leader appears to be broadly determined by personality and situational factors. More specifically, leaders can vary in the style they adopt. Leaders can be *autocratic*, *democratic*, or *laissez-faire*. Autocratic leaders are high in *task focus*, but low in *socio-emotional focus*; laissez-faire leaders are high in socio-emotional focus, but low in task focus. Democratic leaders have a high task focus and high socio-emotional skills. Irrespective of whether leaders have either type of focus, they can be transformational, able to take the group in a dramatic *new direction* due to their *charisma* and ability to *motivate* members (either via a task-focus or socio-emotional focus).

Finally, we examined two approaches that argue that in order to fully understand leadership processes, we need to look at the interaction between leaders' style and the situation. *Contingency theory* argues that the effectiveness of leaders depends upon an interaction of their leadership style (task-focused or socio-emotional) and the degree of *situational control* they have. Two other theories focus on the interaction between the leader and the group. *Leader-member exchange theory* argues that leaders who engage in material and psychological exchange are more successful. Finally, the *social identity* approach argues that successful leaders are initially *prototypical* of the group before deviating from the prototype in order to take the group in a new direction.

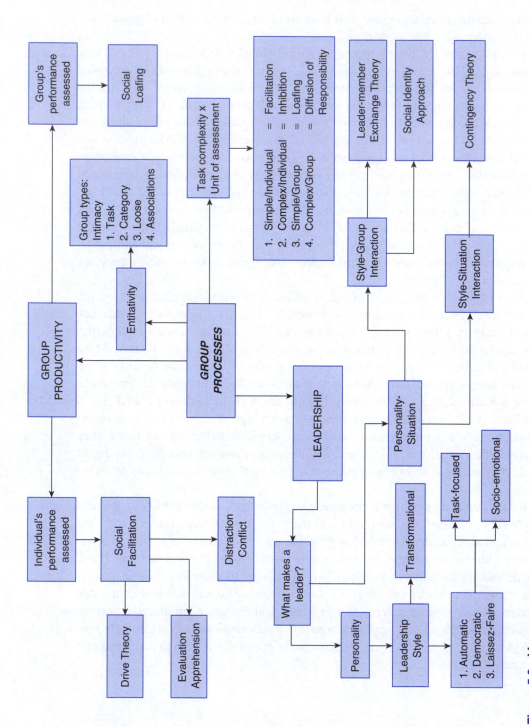

Figure 5.9 Memory map

Taking it Further

Try This

Have you ever been a social loafer? Think back to times when you've been in a group (e.g. a tutorial group, or with your friends on a night out just deciding where to go). Can you identify times when the groups you've been in have worked well together, and times when they have not? Think of the criteria for determining facilitation or inhibition effects on performance (simple vs. complex task; individual vs. group assessment) and map them on to your own experiences. The next time you're in charge of a group (e.g. leading a seminar, organizing a night out) what would be the best way to get the outcome you're looking for?

Debate This

What sort of leader is Barack Obama? Remember that there are three key leadership styles – autocratic, democratic, and laissez-faire, but they can all be transformational. Based on what you know, what you have read, and what you can find from sources on the web, come up with evidence to support your point of view. Based on contingency theory, leader-member exchange, and the social identity approach, do you think he's likely to be successful in achieving his goals?

Something for the Weekend

So now you know all about groups and leaders. You also know from Chapter 4 all about how to change attitudes. Leaders often need to change the attitudes of the group they're leading, and you might find yourself in such a position sooner than you think! Can you combine what you've learned about persuasion, and the self, with what you've learned about leadership to come up with a strategy that fits you personally? First off, choose a scenario you might find yourself in – let's say running for office in the student union at a time when student debt is on the rise. What will you need to do and say to get elected and address the key issues facing your voters? Next think about what sort of leader you might be … or what sort of strategies you might use to convince the voters you're the right person for the job (e.g. you could point out your prototypical characteristics, while at the same time your democratic style … if that's what's needed in the current situation). Think about what sort of person you are (looking back at Chapter 1 on the self). Do you think you would be better at persuading people with facts (central route processing), or instead relying on your attractiveness and razor-sharp wit (peripheral route)?

Further Reading

The Essentials

Brown, R.J. (2000). *Group processes* (2nd edn). Oxford: Blackwell.
Chemers, M.M. (2001). Leadership effectiveness: An integrative review. In M.A. Hogg & S. Tindale (Eds.), *Blackwell handbook of social psychology: Group processes*. Malden, MA: Blackwell.

Two contemporary, comprehensive and compelling accounts of the psychology of group processes. As a first step in learning more about group performance and leadership, these are excellent resources.

Next Steps

Latané, B., Williams, K., & Harkins, S. (1979). Many hands make light work: The causes and consequences of social loafing. *Journal of Personality and Social Psychology, 37,* 822–832.
Zajonc, R.B. (1965). Social facilitation. *Science*, *149*, 269–274.

A couple of classics.

Delving Deeper

Levine, J.M. & Moreland, R.L. (Eds.). (2006). *Small groups: Key readings*. Philadelphia, PA: Psychology Press.

Here's a set of key readings that will give you both a breadth and depth of understanding of group psychology from two of the leading experts in the field.

Social Influence

6

Social Influence

When, why and how is people's behaviour influenced by the presence of others? How do other people *influence* our own behaviour? **Social influence** is all about how our thoughts, feelings, and behaviours change when in the presence of others. Social influence is an umbrella term. It refers to any effect that another person or group has on your own attitudes and behaviours. In this chapter, two types of social influence will be discussed: *conformity* and *obedience*. Both are concerned with the same outcome: a change in behaviour. They differ in that **conformity** is used to describe attitude or behaviour change in response to an implied, rather than explicit, social norm. In contrast, **obedience** is attitude or behaviour change in response to a direct, or explicit, order. We will see how both majorities and minorities can exert influence on each other, how there are different motivations for following social norms, and how all these inter-related ideas come together to predict social influence in any given context.

SOCIAL NORMS

Norm Development

Some of the very earliest studies in social psychology were on the topic of social influence. Sherif (1935) carried out a classic study to investigate how groups might come to have what are apparently consensual and homogenized beliefs. His experiment had two phases. Participants were initially led to believe that the experiment concerned 'visual perception', although what Sherif was really interested in was the influence that other people in the context had on reported visual perception. Participants were led to a room which was pitch-black except for a small dot of light on the far wall. The participants' task was to make 100 judgements as to how far the dot was moving in inches. In fact, Sherif was making use of an established perceptual illusion called the 'autokinetic effect'. This effect makes a dot appear to oscillate in a dark room when there is no other point of reference. Because there was no actual movement of the dot, the autokinetic effect provided an excellent experimental control: any observed effects on participants' estimations of how far the dot moved could only be attributable to psychological factors. In this first phase when participants individually made their estimates there was, as expected, some variation in *different* participants' mean estimates of distance moved.

What Sherif was really interested in was what would happen when each participant made their judgements in public (i.e. in a *social* context). Sherif predicted that in such contexts, a group norm would naturally form, with all participants converging (without realizing it) to a common standard. After the individual judgement was given at phase one, participants then had a number of subsequent trials in which they performed exactly the same task but this time in public (there were two or three other participants present). Sherif observed that on successive trials participants' mean judgements converged *away* from the initially disparate estimates in phase 1 to a common standard. Sherif called this common standard a **social norm** (see Figure 6.1). Participants denied that others' judgements had influenced their own: the effect of the social context on their judgements appeared to have worked outside of their awareness. However, in fact others need not be physically present

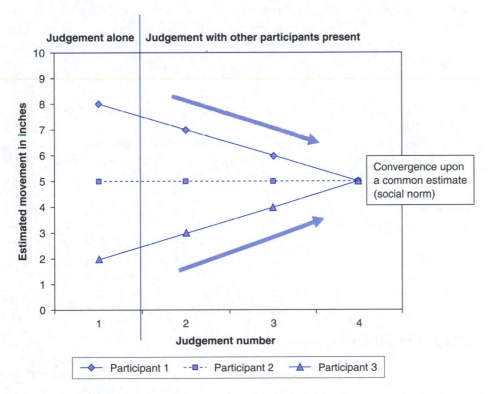

Figure 6.1 Illustration of Sherif's norm convergence results

for social norms to develop. In Text Box 6.1, we describe some recent research on social influence over the internet that has shown that the effects of conformity can also be observed without the actual presence of others.

Text Box 6.1

Influence Over the Internet

Contemporary research has considered whether social psychological processes operate in the same way over the internet as they do in face-to-face social encounters. Postmes, Spears and Lea (2002) investigated whether the convergence of individual attitudes onto a group norm, as demonstrated by Sherif (1935), still occurs when a group interacts 'on-line' rather than face-to-face.

Method

Seventy-two Dutch and English university students were arranged into groups of six (three Dutch and three English) to take part in an internet discussion. In an initial session, participants were introduced on-line to the other participants. In two further sessions, participants were instructed to give their opinions and discuss three issues (the legalization of drugs, the monarchy, and scientific research into homosexuality) on-line for 10 minutes each. After each session, participants completed measures of their personal attitudes regarding each topic. Participants were allocated to one of two conditions. In the depersonalized condition, each participant was identified only by their nationality (Dutch or English) and their initials, whereas in the individuated condition participants were identified by their nationality, their first name, and by photographs taken of them in the first session.

Results

As the figures below show, the attitudes of the two groups converged in the individuated condition, in line with the traditional conformity effect shown by Sherif (1935). In the depersonalized condition, however, group attitudes actually diverged. In other words, when participants did not know much about the other individuals involved in the discussion, they were influenced more by their ingroup than by the discussion group as a whole.

Interpreting the Findings

The individuating condition here mirrors Sherif's original 'autokinetic' social norm experiment, except that participants interacted on-line, rather than physically in a group. As you can see above, in this condition there is the same

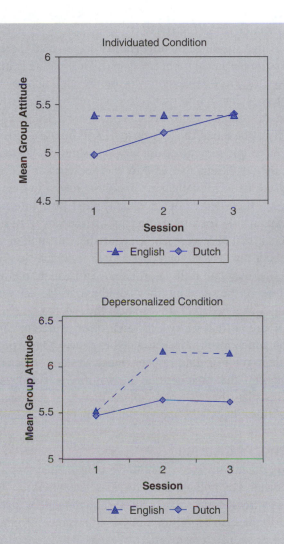

social norm convergence effect as observed when other group members are physically present; both English and Dutch group members came to agree on a common point of view. Interestingly, the opposite effect was observed when the only information participants had about each other was their nationality. This made differences between the participants (i.e. their nationalities) more salient which led to attitudes diverging rather than converging. This study illustrates that whilst social influence processes can occur without the physical presence of others, under such conditions of relative on-line 'anonymity' the tendency to reach an agreed norm may be quite weak and subject to interference from other relevant factors. In this experiment, a social norm only developed when the differences of individuals within the group did not outweigh the similarities.

Uncertainty and Social Norms

Also of interest is that the level of **uncertainty** in the task increased the rate at which convergence on the social norm developed. This finding is important because it suggested a psychological explanation for the development of the social group norm. The argument is that in uncertain situations other people's judgements are a valuable heuristic (or 'rule of thumb'; see Chapter 3 for a detailed description of the function of such heuristics) that can help us to be as accurate as possible. In Chapter 3 we looked at how people sometimes use heuristic short-cuts to make social judgements. Amongst the conditions that tend to lead to heuristic use was 'little information regarding the issue'. In situations like that created in Sherif's experiment, in general there is a high degree of uncertainty (and little information regarding the issue). One explanation for why participants' responses were influenced by the responses of others is that they were using a heuristic. Put another way, participants were uncertain about the task at hand (the degree to which the light was moving was ambiguous), and they had little information with which to engage in a logical and detailed analysis of the situation (they could not, as Heider would say, behave like 'naïve scientists', see Chapter 3). As such, they would be compelled to use a heuristic in this situation; that is, look to some other source of information in the environment upon which to form an estimated response. Other people's responses provide an excellent guide in this respect (most western societies live, after all, under a political system that assumes that the majority is usually right). Given this reasoning, it seems plausible that participants in this experiment would act like 'cognitive misers' (see Chapter 3), and go along with others' judgements.

Norms as Group Attitudes

Sherif's norm experiment involved quantitative judgements: how far a dot of light was moving on a wall. His finding, however, can be applied to attitudes or judgements that people express in any social context (and remember that a social context does not necessarily have to require the physical presence of others; they can be imagined, implied or simply remembered). We can liken a social norm to a group prototype, or *stereotype*, as we discussed in Chapter 3. A group norm is a set of beliefs about one's own group, as opposed to another group, so it is exactly like a stereotype of another group, except that here it refers to people's beliefs about the attitudes and behaviours associated with a group to which they belong. We discussed a number of the factors that influence *self-stereotyping* in Chapter 3. Here, the focus is on the development of those self-stereotypes, and how conformity to such stereotypes varied as a function of the presence of others.

Sherif's findings illustrate how the attitudes that we express, whether they be relating to politics, sport or friends and family, are influenced by who is around us at the time. Broadly speaking, this makes a lot of sense; of course we know that we're more likely to openly express our thoughts and opinions to good friends rather than strangers. What is important about Sherif's study, however, is that it represents how *group* attitudes can be formed – how our individual attitudes can change and adapt to form a set of beliefs that define a group. When we think of attitudes we usually just think of them as being something held by an individual (see Chapter 4). In this chapter we will look at group attitudes – social norms – that exist as the amalgamation of individuals' attitudes, but which are formed from uniquely social psychological processes.

Social norms are attitudes that are consensually held between different members of a group. Importantly, individual or 'private' attitudes can be different from social norms (or 'public' attitudes). In Sherif's experiment, participants were uncertain, and their private judgement was thus undefined (as to the distance the spot of light was moving). They appeared therefore to look to others in the context to define their private judgement. As such, the group judgement and individual judgement converged – they were the same. In some cases, however, people might go along with the social norm, and hold a public (group) opinion that *does not match* their private opinion. This is particularly likely to be the case when the context is not one which the perceiver feels uncertain about, but where individuals have a clear idea of their own point of view. What happens then when people are exposed to others who do not share their point of view? This question was examined in a famous set of experiments conducted by Solomon Asch.

CONFORMITY

From Sherif's experiment we know that social norms may come into play in uncertain situations (such as ambiguous light movements), but what about when we *do* have information about the issue at hand, and are *certain* about the correct answer to give? What happens when our *private opinion* conflicts with the social norm at hand? In such situations the use of a heuristic is not necessary – we do not need to look to others to determine what might be the right answer to give, the right opinion to hold. Under these circumstances would we still expect the social context to exert an influence? Whilst norm development can be seen as a useful and fairly innocuous (possibly beneficial) effect of the presence of other people on our judgements, in some cases the presence of others can lead us to go along with the group norm even though we might not agree with it. Can you remember ever going along with a group at school, perhaps teasing another child, even when you thought it was wrong? Has there ever been a time when, as a student, you have done things you might not have done if you had been on your own? The study we discuss next is all about these types of situation.

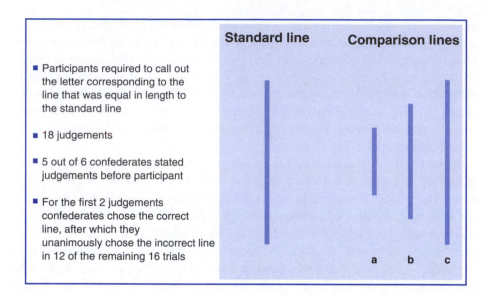

Standard line   **Comparison lines**

- Participants required to call out the letter corresponding to the line that was equal in length to the standard line

- 18 judgements

- 5 out of 6 confederates stated judgements before participant

- For the first 2 judgements confederates chose the correct line, after which they unanimously chose the incorrect line in 12 of the remaining 16 trials

a   b   c

Figure 6.2   Example materials used in Asch's experiment

Asch's Conformity Experiment

In 1951 Solomon Asch carried out a classic and highly influential experiment on social influence. The task was, on the surface, a 'visual perception experiment' but Asch, like Sherif, was interested in something quite different: the effects of others on judgements when the task is easy, and there is a mismatch between public and private attitudes.

In his experiment participants were told that they would be taking part in a study of line length estimation along with six other participants. There are two crucial differences between Asch's experiment and that of Sherif. For Sherif, the task was difficult and the other people making the judgement were simply other participants. For Asch, the task was easy and the other participants were really *confederates* of the experimenter (i.e. they were not really participants at all, but other people pretending to be participants who followed a script to try to influence the one true participant's responses).

During the task participants were presented first with a 'standard line'. Following this three 'comparison lines' were presented (labelled 'a', 'b', and 'c'). The participant's task was to call out, in the presence of the other six supposed participants, which comparison line (a, b or c) was the same length as the standard line. As can be seen in the example in Figure 6.2, the task was really rather easy; in marked contrast to Sherif's autokinetic task, there is really no doubt as to which comparison line is the correct one. The important thing was, however, that not only were the participants' judgements public but they called out their judgement *after* most of the other people present. Four of the confederates gave their judgements before the participant with one confederate after. This was done to make sure that the majority of the group give a consensual incorrect response before the participant, whilst also taking care not to arouse suspicion.

Participants made in total 18 judgements. For the first two judgements the confederates chose the clearly correct line, after which they switched to unanimously choose a clearly incorrect line for 12 of the remaining 16 trials. Asch was interested in what effect this would have on participants' judgements. Would people trust their own eyes and give the clearly correct answer, or go along with the group norm, even though they disagreed with it?

Asch found that when there were no other people present (and participants gave their judgements alone, as in phase 1 of Sherif's study), only 1 per cent of people made any errors. This confirmed that the task really was easy. What was interesting was what happened to this error level in the presence of other people who were clearly giving the incorrect response. Asch found that participants conformed to the incorrect majority of confederates on 37 per cent of trials. This was a considerable increase in error rate that could only be attributable to the presence of other people giving such a response (this was the only thing that was different from the control condition in which participants gave their responses alone). Indeed, 76 per cent of participants conformed on at least one of the trials. Asch had established that even when the task is easy, and people are certain about their private attitude, they will still sometimes conform to the majority's viewpoint.

In Sherif's study perhaps it is understandable for people to conform to the majority; the task is difficult and so it would seem sensible to use other people's responses as a guide. Here, however, participants gave responses that were clearly counter to their own belief. It was clear to the participants that they themselves were correct and all the other participants were wrong. Why then should conformity have occurred in Asch's experiment?

Explaining Conformity

Deutsch and Gerard (1955) suggested two sources of social influence that could account for the convergence on the group norm in *both* Sherif's and Asch's experiments. The first is **informational influence.** Informational influence is conformity to a group norm that occurs as a way of gaining information (i.e. in ambiguous or uncertain situations where people are unsure of their own perceptions). This can account for the conformity observed in Sherif's autokinetic experiment and can be seen as a heuristic 'rule of thumb' that is useful for making a range of judgements. The second source of group pressure can be termed **normative influence**. Normative influence is conformity due to the desire to gain acceptance and praise, and avoid punishment and exclusion, from others. The argument is that people are motivated to be accepted by others – we all want to be liked, included, part of something. We know that when we do not conform to the majority then this can involve social 'sanctions' like name-calling, ridiculing, and exclusion. To avoid these negative consequences of being 'the odd one out', people are motivated to go along with the group norm. This is the type of influence that can explain the conformity in Asch's experiment, where the participant knew they were right, and the majority were wrong, but still they went along with the group in order to 'fit in'.

Deutsch and Gerard (1955) carried out an experiment very similar to Asch's that illustrated both normative and informational influence. As well as replicating the conditions in Asch's original experiment, Deutsch and Gerard also had a condition in which participants were told that the group had the explicit goal of being as accurate as possible. In addition, the nature of the line judgement task was varied. Half the participants made their judgements with the lines still visible (as in Asch's original experiment), and for half the lines were removed prior to judgement. Results revealed that both the explicit group goal (maximizing group pressure and normative influence) and removal of the lines at judgement (maximizing uncertainty and informational influence) increased the level of conformity observed.

Informational and normative influence can be said to produce different types of conformity. Normative influence changes a person's public attitude (what they say is their attitude to others) but it does not change their private attitude (they are simply going along with the majority to avoid social exclusion). This type of conformity can be termed **compliance**. In contrast, informational influence involves changes in both public *and* private attitudes. This is because the perceiver is using other people's opinions as a guide to forming their own attitude. This type of conformity can be termed **conversion**.

Although both informational and normative influence may well be working to differing degrees in most contexts, for simplicity we can outline a model for when we would expect compliance and conversion. In situations where perceivers are uncertain about their own attitude, the task is difficult, or they have little information regarding the issue, then they will be most likely to be subject to informational influence. This will lead to changes in both public and private attitudes and conversion will have occurred. In contrast, where perceivers are clear about their own opinions, the task is easy, or they have lots of information regarding the issue, then they will be most likely to be subject to normative influence. This will lead to a change in public but not private attitudes, and compliance will have occurred. This model is illustrated in Figure 6.3.

Factors that Moderate Conformity

Moderators of Normative Influence

There have been numerous replications and extensions of the classic experiments by Sherif and Asch. These studies have confirmed the robust nature of

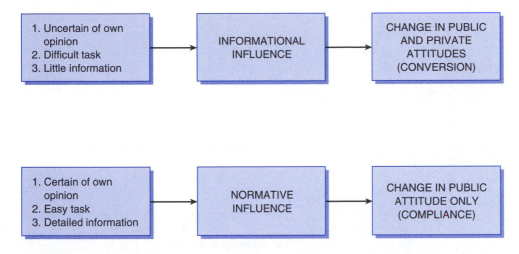

Figure 6.3 Social influence processes leading to compliance and conversion

informational and normative social influence but also identified a number of different factors that either increase or decrease the level of social influence in any given situation. The first of these is *group cohesiveness*. Group cohesiveness is the degree to which a group is perceived to have a strong sense of interconnectedness. The more cohesive the group – that is, the more interdependent its members – the faster the rate of conformity (Hogg, 1992). This makes sense with respect to normative influence. A cohesive group in which the members have a history of interdependence will likely create conditions under which group members are expected to 'tow the party line'. In Deutsch and Gerard's (1955) study discussed above, the presence of a collective group goal would have maximized the sense of interconnectedness (all members have a common goal) and group cohesiveness.

A second factor that affects the level of conformity is *group size*. The level of conformity that is observed appears to be proportional to the number of confederates; but only up to a point. As groups grow in size, there is a corresponding increase in the level of conformity observed, but there is a levelling off once the group size reaches three people (see Figure 6.4). In an extension to his classic study, Asch (1952) found that when the group size got progressively bigger than three, then conformity remained stable at about 35 per cent. The idea here is that when there are just two people, any disagreement between participants could be regarded as an interpersonal issue (i.e. their 'group' status would not be noticeable). With three, however, there are enough people present for the individual participant to feel that they are outnumbered, and they will begin to feel pressure to conform to avoid possible social exclusion.

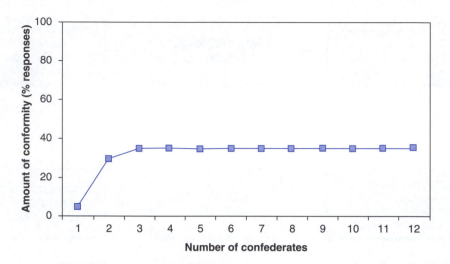

Figure 6.4   Illustration of the relationship between group size and conformity

A third factor that affects conformity is *social support*. This is different from group cohesiveness and group size, because instead of increasing the level of conformity, social support *decreases* the level of conformity. In a further extension to Asch's original study, if just *one* confederate agreed with the participant (i.e. gave the correct answer, rather than the scripted incorrect answer given by the confederate majority) then conformity dropped dramatically (Allen, 1975). The same occurred even if one confederate disagreed with *everyone's* opinion (i.e. they gave a response that was different from the participant but *also* different from the majority; Asch, 1959). This leads to the conclusion that any *breaking of the social consensus* is enough to reduce conformity. The social support must, however, be consistent. When a confederate who initially agrees with the participant switches later on to agree with the majority, conformity returns to normal levels (Asch, 1955). Perceived competence is also important. Allen and Levin (1971) found that when the supporter wore incredibly thick glasses (casting doubt on their ability to be accurate during the visual perception task), conformity actually rose from the typical 36 per cent to 64 per cent.

Moderators of Informational Influence

The former three factors can be seen as primarily (although not exclusively) affecting normative influence. They have all been illustrated using Asch's paradigm, where uncertainty is not a factor, and generally focus on the ability of the group to exert social power in terms of keeping its members 'in line' (i.e. the extent to which it is cohesive, large enough, and has enough solidarity in its ranks). Other factors affect *informational* influence. A distinction between Sherif and Asch's experiment is the degree to which the task might induce uncertainty. Sherif's autokinetic experiment presented participants with a task where they would be uncertain as to the correct response to give. Here then we suppose that informational influence is the driving force for any conformity.

There are two factors that can affect informational influence. The first is located within the *person*, perceived *self-confidence*. The less self-confident participants are, the more likely it is that they will be susceptible to informational influence (Mausner, 1954). This, of course, makes sense. If you are generally unsure about your own attitudes and abilities then it is more likely that you will look to others to guide your judgements in general (i.e. informational influence). The second factor affecting informational influence is located within the *situation*. As *task difficulty* increases, the extent of informational influence will also increase (Baron, Vandello, & Brunsman, 1996). Again, this makes sense. The more difficult a task, the less likely it is that the participant will have a clear idea about what judgement to give, making it more likely that they will look to others to help them give the correct answer.

Finally, another important *situational* factor influencing the level of observed conformity is *cultural norms*. Although it was surprising that Asch's studies led to such a high level of conformity in individualist cultures like the United States, when replicated in more collectivist cultures (like Japan) the level of conformity was substantially higher. In fact, when the extent to which cultures agree with individualist versus collectivist norms was measured, this was the largest influence on the level of conformity (Bond & Smith, 1996). In Text Box 6.2 we describe some recent research that has further explored the impact of norms on the level of conformity by combining work on *stereotype priming* (see Chapter 3).

Text Box 6.2

Anarchy in the Asch Paradigm

Although traditionally conformity has been explained in terms of informational and normative social influence, social identity theorists (Abrams & Hogg, 1990) argue that conformity is also influenced by our group memberships. They propose a process of referent informational influence. This is the idea that when we categorize ourselves as a member of a particular group we tend to follow the prevalent norms of that group. In other words, we are strongly influenced by

(Continued)

the attitudes and behaviour that we believe are expected of group members. Pendry and Carrick (2001) tested whether such group norms would have an impact in the Asch paradigm, but with an interesting twist: would thinking even of groups we don't belong to have an effect?

Method

Forty-eight undergraduate students who believed that they had come to the laboratory to take part in a task on aural discrimination were asked if they would participate in an extra task prior to the start of the experiment. The task was to look at some stimulus materials being used in a different study and check for clarity and focus. In fact, this initial task was actually part of the experiment. In one condition, participants were asked to look at a photo of a neat man with short hair, wearing a suit and glasses. Below the photo a short paragraph described the man as 'Norman, who is an accountant' ('Accountant' condition). In another condition, participants looked at a photo of a man with spiky hair and torn clothes covered in graffiti, described as 'Norman, who is a punk rocker' ('Punk' condition). A further group of participants did not complete the initial task (no prime condition). Participants then went into a room with four other participants (who were actually confederates) to complete the aural discrimination task. They were asked to listen to a series of beeps and count how many they heard. At the end of the series of beeps, the researcher asked each of the confederates and finally the participant to report how many beeps they had heard. While there were actually 100 beeps, confederates reported

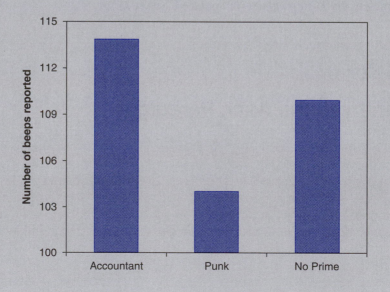

hearing between 120 and 125 beeps. The dependent measure was how many beeps participants reported hearing: Would participants conform to the incorrect group norm or accurately report the number of beeps?

Results

The figure shows what Pendry and Carrick found. In the no prime condition participants' estimates showed the typical Asch conformity effect: responses were inaccurate in the direction of the confederate majority's overestimation. What is interesting is that participants who had also thought about an accountant reported a greater number of beeps than participants in the no prime condition, and participants in the punk condition reported fewer beeps than participants in the no prime condition.

Interpreting the Findings

The social categories of punk and accountant are associated with non-conformism versus conformism norms respectively, and we know from work on social stereotyping (see Chapter 3) that people sometimes, without realizing it, can behave like members of groups they think about (even if they are not a member of such groups). This is precisely what happened here. Participants who thought about a punk were significantly less conforming than participants who thought about an accountant. Participants who thought about an accountant were even more likely to conform to the majority's overestimate.

Impact of Influence on Social Norms

So far we have focused on the effect that social and informational influence can have on individuals, and the factors that determine whether such individuals will go along with the social norms that represent the majority of members in the group. However, these pressures towards conforming – consensus seeking – can also be seen in attitude change at the *group* level. That is, informational and normative influences do not only affect individuals. The social norm *itself* can change as a result of the types of pressures we have been discussing above. The impact of social influence on social norms is illustrated by work on **group polarization**.

Group Polarization

A consistent finding in work on group processes is that when an issue is discussed in a group, then the starting point, or initial attitude, tends to become exaggerated or polarized after a period of discussion, especially with respect to important issues (Kerr, 1992). Turner (1991) describes group polarization in terms of **depersonalization**, a concept that is central to *self-categorization theory* (Turner, Hogg, Oakes, Reicher, & Wetherell, 1987; see also Chapter 1). Depersonalization describes the tendency for people to categorize themselves in terms of their salient group memberships. In a context where someone is aware of their category membership, they automatically assign the category prototype to self as a means of self-definition (Hogg, 2001). Applying this to a situation in which a group is discussing their opinion on a particular issue when it is clear what the group's position is, group members will converge their views upon this group norm. In so converging the consensus of the group will become stronger, and it is likely that polarization will occur (the initial attitude will become more clearly espoused by the group).

We can explain group polarization with reference to both *normative* and *informational* influence. In order to meet normative concerns and fit in with the majority of group members, each member will move towards the group norm and express public attitudes in line with the group (normative influence). Informational influence will also occur. The group offers a valuable source of information by which to arrive at a decision. In group discussion people learn more information (encounter more arguments) that supports the initial group position. As a consequence they are more persuaded by that position. This enables the group to achieve the consensus which is so valued for making the world a predictable and stable place. For an illustration of how group polarization can affect judgements in one very important domain, see Text Box 6.3. These pressures towards conformity are sometimes so strong that significant problems for group decision-making may arise.

Text Box 6.3

Decision-Making in the Criminal Justice System

Group processes play a major role in many aspects of the criminal justice system. Given that this system determines whether the perpetrators of crime are caught and appropriately punished for their actions, it is important that we understand the impact of group processes in this domain. Here we discuss the implications of group processes for two particular aspects of the criminal justice system: eyewitness testimony and jury decision-making.

Eyewitness Testimony

The accuracy of eyewitness testimony is particularly important given that the accounts of witnesses have a powerful influence on whether a defendant is found guilty or not. Research has shown that people who are required to recall information about an event while in a group respond quite differently from individuals who recall the same information on their own. Alper and colleagues (1976) staged a theft in front of an audience of students, and then asked individual students to describe what they had seen. They then divided these students into groups and asked each group to come to an agreement about what had happened. Although groups recalled *more information* about what had happened than individuals, they also made *more errors*, introducing details that had not actually occurred. The authors argued that participants may have felt pressured into making additional inferences in a group setting, possible due to group polarization pressures. These pressures can also be seen in jury decision-making processes.

Jury Decision-Making

Juries are one of the most influential decision-making groups in society, influencing the lives of the suspected perpetrators of crime, the victims of crime, and the community at large. As a result it is essential that we understand how juries make their decisions and ensure that this process is as objective and accurate as is possible. However, as with any group, the decision-making process in a jury is not infallible. Empirical and anecdotal evidence point to a number of problems with the process:

1. As with any group, juries are susceptible to group polarization; their initial attitude is likely to become more extreme in the direction of that viewpoint in the course of their discussions (Kerr, 1992).
2. Jurors often have to take in and disseminate a large amount of information. There is evidence that there is often a recency effect: information delivered later in the trial has a more powerful influence on the decision made than information delivered early in the trial (Horowitz & Bordens, 1990).
3. Jurors are at times required to deal with extremely complex information, for example the testimony of expert witnesses, and the use of legal terms. This is despite the fact that jurors are normal members of the public; they are not necessarily scientists or lawyers. Complex evidence is associated with greater difficulties in making decisions among jurors. Heuer and Penrod (1994), for instance, found that the more complex the law was in a case, the less confidence jurors had that their verdict was based upon a proper understanding of the judge's instructions. This type of finding seems to be echoed in recent debates. In March 2005, for example, a group of British MPs (the Commons Select Committee on Science and Technology) called for juries to be dropped from trials

(Continued)

involving complicated scientific evidence because they would be unable to distinguish between the strength of evidence and the charisma of an expert witness.

4. Characteristics of the defendant have been shown to influence jury members. Stewart (1980) had observers rate the physical attractiveness of young white and non-white defendants in a criminal court. The more attractive the defendant, the less severe the sentence passed. Moreover, race appears to be influential; non-white defendants were consistently given more severe sentences than white defendants.

Groupthink

Groupthink is an extreme form of group polarization (Janis, 1982). It is deterioration in mental efficiency, reality testing, and moral judgement in groups due to an excessive desire to achieve consensus. Groupthink is caused by high group cohesiveness (a factor we discussed above which increases conformity) and a threatening situational context (where stress leads to people valuing speed over accuracy). The symptoms of groupthink are increased conformity, an overestimation of the competence of the group, and close-mindedness. Groupthink has been identified in the procedures that led up to a number of well-documented tragedies such as the Space Shuttle *Challenger* disaster in 1986 (see Text Box 6.4).

Text Box 6.4

A Catastrophic Consequence of Groupthink

The *Challanger* Shuttle Disaster

On the morning of 28 January 1986, the space shuttle *Challenger* was launched as the families of those on board watched from the ground and millions around the world watched live on television. Seven astronauts were on board, including schoolteacher Christa McAuliffe who had won her place on the flight through a competition. Tragically, just 73 seconds after take-off the shuttle exploded, as audiences watched in shock and disbelief. All seven crew members died in the blast.

An inquiry into the disaster determined that the primary cause of the accident was a problem with the rubber ring which joined together two sections of the rocket. Because the joint was not sealed properly, rocket fuel escaped and was ignited, causing a huge explosion. But why did this problem go unnoticed by the team responsible for the shuttle and its launch?

A Highly Flawed Decision-Making Process

The enquiry into the disaster concluded that the decision-making process preceding the launch was severely flawed. The day before the launch, engineers were concerned about the cold weather, arguing that the rubber rings had never been tested at such low temperatures. NASA officials were, however, sceptical and urged the engineers to reconsider. Rather than sticking to their position, the engineers changed their mind, agreeing that the shuttle was ready to launch. Jesse Moore, the commander of NASA who made the ultimate decision to launch, was never informed of the problem with the rubber rings by his staff so could not take this information into account when making his final, fateful, decision.

An Example of Groupthink

The decision-making process at NASA in January 1986 is an example of groupthink. The situation was characterized by high group *cohesiveness*, as NASA officials and engineers worked together on an important and high profile project. NASA was also in a highly *stressful* situation; the flight had already been delayed several times and the agency was worried that the American public would start to lose faith in them. NASA responded with typical symptoms of groupthink: the engineers felt pressure to *conform* to the group norm (a desire to launch) rather than sticking to their true attitudes; NASA were *overconfident*, arguing that any risks were no greater than for any of the previous successful flights. Finally, they were *close-minded*, failing to listen to outsider recommendations and failing to pass on vital information to the head of command.

Summary

So far we have focused on two types of social influence: *informational* and *normative* influence. Both types of influence describe the impact that other people have on the expression of our own attitudes and beliefs, but they occur as a result of two different underlying motivations. Informational influence occurs when we are influenced by others because they provide us with information as to the right answer to give. This is especially likely in *uncertain* situations where we do not know what to do or what the right response is (for example, in Sherif's autokinetic experiment). In such situations other people are a useful heuristic that can be used to guide the formation of our own attitudes. *Social norms* can also be created when people disagree

(Continued)

with the majority of other people but want to avoid being excluded from the group, or singled out for deviating from the rest of the group. When people conform for this reason, it is an example of normative social influence; Asch's line experiment is illustrative of this type of influence. Whereas informational influence leads to *conversion* – a change in both publicly expressed and privately held attitudes – normative influence is a change in publicly expressed attitudes only – *compliance* – and is typically defined by a mismatch between public and privately held beliefs.

A number of factors can increase or decrease both normative influence (*group cohesion, group size*, and *social support*) and informational influence (*self-confidence, task difficulty*, and *social norms*). Whilst the above refers to the impact of groups on individual attitudes, normative and informational influence can also be seen in attitude change at the group level. The influence of others leads to pressures towards *consensus*. Moreover, the social norm itself can *polarize*; that is, change to be more extreme when the above factors that lead to social influence are in operation. Finally, when informational and normative influence is taken to the extreme (e.g. when there is excessive group cohesiveness), then *groupthink* can occur, which results in procedural errors that often characterize large-scale disasters.

So far we have discussed the influence that majorities have on minorities. In other words, we have looked at how individuals change their attitudes to fit in with the rest of the group, but not at whether individuals, or smaller groups of individuals, can ever convince larger, majority groups to change their point of view. A classic 1957 film, *12 Angry Men*, is based on this premise. The film featured Henry Fonda as a dissenting juror, a man who – in contrast to the other 11 jurors – proposed that the defendant in what appeared to be an open-and-shut murder case was in fact not guilty. Over the course of the film, he manages to convince the other 11 jurors to cast a *not guilty* vote. But does this cinematic example of a minority influencing the majority reflect reality? From Asch's studies, we may be forgiven for thinking that the minority doesn't stand a chance against the full force of normative and informational influence. Will the lone dissenter ever be able to change the view of the much more powerful majority?

It is worth noting that the conformity observed by Asch was far from *complete*. For instance, in his original experiment, 24 per cent of participants did not conform even once. These lone individuals appeared to stand up to the majority, and stuck resolutely to their own beliefs. In fact, social psychologists have discovered that social influence can work both ways: in some cases minorities can change the attitudes and behaviours of majorities. Although this only occurs under a number of specific conditions, the impact of minorities in group decision-making appears to be highly important for understanding how groups work. Minorities may be able to counteract some of the negative consequences of majority influence (such as groupthink) by promoting more in-depth and careful consideration of whatever issue is at hand. Below we look at the research that has shown us how minorities exert their influence.

MINORITY INFLUENCE

Consistency and Confidence

Sometimes a minority can shift the views of the majority, but they will only have an influence when they are *consistent and confident* (Maass & Clark, 1984). This was demonstrated in a classic study by Moscovici, Lage, and Naffrechoux (1969). Once again, this was ostensibly a 'visual perception experiment'. The task was to judge the colour of a series of slides (either green or blue). As with the Asch experiment, the task was unambiguous and relatively easy; the slides were always perceived as blue when participants were tested in a control condition (i.e. alone). This time there were four *real* participants and two confederates. So in this case the confederates were in the minority and the aim was to see what effect the minority giving obviously incorrect answers (i.e. saying that the slide was green) would be on the responses of the majority. From Asch's experiments we might expect that the minority would have little influence on the majority. The majority can exert both informational and normative influence so why should they be concerned with a minority who might deviate from their group norm? However, Moscovici et al. hypothesized that in *certain* situations the minority may be able to exert some influence on the majority.

Figure 6.5 shows what Moscovici et al. (1969) found. Compared to a control condition where participants gave their judgements alone and where the error rate

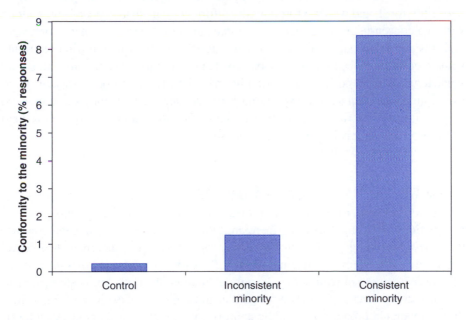

Figure 6.5 The effect of consistency on minority influence. Data from Moscovici et al. (1969)

(green responses) was negligible, Moscovici et al. found that a minority did indeed have an effect on the majority participants when they were consistent in giving the incorrect green response. The number of participants (in the majority) that went along with this clearly incorrect judgement increased from almost 0 per cent to 8 per cent. However, a third condition illustrated that the influence of the minority was subject to certain conditions. When the minority gave the green incorrect response only some of the time (i.e. when they were inconsistent) then there was no influence on the majority, and no shift in responses from blue to green. This significant influence of the minority, when consistent, demonstrates that in some situations a minority can change the view of the majority.

Minority influence can be explained with reference to the two types of social influence processes outlined by Deutsch and Gerard (1955). Given the normative consequences (social exclusion and punishment) and informational advantages (confirmation) of conforming, if a minority consistently sticks to its guns then others in the majority might then *attribute* some degree of credibility to the minority argument (see Chapter 2 for how people make attributions about the characteristics of others). That is to say that the majority observing a minority *consistently not conforming* knows that the minority will experience social exclusion and derogation for not 'toeing the line' (normative influence), and also that they appear to be ignoring the benefits of going along with what most people believe is the normally correct majority (informational influence). As such, the impression might develop that the minority, who are consistently going against the majority view despite getting a hard time for it, and who are forgoing the informational advantages of going along with the consensus, *know something that the majority doesn't* (i.e. have some special 'insider' knowledge). If this is the case then the majority may begin to attribute some credibility to the minority's perspective and consequently begin to shift somewhat towards their position. Importantly, the minority has to be consistent (and, by implication, *confident*) in expressing their 'deviant' view. If they sometimes go along with the majority and sometimes do not, then the majority may regard them as 'quirky' and simply dismiss their responses.

How Minorities Exert Influence

Do majorities and minorities exert their influence through the same process? Moscovici (1980) suggested that there are two processes at work in such contexts that vary depending on the numerical size of the groups concerned. Moscovici argues that majorities produce conformity through a *social comparison* process. This process does not require any deep thought about the issue but is characterized by normative concerns (i.e. the desire to fit in and avoid social exclusion). Majorities therefore should produce *only* public conformity: compliance. In contrast, minorities who are consistent and confident will encourage majorities to think more deeply about the position they are taking (in order to try to work out why they are 'sticking to their guns'). This process should involve some assessment of the minority's arguments and correspondingly some acceptance of their position: private conformity. People in majorities, however, are all subject to normative influence, and thus unlikely to express any change of opinion publicly for fear of being excluded from the group. As such, minorities should produce *only* private conformity: conversion, but without a change in public attitude.

Similar to Moscovici's theory, Nemeth (1986) has suggested that minorities exert their influence more broadly via increased **divergent thinking**. Nemeth argues that minorities will lead to more cognitive processing than majorities (which is in line with Moscovici's ideas regarding conversion and the notion that the majority will try to explain why the minority is going against the majority's position). However, she argues that the direction of the thought processes need not always be towards the minority viewpoint, but rather it is increased thought about the issue *per se* that is important. The outcome of considering a minority's viewpoint may not, therefore, be a change in attitude (although it could do so), but in general qualitatively *better* judgements by the majority because by considering the minority's alternative point of view they will think in a more elaborate way about the issue at hand (see Nemeth & Wachtler, 1983, for experimental evidence). Nemeth (1977) also observed that mock juries forced to come to unanimous decisions (so having to consider minority viewpoints) tended to consider evidence in more detail and take longer to reach a decision than juries who could arrive at a majority decision. Minorities can, therefore, be a highly useful force in group decision-making contexts. They provide a counterpoint to the majority viewpoint, and a safeguard against *groupthink* by encouraging more divergent thought on the issue at hand. Even if the eventual view of the majority does not change, they are likely to have considered the arguments in more detail and in more depth, and so are more likely to make a well-considered judgement.

OBEDIENCE

So far in this chapter we have talked about how social norms develop within groups, and the pressures that individuals (minorities) face to conform to the majority social norm, but also the conditions under which sometimes a consistent and confident minority that sticks to its guns can have an influence on majorities. Everything we have looked at so far has, however, considered the effects of 'implicit' social influence – people going along with what they perceive to be a group norm based on observing other people's responses. However, sometimes people try to exert social influence on others in more direct, blatant, and explicit ways. Is there a difference in the social psychology of social influence when pressures to conform are explicit versus implicit? Put another way, is there a difference between conformity (complying with an implicit norm) and obedience (complying with an explicit order)? In the next section we find out by looking at one of the most talked about psychology experiments ever.

Milgram's Study of Obedience

Work on obedience was inspired by the atrocities observed in the Second World War. Stanley Milgram was interested in what made Nazi guards go along with orders to commit atrocities against the Jews. Milgram did not think that a whole nation of people could be inherently evil, but rather that there might be conditions under which anyone might abandon their own sense of right and wrong and go along with an immoral order. This was the motivation for his classic studies on obedience. These studies are today considered unethical but nonetheless are highly informative and were highly influential in subsequent theoretical and empirical work on social influence.

Milgram's (1963) experiment went like this. Participants were told that the study concerned the effects of punishment (negative reinforcement) on learning, although this was just a cover story. The participant entered the laboratory ostensibly with a second participant who, like in Asch and Moscovici's experiments, was actually a confederate. The experimenter then allocated them to two roles, ostensibly on a random basis, but in fact set up so that the participant was always the 'teacher' and the confederate always the 'learner'. The task for the learner was to learn word pairs (i.e. on presentation of one word the learner had to give a second word with which it had previously been paired in an earlier learning phase). Each time the learner made a mistake they were supposedly given an electric shock by the teacher (the participant). The intensity of this shock increased each time the learner made a mistake. The confederate explained that they were 50 years old with a heart problem but the experimenter at this point said that this would not be a problem and strapped the learner into the chair, attaching the electrodes that would apparently deliver the shocks. At this stage the participant received a real 15 volt shock from these electrodes to enhance realism, but in fact none of the subsequent shocks were real.

During the experiment the confederate, in another room, answered each question through an intercom. The participant asked the questions, recorded whether the answer was correct or incorrect, and administered the electric shock if the answer was incorrect. At any query from the participant the experimenter simply said please continue (and had a script for subsequent responses). During the course of the task the confederate made several deliberate mistakes so that Milgram could see how far the participant would go in obeying the experimenter and supposedly shocking the 50-year-old learner. The script that the experimenter and confederate adhered to was critical to Milgram's experiment. It ensured experimental control (i.e. all participants were exposed to precisely the same situation) and also allowed Milgram to record at a number of specific points the reaction of the participants. Key points in the script went something like this:

> At 150 volts the learner demanded to be released, shouting: "Experimenter! That's all! Get me out of here … My heart's starting to bother me now. I refuse to go on!'

> At 180 volts the learner shouted that he could no longer stand the pain.

> At 300 volts the learner refused to give any more answers – which the experimenter said to simply treat as incorrect answers.

> There were screams of agony at each subsequent shock, and then from 330 volts onwards just silence. The last switch was labelled '450 volts: XXX – danger severe shock'.

Milgram was interested in how far participants would go. Looking at this script one cannot imagine participants happily continuing to shock the poor learner, given all the protestations and apparent medical emergency that ensued at 300 volts. Milgram wanted to confirm the expectation that 'reasonable' people would refuse to obey such apparently irresponsible orders. Prior to the experiment he obtained predictions from college students, middle-class adults, and psychiatrists. All of these groups predicted that all participants would refuse to continue well before the 450 volt limit. In fact the psychiatrists predicted that only 0.1 per cent of participants would obey the experimenter completely; such behaviour would surely indicate some sort of mental problem that one would expect only in a tiny proportion of the population. What Milgram actually found in this experiment was astonishing.

In Figure 6.6 you can see Milgram's findings. As you can see, there is a massive discrepancy between what people expected to find and how participants actually responded to the orders given by the experimenter. At 210 volts everyone had predicted that the majority of participants, 86 per cent, should have refused to go on. This is well after the learner has complained about his heart and shouted out in agony. Surely no-one would continue to shock this poor man? In fact, at 210 volts not a single participant had defected. After this point some participants did begin to question the experimenter, but only a tiny minority. At 315 volts 96 per cent of people should have defected, but only 22.5 per cent had done so. At this point the learner was screaming with agony at each shock. Overall, 65 per cent of participants (24 out of 30) obeyed the experimenter right up to the maximum 450 volts switch labelled 'XXX – danger severe shock'.

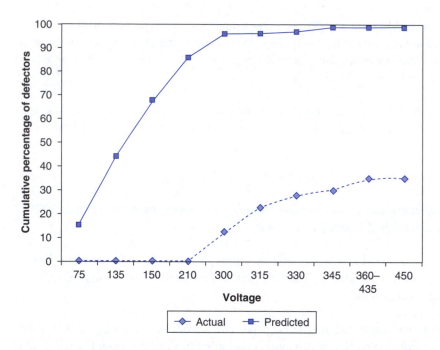

Figure 6.6 Levels of predicted and actual obedience in Milgram's study. Data from Milgram (1963)

Milgram's findings caused quite a stir, not just in the psychological community but in society at large. Were people really so savage that they would happily engage in apparently immoral acts simple because they were being told to do so by someone else? The findings raised issues that cut to the core of human nature. Could so many people be willing to do serious harm to an innocent person?

Explaining Obedience

How can we explain Milgram's findings of obedience to authority? Milgram argued that three factors are at work in contexts where obedience is high. First, there is a general *cultural norm* to obey authority. People are generally rewarded for obeying authority (see Chapter 4 on operant conditioning explanations for attitude formation). People expect authority figures to be trustworthy and legitimate. Second, in his experiment the requests to obey increasingly immoral acts were *gradual*. People were led into shocking at potentially lethal levels over a relatively long time so that before they knew it they were administering apparently lethal shocks. Third, Milgram argued that there is a shift in '*agency*', so that people no longer regard themselves as personally responsible but attribute responsibility (agency) to others in the context (this is similar to 'diffusion of responsibility' which we discuss in Chapter 10, which can explain why people do not go and help others in emergencies).

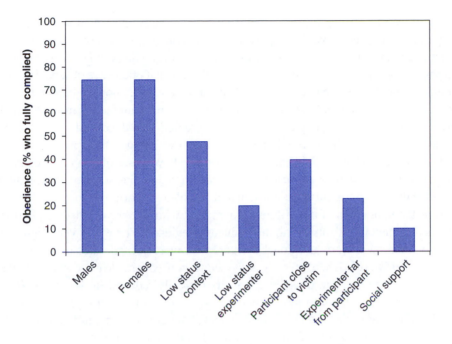

Figure 6.7   Context effects on level of obedience. Data from Milgram (1963)

Determinants of Obedience

Social psychologists were understandably very keen to understand why Milgram had observed such … shocking levels of obedience, but also how such high levels of obedience could be *reduced*. In the studies that ensued, we began to understand a little more about the psychological factors that led to such high levels of obedience in Milgram's experiment. Figure 6.7 summarizes the effects of different conditions subsequently introduced to the Milgram experiment that help to explain when and why people are obedient.

In Milgram's original experiment all the participants were male, so one possibility was that there was a *gender difference*; perhaps males are inherently more aggressive than females, and this can explain the willingness to inflict apparent harm on the learner. However, studies that compared the reactions of males and females to the Milgram experiment revealed no difference.

More enlightening were comparisons on obedience in different contexts and with different experimenters. The original experiment was carried out at Yale University with Milgram, a respectable scientist (dressed smartly in a lab coat, exuding confidence and authority). When the experiment was carried out in a run-down office block, the level of obedience dropped dramatically. The same effect was observed when instead of Milgram, the experimenter was a scruffy individual who, far from inspiring confidence, gave the impression of someone who was not entirely sure of what was going on. The impact of the *status* of the surroundings and the experimenter go some way to helping explain the relatively high level of obedience observed in Milgram's original experiment, and suggest that participants were not just blindly following the orders of someone else but in fact taking other relevant factors into account. It makes a lot of sense that people would attribute credibility to the experimenter and the setting, and so might be more willing than usual to go along with apparently bizarre instructions (see Chapter 2 for more discussion of how the attribution of credibility makes us more likely to be persuaded, and earlier in this chapter when we talked about the attribution of credibility to consistent and confident minorities).

A neat combination of the Milgram experiment with the Asch conformity experiments also uncovered something that reduces obedience. There was very high obedience when there were additional teachers who were confederates and also fully obedient. However, when there was a second confederate learner who rebelled against the experimenter, obedience was dramatically reduced (to less than 20 per cent). As in the Asch conformity experiments, a source of *social support* is a powerful antidote to social influence. In fact, social support is apparently so powerful that it helps people resist compliance when faced with both implicit pressures to conform to social norms as well as explicit orders from an authority figure.

One final set of conditions to note are the effects of *proximity*, both between the source of influence (the experimenter) and the learner. When the participant and the victim were in the same room, this reduced obedience to 40 per cent. Obedience was reduced further when the participant was required to physically touch the victim by placing their hand on an electric plate in order to receive the supposed shock. In addition, proximity of the experimenter was important, with obedience dropping to just over 20 per cent when the orders were given by phone. The effects of proximity on social influence is central to the final theory we will discuss in this chapter – a theory that unifies all of the effects of conformity and obedience we have discussed so far.

SOCIAL IMPACT THEORY

Latané (1981) devised social impact theory as a general theory of social influence that could account for all of the conformity and obedience findings we have discussed in this chapter. **Social impact theory** attempted to unify and explain the findings from conformity and obedience research, proposing that the amount of social influence that others have depends on their *number*, *strength*, and *immediacy* to those they are trying to influence. Number refers to the number of people in the group exerting power. The more people in the group that is the source of social influence, the more powerful their influence will be. Strength is the status, power, and/or expertise of the person or group exerting the influence. Immediacy is how close the group exerting power is in time and space.

The best way to describe the theory is to make a 'light bulb' analogy. So, for instance, with respect to the number of people exerting influence, social impact theory can explain the 'levelling off' effect in Asch's (1956) conformity study – each successive individual adds less and less to the overall effect (one light bulb has more of an effect than the second, than the third, and so on). Strength is relevant to the findings from obedience research. The level of obedience was much greater when the person giving the orders appeared to be someone in authority (i.e. a source of social power); Milgram appeared to participants in his experiments as a senior and respectable scientist, hence the high level of obedience. However, when the experimenter wore scruffy clothes and was apparently less confident, the level of influence was much lower. Minority influence can also be accounted for by this model. Minorities who are consistent and confident are attributed credibility, social power and social strength. Immediacy can also be illustrated with reference to Milgram's study. The level of obedience was much greater when the experimenter was in the room with the participant compared to when the orders were given by telephone.

CHAPTER SUMMARY

This chapter has discussed social influence: when, how and why our attitudes and behaviours are influenced by other people. Social influence can be divided up into implicit and explicit forms. *Conformity* research has examined implied pressure from groups to conform to a common standard or *social norm*. Sherif's work illustrated how people can spontaneously conform to a group norm in situations where the correct response is unclear. We can describe this as *informational influence*, and this can lead to *conversion*: a change in both public and private attitudes. Asch's conformity studies illustrate that people also converge upon a common group norm even when they are sure of a response that is counter to the majority. In such contexts we can say *normative influence* is occurring, leading to *compliance* – a change in public but not private attitudes. Normative and informational influence can both lead to *group polarization* and, in extreme circumstances, *groupthink* which is characterized by poor judgements resulting from group discussions. Levels of conformity can, however, vary and the extent to which people conform is dependent on a number of factors such as *group size*, *cohesiveness*, *social support*, *self-confidence*, *task difficulty*, and the presence of different *cultural norms*.

Minorities can sometimes influence majorities, but only when they are *consistent* and *confident*, and can be attributed some *credibility* by the majority. Considering minority perspectives can lead to *divergent thinking*, which can, even if no majority attitude shift occurs, lead to more *systematic* consideration of

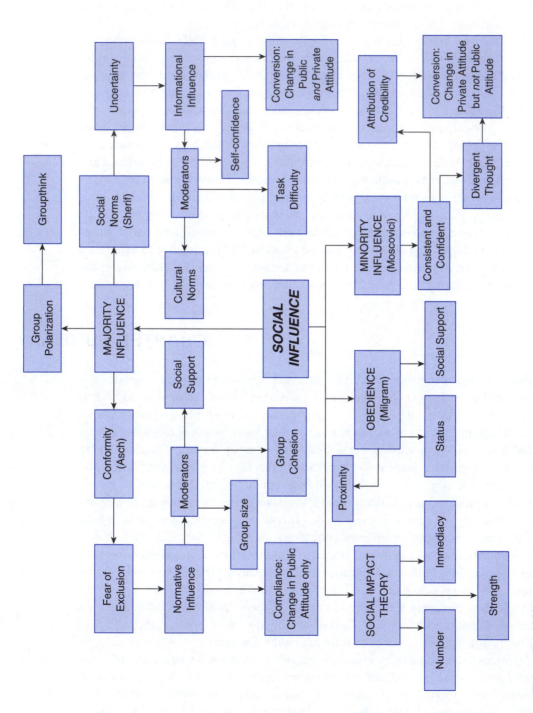

Figure 6.8 Memory map

issue-relevant arguments and avoid the negative tendencies towards group polarization and groupthink.

More explicit forms of social influence are illustrated by work on *obedience*: influence in response to a *direct order*. Milgram's obedience research demonstrated how people can follow orders even when those orders may appear to be questionable and immoral. Obedience is, however, dependent upon a number of factors, and is much less likely when the source of the influence is perceived to be *illegitimate* or *non-credible* and when the source is further away from the participant in time and space. The combined effects of social influence can be understood within the framework of *social impact theory*, which uses a light bulb *analogy* to predict the amount of social influence as a function of the *number* of people exerting influence, the perceived *strength* of those people (*status*, *power*, *credibility*), and *immediacy*.

Taking it Further

Try This

Have you ever been in a minority? Can you recognize normative and informational influence? Think back to a time when you have been quite certain of your own opinion (e.g. you knew what pub *you* wanted to go to) but where you were in the minority (compared to your friends, your tutor group). Did you go along with what everyone else wanted to do and, if so, how did you feel? Did you feel normative influence? Similarly, think back to a time when you've been uncertain about a decision, or course of action (e.g. how to write an essay, whether to change your hair colour). Did you seek advice from others, and, if so, can you identify common bonds between the people you asked (perhaps they were not physically present as a group, but were the people you asked all friends, family, your peer group of students?). Thinking about the people you ask advice of typically, can you say how entitative they are, and do you think you are more likely to feel informational influence from highly entitative groups? (think back to Chapter 5)

Debate This

Social influence is all about changing attitudes, and we've already talked a bit about this in Chapter 4. Can you apply any of the models we talked about in Chapter 4 to the sorts of social influence situations we've described in this chapter? For instance, is minority influence just a particular example of the workings of the elaboration likelihood model (and, if so, how?). Can the ELM or other models of attitude change explain all of the effects we have discussed in this chapter, or are there any unique impacts of the sort of social influence we have described here that go beyond the scope of these attitudinal models?

Something for the Weekend

Choose one behaviour that, as a society, we would like to encourage (e.g. giving blood), and one behaviour that we would like to discourage (e.g. prejudice). Using what you now know about social influence, devise an educational intervention to tackle both. It could, for instance, be a poster campaign highlighting the issue; or a series of workshops held in schools. When devising your strategies, draw upon the light bulb model (social impact theory) and say how you can capitalize on factors such as number, strength, and immediacy. Can you draw on what you know of the following to enhance the attitude change: social support, faster convergence on norm under uncertainty, group cohesiveness, consistent and confident minority influence to promote divergent thinking?

Further Reading

The Essentials

Martin, R. & Hewstone, M. (2003). Social influence processes of control and change: Conformity, obedience to authority, and innovation. In M.A. Hogg & J. Cooper (Eds.), *The Sage handbook of social psychology* (pp. 347–366). London: Sage.

This is a superb review of social influence research developing all of the themes we have discussed in this chapter.

Next Steps

Milgram, S. (1974). *Obedience to authority: An experimental view*. London: Tavistock Publications.

These days you just couldn't do this sort of study (it would be considered highly unethical) – nonetheless, it's a classic, and reading the original (one of the most famous studies in psychology) will give you a unique historical perspective on the development of social influence research.

Delving Deeper

Crano, W.D. & Prislin, R. (2006). Attitudes and persuasion. *Annual Review of Psychology*, *57*, 345–374.

Wood, W. (2000). Attitude change: Persuasion and social influence. *Annual Review of Psychology*, *51*, 539–570.

These are two excellent reviews of social influence research that integrate the work we've covered in this chapter with research on attitudes and persuasion (covered in Chapter 4). The authors expertly weave the two areas together as well as drawing on research on social identity (Chapter 1) and social cognition (Chapter 3), illustrating just how many of the concepts we have discussed link together.

Prejudice

7

Prejudice

Text Box 7.1

Account of a Racist Murder

One night in July 2005, an 18-year-old college student, Anthony Walker, was spending the evening at his Huyton home with girlfriend Louise Thompson. They were babysitting his two-year-old nephew, Reuben.

At around 11pm, Mr Walker and his cousin Marcus Binns offered to walk Louise to her bus stop, close to the Huyton Park pub. Standing outside the pub was Michael Barton, dressed in a hooded top with a scarf or ski mask covering his face. He began hurling racist abuse at Mr Walker and Mr Binns, telling them: 'Walk, nigger, walk'.

Mr Walker, a devout Christian, walked away. He intended to take a short-cut to a different bus stop through McGoldrick Park.

As they walked away, Barton told his friend Paul Taylor that he had 'lost face' during a row.

They got into a car, drove to the entrance to the park and hid in bushes before ambushing Mr Walker and his friends. Ms Thompson and Mr Binns escaped but Mr Walker was trapped. Taylor drove a mountaineering axe into the teenager's head with such force that the adze end was embedded 6cm into his skull.

While their victim lay unconscious on the ground, Barton desperately tried to retrieve the weapon, but it was stuck fast in Mr Walker's skull. Even doctors struggled later to remove it.

Barton fled with his hands covered in Mr Walker's blood. By the time Mr Binns returned with help, there was little anybody could do. Mr Walker was taken to Whiston hospital, then transferred to Walton neurological centre.

Mr Walker died at 5.25am, with his family at his bedside.

Source: *The Guardian*, 30 November 2005

Text Box 7.1 gives an account of the racially-motivated murder of college student Anthony Walker by four white men in Merseyside in July 2005. This was a shocking, tragic event that vividly illustrates the very worst consequences of racial prejudice. Such acts are not representative of attitudes held by the general population, but simple statistics show us that less savage, but nonetheless highly divisive, forms of prejudice persist. In the 20th British Social Attitudes report (Park et al., 2003), the percentage of respondents who openly admitted being racially prejudiced was 31 per cent (a figure that has generally stayed the same since 1987). Prejudice is a fundamental social problem, and one that remains so even in the light of apparent widespread egalitarian beliefs. Social psychologists have therefore been very much concerned with understanding the psychological processes that can explain such pervasive, destructive human tendencies. This chapter is about what psychologists have learned about the nature of prejudice, and what we can do to fight against it.

PREJUDICE: OLD AND NEW

Prejudice, Discrimination and Intergroup Bias

This chapter introduces what social psychologists have learned about prejudice, intergroup discrimination and social conflict. We will be talking about *ingroups* and *outgroups*. Ingroups are social categories (see Chapter 3) to which you belong. Other people who share your category membership are ingroup members. Outgroups are social categories to which you do not belong. People who are members of categories that don't include you are outgroup members. While not terms typically used in common language, we make reference to ingroups and outgroups all the time. Generically speaking, whenever we refer to 'us' or 'we', 'they' or 'them', all of these terms denote shared versus non-shared category membership (and this fundamental role that group referents have in everyday language suggests some of the psychological causes of prejudice that we discuss later on). We are going to be talking about people seeing their ingroup as more positive than their outgroup, something we call **ingroup bias** (sometimes also referred to as *ingroup favouritism* or *intergroup bias*). Ingroup bias is an umbrella term that includes different manifestations of bias in favour of one's own social category. This brings us to prejudice, which is defined as a negative *attitude* or *feeling* held towards members of an outgroup. Intergroup discrimination is the *behavioural* manifestation of prejudice. That is, people who hold prejudiced attitudes might be those more likely to show discriminatory behaviour. We will refer to experiments that measure prejudice or discrimination, and for the purposes of this chapter we can treat them both as manifestations of the same intergroup bias. However, it is important to remember that attitudes do not *always* predict behaviour (see Chapter 4 and the discussion of the attitude-behaviour relationship).

Given these basic definitions, how can we start trying to understand the nature of prejudice? In Chapter 3 we talked about how people use social categories to make the world easier to understand; they are heuristics that help people make cognitively efficient judgements and better understand the world by providing information in the form of norms and stereotypes. It is this tendency to use categories to define our worlds that belies the most talked about forms of prejudice – racism and sexism. Racism is prejudice against someone based on their race; sexism is prejudice against someone on the basis of their sex. We saw in Chapter 3 that people appear to use categories such as race and sex chronically; that is, they spontaneously categorize others along these dimensions without even realizing it. This tendency to use race and sex in defining others is a problem because membership of these categories can come with stigma attached (Crocker et al., 1998). **Stigmatization** is when a person's social category puts them at a lower status than a dominant group and ascribes to them negative characteristics (or *stereotypes*). In this chapter we chart psychologists' understanding of racism and sexism, how the expression of these most common forms of prejudice have developed over time, how the development of societies' egalitarian norms have had a key defining role, and how new technologies have helped identify contemporary and more subtle forms of prejudice.

Racism

There are two types of racism: *old-fashioned* racism and *aversive* racism. Old-fashioned racism is the blatant expression of negative and unfair stereotypes of others based on their category membership. For instance, African Americans have been seen as aggressive (Devine, 1989) and of low intelligence (Steele & Aronson, 1995). Although we periodically read about racially-motivated violence in our newspapers, we may regard these as acts carried out by a small criminal minority. You may think that because blatant racist attitudes are rarely expressed, and only by a small minority of people, that prejudice is decreasing. To some extent this is true; we now have societal norms that largely prohibit the blatant expression of prejudiced beliefs. However, psychologists have identified a second, more pervasive, manifestation of racism that people do not admit to, and which is therefore much more difficult to detect: *aversive* racism.

Aversive racism describes the type of racism that is defined by having *both* egalitarian attitudes and negative emotions towards members of different groups. Gaertner and Dovidio (1986) argue that modern racism is best described by this conflict between modern egalitarian values (such as equal treatment of all people and sympathy for victims of racial prejudice) and the more explicit forms of prejudice that are perpetuated by images of minority groups as conforming to negative stereotypes. The result of this conflict is the experience of negative emotions such as uneasiness, fear and discomfort. Because egalitarianism is important to many people, these negative emotions arouse feelings of shame and guilt in those who experience them, leading them to avoid publicly acknowledging these feelings, and to avoid intergroup encounters that might mean having to face up to this conflict. The consequences of aversive racism are clearly demonstrated in a study reported in Text Box 7.2 which shows that while people may report holding egalitarian attitudes, their behaviour towards the ingroup and the outgroup can vary dramatically. These implicit prejudiced attitudes can also be understood in terms of the automatic stereotyping processes which we discussed in Chapter 3. We return to consider these processes in more detail later in this chapter.

Text Box 7.2

The Effect of Race on Helping Behaviour

The majority of studies on racism and discrimination involve participants directly reporting their outgroup attitudes. However, people may not always be completely honest when reporting such attitudes, because of a fear of violating the egalitarian norms of modern society. Gaertner and Bickman (1971) used a subtle measure of discrimination, investigating whether people are more likely to help ingroup members than outgroup members.

Method

1,109 residents of Brooklyn, New York (approximately half of whom were black and half of whom were white) were called by either a Black or a White confederate. To ensure that their ethnicity was obvious to the caller, the confederates used an accent that was typically associated with their ethnic group. When a participant answered the phone, each confederate used the following script:

Caller:	Hello … Ralph's Garage? This is George Williams … listen, I'm stuck out here on the parkway … and I'm wondering if you'd be able to come out here and take a look at my car?
Expected response:	This isn't Ralph's Garage … you have the wrong number.
Caller:	This isn't Ralph's Garage! Listen, I'm terribly sorry to have disturbed you, but listen … I'm stuck out here on the highway … and that was the last dime I had! I have

(Continued)

bills in my pocket but no more change to make another phone call … Now I'm really stuck out here. What am I going to do now? … Listen … do you think you could do me the favour of calling the garage and letting them know where I am? I'll give you the number … They know me over there.

If the participant agreed to help, the caller gave him the telephone number of the garage. Calls were actually received by a research assistant, posing as a garage attendant, who logged the calls.

Results

- White participants showed ingroup bias; they were more likely to help a White caller than a Black caller.
- Black participants were actually more likely to help a White caller than a Black caller, although this difference was not statistically significant.

Interpreting the Findings

People have a general tendency to help those in need, because we hold a 'social responsibility norm'; we feel we should help others even if it is of no personal benefit. For White people, however, this norm was violated more frequently when the person in need of help was in the outgroup; White people were more likely to help ingroup members than outgroup members.

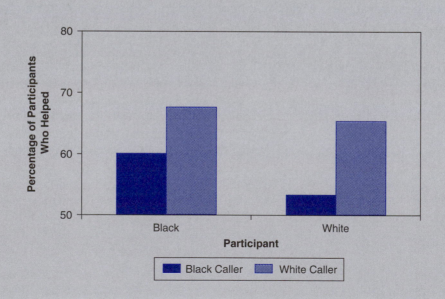

One can conceptualize a society's progression towards **egalitarianism** as moving through stages defined by these different types of racism, from old-fashioned blatant racism, through to aversive racism, where both egalitarian and prejudiced attitudes co-exist, through to full egalitarianism, where there is no longer any conflict (Kleinpenning & Hagendoorn, 1993). Where is our society on this continuum? Many commentators believe that western societies are at stage two: aversive racism. We have a society that acknowledges the importance of egalitarian values, but there are still pervasive biases evident in all strata of social life, from the sort of violent racist murder described at the beginning of this chapter through to less obvious, but still destructive, forms of prejudice such as institutional racism. In the second half of this chapter we talk about how social psychologists are developing interventions to help us move to stage three, total egalitarianism. Next, however, we discuss another type of prejudice that has proved difficult to eradicate: sexism.

Sexism

Sexism is the subordination of someone on the basis of their sex. Typically this is defined as male domination of females, and can be exemplified in sexual harassment through to institutional discrimination and the 'glass ceiling' effect (Hymowitz & Schellhardt, 1986). Like racism, sexism can be divided into two components: *hostile sexism* and *benevolent sexism*. Hostile sexism is what we typically think of as sexist attitudes towards women, the view that women are inferior, irrational, and weak. However, there is also a less blatant, more benevolent side to sexism. Benevolent sexist attitudes are positive in valence and are characterized by idealizing women in traditional female roles such as 'homemaker' or 'mother'. Although these are positive stereotypes they restrict women to specific roles, justifying male social dominance (Sidanius, Pratto, & Brief, 1995). Modern forms of sexism, just like modern racism, can be characterized by the conflict between positive (egalitarian) and negative (prejudiced) attitudes.

Interestingly, it seems possible for sexist men to possess both hostile and benevolent attitudes towards women. Glick, Diebold, Bailey-Werner, and Zhu (1997) found that men high in ambivalent sexism had polarized views of women that fell into the two types of sexism. Men high in ambivalent sexism who were asked to think about a woman transcending traditional roles (e.g. a career woman) reported negative feelings such as fear and envy. These negative feelings were correlated with hostile sexism, but *not* with benevolent sexism. Men high in ambivalent sexism who thought about a woman in a traditional role (e.g. a homemaker) reported positive feelings (warmth, trust, etc.) which were correlated with a measure of benevolent sexism but *not* hostile sexism. These findings suggest that ambivalent sexist men can hold simultaneously positive and negative attitudes about different subcategories of women, which may help to explain why sexism has been hard to counteract. It is harder to show someone that their negative stereotype is unjustifiable when they can counter with the argument that they do have a positive view of women (albeit along restrictive and inherently biased dimensions).

Explicit and Implicit Prejudice

Until quite recently, research on prejudice focused on people's explicit attitude towards members of other groups. Explicit attitudes are conscious, deliberative and controllable and are usually captured by getting participants to report in a question-naire how positive or negative their attitudes, feelings, or stereotypes are towards members of another group. Although these measures have been used widely in investigations of prejudice, they have a notable limitation: they are influenced by *social desirability*. We have a general desire to be perceived positively by others. At the same time, there is a strong contemporary norm for equality and intergroup tolerance. It may therefore be the case that people do not report their true intergroup attitudes because they fear that those attitudes are not socially desirable. To some extent, this problem has been dealt with by getting participants to complete ques-tionnaires anonymously. However, it may be that people do not want to admit the extent of their prejudices, even to themselves.

Recently, however, the development of millisecond reaction time methodology (measuring how long respondents take to answer questions relating to prejudice) has allowed us to measure implicit attitudes. **Implicit attitudes** are attitudes that are unintentionally activated by the mere presence of an attitude object, whether actual or symbolic. So implicit intergroup attitudes may be triggered by seeing someone from another group, or even simply seeing something that we associate with that group, such as a religious icon or symbol.

One of the most frequently used measures of implicit attitude is the **implicit association test** (IAT; Greenwald, McGhee & Schwartz, 1998). This is a task that identifies the speed with which participants can categorize positive or negative stimuli (e.g. positive or negative words) alongside ingroup or outgroup stimuli (e.g. names or faces). It typically demonstrates that people show an implicit intergroup bias. Specifically, people find it easer to associate their own group (compared to the outgroup) with positive stimuli, and the outgroup (compared to the ingroup) with negative stimuli, indicating implicit bias in favour of one's own group. The IAT has been used to measure a whole range of different types of ingroup favouring bias, including male-female, Black-White, and Christian-Muslim bias, to name just a few. For a demonstration of this test, you can visit the website implicit.harvard. edu and try it out for yourself. Initially, psychologists believed that while explicit attitudes change relatively easily, implicit attitudes were like old habits which are much more difficult to change (e.g. Wilson, Lindsey, & Schooler, 2000). However, recent evidence suggests that current events can have a powerful effect on implicit attitudes (see Text Box 7.3).

So why is it important to measure implicit, as well as explicit, prejudice? Well, first of all implicit measures like the IAT do not require participants to report their attitudes directly, which means they are less likely to be influenced by social desirability than are explicit measures. They are therefore particularly interesting to study in the context of prejudice towards social groups towards whom it is no longer socially acceptable to express negative attitudes. Second, there is evidence that although explicit and implicit prejudices both influence behaviour, they do so in different ways. While explicit prejudice might lead to conscious and deliberative behaviours, for example being blatantly unpleasant to outgroup members, implicit prejudice is more likely to lead to subtle, indirect and spontaneous biased non-verbal behaviours, such as avoiding eye contact, increasing physical distance from outgroup members, and hesitating during speech (e.g. Fazio et al., 1995; McConnell & Leibold, 2001). These subtle behaviours can damage interactions between members of different groups without the participants even realizing it.

Text Box 7.3

The Obama Effect: Does Exposure to a Counter-stereotypical Political Figure Reduce Implicit Bias?

Research conducted over the last decade has shown that the majority (75–85%) of White people show a bias in favour of White people over Black people on the implicit attitude measure, the IAT. In 2008, however, Barack Obama ran a high profile campaign which resulted in his election as the 44th president of the United States on 20 January 2009. During this time, Americans had an unprecedented level of exposure to Obama, whose qualities – well educated, motivated, and articulate – contradict the negative stereotypes that typically exist towards African Americans. Plant and colleagues (2009) investigated whether this exposure had changed the implicit attitudes of White Americans towards African Americans, and if so, what might be causing this change.

Method

Two hundred and twenty-nine predominately White American students completed a Black–White version of the IAT during the 2008 election campaign.

(Continued)

Participants then listed the first five thoughts that came to mind when they thought of Black people. The researchers recorded how many positive examples of Black people were mentioned (e.g. Barack Obama, Martin Luther King).

Results

In stark contrast to the previous finding of consistent anti-Black implicit bias, there was no evidence of anti-Black bias on the IAT. In fact, a considerable proportion of participants actually showed a pro-Black bias. These findings were replicated in a follow-up study. Moreover, when asked what thoughts came to mind when thinking about Black people, participants who listed a positive exemplar (such as Barack Obama) were less likely to respond with anti-Black bias.

Summary

These findings suggest that media coverage of the election of Barack Obama may have led to a general change in White participant's implicit responses to Black people by repeatedly exposing them to a counter-stereotypical Black exemplar. While Obama's election has positive implications for intergroup relations in the United States, Plant and colleagues acknowledge that it is not clear how long this effect will last. If Obama's term of office continues to be perceived as a success, levels of implicit bias may remain low, but should his presidency prove less successful, there could be a backlash, resulting in an increase in anti-Black bias.

Summary

In this section we have seen how, at first glance, racism and sexism appear to be in decline. This may be because we live in societies that encourage egalitarianism as a universal value and where there are now laws against the expression of extreme racist and sexist views. However, when we take a closer look we can see how such prejudices have adapted and live on in different forms. *Aversive racism* and *ambivalent sexism* show us that prejudice still exists and can have a profound negative impact on people's lives (from experiencing racist taunts in the street through to gender discrimination at work). There is, of course, also prejudice apparent against many other groups, including gay men and women, immigrants and asylum seekers, Muslims, Jews and other religious groups. Social psychologists have sought to understand why these prejudices occur, and why they prove so pervasive. There is also an *implicit*, as well as an *explicit*, component of prejudice. While implicit prejudice was initially believed to be very difficult to change, recent research suggests that exposure to positive outgroup exemplars may help to eliminate it. The research we discuss above on ambivalent sexism suggests that, at least to some extent, prejudice might be the result of individual differences. In other words, some people may simply have personalities that lend them to possessing prejudiced views. We discuss this possibility in the next section.

INDIVIDUAL DIFFERENCES IN PREJUDICE

The Authoritarian Personality

An obvious place to begin any examination of the causes of prejudice is to ask the question: are some people more prejudiced than others? Perhaps understanding prejudice is simply a matter of personality. Adorno, Frenkel-Brunswick, Levinson, and Stanford (1950) thought just this, and put forward a theory of prejudice as a personality type. They argued that some people were more prejudiced than others because of the way they had been brought up. According to their theory, which was heavily influenced by the writings of Freud, an **authoritarian personality** arises as a defensive reaction against over-strict parenting methods. Having over-strict parents means the child is unable to express any natural hostility towards their parents, and as such transfers this aggression elsewhere (to weaker, easier targets). This displaced aggression is thus targeted towards minority or low status groups. These tendencies are then said to continue into adulthood, along with other, associated characteristics, like an overly-deferential attitude towards authority figures (who represent the parents).

Although intuitively appealing, this explanation of prejudice can be criticized in two major ways. First, it did not receive unequivocal empirical support. The F-scale, the measure devised by Adorno et al. (1950) to measure if someone had an authoritarian personality, did not predict racism in South African in the 1950s (Pettigrew, 1958), but this is a social setting where prejudice was self-evident. Second was the bigger, conceptual, problem. Personality theories, by definition, explain individual variation in attitudes and behaviours. As such, they have difficulty as explanations of widespread and uniform prejudice. For example, in the 1990s there was clear prejudice in former Yugoslavia, evident in an extreme and brutal form, ethnic cleansing. Is one to conclude that a whole generation of people in this context were raised in the same way by authoritarian parents, and thus ended up all with the same prejudiced tendencies?

We can therefore question the specific Freudian basis for research on the authoritarian personality. But does this mean people do not vary in the level of prejudice they are likely to express? Common observation would tell us that there is significant variation across different people in terms of how willing people are to express prejudiced views. If this is the case, then how can we explain these individual differences? An idea that has been the subject of much recent attention by social psychologists is that the extent to which people hold broad ideologies about the nature of society can predict differences in prejudice.

Social Dominance Orientation

Sidanius (1993) argued that people vary according to something called **social dominance orientation**. This is the idea that our societies are defined in part by implicit ideologies that either promote or attenuate intergroup status hierarchies, and that people can vary in the extent to which they either accept or reject these ideas that are ingrained in society. According to Sidanius, people who are high in social dominance orientation favour intergroup hierarchies – this means that people who are in high *or* low status groups should favour the high status group (i.e. it can explain both ingroup and outgroup favouritism). Empirical evidence is more supportive of social dominance orientation than it was for the authoritarian personality. Social dominance orientation has, for example, been found to predict sexism, nationalism, and ethnic prejudice against a range of different minority groups and among samples from a range of countries including the US, Canada, Mexico, Israel, Taiwan, China and New Zealand. There is also evidence that people high in social dominance orientation support suspension of civil liberties, and are opposed to immigration and gay rights (Pratto, Sidanius, Stallworth, & Malle, 1994; Sidanius & Pratto, 1999). The effect of social dominance orientation on prejudice remains even after controlling for a wide range of other individual difference factors including self-esteeem, need for structure, neuroticism, psychoticism, traditionalism, and several demographic factors.

   Overall, then, there does seem to be something in the idea that the extent to which people endorse authoritarian beliefs, the extent to which they agree with prevailing status hierarchies, and a general tendency towards accepting the dominance of some groups over others, provides some basis for individual differences in the expression of prejudice. When we discussed aversive racism above we noted how modern racism is defined by the internal struggle between the desire to conform to positive egalitarian norms and negative prejudiced attitudes. Social dominance orientation explains why we might observe individual differences in tendencies to express prejudiced attitudes, but what about the opposite perspective: do people differ in the extent to which they are motivated to go along with egalitarian social norms? Below we examine the psychological processes that can predict how some people come to question prejudiced attitudes, and modify their own behaviour accordingly.

Prejudice and Self-Regulation

We discussed how people can be more or less sexist or racist in the earlier sections of this chapter, and it is evident from this research that people do vary from one another in terms of how racist or sexist they are. But since the end of the Second World War, there has been increasing opposition to the expression of such prejudiced attitudes (Condor et al., 2006). Accordingly, there is evidence that people can develop a motivation to control prejudice (e.g. Fazio, 1990). When someone becomes aware that they may have acted in a prejudiced way, they may feel guilty about this because it violates other beliefs based on shared egalitarian values (see the discussion of aversive racism above). We know this kind of discrepancy between attitudes and behaviours can motivate people to change their attitudes (this is *cognitive dissonance*; see the discussion in Chapter 4). Devine and Monteith have suggested that a similar desire to deal with this dissonance in terms of prejudiced attitudes and behaviours can result in attitude change, and individuals ultimately becoming less prejudiced. They argue that people who detect such discrepancies (and who are motivated to control their prejudices) then engage in a deliberate *self-regulation* process, to monitor and consistently inhibit prejudice-related thoughts (Devine & Monteith, 1999), replacing them with a low prejudiced response (Plant & Devine, 1998) until ultimately they no longer think prejudiced thoughts or behave in prejudiced ways. On an individual level this idea that people can choose to self-regulate to avoid prejudiced thoughts shows us how people can become less prejudiced (Monteith, 1993). This theory describes how individuals, once they decide to become less biased, can achieve that goal.

Regulation of Prejudice Through Socially Interactive Dialogue

Condor and colleagues (2006) have argued that societal regulation of prejudice does not only happen at an individual level, but is a dialogic process that involves two or more people. By carefully analysing dialogues taken from a number of data sources, including academic interviews and television debates, Condor and colleagues found that people do not regulate prejudice in isolation. Instead, there are at least two types of *interactive* prejudice suppression. First, it emerged that in addition to denying their own prejudice, people often defend absent others who are being accused of prejudice. In one example, a woman argued that her mother was subject to prejudice because of her nationality, but her interaction partner argued that the woman might be being over-sensitive, and that the supposed protagonist might not have even realized that the alleged victim belonged to a different national group. Second, the researchers found that we have a tendency to act on the behalf of other individuals present in order to ensure that they do not come across as prejudiced. For example, when an older man stated in an interview that 'we already have enough low-life here without importing other peoples', his wife quickly interrupted to say

'He's not xenophobic' (p. 452). In another interview, an older woman was talking about her hip replacement operation and says of her doctor that he was 'a big black man', and her daughter exclaims, 'Oh Mum, you can't say that!' (p. 454). Condor and colleagues argue that while research typically focuses on strategies adopted by individual actors, these findings suggest that prejudice suppression may occur in a collaborative, interactive manner.

REDUCING PREJUDICE

The Contact Hypothesis

According to the **contact hypothesis,** contact between members of different social groups, under appropriate conditions, can lead to reductions in intergroup bias. Allport (1954) argued that a number of conditions were necessary for contact to be successful at reducing intergroup bias. First, social norms favouring equality must be in place. In other words, the social conditions (government policy, schools, and laws) should all promote integration. We can make a link here with cognitive dissonance (Festinger, 1957) which we discussed in Chapter 4 on attitudes. When attitudes are not in line with behaviour this causes an unpleasant internal state. People are motivated to avoid this dissonance. So they change their attitudes to be in line with behaviour. It follows that laws which prevent discriminatory behaviour can therefore eventually lead to changes in attitudes. Second, contact must occur under conditions of equal social status. If the minority group has contact with the majority group as a subordinate then this is likely to perpetuate negative stereotypes of inferiority. Third, contact must involve cooperation to achieve a common goal. Sherif (1966) showed that cooperation and common goals were necessary for reductions in bias. However, Blanchard et al. (1975) found that cooperation worked best when the outcome of the superordinate goal is successful.

Intergroup contact is now one of the most widely used psychological interventions for the reduction of prejudice and the improvement of intergroup relations (Oskamp & Jones, 2000). But despite its successes, the contact hypothesis has often been subject to two major criticisms, although both of these have now been addressed in contemporary research. The first criticism was that the contact hypothesis failed to specify how the effects of contact would generalize beyond the immediate situation to other situations and from the individuals involved in the contact to the entire outgroup. For instance, if a white person and a black person have a friendly, positive interaction with one another, although they will likely develop a positive opinion of one another, how can we be sure that (a) they would be nice to members of the other ethnic group in other situations, and (b) they would have a more positive attitude towards the other ethnic group *in general*? Contact may also lead to *subtyping* of individuals involved in the contact away from the group representation. The white person in the previous example may, for example, decide that although they like the black person they met, this person is unusual, an 'exception to the rule', and therefore cannot be considered representative of black people in general. As a consequence, category-based prejudice would remain.

Hewstone and Brown (1986) have argued, however, that contact can generalize to the outgroup as a whole when the ingroup and outgroup members taking part in the contact encounter are regarded as sufficiently typical or representative of their groups, and so cannot be subtyped away from the group so easily (Wilder, 1984). They argued that for this to happen, group memberships must be psychologically salient during contact (Johnston & Hewstone, 1992). In other words, group members must be aware of their respective group memberships during the interaction. This fits in with the 'multicultural perspective': the idea that 'colour-blind' policies (ignoring group membership) are not effective and that group differences need to be embraced, and seen in a positive light.

A second criticism of the contact hypothesis was that it became overly complex, as a result of researchers specifying many conditions that need to be met for intergroup contact to reduce prejudice. It was, for example, suggested that for contact to be effective at reducing prejudice, initial intergroup attitudes should be favourable, there should be a common language, a prosperous economy, and the contact should be voluntary rather than forced (Wagner & Machleit, 1986), to name but a few such conditions. The theory became essentially unfalsifiable, as few contact situations would meet all the conditions specified (Hewstone, 1996). Recently, however, a number of theorists have argued that none of the proposed conditions are *essential*; instead, they *facilitate* the effect of intergroup contact in reducing prejudice (e.g. Brown & Hewstone, 2005). Supporting this argument, in a meta-analysis of 515 contact studies, Pettigrew and Tropp (2006) found that although contact which met Allport's original conditions led to the greatest reductions in prejudice, prejudice reduction still occurred in their absence.

Contemporary research on intergroup contact has moved on to consider whether certain types of contact, such as *cross-group friendship*, are particularly effective at reducing prejudice. This is the idea that people who have friends in an outgroup are likely to hold more positive attitudes towards that outgroup in general, and it has received considerable support. In a survey of 3800 participants from all over Europe, Pettigrew (1997) found that the more friends from minority groups participants had, the less prejudice they showed and the more sympathy and admiration they had for those groups. The relationships between both neighborhood and co-worker contact and lower prejudice were considerably weaker. Pettigrew and Tropp's (2006) meta-analysis also supported the idea that friendship is a particularly effective form of contact. They found that studies where intergroup friendship was used as the measure of contact had a markedly stronger effect on prejudice than those that did not.

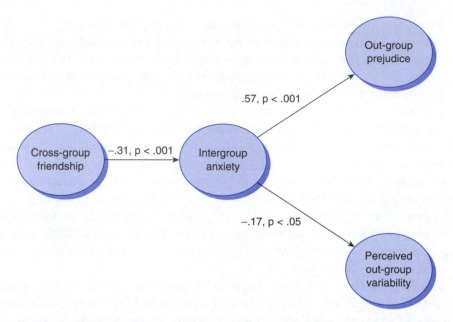

Figure 7.1 Path model of the relationship between cross-group friendship, outgroup attitude, and outgroup variability among Catholics and Protestants in Northern Ireland, showing mediation via reduced intergroup anxiety

So how exactly does cross-group friendship lead to more positive intergroup attitudes? Paolini, Hewstone, Cairns, and Voci (2004) asked Catholics and Protestants in Northern Ireland to fill out a questionnaire about their experiences with, and attitudes toward, the other community (i.e. Catholics answered questions about Protestants, and Protestants answered questions about Catholics). They found a positive relationship between cross-group friendship and two outcomes, outgroup attitude and perceived outgroup variability (the latter being the extent to which the outgroup is seen as including many different types of people, rather than being seen as all the same as one another – see Chapter 3). But these relationships operated via an underlying mediating mechanism, *intergroup anxiety*, which is the negative arousal experienced at the prospect of contact by individuals who have little experience with the outgroup (Stephan & Stephan, 1985). It emerged that the more friends participants had in the other community, the less anxious they were about interacting with members of that community. In turn, participants with lower levels of anxiety tended to have more positive outgroup attitudes and were more likely to perceive variability among the outgroup (see Figure 7.1).

Other research has shown that *self-disclosure*, the sharing of personal information between two people, can explain why people who have cross-group friends are less prejudiced. Turner, Hewstone, and Voci (2007) investigated cross-group friendship between the South Asian and White communities in the UK and found that the more outgroup friends participants had, the more they engaged in self-disclosure with outgroup members. Moreover, the more participants engaged in this self-disclosure, the more likely they were to have a positive attitude towards the outgroup in general. Self-disclosure seems to be associated with more positive outgroup attitudes for two reasons. First, it leads to empathy towards outgroup members, and second, it helps to generate mutual trust.

Indirect Contact

Despite the benefits of cross-group friendship as a means of reducing prejudice, it has one inevitable limitation: it can only be used as an intervention to reduce preju-dice when group members have the *opportunity* for contact in the first place. That is, unless an individual lives in the same community, attends the same school, or works in the same place as outgroup members, they will not be able to form friend-ships with them. As a result, cross-group friendship may not be useful in segregated settings. Fortunately, recent research on *indirect contact* may provide a solution to this dilemma. There are two types of indirect contact which have been investigated to date: *extended contact* and *imagined contact*.

Wright, Aron, McLaughlin-Volpe, and Ropp (1997) showed that *just the knowl-edge* that other people in your group have friends in the outgroup can reduce inter-group bias, a phenomenon referred to as **extended contact**. In the first phase of an experiment designed to illustrate this effect, participants were divided into two small groups (formed ostensibly on a random basis). Ingroup solidarity was created by having group members work together on a series of cooperative tasks designed to create ingroup familiarity and liking. In the second phase of the experiment, intergroup rivalry was generated by having the two groups compete against one another on a series of tasks. To enhance intergroup conflict, each team was given a negative evaluation from the opposing group following each task. In the third phase of the experiment, one participant from each group was randomly chosen to take part in what they were led to believe was a different study. The chosen participants together completed a closeness-building task (Aron et al., 1997) that had previously been shown to create high levels of interpersonal closeness among pairs of strangers in a short period of time. Finally, these two participants returned to their previous groups and were asked to discuss the experience with the rest of the group, in order to 'bring everyone up to date'.

At each stage of the experiment, participants were asked to divide $500 between the two teams. The findings revealed that participants showed intergroup bias (allo-cating more money to the ingroup than the outgroup) after phase 1; that is, follow-ing categorization but before the introduction of intergroup competition. Intergroup bias was even greater following the introduction of competition in phase 2. How-ever, after learning about the positive intergroup contact experience of one group

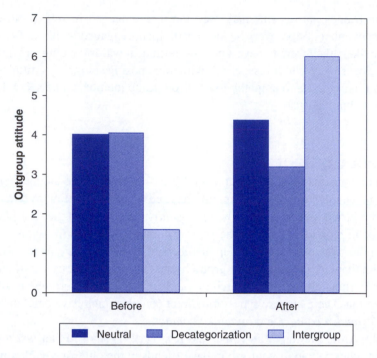

Figure 7.2 The effect of extended contact stories involving disabled and non-disabled children on outgroup attitudes towards the disabled among primary school children. Data from Cameron and Rutland (2006)

member in the final phase of the experiment, even participants not directly involved in the closeness-building task showed a reduction in intergroup bias (see Text Box 1.2 in Chapter 1 for more details about Wright and colleagues' research).

Extended contact has been successfully applied with children in educational contexts. Cameron and Rutland (2006) asked non-disabled children aged between 5 and 10 years to take part in a 6-week intervention study which involved them being read weekly stories featuring disabled and non-disabled children in friendship contexts. Participants were assigned to one of three conditions: an extended intergroup condition, in which the stories emphasized the group memberships of the characters and highlighted their typicality as group members, a depersonalized condition in which stories emphasized individual characteristics of the protagonists, and a neutral condition in which neither group membership nor personal characteristics were highlighted. Attitudes towards the disabled became more positive after the intervention, but only in the intergroup extended contact condition (see Figure 7.2). This finding is important, because it illustrates that the group membership of those involved in extended contact should remain salient if the interventions are to lead to more positive attitudes towards the outgroup in general (consistent with Hewstone & Brown's, 1986, *mutual intergroup differentiation model*).

Extended contact, like cross-group friendship, improves outgroup attitudes by reducing intergroup anxiety (Paolini et al., 2004; Turner, Hewstone, Voci, & Vonofakou, 2008). The more ingroup members participants know have outgroup friends, the less anxious they are at the prospect of interacting with outgroup members themselves, and in turn, the more positive their outgroup attitudes become. This is because observing a positive relationship between members of the ingroup and outgroup is likely to reduce negative expectations about future interactions with the outgroup. Extended cross-group friendship may be especially useful in situations where there is less opportunity for contact, as an individual does not need to *personally know* an outgroup member in order to benefit from it (Turner et al., 2007).

But what about *very* highly segregated settings, where people may not know *anyone* who has outgroup friends? In this situation, even extended contact may run into problems. A second type of indirect contact, however, does not suffer from this limitation. **Imagined contact** is the mental simulation of a social interaction with a member or members of an outgroup (Crisp & Turner, 2009). The basic idea is that mentally simulating a positive contact experience activates concepts normally associated with successful interactions with members of other groups. These can include feeling more comfortable and less apprehensive about the prospect of future contact with the group, and this reduced anxiety should reduce negative outgroup attitudes. Imagery works because it increases the accessibility of thoughts and feelings that are typically associated with the social situation at hand. Imagining being in a crowd, for example, has been shown to activate feelings of being 'lost in a crowd' and 'unaccountable', feelings which are associated with less helping behaviour in real situations (Garcia et al., 2002). Similarly, when people imagine intergroup contact they should engage in conscious processes that parallel the processes involved in actual intergroup contact. They may, for example, actively think about what they would learn about the outgroup member, how they would feel during the interaction, and how this would influence their perceptions of that outgroup member and the outgroup more generally. In turn, this should lead to more positive evaluations of the outgroup, similar to the effects of face-to-face contact.

To test this idea, Turner, Crisp, and Lambert (2007) asked young participants to spend a minute imagining a positive interaction with an elderly stranger. Participants in a control condition were asked to imagine an outdoor scene instead. After writing down what they had imagined, participants were told about a future study in which they would be asked to interact with either an elderly person or a young person, and were asked to indicate how keen they would be to take part in these two interactions. While participants in the control condition were biased in favour of young people, preferring to interact with a young person rather than an elderly person, those who had previously imagined interacting with an elderly person were equally happy to interact with an elderly person or a young person. Imagining intergroup contact was

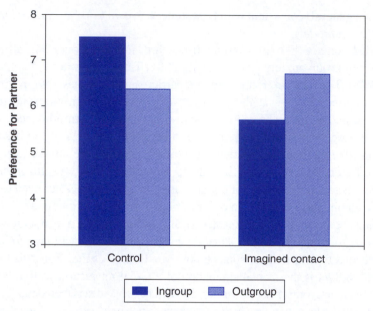

Figure 7.3 The effect of imagined contact on intergroup bias against the elderly. Data from Turner, Crisp, and Lambert (2007)

therefore effective at reducing intergroup bias (see Figure 7.3). Imagined contact has subsequently been shown to improve attitudes towards a variety of target groups including gay men (Turner, Crisp, & Lambert, 2007), Muslims (Turner & Crisp, 2009), and Indigenous people in Mexico (an ethnic minority compared to the majority Mestizo group; Stathi & Crisp, 2008).

So how do direct and indirect forms of contact compare to one another? On the one hand, indirect forms of contact are more versatile because they are not reliant on opportunity for contact, which means they can be used to improve attitudes even in segregated settings (e.g. Turner, Hewstone, & Voci, 2007; Turner et al., 2008). On the other hand, attitudes based on direct experience are thought to be longer-lasting and more powerful than attitudes based on indirect experiences (Fazio, Powell, & Herr, 1983; Stangor, Sullivan, & Ford, 1991). Research comparing actual and extended contact, for example, typically shows actual contact to have the stronger impact on prejudice (Paolini et al., 2004; Turner, Hewstone, & Voci, 2007).

Crisp and Turner (2009) have proposed an integrative model that incorporates these different types of contact, arguing that imagined, extended and actual contact form a *continuum of contact* interventions, with each recommended depending on how much opportunity for contact there is in a particular context (see Figure 7.4). In situations where there is high segregation and little opportunity for contact, imagined contact may be the only viable intervention to help encourage attitude change and intentions to engage in preliminary contact, or ensure that when that contact

Figure 7.4   Continuum of contact (Turner & Crisp, 2009)

does occur, it does so with open minds and an increased chance of success. When boundaries have begun to permeate, and there are some positive interactions initiated between members of different groups, extended contact will work well to reinforce the impact of isolated contact encounters. Increasing extended contact may lead to the development of friendship networks which include people from different social groups. This may then lead to a cascade of positive direct interactions, with further benefits for intergroup relations.

Summary

In this section, we talked about intergroup contact as a means of prejudice reduction. According to *the contact hypothesis*, contact between members of different social groups can lead to reductions in intergroup bias, but only if there are *social norms* favouring equality, if the groups are of *equal social status*, and if group members *cooperate* to achieve common goals. Although the contact hypothesis has been criticized for failing to specify how the positive effects of contact *generalize* from individual outgroup members to the entire outgroup, and for being overly complex, recent reformulations of the theory have helped deal with these criticisms. More recently, research has suggested that friendship contact is most likely to reduce prejudice towards other groups, but only in settings where there is the opportunity for contact. On the other hand, indirect forms of contact, such as *extended contact* and *imagined contact*, can be useful even in segregated settings.

CHAPTER SUMMARY

In this chapter we have discussed the psychological processes that can help us to explain prejudice, discrimination and social conflict. We first saw how pervasive kinds of prejudice in the form of racism and sexism have evolved to take account of the development of egalitarian social norms. *Aversive racism* and *ambivalent sexism* are characterized by people holding conflicting positive and negative views about groups at the same time. Prejudice can also be explicit or implicit in nature.

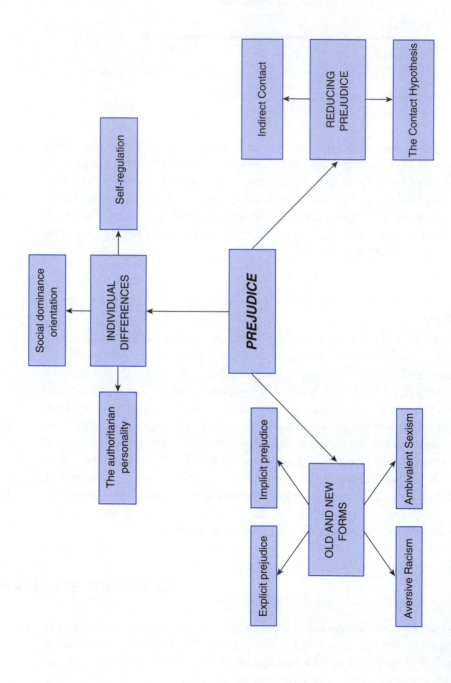

Figure 7.5 Memory map

Although there is not much evidence that individual differences in authoritarianism can explain prejudice, differences in the degree to which individuals have a *social dominance orientation* appear to have a role in explaining why some people are more biased than others. Modern forms of prejudice are characterized by a desire to be egalitarian but with implicit negative attitudes, and individuals can become more egalitarian via a process of *self-regulation*, both through internal regulation and via interactive dialogue with others. On the basis of this knowledge about the nature of prejudice, psychologists have sought to develop ways of reducing intergroup bias and encouraging more egalitarianism. *Intergroup contact* works by getting members of ingroups and outgroups together under conditions that favour positive outcomes (e.g. cooperative goals). *Cross-group friendship* is a particularly effective form of contact, although it is only useful in settings where there is the opportunity for contact, for example in multicultural communities. Indirect forms of contact, such as *extended contact* and *imagined contact*, can be utilized in settings where there are higher levels of segregation in order to reduce prejudice.

Taking it Further

Try This

Several different interventions have been devised by social psychologists to reduce prejudice. In this chapter, we discussed contact-based interventions, which have been developed on the premise that people are prejudiced in part because of lack of experience with other groups. However, research findings suggest that personality also plays a role in explaining prejudice. Try devising an intervention strategy to reduce prejudice in an educational setting, based on what you have learnt about the psychological bases of prejudice in this chapter. Use a form or forms of contact in your intervention, but make sure your intervention takes personality factors into account (for instance, will your form of contact work as well for people with high as with low social dominance orientation, and if not, what could you do to compensate?).

Debate This

Although the expression of prejudice has become less socially acceptable over time, there is nonetheless evidence that different forms of prejudice, including sexism, racism, and homophobia, still exist. Will society ever be completely rid of prejudice? Or is prejudice a 'normal' aspect of society that we can try to reduce, but that we will never be able to eliminate? Based on what we know about prejudice and prejudice reduction, what are our best hopes of eliminating prejudice?

Something for the Weekend

We have been focused in much of this chapter on reducing prejudice via contact, but in essence what we are talking about is attitude change. Contact is therefore a distinct way of persuading someone to change their negative attitude towards a certain group into a positive one. But if you think back, every single chapter so far has something to contribute to our understanding of attitude change. Come up with a mental map that links prejudice to one concept, phenomenon or theory from each chapter that we've covered so far, and say why the link is there. This could be to do with majority influence (societal changes in explicit prejudice), cognitive dissonance (if anti-racist laws make egalitarian behaviour more likely, this will lead to internal attitude change) or even leadership (Barack Obama represents an inherently non-racist choice by American society). Compare your mental map with others in your class – you'll be surprised at how many different links you can make between all of the topics and issues we've covered so far in the book (and we're only half way through!).

Further Readings

The Essentials

Hewstone, M., Rubin, M., & Willis, H. (2002). Intergroup bias. *Annual Review of Psychology*, *53*, 575–604.

This review article will tell you everything you need to know about different forms of intergroup bias, their causes and their consequences.

Next Steps

Turner, R.N., Hewstone, M., Voci, A., Paolini, S., & Christ, O. (2007). Reducing prejudice via direct and extended cross-group friendship. *European Review of Social Psychology*, *18*, 212–255.

Crisp, R.J. & Turner, R.N. (2009). Can imagined interactions produce positive perceptions? Reducing prejudice through simulated social contact. *American Psychologist*, *64*, 231–240.

These two recent review articles focus more specifically on the different types of intergroup contact discussed in this chapter (direct, extended, and imagined contact), explaining how they reduce prejudice and when they are most effective at doing so.

Delving Deeper

Brown, R.J. (1995). *Prejudice: Its social psychology* (chp. 8). Oxford: Blackwell.

This comprehensive book is written by one of the leaders in the field. It will give you an exhaustive account of all the key areas of research on prejudice, and is written in an engaging and accessible style.

Intergroup Relations

8

Intergroup Relations

In the previous chapter we focused on prejudice as an attitude, and contact as a way of changing that attitude towards a particular group. In this chapter we will examine prejudice from a different perspective, not so much as an attitude, but more in terms of social categorization and the psychological representation of the relationship between 'us' and 'them'. As you will see, there are clear points of convergence between the work we will discuss here and that discussed in Chapter 7. However, it might be useful to think about prejudice research as focused on improving the attitudes held by majorities towards minority groups, while research on intergroup relations as about taking a step back and looking at what we can do to understand and alleviate the forces that compel groups to come into conflict, or hold negative views of one another, in the first place.

So we'll start with social categorization (you might want a quick refresher at this point – we talked about the basics in Chapter 3). Social categorization is central to explaining intergroup relations, because without it, there would be no conflicts or difficulties between different groups. Put quite simply, poor intergroup relations arise because of a negative view of 'them' relative to 'us', based on the recognition that some people are in the same social category as ourselves and some people are not. This self-inclusion and the distinction between ingroups and outgroups is critical to understanding intergroup relations. In this chapter we consider how social categorization affects relations between people belonging to different social groups. We also consider how *changing* the way in which these social categories are perceived can alleviate poor intergroup relations. We begin by discussing a classic study of intergroup relations carried out by Muzafer Sherif and colleagues in the 1950s that set the agenda for the next 50 years of research into intergroup relations, before next discussing the theories that emerged from this pivotal research.

THEORIES OF INTERGROUP RELATIONS

Sherif's Summer Camp Studies

Sherif and colleagues (Sherif & Sherif, 1953; Sherif, White, & Harvey, 1955) realized that a long-standing American tradition could provide an ideal setting in which to observe intergroup behaviour from inception to dissolution (and thus avoid any of the typical confounding influences with real and established social group memberships, such as political, economic and historic relational factors, all of which can obscure the psychological elements in group processes). Their idea was to take over a boys summer camp at Robbers Cave State Park (150 miles south of Oklahoma City) where 20 white, middle-class 11- to 12-year-old boys would go to take part in varied outdoor pursuits.

The study worked in three stages. In Stage 1, Sherif wanted to observe the immediate effects of group formation; in Stage 2, the effects of introducing competition between the groups was studied. In Stage 3, he wanted to see whether certain factors could reduce any conflict that had occurred at stages 1 and 2. In this way, Sherif planned to obtain a model of intergroup behaviour at all the stages from group formation to interaction and eventual dissolution.

At Stage 1 the boys had just arrived at the camp and knew nothing of each other. The first thing that happened was that they were placed, on a purely random basis, into two groups for the remainder of the two weeks at the camp (this was not an unusual thing; such camps are based on team competition but this division into arbitrary groups suited the interests of the psychologists perfectly). On doing this, Sherif immediately observed *spontaneous suggestions for competition* between the two groups, *spontaneous social comparisons* and *the development of group icons*. That is to say, as soon as the group of boys was split in two, and allocated different group labels, they began to suggest that the two groups compete against each other. They began to throw verbal taunts at each other (along the lines of, 'Our group is better than yours!'). One group called themselves the 'Rattlers' and the other the 'Eagles'. Interestingly, within a short time the boys in the respective groups had made some icons to represent the animal name of their group, and put it above their (separate) dormitory huts. This was a first indication of the development of a group norm and *social identity* (a term that we heard first in Chapter 1, and that we'll discuss later on in this chapter).

Having observed these immediate behavioural effects, Sherif wanted to introduce a particular element into the context that he believed might be a key determinant of intergroup hostility. Again, he took advantage of a typical element of the summer camp experience: the introduction of competitive games between the groups. The introduction of these games (including baseball and tug-of-war) had some expected effects. Sherif and colleagues observed a dramatic rise in derogation between the two groups. This culminated in the groups even physically attacking each others' 'icons' (including burning their flag and ransacking their cabin). Another consequence of imposing the group labels and the competition was that interpersonal affiliations gave way to intergroup concerns; by Stage 2, 93 per cent of friendships were defined by ingroup affiliation (i.e. friends were almost exclusively within-group, and rarely crossed the intergroup boundary). This supports Tajfel's (1978) idea that there are two ways to define social encounters: from interpersonal through to intergroup. In the case of the summer camp, relations had become very much defined at the intergroup end of this continuum. This intensification of ingroup loyalty and increase in hostility towards the outgroup is called *ethnocentrism* (Sumner, 1906).

Having observed a dramatic increase in bias following the introduction of competition, Sherif was then interested in seeing whether changing other aspects of the group context could attenuate this intergroup hostility. The psychologists arranged for the boys' bus to break down on their way back from a competitive activity one day (this was, of course, a set-up). They arranged it so that only if the two groups worked together – cooperated – could they push start the bus in time to get back for lunch. Here, then, Sherif had introduced a cooperative goal in order to gain a reward that would be beneficial for both groups. Cooperation between the groups did indeed lead to a reduction in intergroup conflict and a considerable reduction in the observed derogation between the two groups.

Realistic Group Conflict Theory

Sherif's summer camp studies were hugely influential. They were the first time that anyone had attempted to systematically examine the psychological and behavioural consequences of group formation, competition, and cooperation whilst controlling for other possible factors. These findings supported an explanation for prejudice, discrimination and intergroup conflict called **realistic group conflict theory** (Levine & Campbell, 1972). According to this theory, conflict between groups is the result of the perception of scarce resources. The theory would predict, for instance, that under conditions of economic deprivation intergroup conflict would increase (this is similar to the frustration-aggression hypothesis described in Chapter 9). Outgroup derogation and ingroup favouritism as observed in Sherif's summer camp studies supports this contention; once competition had been introduced at Stage 2, conflict and examples of ingroup bias dramatically increased. The conflict can be seen as 'realistic' because it is based on a real competition for resources (in Sherif's case, competition for prized rewards such as medals and penknives). But does this mean that all conflict is due to competition for scarce resources? In Sherif's studies, spontaneous derogation of the outgroup occurred at Stage 1, when all that had happened was that the groups had been divided into two groups. Could *mere* categorization therefore be enough on its own to incite intergroup bias? Some years later the idea that *just being categorized* could lead to prejudice was addressed experimentally in what would become one of the most influential experiments in social psychology.

The Minimal Group Paradigm

Henri Tajfel was interested in systematically finding the baseline conditions under which people would prefer their own group over other groups. Put another way, he wanted to find, under highly controlled experimental conditions, what might be the *minimal* conditions necessary to observe prejudice (Sherif's summer camp studies were observational, and so less powerful than experimentally controlling the context). In order to do this he created a paradigm that removed all the possible factors that might accentuate intergroup bias, so that all that was left was mere categorization as ingroup and outgroup. Tajfel wanted to know whether simply being categorized into one group versus another would be *sufficient*, without any differences in political or religious ideology, economic imbalance or a history of conflict, to elicit intergroup bias. In actuality, Tajfel did not expect mere categorization to elicit bias; he was simply trying to find the baseline no-bias conditions from which to incrementally add further possible contributing factors. However, to his surprise he found that the conditions that could lead to intergroup bias were far more minimal than anyone could have imagined.

Tajfel's **minimal group paradigm** (Tajfel, Billig, Bundy, & Flament 1971) describes an experimental context that creates an ad hoc basis for categorization and includes measures of evaluation of, and discrimination between, the groups involved. In Tajfel's original experiment the participants, who were schoolchildren, were allocated to two groups on an arbitrary basis (rather like they were in Sherif's summer camp studies). The allocation into the two different groups was done by showing the participants a number of slides of abstract paintings. These were by the painters Paul Klee and Wassily Kandinsky who, to the participants, were unfamiliar, and had broadly similar abstract styles. Participants noted for each slide which one they preferred. After all the slides had been shown the experimenters pretended to go away and compare each person's responses. After a short while they came back and told each participant that they were either in the 'Klee' or 'Kandinsky' group. This feedback was, however, contrived by the experimenter, and allocation to groups was in fact random and meaningless.

Participants then completed a task in which they were required to allocate points (via code numbers) to people in the two groups. The points represented money and participants were told that at the end of the task they would receive the money allocated via points to their code number by the other people doing the task. The idea was that this allocation of points would represent behavioural discrimination (more points given to members of the ingroup compared to the outgroup represents ingroup favouritism). Allocation was completely anonymous; participants did not know who was in which group nor to whom they were allocating points. Participants could not allocate points to themselves, thus removing any element of self-interest from the task. The points were allocated via a series of decision matrices on which participants indicated with a cross through one column how much the ingroup and how much the outgroup member should receive. There were different types of matrix which were used to assess different 'strategies' of allocation (we discuss these strategies in more detail below). For now, the important thing is that the total amount of points allocated to the ingroup and outgroup could be calculated from these matrices, and from this the experimenters could assess whether there was an ingroup favouring bias.

The unique characteristic of this minimal group paradigm was that the groups really did represent the most basic form of social categorization. Unlike real social groups defined by nationality, religion, or age, there was no economic imbalance, political motivations, past interaction, or even any meaning ascribed to these groups. They were the most basic form of group membership, based on simply being in one group or the other.

So what would happen in this experiment? Just for a moment put yourself in the position of someone taking part. You have to allocate points to anonymous others. You can't give points to yourself, so any money you receive at the end of the experiment will be down to what other people give to you. But they don't know who you are. The only thing you know about the people listed on each matrix that you fill in is that they are in one group (your group) or the other group. There's no objective reason to give more points to someone just because they are in your group and not the other (the group labels have no impact on how much money you personally will receive at the end), so what would you do?

Well, even in this most minimal of group contexts, Tajfel and colleagues observed a persistent tendency for participants to allocate more points to people in their own group compared to people in other groups. Remember that the allocation of points to individuals was anonymous (otherwise people may have recognized their friends and given them more points) and all that distinguished people was a random code number (e.g. person number: 419) and their group membership (e.g. Klee or Kandinsky). Amazingly, Tajfel and colleagues found that mere categorization – simply knowing that someone is in the same group as you – was sufficient to elicit intergroup bias. People ignored the logic that told them that the group labels made no difference to how much money they would receive at the end; for some reason they used the category labels to guide their allocations. Importantly, if different allocation of points to the two groups had no impact on the objective of the exercise (i.e. to amass money for oneself), then this suggests that there must be some other more implicit *psychological* motivation that differential allocation of points served.

This *mere categorization effect* has been replicated many times using many different ways to categorize people and many different measures of evaluation. It is a very robust finding (Brewer, 1979; Mullen, Brown & Smith, 1992). This finding is so important because it suggests that there is a psychological component to prejudice, beyond any economic, political, or historical factor. Tajfel et al. demonstrated that the mere recognition that someone is in a different group to oneself is enough for us to like them less, quite independent from the apparent goals and aims of the task at hand. This suggested a then unknown psychological motivation pushing people to differentiate their own group from others. In the next section, we introduce the theories that have been put forward to explain the mere categorization effect, and therefore how categorization can lead to intergroup bias.

The Category Differentiation Model

Doise (1978) suggested a model of categorization effects that can explain why we observe differential allocation of points as a function of group membership in the minimal group paradigm. The **category differentiation model** specifies that imposing a system of classification on a series of previously unordered stimuli can lead to an accentuation of the differences *between* categories and an attenuation of similarities *within* categories. Put another way, when category labels are made salient (such as in the minimal group paradigm), according to Doise there is then an automatic tendency to think of all people who are in the same category as being similar to one another, and a corresponding automatic tendency to think of all people who are in different categories as being different from one another (see Figure 8.1). As discussed in Chapter 3, people are sometimes *cognitive misers*; they have a general motivation to simplify their view of the world by using broad generalizations – social categories. The category differentiation model describes how this process works when there is an ingroup and a corresponding outgroup category. The accentuation of similarities within categories, and the accentuation of differences between categories, simplifies things so that information about people in the immediate context can be more efficiently processed, enabling judgement to be made more easily and with less effort.

The power of this categorization process has been consistently and reliably demonstrated in a number of domains including judgements of both physical and social stimuli (e.g. Crisp & Hewstone, 1999; Eiser, Van der Pligt & Gossop, 1979; Tajfel & Wilkes, 1963). But how does this apparently basic-level cognitive mechanism help to explain allocation of points in the minimal group paradigm? If we examine the procedure in Tajfel et al.'s experiment we can see how Doise's (1978) proposed mechanism might apply. In the minimal group paradigm participants are faced

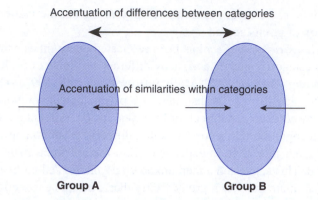

Figure 8.1   Representation of category differentiation (ovals represent all the groups' attributes)

with a decision regarding how they should allocate the points. They know that they can't allocate points to themselves, and that there is really nothing they can do to maximize the potential reward they will gain at the end of the experiment when the money is distributed. There is, however, still this observed tendency for people to allocate more points to ingroup members than outgroup members (even though this doesn't help them achieve the objective goal of the task, to maximize their personal profit). The category differential model offers the implicit psychological motivation that can explain the mere categorization effect. If people are implicitly motivated to simplify their perception of social contexts (see Chapter 3) they should use some functional mechanism, such as the mechanism specified by the category differentiation model, to achieve this aim. The only way they can express this desire to classify and simplify is to use the only thing in the minimal context that lends itself to this aim: the point allocations. Allocating more points to one group compared to another group is an expression of category differentiation: it accentuates the differences between people in two categories.

The way the matrices were used in the minimal group paradigm offers a means to test directly the predictions derived from the category differentiation model. As we mentioned above, there were different versions of the matrices which assessed different allocation strategies. Two strategies are of primary interest for distinguishing support for the category differentiation model. On some matrices the participant had the choice between choosing either of two boxes, both of which allocated more points to the ingroup than the outgroup. The difference between these two boxes was defined in two ways: the total number of points that would be given to the ingroup and the difference between the number of points given to the ingroup *compared* to the outgroup. Importantly, choosing to maximize the number of points going to the ingroup would *minimize* the difference in the number of points going to the ingroup compared to the outgroup. In other words, allocating more points to the ingroup would also mean allocating more points, in relative terms, to the outgroup. Maximizing ingroup profit could only be achieved by sacrificing the amount of differentiation (the difference in points given to the ingroup and outgroup). It was therefore possible to identify two different strategies participants were using in their allocations.

To illustrate, Box 1 might indicate 25 points for the ingroup member and 21 points for the outgroup member. Box 2, on the same matrix, might indicate 7 points for the ingroup member and 1 point for the outgroup member. The choice of the Box 1 (25/21) would indicate that the participants are mostly concerned with maximizing the total number of points allocated to their group. In contrast, the choice of the second allocation (7/1) would indicate that participants were not interested in maximizing their group's profit overall, but rather in maximizing the *differentiation* between the ingroup and the outgroup in terms of points allocated. This is because although the first allocation would give the ingroup 25 points, it would also give the outgroup 21 points, leaving the outgroup with only 4 points less than the ingroup. But, if the ingroup sacrificed having more points overall and went for the 7 points, this would mean that the outgroup would only get 1 point, creating a larger *difference* (of 6 points) between the ingroup and outgroup. If differentiating the ingroup from the outgroup was primary in the participants' mind then they would choose Box 2 (7/1), but if they were not particularly bothered about being different from the outgroup then one might expect them to choose Box 1 (25/21) as this overall maximizes the total profit for the ingroup.

Examination of the choices made in the minimal group paradigm reveals a consistent tendency to choose *maximum differentiation*. This therefore supports Doise's idea that giving more to ingroup members compared to outgroup members reflects a fundamental motivation towards categorizing and simplifying.

The elegance of this model makes it very appealing, but it cannot be the whole story. Although there is undoubtedly a drive towards maximal differentiation in the minimal group paradigm, this is not the only observed tendency. As well as going for distributions of points that differentiate the ingroup from the outgroup to the greatest extent, participants also showed a strong tendency to *favour* their own group over the outgroup. If all that was important was maximizing the difference between the ingroup and outgroup then why not allocate more points to the outgroup than the ingroup? This would satisfy the same drive towards differentiation as giving more to the ingroup than the outgroup. However, this does not happen; the differentiation is always ingroup favouring. In order to explain this persistent ingroup favouritism we require another theory. This theory, which we describe below, makes specific reference to something the category differentiation model ignores: self-inclusion.

Social Identity Theory

The finding that mere categorization can lead to ingroup favouritism has implications for every aspect of our understanding of intergroup relations. The fact that social categorization was apparently so important in determining discrimination between ingroups and outgroups required a theory that could explain ingroup favouritism in the minimal group paradigm. With John Turner, Henri Tajfel came up with such a theory.

Social identity theory (Tajfel & Turner, 1979) is a theoretical account of the relationship between personal (i.e. individual) and social (i.e. group membership) identity. With respect to judgements about people in different groups, the logic goes like this. First, Tajfel and Turner assume that people prefer to have a positive self-concept (i.e. positive self-esteem (feeling good about themselves); we know this is a valid assumption as it had been demonstrated empirically many times, e.g. Baumeister, 1998; Sears, 1983). The theory states that one source of self-esteem is the social groups to which we belong. Put simply, if our social groups are seen as being of high status and positively valued, then by extension we, as members of such groups, can also view ourselves positively (see Abrams & Hogg, 1990). Because of the link between how positive our groups are and how positively we see ourselves, Tajfel and Turner argue that we are motivated to do what we can to increase the status of our own group because, by extension, if our group does better than others then we also look good as individual members of that group. In the minimal group paradigm, social identity theory can explain why people have a tendency to award more points to their own group compared to the other group. In so doing, this will increase the status of the ingroup, relative to the outgroup, and as such increase the self-esteem of the group members (see Rubin & Hewstone, 1998, for a review of research into this self-esteem hypothesis).

Category differentiation can therefore satisfy the motivation to clarify and simplify, whereas social identity theory can provide the motivational explanation for the ingroup favouring direction of differential points allocation. We can refer to this combined desire to be differentiated from outgroups, and to be differentiated in a way that is ingroup favouring, as a desire for *positive distinctiveness*. Broadly speaking, there is much evidence that there is a strong motivation to achieve such positive distinctiveness from outgroups. Indeed, anything that threatens this distinctiveness can increase intergroup bias, apparently in a desire to re-establish positive differentiation, in the same way as participants in Tajfel et al.'s original experiment appear to use points allocation as a means of differentiating the ingroup from the outgroup (Jetten, Spears, & Postmes, 2004). However, despite the appeal of the social identity theory explanation, the strength of the mere categorization effect has meant a proliferation of theories as alternatives to the category differentiation and social identity perspectives. Below we outline some of these alternatives.

Belief Similarity

One criticism of the original Tajfel et al. (1971) minimal group paradigm experiment was that allocation to the two groups was not, in fact, entirely minimal, but that there was a basis for **belief similarity** that could have accounted for liking. Recall that participants were allocated to different groups on the basis of their apparent preference for the Klee or Kandinsky abstract paintings. Although these ad hoc social categorizations were largely meaningless, participants could have inferred that people who were allocated to the same group as them, because they liked the same painting style, perhaps shared other beliefs in common. In Chapter 11 on affiliation and attraction we will see how belief similarity can account for some degree of interpersonal attraction. Perhaps intergroup bias in Tajfel's experiment was not, therefore, to do with intergroup processes at all, but with *interpersonal* processes of belief similarity. To test this hypothesis Billig and Tajfel (1973) carried out a replication of the original minimal group paradigm experiment but made some important changes. In the new condition participants saw clearly that they were allocated to groups on a purely *random* basis: the toss of a coin. This random allocation was then compared with categorization based on belief similarity, that is, allocation on the basis for apparent liking of the Klee or Kandinksy abstract paintings. Billig and Tajfel's findings can be seen in Figure 8.2. Quite clearly, there was more intergroup bias in the belief similarity condition compared to the random allocation condition. However, what is important is that although there was less bias in the random allocation condition, there was *not* an elimination of bias. In other words, even when participants were allocated to the minimal groups on the basis of a toss of a coin, they still gave more points to members of their own group compared to members of the outgroup. This suggests that while belief similarity can increase intergroup bias, just like competition between groups, it is not a *necessary* precondition to observe bias. Mere categorization, even when it is ostensibly based on purely random criteria, is enough for people to favour their own group over others.

Self-Categorization Theory

Self-categorization theory (Turner, Hogg, Oakes, Reicher, & Wetherell, 1987) is based on social identity theory but re-emphasizes the cognitive processes associated with contextual affiliation to social groups. Rather than focusing on motivational processes (as social identity theory does), *self-categorization theory* outlines how identity salience leads to depersonalization, assimilation to group norms, and self-stereotyping, and how these cognitive processes can impact on intergroup behaviour such as prejudice and discrimination. In a salient group context, Turner et al. argued that people depersonalize and take on the characteristics associated with the prototypic qualities of their groups (see Chapter 3 for a discussion of category structure,

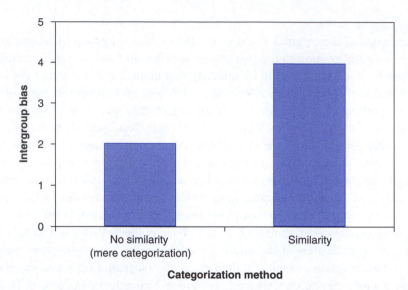

Figure 8.2 Effects of belief similarity on points allocations in the minimal group. Data from Billig and Tajfel (1973)

prototypes, and stereotypes). Similar to the category differentiation model (Doise, 1976), self-categorization theory specifies a *meta-contrast principle* that describes the perception of increased similarity within, and increased differentiation between, ingroup and outgroup categories (Oakes & Turner, 1990). Self-categorization theory states that social categorization and intergroup discrimination are (a) context dependent and (b) involve a search for meaning.

An elaboration of the motivational component of self-categorization theory is offered by Hogg's (2001) **subjective uncertainty reduction hypothesis**. Social categorization clarifies and defines social situations, providing a means for predicting how outgroupers will behave, and providing a set of prescriptive ingroup norms to guide perceivers. Group members are thus motivated to maintain the distinctiveness of their own groups from others in order to reduce subjective uncertainty (Hogg, 2001; Hogg & Mullin, 1999). The motive of reducing uncertainty via self-categorization and meta-contrast will lead members of valued groups to compare the ingroup with the outgroup, particularly when positivity and distinctiveness are threatened. The reduction of uncertainty caused by ingroup identification imbues people who are associated with this reduction (i.e. ingroup members, including the self) with a positive valence. Ingroup favouritism is explained as a reflection of the resulting perceived differences in intergroup positivity (Hogg & Abrams, 1993).

An elaboration on the idea that people have a need to differentiate their social identities can be seen in the form of Brewer's (1991) **optimal distinctiveness theory**. This theory argues that people are motivated to satisfy *two* needs which conflict with one another. These are the need for assimilation *and* the need for differentiation. People seek out groups that provide a balance in satisfying these two motives. This theory argues that bias will result when the need for differentiation is not fulfilled, and so can be seen as a further specification of the distinctiveness motivations outlined above.

Self-Anchoring Theory

An explanation of intergroup bias that is applicable particularly to the minimal group paradigm is **self-anchoring theory** (Cadinu & Rothbart, 1996). The foundation for the idea that the self can be used as an informational base in social judgement is outlined more generally by the concept of *social projection* (Clement & Krueger, 2000; Krueger & Clement, 1996), which refers to people's tendency to predict the feelings, thoughts and behaviours of others based on their own feelings, thoughts and behaviours (see Chapter 2's discussion of attribution theory). Social projection is stronger when the target person is similar to self. In an intergroup context this suggests that people will project self attributes onto the ingroup to a greater extent than the outgroup (Marks & Miller, 1987). This ingroup-outgroup projection asymmetry may help to explain intergroup bias in the minimal group paradigm. Since people generally have a favourable self-concept (Baumeister, 1998; Sears, 1983), projection of positive self-beliefs onto others in one's ingroup (but not outgroup) leads to a perception that the ingroup possesses more favourable attributes than the outgroup (see Otten & Wentura, 1999). Previous demonstrations of this theory have been restricted to minimal group settings, where ingroups are not defined by an existing knowledge base, and where projection is functional because it provides information about groups where there is none (satisfying drives towards uncertainty reduction and cognitive efficiency). As such, it may be more applicable when groups are new to people (e.g. when going to university and figuring out what it means to be a university student – what attitudes and behaviours one is supposed to have).

Terror Management Theory

A rather different approach to intergroup relations is offered by **terror management theory** (Greenberg, Pyszczynski, & Solomon, 1986). According to this theory, humans have a strong survival instinct. Unlike other animals, however, we also possess the intellectual capacity to realize that one day we will die, a fact that can paralyse us with fear at the prospect of our own mortality. Terror management theory argues that, to manage our terror, we adopt a cultural worldview (a set of values, for example religious beliefs and social norms) that provides a sense of meaning to the world and helps us maintain our belief that our lives are important and significant. Our cultural worldview is important because it allows us to transcend death, either literally, through a belief in an afterlife, or symbolically, through lasting cultural achievements, so that we will not be forgotten. According to the theory, people who believe they are meeting the values of their cultural worldview have higher self-esteem because they are more confident about attaining immortality in some form. If belief in a cultural worldview provides protection against fear of death, reminding someone of their mortality will increase their need for that worldview, and therefore increase efforts to protect it from those who violate it. In these circumstances, the theory predicts that people will evaluate ingroup members more positively because they validate an individual's personal worldview, but outgroup members more nega-tively because they are dissimilar and therefore seen as a threat to an individual's worldview.

To test this premise, Greenberg et al. (1990) asked Christian participants to form impressions of Christian and Jewish individuals after heightening 'mortal-ity salience'; that is, reminding people of the prospect of their own death. They found that mortality salience predicted a more positive evaluation of the Chris-tian individual and a more negative evaluation of Jews. Harmon-Jones, Green-berg, Solomon, and Simon (1996) conducted a similar test using the minimal group paradigm. Participants who were assigned at random to groups wrote about death or a neutral topic prior to a resource allocation task. Participants in the mortality salience condition showed higher intergroup bias than those in the control condition.

Terror management theory might help to explain extreme intergroup behav-iour as well as simple outgroup derogation. Hayes, Schimel, and Williams (2008) argue that during severe conflicts between members of groups with opposing worldviews, group members may resort to the annihilation of outgroup members. This might occur for two reasons. First, if outgroup members die while ingroup members continue to exist, group members may infer that their own beliefs must be correct in their worldview: the opposing group's beliefs were insufficient to protect them from death. Second, by killing outgroup members, the number of people holding the threatening worldview can be reduced or even eliminated. In sum, the annihilation of outgroup members should reduce anxiety about death by protecting one's conception of reality. Hayes and colleagues conducted a study to test this idea.

Christian participants were assigned to one of three conditions. In the *worldview threat condition*, they read a news article about how Muslims were

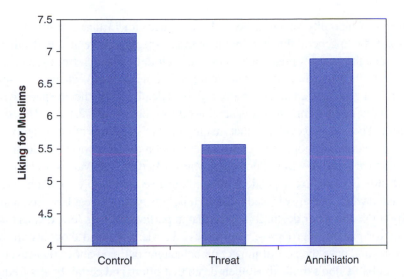

Figure 8.3 Data from Hayes, Schimel, and Williams (2008) showing the effects of worldview threat on liking for Muslims

actively threatening the Christian population of Nazareth, the childhood home of Christ. In the *annihilation condition*, participants read the same article but were informed at the end of it that, in related news, a number of Muslims had died in a plane crash on route to Nazareth. Participants in the *control condition* read a neutral article. Following the article, participants completed a measure of 'death-thought accessibility' (which assessed how many death-related words they produced on a word-completion task), and were also asked to indicate how much they liked Muslims in general. While participants were significantly more likely to think of death following the article in the worldview threat condition compared to the control condition, learning about the death of some outgroup members significantly reduced death-thought accessibility. Moreover, while participants liked Muslims less in the worldview threat condition than in the control condition, when participants learned about outgroup annihilation, they liked Muslims just as much as participants in the control condition who had not had their worldview threatened (see Figure 8.3). In sum, learning about the annihilation of outgroup members buffered people from death-related anxiety and resulted in less subsequent outgroup derogation. These findings have clear relevance for understanding why people sometimes engage in extreme actions to protect their worldview (for instance, acts of terrorism).

Despite this evidence, there are two concerns with terror management theory as a means of explaining prejudice. First, there are alternative possible interpretations for the effects of mortality salience. Some have argued, for instance, that the observed effects are due to general threat, rather than threat specifically related to death, which would make the theory's predictions more difficult to distinguish from social identity theory. It is therefore important that future research identifies whether self-esteem stems from a general need to reduce anxiety about death, or whether the need to reduce anxiety about death stems from a general need for positive self-esteem (Hewstone et al., 2002). There is also evidence that making people's feelings of uncertainty salient is more predictive of people's reactions to a violation of their worldview than is mortality salience (Van den Bos, Poortvliet, Maas, Miedema, & Van den Ham, 2005). Second, this is a context dependent effect: Negative outgroup evaluations are only accentuated when mortality is made salient. It is, however, not clear how frequently we actually think about our death. It may be that at particular times (e.g. deaths of loved ones) or for particular groups (e.g. terrorists) that death-related thoughts are highly accessible, and have the sort of impact on behaviour outlined above. However, most people probably don't think about their death that often, and certainly less frequently than would be required to explain the wide prevalence of prejudice and discrimination in society. As such, terror management theory cannot offer a fully inclusive account of why people are prejudiced, only how prejudice can be heightened in contexts where they think about, or experience, a fear of death.

Summary

In this section we have talked about intergroup theories of prejudice. We have described Sherif's classic summer camp study. This observational study showed us that competition between groups for scarce resources can accentuate intergroup conflict (as outlined by *realistic group conflict theory*), but that there were also spontaneous social comparisons as soon as the groups were formed, before any competition. This suggested that perhaps there was something simply about being categorized that leads to some level of ingroup bias. In subsequent more controlled experiments carried out by Tajfel in his *minimal group paradigm*, the idea that mere categorization was enough to elicit some degree of bias was confirmed. So, even though the ingroup and outgroup labels used in these experiments had no implications for the aims of individuals (to amass money), participants still allocated more points to the ingroup than the outgroup. Analysis of the matrices used to measure the points allocations suggested that maximal differentiation was more important to participants than maximal ingroup profit – that is, participants appear to be driven more by a desire to differentiate themselves from the outgroup than to amass most points for the ingroup. Doise's *category differentiation model* provides an account of how the desire to create a simplified, meaningful impression of the social context leads to differentiation, but it cannot account for the ingroup favouring direction of this differentiation. For this we need other theories, such as *social identity theory*, which argues that people want positive distinctiveness from outgroups, so as to acquire a positive social identity (positive self-esteem via association with a positively valued group). There are other theories that can also, however, explain why ingroups are persistently seen as more positive than outgroups. These include *self-categorization theory* and the idea that a positive and distinct social identity reduces *subjective uncertainty* by providing normative expectancies about ingroups and outgroups. *Self-anchoring theory* argues that for novel ingroups, we project our own positive attributes to create a positive norm, but we don't do this for outgroups. Finally, *terror management theory* argues that a fear of death may also motivate us to favour ingroups over outgroups. Having outlined the major theoretical explanations for the emergence of prejudice and discrimination between groups, in the second half of this chapter we now return to what Sherif tried to do in Stage 3 of his summer camp studies: *improve* intergroup relations.

IMPROVING INTERGROUP RELATIONS

In Chapter 7, we talked about intergroup contact as a means of reducing prejudice. Intergroup contact improves intergroup relations primarily by changing how we think and feel about the *outgroup*. There are, however, a number of alternative approaches to improving intergroup relations based on the social categorization perspectives that we have been discussing in this chapter. These interventions change our perception of the relationship between the outgroup *and* the ingroup. Here we will talk about three such approaches to improving intergroup relations: the common ingroup identity model, crossed categorization, and multiple categorization.

The Common Ingroup Identity Model

According to the **common ingroup identity model** (Gaertner & Dovidio, 2000), one way of improving intergroup relations is through *recategorization* from a two-group ('us' vs. 'them') representation to a one-group representation. Recall that category differentiation between ingroups and outgroups is a prerequisite for intergroup bias (Doise, 1978): 'we' cannot discriminate against 'them' if they are not

seen as different and distinct from 'us'. Gaertner and Dovidio argue, based on principles outlined by self-categorization theory (Turner et al., 1987), that when members of two groups form a new common ingroup identity that includes both ingroup
and outgroup members (remember Stage 3 of Sherif's summer camp study, where
the two groups of boys had to work together to get the bus back to camp in time
for lunch), intergroup bias will be reduced. By working cooperatively, or by being
reminded that both groups belong to an overarching group, a new ingroup is formed
and as such the same processes that lead to ingroup favouritism in the first place will
now apply to the new common ingroup – which includes the former outgroup members. For all the reasons why ingroups are evaluated more positively than outgroups
that we have discussed earlier, everyone – including the former outgroupers – will
be seen as positive in the recategorized common ingroup.

Gaertner, Mann, Murrell, and Dovidio (1989) carried out a minimal group paradigm experiment to test their model. Two minimal groups were formed in the same
way as described earlier in this chapter. There were three conditions: two-groups
versus one-group versus individuals. Gaertner and Dovidio wanted to test whether
forming a common ingroup would reduce bias in a way that was distinct from something called *decategorization*. Decategorization describes when people stop using
categories to form an impression of others, and instead see them as individuals. This
is like moving from thinking about others in intergroup terms to interpersonal terms
(Tajfel, 1978; see the discussion earlier in this chapter) or shifting from a categorical mode of perception to a individuated mode of perception (see Chapter 3 and the
discussion of dual process theories). Although decategorization should reduce bias,
because it implies a focus on individual characteristics rather than using stereotypes
(see Chapter 3), it is limited in that it only applies to the specific outgroup member
involved in the task – there is no generalization of positive affect to other outgroup
members, and so no overall improvement in intergroup relations (see the discussion
of subtyping above). Gaertner and Dovidio argued that recategorization would not
be limited in such a way because a common ingroup reduces bias by recategorizing
at a new level, rather than abandoning categorization altogether.

In Gaertner et al.'s (1989) experiment participants either sat round a table in a
segregated (AAABBB) or integrated (ABABAB) pattern. In these seating patterns
participants had to take part in a problem-solving exercise requiring either the original (segregated seating) group's decision, a decision to be given by each individual
(integrated seating), or an aggregated group's decision (integrated seating). In the
problem-solving phase the participants in the two-group (segregated seating) condition retained their original group names (A vs. B). In the individuals condition
participants had individual nicknames, and in the one-group (integrated seating)
condition participants were given a new single name than included everyone who
had been in the original two different groups.

The findings are illustrated in Figure 8.4. The first thing to note is that reduced
bias was observed in both the one-group and individuals conditions compared to the

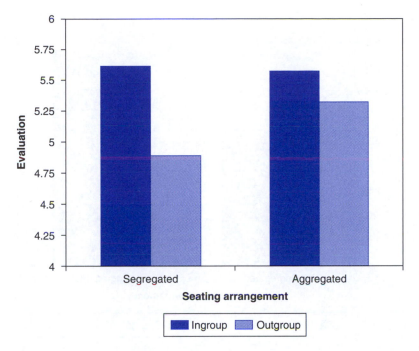

Figure 8.4 Intergroup evaluations as a function of common ingroup categorization. Data from Gaertner et al. (1989)

baseline condition. What is interesting is that this was achieved in two distinct ways. In the individuals condition bias was reduced due to a decrease in the evaluation of the ingroup. This is consistent with decategorization: if the context has moved from being intergroup to interpersonal then the typical boost in evaluation enjoyed by ingroup members when group contexts are made salient will be reversed (Brewer, 1979). In contrast, bias was reduced in the one-group condition due to an increase in the evaluation of the outgroup. This is consistent with the predictions of the common ingroup identity model. Bias is reduced because former outgroup members come to be seen as new ingroup members in the recategorized common ingroup. When groups are formed, bias is created because ingroups are evaluated more positively than outgroups. Following recategorization, however, the former outgroups, who are now in a new common ingroup, will be evaluated positively. In further support of the idea that recategorization and decategorization represent different processes, some additional measures that directly assessed whether participants perceived people as two groups, one overall group, or individuals shows precisely what would be predicted (see Figure 8.5).

Subsequent research has offered much support for the idea that creating a common ingroup can reduce intergroup bias. Importantly, it is not only contact that can lead to the formation of common ingroups, but a range of other factors from simply

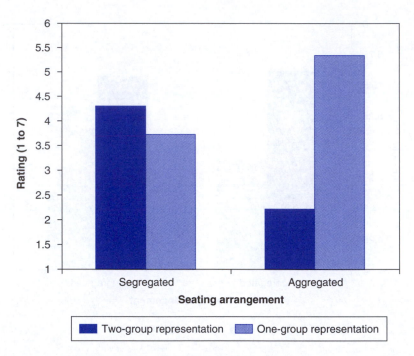

Figure 8.5   Perception of the experimental context as a function of common ingroup categorization. Data from Gaertner et al. (1989)

getting people to wear the same coloured lab coats (Worchel et al., 1978) through to making them more aware of a superordinate inclusive identity (Crisp, Stone, & Hall, 2006). Even putting people in a good mood, by giving them a chocolate bar, can create a common ingroup identity (Dovidio, Gaertner, Isen, & Lowrance, 1995).

Despite the advantages of encouraging a common ingroup identity, Hewstone (1996) questioned whether recategorization can overcome powerful ethnic and racial categorizations on more than a temporary basis, or work where there is intense intergroup conflict. One cannot, for example, imagine Catholics and Protestants in Northern Ireland relinquishing their religious group membership – an important aspect of their identity – to be known simply as 'Northern Irish'. There may also be strong resistance to changes in category boundaries where the two groups differ in size, power or status (Brewer & Gaertner, 2001). British Asians, for example, might be reluctant to accept a superordinate identity of 'British' that is dominated by the majority group, and is seen by many as synonymous with 'white' (Simon, Aufderheider, & Kampmeier, 2001). Applying a common ingroup identity to two groups may be particularly problematic for individuals who highly identify with their initial group membership, because they have a desire to maintain the distinctiveness of this group. In fact, this desire to retain the salience of one's identity can be seen even with relatively short-lived groups (let alone racial or ethic identities).

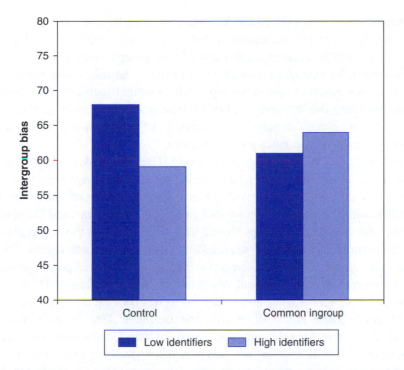

Figure 8.6 Intergroup bias as a function of common ingroup categorization and ingroup identity. Data from Crisp and Beck (2005)

Crisp and Beck (2005) asked students at the University of Birmingham in the UK to indicate how much they identified themselves as a University of Birmingham student. Next, participants were assigned to either a common ingroup condition, or a control condition. In the common ingroup condition, participants were asked to think of five things that University of Birmingham and Aston University students had in common (the latter being a local rival college), while in the control condition, participants did not read this statement. Participants then indicated their attitude towards Birmingham and Aston University students. It emerged that while for low ingroup identifiers this common ingroup task reduced intergroup bias, for high ingroup identifiers it had no effect (see Figure 8.6). Moreover, a similar study by Crisp, Stone and Hall (2006) showed that high identifiers can sometimes react with an increase in intergroup bias following recategorization.

Crossed Categorization

An alternative approach, which also involves changing the way we categorize people into groups, is **crossed categorization**, which entails making two bases for group membership simultaneously salient. For example, for a British white person, rather than thinking about their relationship with the Asian community as *just* white versus Asian, they might be encouraged to think of both groups along a second categorical dimension, for example nationality (for example, British versus French). This creates the perception of four subgroups; British white (double ingroup members, sharing two categories in common), British Asian and French white (partial ingroup members, sharing one category in common), and French Asian (double outgroup members, sharing neither category in common).

According to the category differentiation model (Deschamps & Doise, 1978), which we discussed earlier in the chapter, categorizing stimuli into groups leads to an accentuation of the differences *between* categories and an attenuation of similarities *within* categories, which provides a basis for intergroup bias. Deschamps and Doise argued, however, that cross-cutting groups should lead these processes to work against each other. So when a British white person thinks about the British Asian community, there will be convergence *between* the categories because of the shared group membership (British), increasing perceived similarity between whites and Asians. There will also be divergence *within* the white and British categories because they now each contain two subgroups. These processes should minimize the tendency to think in terms of 'us' and 'them', removing the categorical basis for bias. Quite simply, one cannot be biased against 'them' if 'they' are not seen as psychologically distinct from 'us'. These predictions have been supported in numerous studies (see Crisp & Hewstone, 1999).

But despite the benefits of crossed categorization for reducing prejudice, it is clear that this intervention must be utilized very carefully. For every shared identity that is made salient, a non-shared identity might also be highlighted, resulting in a potential exacerbation of prejudice towards 'double outgroups'. For example, a British white person may feel more positive toward a British Asian person by virtue of a shared British group membership, but they may therefore be more negative towards French Asians, with whom they do not share *any* common category. A second limitation of crossed categorization is that it is a very simple version of *multiple categorization*. The approach suggests that the ingroup and outgroup share just *one* additional basis for categorization. However, this may not be an accurate reflection of the increasingly multicultural, multiethnic and multiracial world in which we now live, where many different and varied ways of defining ourselves and others are available. Accordingly, recent research has shifted focus to exploring the effects of making multiple identities salient more generally.

Multiple Categorization

A third approach to reducing prejudice is based on encouraging people to use many different ways of categorizing people, rather than thinking about others all the time in terms of race, gender or age. According to Crisp, Hewstone and Rubin (2001)

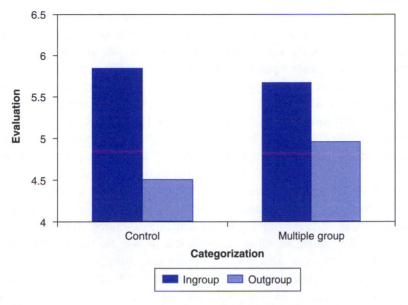

Figure 8.7 Intergroup evaluations as a function of multiple categorization. Data from Crisp, Hewstone, and Rubin (2001)

getting people to realize that people should not be pigeonholed into just one category, that there are all sorts of other ways they can be described, should reduce bias according to any single basis for categorization. Rather than applying a negative stereotype to someone just because they are a member of a stigmatized group, people will come to realize that social categories are fluid, flexible and dynamic, and that there are many different (and positive) ways in which anyone can be described. As such, the impact of any one negatively-valued identity should be reduced.

There are a number of studies that support the idea that getting people to appreciate the complexity of social categorization can reduce intergroup bias. Crisp, Hewstone and Rubin (2001) asked university students to think about a number of different categorizations that they could use to describe someone from a rival university, other than this simple outgroup status. Their findings can be seen in Figure 8.7. In line with predictions, thinking about the multiple different ways that others can be construed did indeed reduce intergroup bias. Similarly, Hall and Crisp (2005) asked participants to think about people who shared their university membership and people who did not. They then asked participants to think of other groups that university students can use to define themselves. Intergroup bias in favour of members of their university over another university was significantly lower following the generation of multiple alternative categorizations than in a control condition.

So how exactly does making multiple categorizations reduce intergroup bias? In contrast to crossed categorization, which reduces bias by increasing perceived similarity to the outgroup, making multiple group memberships salient is thought to reduce intergroup bias because the increased complexity of the intergroup context means that perceivers may be unable to use, or combine, social categorizations in any meaningful ways. Perceivers may, for example, be able to cognitively combine categories such as 'single mother' or 'working parent', but may find 'single, black, educated, working mother' too difficult to process. When categories have become too complex to use as a cue for evaluative judgement, the perceiver may be forced to seek alternative ways of forming an impression of a person. Theories of impression formation (Brewer, 1998; Fiske & Neuberg, 1990) suggest that although people tend to use categories to process information, where there is a poor fit between the category and the target, there is a shift towards an individuated mode of processing (Fiske, Lin, & Neuberg, 1999; see our discussion of dual process theories in Chapter 3), leading to *decategorization* and a more comprehensive, differentiated perception of the individual, reducing stereotyping and alleviating intergroup bias.

Related to the approach outlined above is Roccas and Brewer's (2002) model of social identity complexity. This model proposes that changing the way we perceive *ourselves* – so we come to define ourselves as having multiple non-overlapping identities – can have benefits for intergoup relations. Roccas and Brewer propose that individuals' representations of their multiple group memberships can vary along a dimension they call *complexity*. **Social identity complexity** refers to an individual's subjective representation of the interrelationships among his or her multiple group identities. It refers to the degree of overlap perceived to exist between groups of which a person is simultaneously a member. When one's representation is low in complexity, it is an indication that one perceives a high overlap between both the typical characteristics of one's various social category memberships, as well as an overlap between the actual members of those same categories. In other words, low complexity is represented by high overlap between membership and characteristics. High complexity, by contrast, is the opposite. It implies that the representation of each ingroup category is distinct from the others, both in characteristics as well as membership. Brewer and Pierce (2005) have shown that higher levels of social identity complexity (more cross-cutting category memberships) are associated with greater outgroup tolerance, including greater support for affirmative action and multiculturalism.

Finally, there has also been some work applying this multiple categorization approach to educational settings in an attempt to develop interventions to reduce prejudice. According to cognitive-developmental theory, the categorization process is somewhat rigid during early childhood, particularly regarding the ability to classify objects into categories (Piaget, 1965). In order to try to better develop the ability to see others as being potentially classifiable along multiple dimensions, Bigler and Liben (1992) created a task through which primary school children were taught to classify along multiple dimensions. Every day, for a period of one week, participants were given one set of 12 pictures of men and women engaging in stereotypically feminine (e.g. hairstylist, secretary) and stereotypically masculine (e.g. construction worker, truck driver) occupations. Children then practised sorting these pictures along both gender and occupation dimensions.

Bigler and Liben (1992) tested their multiple classification training method among 5-to 10-year-old children attending a summer school programme. They found that while before the training, less than 3 per cent of participants were competent at multiple classification, after training 95 per cent were able to classify a long multiple dimension. Importantly, participants who had acquired multiple classification skills showed significantly less gender stereotyping than participants who had not acquired multiple classification skills. This research shows that multiple classification skills may become an important thing to include in our curriculum if we are to achieve the aim of a more egalitarian society.

Summary

The *common ingroup identity model* proposes that intergroup relations can be improved through recategorizing two groups into one all inclusive group. The *crossed categorization* approach, in contrast, suggests that rather than focusing on intergroup similarities, cross-cutting two categorical dimensions can reduce intergroup bias. Finally, prejudice can be reduced through multiple categorization: by encouraging people to use many different ways of categorizing people, rather than thinking about others in terms of simple social categories.

CHAPTER SUMMARY

This chapter reviewed several theories of intergroup relations which are based on social categorization. Sherif's summer camp studies suggested that competition for scarce resources accentuated intergroup conflict, but later Tajfel showed that even mere categorization can be enough to elicit intergroup bias. Mere categorization can be explained by a combination of drives towards category differentiation and positivity as outlined by *social identity theory* and *self-categorization theory*. For novel ingroups, where there is not an established group prototype, *social projection* can explain why ingroups are viewed as more positive than outgroups. For established groups, associative learning can help explain prejudice, and such implicit bias can be measured using response times to cognitive tasks. On the basis of this knowledge about the nature of prejudice, psychologists have sought to develop ways of reducing intergroup bias and encouraging more egalitarianism. The *common ingroup identity model* argues that getting people to appreciate that they can all be within an inclusive superordinate group can reduce bias by recategorizing former outgroupers as new common ingroupers. Finally, the *crossed categorization* and *multiple categorization* approaches suggest that getting people to appreciate the multiple different ways in which anyone can be categorized – not just according to race, gender, age, and so on – can improve intergroup relations.

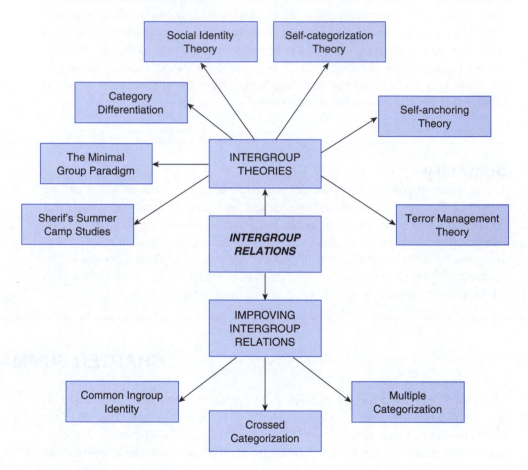

Figure 8.8   Memory map

Taking it Further

Try This

In this chapter we have discussed several theories that attempt to explain the psychological basis for intergroup relations. Many of these theories have been developed on the basis of laboratory-based studies, but how well can they be applied to the real world? Realistically, what can studies with 'made-up' groups, such as those used in the minimal group paradigm, tell us about pervasive and destructive conflicts around the world, that are often based on years of poor relations, or woven into religious or cultural worldviews? Choose an example of a real-life intergroup conflict (for example, the Arab-Israeli conflict, tensions between Catholics and Protestants in Northern Ireland) and try to account for some aspect or aspects of this conflict with reference to the theories we've talked about in this chapter. How well does each of these theories explain the conflict? Which theory do you think can *best* explain the conflicts that arise between different groups? Do different theories work better for different conflicts, or is there one that is overall the best account across different situations?

Debate This

Terror management theory is one of the more controversial theories of intergroup relations. Does mortality salience really explain why we show intergroup bias, or might there be some other explanation for this effect? How useful is this theory as either (a) a broad account of intergroup relations or (b) a very powerful account of a specific type of intergroup conflict?

Something for the Weekend

In this chapter, we have discussed approaches to improving intergroup relations that focus on changing the way we perceive social groups in general, including both the ingroup and the outgroup. This contrasts with the intergroup contact approach, outlined in Chapter 7, which focuses primarily on changing perceptions of the outgroup. How do these two approaches compare to one another? Which do you think will have the best consequences for intergroup relations? And can you think of a creative intervention that combines these two types of approach in order to have the most powerful possible impact on intergroup relations?

Further Readings

The Essentials

Brown, R. & Gaertner, S. (Eds.). (2001). *Blackwell handbook of social psychology: Intergroup processes*. Malden, MA: Blackwell.

This accessible and well-written handbook covers a whole range of topics relating to intergroup relations, including categorization processes, social identity theory, and changing intergroup relations.

Next Steps

Das, E., Bushman, B.J., Bezemer, M.D., Kerkhof, P., & Vermeulen, I.E. (2009). How terrorism news reports increase prejudice against outgroups: A terror management account. *Journal of Experimental Social Psychology, 45,* 453–459.

Check out this hot-off-the-press article on terror management theory, which looks at how learning about terrorism in the news can affect our perceptions of other groups.

Delving Deeper

Crisp, R.J. & Hewstone, M. (2007). Multiple social categorization. In M.P. Zanna (Ed.), *Advances in Experimental Social Psychology* (vol. 39, pp. 163–254). Orlando, FL: Academic Press.

This article provides a comprehensive review of multiple social categorization, including a discussion of the common ingroup identity model, crossed categorization and multiple categorization approaches to reducing prejudice.

Aggression

9

Aggression

In May 2005, 16-year-old schoolgirl Becky Smith suffered severe head injuries and temporary paralysis after being attacked near her Manchester home. The attack was filmed on a mobile phone, an incident of a disturbing act of violence that has become known as 'happy slapping'. The craze, which began in south London in early 2005, quickly became a nationwide phenomenon, with groups of teenagers with camera phones attacking passersby without provocation and then filming the incidents. Academics and social commentators have blamed popular television shows in which pranks are carried out on members of the public for providing the inspiration for such attacks.

In July 2002, Deborah Broad was jailed for three months after pleading guilty to hitting a pregnant primary schoolteacher. She had been angry that she was being asked to pay an extra £1.50 towards a school trip which had already cost £4 for her seven-year-old child. The National Union of Teachers reported that assaults on teachers in England and Wales rose from 34 in 1988 to 130 in 2001.

In 2001, violent riots occurred in close succession in three towns in the north of England, as tensions between the South Asian and white community came to a head. This 'Summer of Violence', as it has become known, is described in more detail in Text Box 9.1. It resulted in millions of pounds worth of damage to property and the injury of members of the community and the police force.

Text Box 9.1

A Summer of Violence

In the summer of 2001, a series of riots occurred in the north of England. The unrest began in May 2001 when hundreds of youths clashed with police during a weekend of rioting in Oldham. Fifteen officers were injured and 29 people were arrested after weeks of racial tension between white British National Party supporters and Asian youths erupted into violence.

This riot was followed in late June 2001 by further violent clashes between groups of Asians, whites and police in Burnley, following a fight between gangs of Asian and white men. An Asian taxi driver was attacked with a hammer, cars and businesses were set alight and 22 people were arrested.

These outbreaks of violence were severe enough. But the worst was yet to come. These earlier incidences culminated in the most severe of the riots, in Bradford on Saturday, 7 July 2001.

On 7 July members of the racist 'National Front' party demonstrated in Bradford, leading to a counter-demonstration by the Anti-Nazi League. Trouble flared up after a group of white youths began shouting racial insults at the crowd. A riot developed, with petrol bombs thrown at police and burning barricades set up, leading to the arrest of 36 people. Together, this series of riots were some of the worst ever seen in mainland Britain, with the Bradford violence alone causing damage estimated at £25 million, and injuring 300 police officers.

These cases are all illustrations of **aggression**, a verbal or physical act intended to cause harm to people or property. We do not have to look far to find many other examples of aggressive behaviour. From a cursory glance through any newspaper, we see evidence of aggression by individuals, for example child abuse, robbery and sexual assault, and aggression by groups, including riots, terrorism, and war. Some sources indicate that aggression is on the increase; between 2004 and 2005, police recorded 1,184,702 violent crimes in England and Wales, an increase of 7 per cent on the previous year. Other reports are more optimistic; the British Crime Survey – which involves interviews with members of the public – reported an 11 per cent drop in violent crime in the same time period. Nevertheless, there is no denying that aggression is a pervasive feature of the social world we inhabit. Although these violent acts are, thankfully, committed by a small minority, most people probably admit to feeling or behaving aggressively towards others on occasion. Given this pervasiveness, social psychologists are particularly interested in understanding what underlies the tendency to aggress against others.

In this chapter, we will talk about the different theories that try to explain, in a broad sense, why humans are aggressive. We then focus more specifically on the factors that determine why someone behaves aggressively. These can be divided into person-centred determinants (relating to the characteristics of the aggressor) and situation-centred determinants (relating to the situation and how it can provoke aggression). We also talk about disinhibition, the process by which people ignore societal norms of non-violence to commit an aggressive act. Finally, we focus in detail on three specific examples of aggressive behaviour which have been investigated by social psychologists: domestic violence, sexual violence and terrorism.

THEORIES OF AGGRESSION

Theories of aggression fall into one of two categories. According to a biological perspective, we are born with a tendency to behave aggressively. In contrast, the social perspective argues that aggression is social behaviour that we learn from those around us.

Biological Theories of Aggression

Biological theories argue that we are genetically predetermined to be aggressive. Here we describe two perspectives that propose that aggression is innate: *psychodynamic theory*, and the *evolutionary* approach.

Psychodynamic Theory

The psychodynamic perspective, which was dominant at the start of the 20th century, proposed that people hold two innate, but opposing, instincts: an instinct for life or 'Eros', and an instinct for death or 'Thanatos'. Freud (1930) proposed that although the death instinct initially led to self-destructive behaviour, it later become redirected from the self towards others, as aggressive behaviour. It was believed that aggressive behaviour would occur as a result of a natural build up of tension in the body, which eventually needed to be released to restore balance. Although quite creative, there is, however, little empirical evidence for the psychodynamic approach.

Evolutionary Approach

Evolutionary social psychologists claim that social behaviour has evolved over time, passed down from generation to generation (Simpson & Kenrick, 1997). Proponents of this approach argue that social behaviour exists to ensure that an individual's genes survive for long enough to be passed on to their offspring. The use of aggression in ensuring genetic survival is particularly evident in animals: males fight other males for mating rights and hunt for food to ensure their survival, while mothers protect their young by fighting off predators. Among humans, aggressive behaviour can be used to secure social and economic advantage. A high-flying business executive may, for example, argue with other colleagues to defend their existing position or to gain a promotion. There are, however, two clear problems with this approach. First, it is inherently difficult to provide supportive evidence because evolutionary tendencies have presumably developed over many thousands of years, making them hard to test over a short time-scale in a laboratory. Second, we are not only aggressive in order to protect ourselves and our offspring. Indeed, as we shall see later in the chapter, people sometimes show aggression towards their closest relatives rather than protecting them through aggression towards others. Explaining these examples of aggressive behaviour presents a tangible challenge to evolutionary accounts.

Social Theories of Aggression

According to social psychologists, the social context in which we exist can also explain aggressive behaviour. It is worth noting here that these theories do not deny that we often have a general biological tendency to show aggression. Rather, they focus more specifically on how the social environment shapes these tendencies.

Frustration-Aggression Hypothesis

In the 1930s, social psychologists at Yale University noticed that people seemed to display aggressive behaviour more at some times than others. They became interested in explaining why this was the case. Dollard and colleagues (1939) argued that aggression resulted from frustration at a particular person or event. If aggression cannot be directly targeted at the cause of the frustration because they are too physically or socially powerful, or because the cause is a situation rather than a person, it may be redirected onto a more realistic target. This highly influential idea has become known as the **frustration-aggression hypothesis**. Hovland and Sears (1940) proposed that the frustration caused by economic downturn (a situational cause) would produce aggressive impulses that would be directed at vulnerable targets, such as minority groups, even when those groups bear no responsibility for the economic decline. Accordingly, they found a strong statistical relationship between the lynching of blacks in the American South and economic downturns, assessed by looking at cotton prices and economic growth from 1882 and 1930 (see Figure 9.1).

The role of frustration continues to be cited when explaining acts of aggression today. Government reports following the summer of violence in the north of England in 2001 (see Text Box 9.1) suggested that poverty, deprivation and disillusionment contributed to the riots, while social and economic deprivation were argued to play a role in the atrocities committed in the former Yugoslavia (Staub, 1996). Since its conception, however, the theory has been criticized on a number of fronts. First, there has been little subsequent empirical evidence to support the findings of Hovland and Sears (1940). Green, Glaser, and Rich (1998) reanalysed the original data used by Hovland and Sears, as well as looking at new data from New York. They found very limited evidence for a link between the economy and hate crimes. Second, where a link between frustration and aggression does exist, it is unlikely to be spontaneous or direct. Instead, right-wing racist groups like the British National Party exacerbate people's existing frustrations by attributing blame and encouraging public resentment towards minorities in times of economic decline. In sum, although frustrations may be one contributing factor, a full account of aggression is likely to be much more complex.

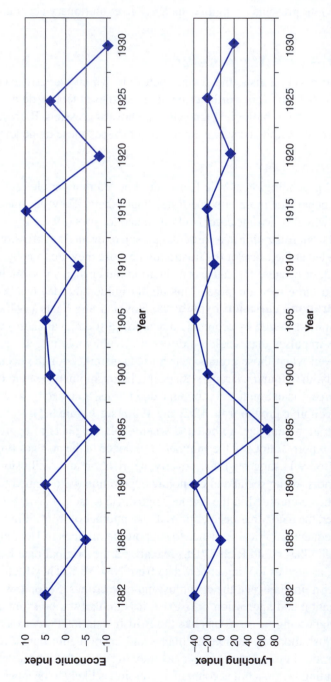

Figure 9.1 The relationship between economic conditions and lynchings of African Americans in the US between 1882 and 1930. Illustration of the findings of Hovland and Sears (1940)

Cathartic Hypothesis

Closely related to the concept of frustration-aggression is the **cathartic hypothesis**. This is the somewhat Freudian idea that when faced with a frustrating or irritating situation, we experience a build up of negative emotions. In order to rid ourselves of these emotions, we need to act them out. Only then will we be able to return to our normal, balanced state. We can probably all think of examples of wanting to scream, shout, or hit a punch bag to get our feelings of anger out of our system. But does catharsis really lead to the dissipation of anger and aggression? While some studies have shown that it reduces aggression, others show that catharsis is ineffective. Bushman, Baumeister, and Stack (1999), for example, found that angry participants who had read a pro-catharsis newspaper article continued to show aggression towards the person who had caused the anger even after engaging in the cathartic exercise of hitting a punch bag.

Cognitive Neoassociationalist Model

Berkowitz's (1969, 1989) **cognitive neoassociationalist model** provides an explanation for aggression that also takes into account environmental conditions, or 'cues', that are generated by a frustrating situation and subsequently lead to aggressive behaviour. In line with the frustration-aggression hypothesis, Berkowitz argued that frustration generates anger, which in turn increases the likelihood of aggressive. behaviour. However, he noted that aggressive behaviour would only arise if there were appropriate cues in the environment. Any object or person can provide a cue for aggression if it has been linked repeatedly with anger and aggression in the past, for example, a disliked person.

Berkowitz and LePage (1967) conducted a study to see if situational cues lead to aggression when a person is angry, as predicted by the cognitive neoassociationalist model. Male college students were given varying numbers of electric shocks by a confederate as part of an 'evaluation' for a task they had previously completed. The more electric shocks a participant had received, the angrier they reported being. Participants were then given the opportunity to evaluate the performance of the confederate by giving them electric shocks in return. In the *situational cue condition*, a shotgun and revolver were placed on a nearby table, while in the *control condition*, there was nothing on the table. The results of this study can be seen in Figure 9.2. Among participants who were not angry, the weapons (aggressive situational cues) had no effect on the number of shocks administered. However, participants who were angry gave more shocks in the presence of the weapons. Berkowitz called this phenomenon the weapons effect, arguing that weapons not only provide the means to cause violence but also increase the likelihood that an act of violence will occur.

Excitation-Transfer Model

While Berkowitz (1974) focused on the effect of specific arousal (anger), others have argued that non-specific arousal can inadvertently influence aggression. We

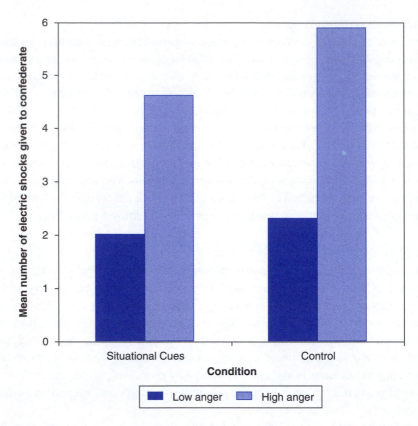

Figure 9.2 The effect of situational cues on aggression. Data from Berkowitz and LePage (1967)

experience physiological arousal in a variety of contexts. For instance, we may experience an elevated heart rate not only when we have had an argument with someone, but also in the presence of someone we find attractive, or when we have been on a rollercoaster ride (see Chapter 12 for a discussion of how this model can apply to the formation of romantic attachments). Some social psychologists believe that the physiological reaction we have is similar in each of these situations, but we differentiate them by giving them different labels: anger, attraction, or exhilaration, depending on the external cues in a particular context. We also have certain repertoires of behaviour that are associated with how we label the arousal. For instance, when we attribute arousal to attraction we might flirt, but when we attribute arousal to anger, we might instead behave aggressively. Furthermore, according to the **excitation-transfer model** (Zillman, 1984), arousal in one situation can carry over into a completely different situation. This is called residual arousal. For instance, residual arousal from one situation can increase the likelihood that we will behave aggressively in another situation.

To illustrate, imagine that you have been writing an essay all morning when your computer crashes – and you have forgotten to back-up your work. You might then feel annoyed and upset that you have lost several hours worth of work. If, soon afterwards, your roommate asks you when you plan to do the washing up, you might snap angrily at her. Ordinarily, this situation would not have elicited an aggressive response. However, according to the excitation-transfer model, residual arousal from the earlier event can trigger aggressive behaviour. It is easy to see how this model can be applied to other situations. For example, during the Euro 2000 football championships English football fans in Charleroi, Belgium, attending the England-Germany match clashed with police and German fans, resulting in the arrest of 131 people and the deportation of 300 English fans. It may be that high levels of excitement and tension at the prospect of the match was misattributed to anger and aggression in the presence of police and fans. While this is probably an overly-simplified explanation for the complex problem of football hooliganism, excitation-transfer may have a partial role to play. For a recent study that has also investigated the role of emotions in producing aggression among football fans, see Text Box 9.2.

Text Box 9.2

Seeing Red or Feeling Blue: Routes to Aggression in Soccer Fans

Soccer tournaments have frequently been blighted by anti-social behaviour among the crowds of attending fans. British fans overseas – for example those attending the World Cup in France in 1998 and Euro 1996 in Belgium and the Netherlands – have acquired a reputation as 'hooligans', starting fights with opposing teams which often result in costly damage to property, injuries, arrests and deportations. But why do soccer fans sometimes behave in this way? Crisp, Heuston, Farr, and Turner (2007) investigated the effect of the emotions fans experience when their team loses a match on their subsequent actions towards fans of the opposing team.

Method
Sixty male supporters of a small amateur football team in the city of Birmingham, England were approached as they left the team's football ground following a loss. Each supporter completed a questionnaire in which they were

(Continued)

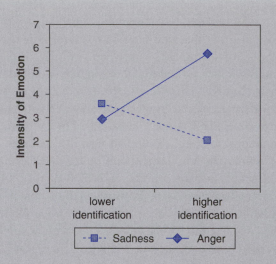

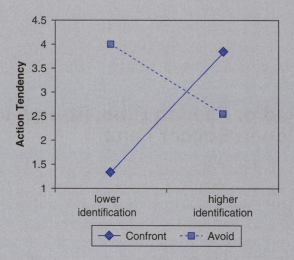

asked how much they identified with the team (how important the team was to them), the extent to which they experienced the emotions of anger and sadness as a result of the loss, and whether they intended to confront (for example, argue with) or avoid the fans of the opposing team.

Results

The results of the study are illustrated below. Participants who highly identified with their team – in other words, their team was very important to them – were more likely to experience the emotion of anger, and were more likely to instigate a confrontation with the fans of the opposing team, when they had lost a match. In contrast, participants who did not strongly identify with the team – those who were less 'die hard' – were more likely to just feel sad and do their best to avoid the fans of the opposing team.

Interpreting the Findings

These findings may help us to understand why football fans sometimes behave anti-socially, getting into fights with the supporters of other teams during international matches. Fans who highly identify with their sports team – as is likely to be the case for individuals who travel across the world to see their team play – are likely to respond with anger and confrontation when their team does not do as well as they expected. According to social identity theory, when people highly identify with a particular group, it forms an important part of their self-esteem. If the group performs poorly compared to another group, this has a negative effect on self-esteem. Unlike less committed fans (lower identifiers) they cannot distance themselves from the loss by avoiding the other team. To maintain self-esteem they therefore need to use another strategy, such as confronting the other group to try to restore a positive group image (e.g. by 'winning' a violent confrontation).

Learning Theories of Aggression

Our behaviour is undoubtedly influenced by the social world that we inhabit. Not only do we observe how others react to our behaviour and adjust our behaviour accordingly, but we also observe – and are influenced by – the behaviour of others. Here, we describe two ways in which we may learn to behave aggressively.

Operant reinforcement. Skinner (1953) was a behaviourist, a psychologist who believed that people are born 'blank slates' – and that our minds develop as a result of environmental influences (in stark contrast to the *evolutionary* approach discussed earlier). Skinner argued that changes in behaviour result from the response to stimuli in a person's environment, a process he called *operant reinforcement*. When a particular stimulus-response pattern is positively reinforced, by rewarding it rather than punishing it, the link between the stimulus and the response is strengthened. Imagine an incident in which one child hits another child for stealing their favourite toy. If the thief gives back the toy and no one admonishes the aggressor for their behaviour, the link between stimulus (having a toy taken) and behaviour (hitting the offender) will be strengthened, and the child might be more likely to respond with aggression if their toy is taken in the future.

Social learning theory. Bandura (1977) also believed that people are not born with a ready-to-use repertoire of behaviour. In contrast to Skinner, however, he proposed that behaviour could also be learnt *indirectly*, by observing the behaviour of others. Bandura's **social learning theory** argued that although behaviours can be learnt through direct experience, if people had to rely solely on their own previous behaviour to inform them of how to act, learning would be time-consuming, error-prone, and limited to the situations of which we have already had experience. He argued that for these reasons, much human behaviour is learned through observing the behaviour of others and that subsequently this information is used as a guide for one's own actions. Bandura called this process observational learning or *modelling*.

Bandura applied social learning theory to our understanding of aggression. He argued that whether a person is aggressive in a particular situation depends upon the person's direct and indirect experiences of aggressive behaviour, and the outcomes of that aggressive behaviour: Did the observed behaviour achieve its goals? Was it rewarded or punished? Based on this information people decide whether an act of aggression would be likely to have positive or negative consequences. The more positive the perceived outcomes of the observed behaviour, the more likely it is that the observer will emulate the behaviour themselves. In Text Box 9.3, we describe research by Bandura, Ross, and Ross (1961) which supports the idea that observing aggressive behaviour increases aggression among children.

Text Box 9.3

Learning Aggressive Behaviour Through Modelling

In a classic study, Bandura, Ross, & Ross (1961) tested the hypothesis derived from social learning theory that people may behave aggressively simply because they have observed the aggressive behaviour of others.

Method

Thirty-six boys and 36 girls, aged between 3 and 5, took part in the study. One at a time, children were invited by the experimenter to sit in a play area in one corner of a room and take part in a fun activity (making pictures using potato prints). Once the child was settled, the experimenter escorted a male or female adult model to the opposite corner of the room, where there was a table and chair, and some toys: a toy set, a mallet, and a 5-foot inflatable Bobo doll, a popular toy in the 1960s. The experimenter then left the room. Children were randomly assigned to one of two conditions.

Aggressive Model Condition: The model first started assembling the toys, but after a couple of minutes, he or she turned to the Bobo doll and spent the rest of the session displaying physical and verbal aggression towards it. Acts of physical aggression included sitting on the doll, repeatedly punching it in the nose, striking it on the head with a mallet, throwing it in the air and kicking it around the room. Acts of verbal aggression included phrases such as 'Sock him in the nose', 'Hit him down', 'Kick him', and 'Pow'.

Non-aggressive Model Condition: The model ignored the Bobo doll for the entire session, instead quietly assembling the toy set.

To discover the impact of observing the model, children were later seated in a different play room, and were told that they could play with any of the toys in the room. The room included toys that could be used in a non-aggressive way (e.g. a tea set, crayons and paper, dolls and bears) and toys that could be used in an aggressive way (e.g. Bobo doll, a mallet, a dart gun). The behaviour of the children was then subtly observed and recorded. Would children who had observed aggressive behaviour subsequently behave more aggressively themselves?

The graph illustrates the effect of observing aggressive and non-aggressive female models (FM) and male models (MM) on the behaviour of female participants (FP) and male participants (MP).

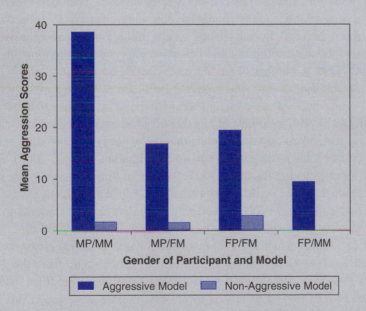

Children who had observed an aggressive model imitated the model, showing significantly more verbal and physical aggression towards the Bobo doll than those who had observed a non-aggressive model.

(Continued)

Results

Although boys showed more aggression than girls overall, boys were more likely to show aggression when the model was male, whereas girls were more likely to show aggression when the model was female.

Interpreting the Findings

Children who were given an opportunity to observe aggressive behaviour later showed aggressive behaviour themselves, supporting social learning theory. The fact that girls were more responsive to female models and boys were more responsive to male models shows that behaviour is observed and copied *selectively*. Put another way, certain models are likely to be more influential than others.

Social learning theory remains influential today, particularly in discussions of the contribution of the mass media to violent crime. The recent wave of 'happy slapping' discussed at the beginning of this chapter has, for instance, been blamed on children and teenagers observing, and then imitating, behaviour on prank TV programmes like the MTV show 'Jackass'. Recent studies which consider the effect of the mass media on aggressive thoughts, attitudes, and behaviours appear to corroborate these commonly-held views. A number of studies have considered the effect of violent video games in causing aggression. Anderson and Bushman (2001) reported that children who play violent video games even for short periods are more likely to behave aggressively in the real world, regardless of whether they had aggressive tendencies to begin with. This is particularly worrying, given that the majority of top-selling games, and most of children's favourite games, are violent in nature (Vargas, 2007). Similarly, Anderson, Carnagey, and Eubanks (2003) found that violent music lyrics increased aggressive thoughts and hostile feelings among 500 college students.

Coyne and colleagues (2008) asked female undergraduate students to watch a film clip showing either physical aggression (taken from the 2004 film, *Kill Bill*), relational aggression, which refers to manipulation and social exclusion (taken from the 2004 film *Mean Girls*), or no aggression (a séance scene from the 2000 film *What Lies Beneath*). After answering some questions about the films, participants were asked to take part in what was ostensibly an unrelated study. This involved completing a task with a confederate who was posing as another participant. The confederate behaved antagonistically towards the participant in order to induce aggression. Physical aggression was assessed by monitoring how many times the participant administered an unpleasant level of noise to the confederate on a subsequent competitive time reaction task, whereas relational aggression was assessed by asking participants to complete an evaluation of the confederate. It emerged that, compared to the no-aggression condition, viewing media which contained physical and relational aggression were associated with administration of more painful noise (more physical aggression) *and* a harsher assessment of the confederate (relational aggression). This suggests a 'cross-over' effect, whereby observing physical aggressive media can lead to relational aggression, and watching relational aggressive media can lead to physical aggression.

These findings are rather worrying, because they suggest that the effect of viewing one type of aggression can lead to not only more of that *same* type of aggression, but also generalizes, resulting in more of *other* types of aggression too. Fortunately, social learning theory has positive applications for interventions to reduce aggression. If observing aggressive behaviour can lead to increased aggression, it follows that observing *non*-aggressive behaviour should have the opposite effect (e.g. Bandura et al., 1961). Supporting this idea, Greitemeyer and Osswald (2009) found that playing 'Lemmings', a prosocial video game in which players are required to save small beings from death by leading them through successive levels, decreased the accessibility of antisocial thoughts, and reduced the likelihood of participants rating ambiguous behaviour as aggressive (see also Chapter 10, to learn more about recent findings showing how prosocial video games might be used to increase helping behaviour).

Despite its intuitive appeal, social learning theory has faced some criticism. First, it does not sufficiently take into account the role of individual differences in aggression that result from genetic, neuropsychological and learning differences. Second, many studies have not replicated the effect of televised aggression shown by Anderson and colleagues. Indeed, Feshbach and Singer (1971) found that juvenile delinquents who watched violent programmes showed less subsequent aggressive behaviour than those who watched non-violent programmes on TV, arguing that watching violence provided viewers with the opportunity to release their aggressive tendencies without acting upon them.

Summary

The competing explanations for aggression that we have discussed above reflect the *nature versus nurture debate* that exists throughout psychology. Although these two approaches appear to be contradictory, most psychologists accept that aggression has *both* a biological and a social component. Put another way, although we may be born with an innate tendency to behave aggressively, the strength of these tendencies and the extent to which we act on them is undoubtedly influenced by the social world in which we live.

The theories we have discussed so far illustrate two broad approaches to the study of aggression: biological and social. They tell us *how* aggressive behaviour might

(Continued)

come about, for instance, due to *frustration*, or because of *learned associations*. We now turn to specific factors that can help us to predict when people might be more or less aggressive. Put another way, the previous section has outlined the processes that explain why *any* of us might, in *any* situation, become aggressive. In the next section we discuss more specifically why some people might be *more* aggressive than others, or why any of us might be *more* aggressive in some situations than others. We divide the factors that predict variations in aggressive tendencies into person-centred and situation-centred determinants of aggression.

PERSON-CENTRED DETERMINANTS OF AGGRESSION

We can probably all think of people we know who are considered to be volatile and aggressive, while there are others who rarely show outward signs of anger even in the most testing of circumstances. Although, as we will see later in the chapter, situational factors can contribute towards whether any individual displays aggression in a given situation, there do also seem to be individual differences in how aggressive people are *in general*. Here we discuss two factors that may explain individual differences in aggression: gender and personality. We also discuss the effect of alcohol consumption on an individual's tendency to behave aggressively.

Gender Differences

Ask anyone which is the more aggressive sex, and the majority of people will say males. On the surface, it appears that this view has some truth to it. Eagly and Steffen (1986) found that men were more likely to engage in physical aggression than women, while Bettencourt and Miller (1996) found that men were more likely to show unprovoked aggression than women. There may be a hormonal explanation for these gender differences. Men typically have a higher level of testosterone than women, and recent studies have investigated whether aggression and testosterone levels are related. Berman, Gladue, and Taylor (1993) found that men with high levels of testosterone were more likely to show aggression (measured in this case as their likelihood of administering an electric shock) towards an opponent during a competitive task. Other studies have found a modest, but significant, correlation between elevated testosterone levels and aggression (Book, Starzyk, & Quinsey, 2001). Hormonal differences cannot, however, provide a full explanation for gender differences in aggression. This is because differences in hormone levels do not take into account social influences on development.

The important point here is that boys and girls do not only differ in terms of hormones, but also gender socialization. Females and males are treated very

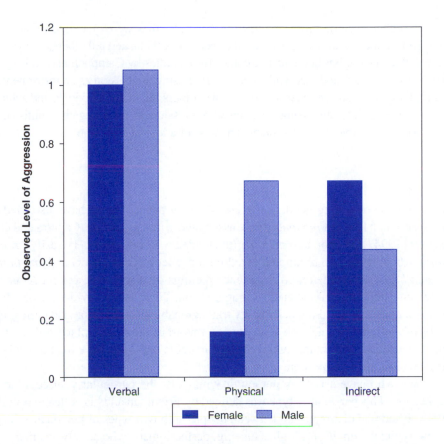

Figure 9.3 Gender differences in aggression. Data from Björkqvist et al. (1992)

differently by their family, peers, societal institutions and the media, treatment which has a profound impact on their behaviour. Girls, for example, are encouraged to be passive and gentle whilst boys are encouraged to be forthright and aggressive. For this reason, girls may be less likely to engage in direct acts of aggression, instead relying more on verbal and other indirect forms of aggression which are deemed by society to be more socially acceptable. This means that gender differences could come about due to *learning* what are believed to be gender-appropriate behaviours, rather than hormonal differences.

If socialization can account for gender differences in aggression, then we should be able to observe not only differences in the *amount* of aggression exhibited by men and women, but also the *type* of aggression exhibited. A study by Björkqvist and colleagues (1992) illustrated differences in the type of aggression reported by male and female adolescents in Finland (see Figure 9.3). While boys tended to show higher levels of physical aggression than girls, such as hitting and kicking, there were no gender differences in verbal aggression, such as shouting and name-calling. Interestingly, girls showed higher levels of *indirect aggression* than boys; they were more likely than boys to spread rumours, malevolently reveal the secrets of others, and tell others not to associate with a person. Further evidence comes from studies by Campbell and colleagues (1996, 1997) who found that while men reported using aggression as an instrument to realize their goals, such as exerting control over others, maintaining power, and achieving positive self-esteem, women perceived aggression to be a negative, anti-social behaviour, which they tended to blame on stress or a loss of self-control.

Personality

As well as investigating gender differences, social psychologists have also tried to uncover which types of *personality* are associated with aggression. Caprara and colleagues (1994, 1996) found *irritability* (the tendency to get angry very easily), *rumination* (the tendency to retain and dwell on those feelings of anger) and *emotional susceptibility* (the tendency to experience feelings of discomfort and inadequacy) to be consistent traits associated with aggression. There is also evidence for a link between aggression and the personality trait agreeableness. Gleason and colleagues (2004) found that people who score low on this trait, those who place self-interest above getting on with others and tend to be irritable and rude, have higher levels of direct and indirect aggression.

People who have a **type A personality** may also be particularly susceptible to aggression. This personality type was defined by Friedman and his colleagues in the 1950s. Friedman distinguished between people with two types of personality. Type As are typically ambitious, high achieving, perfectionists, who are always in a rush to achieve their goals and compete with others. Research has shown that such individuals are at greater risk of coronary heart disease. In contrast, type Bs are relaxed, uncompetitive and creative. Carver and Glass (1978) tested the hypothesis that type A personalities would show more aggression under threatening circumstances. Male undergraduates were exposed to a confederate who threatened their sense of competence by denigrating their performance on a perceptual-motor task. They were then given the opportunity to administer an electric shock to the confederate. Participants with type A personalities administered a larger electric shock than those with type B personalities if their sense of competence had been threatened (see Figure 9.4).

Finally, there is evidence that self-esteem is implicated in aggression. Traditionally, low self-esteem was considered to be a primary cause of aggression. Social psychologists have used low self-esteem to explain the behaviour of violent gang members (Anderson, 1994; Jankowski, 1991), perpetrators of domestic violence (Renzetti, 1992) and even terrorists (Long, 1990). People with low self-esteem were thought to use aggression and violence as a means of boosting their self-esteem to a desirable level. Despite this speculation, however, there is little direct evidence for a causal relationship between low self-esteem and aggression.

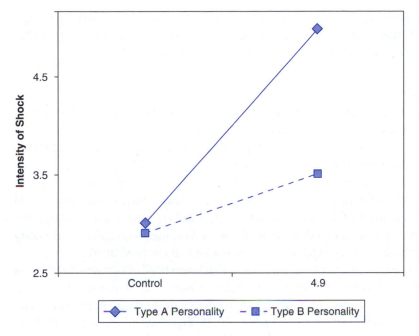

Figure 9.4 Differences in aggression between men with type A and type B personalities. Data from Carver and Glass (1978)

There are also psychologists who argue against the view that low self-esteem causes aggression, and who in fact propose that people with *high* self-esteem are more likely to act aggressively. Such individuals are likely to feel little guilt about treating badly those who they consider to be of lesser importance. People who view themselves very positively are also likely to be more confident that their aggressive behaviour will have positive outcomes – for example, they are more likely to believe they can win a fight or an argument – and they may therefore be more likely to behave aggressively. In particular, Baumeister, Smart, and Boden (1996) suggested that people who have high self-esteem or egotism are more likely to show aggression than those with low self-esteem because they regard themselves as superior, and will therefore be more sensitive to threats to that superiority. Baumeister and his colleagues (1996) argued that people with high self-esteem would be particularly likely to engage in aggressive behaviour when their ego is threatened. When another person challenges or contradicts the viewpoint, or in any way indicates that they do not share the positive self-appraisal of the egotistic individual, they may react with aggression.

In line with these predictions, Berkowitz (1978) studied British men who had been convicted of assault, and found that most of the assaults had occurred when the offender believed the target had insulted or belittled them in some way, wounding their pride. Similarly, Katz (1988) argued that people convicted of homicide generally held a positive view of themselves but felt that their victim had contradicted this viewpoint. Katz argued that offenders felt humiliated, and this humiliation quickly developed into rage. Gelles and Straus (1988) also found that domestic violence frequently occurred after the perpetrator perceived there to be a threat to their perception of self-worth.

Alcohol

Alcohol can be considered a person-centred determinant because different degrees of consumption can cause individual differences in people's aggressive behaviour. A number of studies have shown that people under the influence of alcohol are more aggressive than those who are not. Bachman and Peralta (2002), for example, found that heavy alcohol and drug use among high school students increased the likelihood of violent offending, even when the effect of home environment and school grades were controlled for. Bushman and Cooper (1990) conducted a meta-analysis of 30 experiments and found that, across those studies, men who had been drinking tended to behave more aggressively than men who had not been drinking.

An experiment conducted by Giancola and Zeichner (1997) illustrates the effect of alcohol consumption on aggression. Sixty males consumed alcohol ostensibly as part of a study into the effects of alcohol on competitive performance. After consuming alcohol, blood alcohol concentration rises as the alcohol is absorbed, and then falls as the alcohol is gradually broken down by the body. To investigate whether there were any differences depending on whether the level of alcohol was rising or falling, half of the participants were tested when their blood alcohol concentration rose past 0.08 per cent, whilst the remaining participants were tested as their blood alcohol concentration fell below 0.08 per cent, as the effects of alcohol were beginning to diminish.

Participants were told that they would be competing against a man in the next room on a reaction time task. In reality, however, there was no opponent and reaction times were not measured; participants were told they had won the trial half of the time and lost the other half of the time. When participants won a trial, they were allowed to deliver an electric shock to their opponent, but when they lost a trial they were given an electric shock, apparently by their opponent. The dependent measure was the intensity of shock that participants delivered to their opponent. The results of this study are presented in Figure 9.5.

Giancola and Zeichner (1997) found that men who had drunk alcohol delivered shocks of greater intensity to their opponent; in other words, they were more aggressive. Intriguingly, however, this effect only emerged when blood alcohol concentration was ascending. When the level of alcohol in the blood was descending, participants did not differ in their level of aggression from control participants who had not been drinking. When alcohol level is on the rise, drinkers experience increases in excitement, extroversion and stimulation, but an increase in impairment of neuropsychological function, for example poorer memory, attention, and reaction time. When alcohol level is falling, on the other hand, drinkers experience the opposite effect: relaxation and fatigue. The fact that aggression was only greater

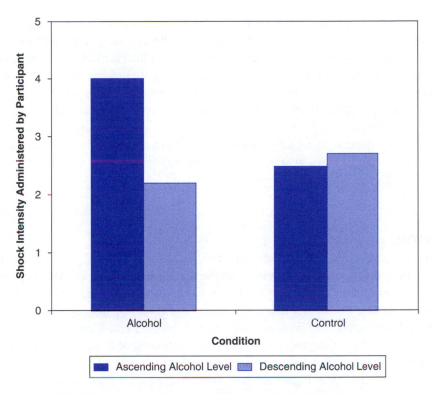

Figure 9.5 The effect of alcohol level on aggression. Data from Giancola and Zeichner (1997)

among drinkers when the level of alcohol in their system was ascending may help us to understand *why* alcohol leads to aggression for two reasons.

First, the increase in *physiological arousal* during the rise of alcohol in the system may have led to greater aggression, in line with the cognitive neoassociationalist (Berkowitz, 1969, 1989) and excitation-transfer (Zillman, 1984) models discussed earlier in the chapter. Second, the impairment in *neuropsychological function* may have resulted in an increase in aggressive behaviour. Alcohol decreases an individual's ability to carefully process information about a situation, increasing reliance upon less effortful, automatic responses to stimuli. An individual will therefore be more likely to engage in aggressive behaviour because they have not systematically evaluated the situation, or thought about the consequences of their actions. As well as failing to attend to external cues, intoxicated individuals also have difficulty in attending to internal cues. Although most people endorse a social norm of non-violence, intoxicated individuals have diminished self-awareness (Hull, 1981) and may fail to behave in accordance with this belief.

An alternative explanation for the effect of alcohol on aggression is offered by **alcohol expectancy theory**. People hold certain expectancies about how alcohol affects behaviour; we generally believe that alcohol leads people to be more extroverted, less inhibited, and more aggressive. For this reason, we are aware that out-of-the-ordinary behaviour while under the influence of alcohol will often be excused; in other words, the alcohol is to blame rather than the individual (recall the discussion of dispositional versus situational attributions in Chapter 2). As a consequence, people may be more likely to behave aggressively because they think they can 'get away with it'. There is some evidence that supports this explanation. Lang, Goeckner, Adesso, and Marlatt (1975) found that people who think they have consumed alcohol, but who actually haven't, also behave more aggressively, although a recent meta-analytic review of the literature has cast some doubts over this so-called placebo effect (Bushman & Cooper, 1990).

Summary

In this section, we talked about three factors related to the individual that influence aggression. First, men tend to be more physically aggressive than women. Thus *gender differences* may reflect the fact that men typically have a higher level of the hormone *testosterone*. Differences in *gender socialization* also appear to play a role; girls are encouraged from an early age to be passive and gentle, while boys are encouraged to be boisterous. However, it is not the case that women do not show aggression. Instead, they display aggression in a different way. Specifically, research shows that females show higher levels of *indirect aggression* than males, for example spreading rumours. Social psychologists have also investigated whether certain personality traits are associated with aggression. Although the evidence is fairly limited, it does seem that *agreeable people* are less likely to be aggressive, and those with a *type A personality* are more likely to be aggressive, especially if their competence is threatened. *Self-esteem* is also implicated in aggression; people with high but fragile self-esteem tend to show higher levels of aggression, particularly if their positive self-concept is threatened in some way. Finally, people under the influence of *alcohol* tend to show heightened aggression. Alcohol impairs neuropsychological function, decreasing an individual's ability to inhibit aggressive responses.

SITUATION-CENTRED DETERMINANTS OF AGGRESSION

Although certain individual characteristics may make some people more likely to behave aggressively than others, these features undoubtedly interact with the situations in which people find themselves. In this section, we discuss the impact on aggression of the physical environment, people's perceived place in society, and the culture or sub-culture in which people live.

Physical Environment

Three aspects of the physical environment have been shown to influence levels of aggression: *temperature*, *crowding*, and *noise*.

Temperature

A number of studies have shown that the higher the temperature, the more aggressive people are. Heat leads to physiological arousal, irritation and discomfort which can spark aggression. Harries and Stadler (1983) looked at the relationship between the weather and the number of aggravated assaults in Dallas over a 12-month period. They found that the hotter and more humid the weather, the greater the number of assaults. Similarly, Anderson and Anderson (1984) studied the rate of murders and rapes over a two-year period and found that as the average daily temperature rose, so did the number of these crimes. Research has also shown that when the weather is hot, there is an increase in collective violence (e.g. riots; Carlsmith & Anderson, 1979) and domestic violence (Cohn, 1993).

This trend does not, however, continue at *extremely* high temperatures. Harries and Stadler (1983) found that the number of assaults did not continue to rise when it was extremely hot and humid. Cohn and Rotton (1997) found evidence for a curvilinear relationship between heat and aggression. They examined crime data from the police department in Minneapolis, looking at the rates of assault, including fights, shootings, stabbings, threats and kidnapping, over a two-year period. They then compared these statistics to the weather each day over that period. Their findings are presented in Figure 9.6. The hotter the weather, the more assaults there were, but as temperatures topped 75 degrees Fahrenheit, the number of assaults began to decrease. This is probably because very high temperatures drain people's energy and make it difficult to do anything, let alone display aggression.

Cohn and Rotton (1997) also found that the relationship between heat and aggression was stronger in the evening, presumably because during the day the majority of people work in air-conditioned buildings and are thus not affected by the outdoor temperature. The relationship between temperature and crime does not, however, hold for all types of crime. According to Anderson, Bushman, and Groom (1997), the link between the two is likely to be stronger for **affective aggression**, where the purpose of the aggression is to cause harm, than for **instrumental aggression**, when the aggression serves a different purpose, for example a robbery.

DeWall and Bushman (2009) observed that the link between heat and aggression has crept into the English language, through commonplace phrases such as 'hot headed', and 'my blood is boiling' used to describe aggression. Accordingly, they wondered whether even simply priming people with words about hot temperatures might activate aggressive thoughts. In order to test this idea, they asked undergraduate students to complete a short word-based problem solving task which was

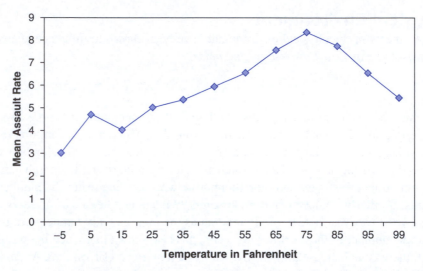

Figure 9.6 The curvilinear relationship between temperature and number of assaults. Data from Cohn and Rotton (1997)

embedded with words associated with heat (e.g. sunburn, roast, sweat, burning), or in a control condition, words associated with cold (e.g. frostbite, cold, shivers, frozen). Next, participants completed a word-stem completion task, in which they had to complete ambiguous word fragments such as 'k- - -' which could be completed as either aggressive ('kill') or non-aggressive ('kiss') words. Supporting their prediction, DeWall and Bushman found that participants primed with hot temperature words used more aggressive words to complete the word-stem completion task than those who were primed with cold words. This suggests a strong association in memory between heat-related words and thoughts of aggression. Moreover, in a follow-up study, it emerged that participants who completed the heat prime were more likely to interpret the ambiguous behaviour of a man presented in a fictional scenario as hostile and aggressive. One limitation of this study, however, is that it did not consider the effect of priming heat related words on *actual* aggressive behaviour.

Crowding

A high density of people can result in aggression. This is evident from the sometimes loutish behaviour of crowds of football fans, and the fights that sometimes break out between drunken revellers in busy bars and nightclubs. As with heat, being crowded is likely to lead to an increase in physiological arousal, and feelings of stress, irritation and frustration, such that the threshold for aggressive outbursts is lowered. People also feel anonymous and therefore less accountable for their actions when in a crowd; their adherence to societal norms of non-aggression is therefore lowered. This process of *deindividuation* that often occurs when in a crowd is explained in more detail later in the chapter.

The effects of crowding on aggression have been found in diverse settings. Ng, Kumar, Ranclaud, and Robinson (2001) examined occupancy levels and incidences of verbal and physical aggressive behaviour in a psychiatric hospital unit. They found that the average occupancy level was 77 per cent when a violent incident occurred, compared with 69 per cent when no incidents occurred. Lawrence and Andrews (2004) investigated the effect of crowding among adult male prison inmates. They found that inmates' perceptions of crowding in the prison were associated with an increase in arousal and stress and a decrease in psychological wellbeing. They also found that inmates who experienced crowding were more likely to interpret the behaviour of others as being aggressive. These changes in perception may also contribute to the outbreak of aggression. According to the *reciprocity principle*, people are more likely to behave aggressively if they feel they have been provoked. If inmates are more likely to view behaviour as aggressive when the prison is crowded, they are more likely to respond with aggression themselves.

Noise

The presence of unwanted sound, particularly when it is too loud or it is unpredictable, can lead to an increase in aggression. Glass and Singer (1973) had participants complete a maths task either under noisy conditions or under quiet conditions. They found that participants in the noisy condition made more mistakes on a subsequent proof-reading task and felt more frustrated, particularly if the noise was very loud, random (and therefore unpredictable) and when they had no control over it. Like heat and crowding, noise probably leads to aggression because it increases physiological arousal and feelings of stress.

Social Disadvantage

Socially disadvantaged groups may react to their standing in society by behaving aggressively, but whether or not they do so depends on their sense of **relative deprivation**. If an individual or group feels that they are being unjustly disadvantaged when compared to other individuals or groups, and believes that they are unable to improve their disadvantaged position by legitimate means, they may instead behave aggressively. This may involve individual acts of aggression like vandalism or assault, or collective acts of aggression, such as the riots that occurred in the north of England in 2001, discussed earlier in Text Box 9.1. Although the explicit cause of these riots was a protest against a British National Party rally, Asian youths also perceived themselves to be *disadvantaged* compared to the white community. Indeed, Lord Hattersley (formerly a British MP) noted in the aftermath of the riots that the underlying causes were alienation and deprivation.

Cultural Influences

Although acts of violence and aggression occur all over the world, the level of aggression appears to differ from culture to culture. It is, however, difficult to compare aggression levels in any absolute sense. Although western cultures like the USA and the UK traditionally endorse non-violence, democracy, and human rights, they have also recently waged war against Afghanistan (2002) and Iraq (2003). While they might argue that their aim was ultimately to reduce repression, violence and terrorism, those at the receiving end probably view western societies as being very aggressive. For this reason, it is probably easier to investigate the effect of culture on aggression *within* a particular society rather than between societies.

Nisbett and Cohen (1996) investigated cultural differences in aggression in the United States. An analysis of crime statistics revealed that the southern and western states had higher levels of violence than the northern states. Moreover, residents of southern and western states were more likely to approve of violence (Baron & Straus, 1989) and become more angry and stressed when insulted than the residents of northern states (Cohen et al., 1996). Nisbett and Cohen explained these differences in terms of the economy in these regions when Europeans first arrived in the US. Settlers in the southern and western states survived by herding animals, while settlers in the northern states farmed the land. Herders' assets (animals) are more vulnerable to theft than the assets of farmers (land). Herders therefore learnt from an early age that it was necessary to be able to respond quickly and aggressively to protect their animals from theft. This created a *culture of honour*, the deep-seated belief that men need to protect their assets, including both their property and their integrity, by resorting to violence. Although most Americans no longer work as herders or farmers, Nisbett and Cohen argue that this culture of honour continues to operate.

The culture of honour is a general set of norms and values that is associated with a higher level of aggression in certain regions, but there are also specific minority groups within a mainstream culture who show particularly high levels of aggression and violence, for example the violent gangs that exist in some urban areas. Groups such as these, with their subculture of violence (Toch, 1969), may perceive aggression to be a legitimate lifestyle choice which will enable them to improve their status and power within wider society. These groups hold a different set of norms and values from most societies, with rewards for aggression and violence and punishments for failure to adhere to this violent *group norm*. Aggression is directed at both outgroup members and ingroup members. There is evidence for a subculture of violence within the Sicilian Mafia in Italy (Nieburg, 1969) and in prison communities (Calkin, 1985). Although the examples we have used in this section have focused on the aggressive nature of some cultures, it is also important to note that group norms can also advocate peaceful and harmonious relations. For instance, Amish communities in the United States still endorse a lifestyle of non-violence and passivity (Gorer, 1968).

Summary

A number of situational factors increase the likelihood that an individual will behave aggressively. Three aspects of the *physical environment* have been shown to influence levels of aggression. A number of studies show that the higher the *temperature*, the more aggressive people are; heat leads to physiological arousal, irritation and discomfort, sparking aggression. People are also likely to behave aggressively when they are in a *crowd*. As with heat, this may be caused by feelings of stress and irritation, but it might also reflect the fact that people feel anonymous and therefore less accountable for their actions. The presence of unwanted *noise*, especially when it is loud or unpredictable, can also increase aggression. Broader societal issues may also be associated with aggression. People who feel *relatively deprived* compared to the rest of society may behave aggressively if they are unable to improve their position by legitimate means. There may also be *cultural differences* in the acceptability of aggression, but it is almost impossible to compare different societies in any absolute sense. Nevertheless, empirical evidence shows that areas of the United States where the economy was initially based on herding tend to be more aggressive than areas that initially farmed the land, because they have a *culture of honour* which requires them to be aggressive in order to protect their property. Some minority groups within a mainstream society, for example urban gangs, have a *subculture of violence* where aggression is a normative act.

DISINHIBITION

So far we have discussed broad theories about why aggression exists, and the specific person-centred and situation-centred determinants of particular aggressive acts. Aggression is, however, something that most people agree is wrong. Indeed, in most societies, *social norms* exist that encourage and reward pleasant and pro-social behaviour, and discourage and punish aggressive and anti-social behaviour. So why, despite these norms, do people sometimes behave aggressively towards others? In this section, we discuss why social norms that exist against aggression are sometimes violated, leading to aggressive behaviour. **Disinhibition** is a weakening of the normative constraints which usually lead to the avoidance of aggressive behaviour. Here we are interested in specifically those determinants of aggression that lead people to disregard pro-social norms. Below we discuss two reasons why people become disinhibited: *deindividuation* and *dehumanization*.

Deindividuation

When an individual is part of a crowd or acting as a member of a large social group, they are less likely to see themselves as an idiosyncratic individual and more likely to see themselves as a relatively anonymous group member. This process of **deindividuation** leads individuals to see themselves as less identifiable and less accountable for their behaviour than normal. As a result, the social norms that normally inhibit them from behaving aggressively are no longer so applicable. Deindividuation processes appear to have been operating in many incidences of aggression. The individuals who caused a riot during the Euro 2000 football championships discussed earlier in the chapter may have done so because they were acting as a crowd, a coherent – deindividuated – group of England supporters. Similarly, the 2001 'Summer of Violence' in northern England described in Text Box 9.1 involved crowds of anonymous individuals. These are both examples of *collective aggression*, an act of aggression committed by a group of individuals, regardless of whether those individuals know one another.

A shocking example of collective aggression is the 'crowd baiting' that sometimes occurs when an individual is threatening to commit suicide by jumping from a high building. Leon Mann (1981) looked at 21 cases reported in newspapers in the 1960s and 1970s, in which crowds were present when a suicidal person threatened to jump off a building, bridge, or tower. He found that in 10 of these cases, the victim was baited (jeered at and encouraged to jump) by the crowd below. Mann was interested in the conditions under which such crowd baiting occurred. He found that baiting tended to occur when the crowd was *large*, when there was a large *distance* between the crowd and the victim, and when the incident occurred at *night*. These factors all share one feature: they all contributed to a sense of deindividuation, providing individuals in the crowd with anonymity. Mann noted that baiting was also more likely to occur when the weather was warm and the victim had been threatening to jump for an extended period of time. These last two factors might be explained by feelings of frustration felt by the crowd and link back to some of the situational determinants of aggression that we discussed earlier.

Despite significant evidence for the role of deindividuation in producing aggression, some social psychologists oppose the idea. According to the **emergent norm theory**, people behave aggressively when they are in a group not because they *ignore* the societal norm of non-violence, but because they *adhere* to a different group norm of aggression that may arise in a particular circumstance. According to social identity theory (Tajfel & Turner, 1979, see Chapter 1), group norms provide a compelling guide for the attitudes and behaviour of individuals when their identity as a group member is salient (e.g. Reicher, Spears, & Postmes, 1995). When some members of a group start to behave aggressively, other members are likely to adhere to this behaviour if they perceive it to be normative. It may ultimately be the case that in group contexts people both disregard non-aggressive norms and adhere to emergent aggressive norms. Mann, Newton, and Innes (1982) found evidence for both theories. Although anonymous individuals were more likely to behave aggressively than those who were not anonymous, this difference was greater when aggressive behaviour was perceived as normative and smaller when aggression was perceived as non-normative.

Dehumanization

Deindividuation leads to disinhibition and aggression because it makes the aggressor anonymous and less accountable. However, disinhibition may also lead to aggression when the *victims* of aggression are anonymous. **Dehumanization** occurs when people fail to see others as unique human beings. By considering someone else to be in some way less than human, a perpetrator is less likely to appreciate the suffering experienced by the target of their aggression. This enables them to legitimize their actions and reduce any feelings of shame or guilt, thereby increasing the likelihood of aggression. Dehumanization often has catastrophic consequences. It is often cited as one of the major causes of genocide (see Text Box 9.4, which discusses the role of dehumanization in the genocide in Rwanda in 1994).

Text Box 9.4

The Rwandan Genocide

In 1994, in the small Central African country of Rwanda, one of the most catastrophic incidences of genocide ever seen unfolded when members of the Hutu tribe began a campaign of violence against the Tutsi tribe.

Origins of the Conflict
Although the majority Hutus and minority Tutsis, the two main ethnic groups in Rwanda, are very similar to one another, living in the same areas and following the same traditions, there has always been simmering ethnic tension between

(Continued)

them. In 1916, when the country was colonized by Belgium, this tension was exacerbated. The Belgians believed that Tutsis were superior to the Hutus and provided them with better jobs and education, generating resentment among the Hutus. When Rwanda was granted independence from Belgium in 1962, the Hutus took over the running of the country, and in the following decades Tutsis were often scapegoats during times of crisis. When the Hutu president was killed in April 1994, reports suggested that a Tutsi leader, Paul Kagame, was responsible, triggering a campaign of violence that spread from the capital to the rest of the country.

The Genocide

The presidential guard along with military officials, businessmen and politicians began a campaign of retribution against the Tutsis. Soon many others joined in, encouraged by radio propaganda, forming an unofficial militant group of up to 30,000 people, known as the 'Interahamwe'.

Hutu civilians were also encouraged to join in, and were given incentives of food, money and land to kill their Tutsi neighbours.

In the space of 100 days, between April and June, approximately 800,000 Rwandans were killed. Most of those who died were Tutsis, killed by members of the Hutu tribe. Moderate Hutus who did not support the genocide were also targeted.

The Role of Dehumanization

It is almost inconceivable that people in such large numbers could murder their fellow countryman and in some cases even their former friends. However, the negative feelings and resentment held by Hutus were so strong that Tutsis came to be seen as less than human. This viewpoint was spread throughout the country through the use of hate propaganda in print and on the radio. After the Hutu president was killed in April 1994, for example, the privately-owned radio station *Radio Television Libre des Mille Collines* called for a 'final war' to 'exterminate the cockroaches'. Later, it proclaimed that Tutsis were being 'killed like rats'. By treating the Tutsis as animals rather than as humans, the normal inhibition against committing murder was eliminated; it was considered that they did not deserve to be treated as humans. Thus, their murder was justified and legitimized in the eyes of the perpetrators.

Dehumanization might also help to explain the treatment of prisoners by members of the occupying British and American armed forces in the aftermath of the invasion of Iraq. In January 2004, it emerged that some of the American soldiers at

Abu Ghraib prison in Baghdad had been abusing Iraqi detainees. An internal criminal investigation revealed that detainees had, among other things, been beaten and electrocuted, and forced to remain naked for long periods of time. It also emerged that some detainees had been forced to walk on their hands and knees and bark like a dog, while others had sandbags put over their heads. British soldiers were found guilty of similar atrocities in Basra, in the south-east of Iraq.

The last two examples of mistreatment mentioned above are powerful examples of dehumanization. By treating prisoners like animals, their human characteristics were ignored. By covering the heads of detainees, they become anonymous. Such treatment undoubtedly made it easier for soldiers to behave aggressively. By not seeing their victims as human, soldiers were likely able to legitimize their actions and ignore the suffering they caused. But what led soldiers to dehumanize their prisoners?

One explanation for the dehumanization of victims, particularly on a group level, is **delegitimization**. In Rwanda, Hutus had come to hold an extreme hatred of the Tutsis (see Text Box 9.4). Although after the invasion of Iraq, Iraqi citizens were initially viewed with sympathy by the West, attitudes became increasingly hostile as the US death toll in Iraq since the invasion topped 1500 in March 2005 and the UK death toll reached 100. When a group is seen in a very negative light, it is placed in a negative social category, labelled as a threat to the norms, values, and the very way of life of the ingroup (Bar-Tal, 1990). By delegitimizing the outgroup in this way, dehumanization of the group and subsequent aggression towards it can be justified.

Summary

Aggression can be caused by *disinhibition*, a weakening of the normative constraints which usually lead to the avoidance of aggressive behaviour (although it is worth noting that disinhibition can also increase prosocial behaviour in certain contexts, as we will show in Chapter 10). People sometimes become disinhibited through a process of *deindividuation*, whereby individuals come to see themselves as less identifiable and less accountable for their behaviour than normal. Deindividuation may explain acts of collective aggression like football hooliganism and 'crowd baiting'. However, *emergent-norm theory* makes the alternative argument that people behave aggressively when they are in a group not because they ignore the societal norm of non-violence, but because they adhere to a different group norm of aggression that may arise in a particular circumstance. Disinhibition may also lead to aggression when the targets of aggression are *dehumanized* and *delegitimized*, sometimes with catastrophic consequences.

Text Box 9.5

An interpretative phenomenological approach to aggression

The majority of research on aggression uses quantitative methodology to understand when and why people are aggressive. But some researchers argue that such methods cannot capture the essence of the aggression; that is, not give us a detailed, vivid account of what it is actually *like* to experience aggression, and all the intense emotions that often accompany it. Psychological research using qualitative methods can, however, help provide an insight into the complexity and vividness of subjective experiences associated with social phenomena like aggression. Eatough and Smith (2006) carried out one such study.

Method

Marilyn, a 30-year-old woman living with her partner in a council home in an inner-city area in the UK, was interviewed by the researcher. Semi-structured interviews were undertaken over a period of three weeks, which resulted in four hours of interview material. The data were then transcribed in full, and analysed using interpretative phenomenological analysis (IPA). This technique is primarily concerned with the subjective experience, or 'lifeworld', of an individual. It is a process in which 'the participants are trying to make sense of their world' and 'the researcher is trying to make sense of the participants trying to make sense of their world' (Smith & Osborn, 2003: 51). The researcher reads through the transcript several times, each time drawing out more detailed observations, and clustering them into higher order themes.

Results

Marilyn described in detail her experience of anger and aggression, with several interesting findings emerging that provide a vivid sense of the subjective experiences that accompany aggressive behaviour. First, Marilyn explained in detail the physical process she goes through as she becomes angry. She described how she begins to tremble, becomes physically very hot, and becomes very tearful. The feelings she experiences are of great intensity, and she repeatedly talks of feeling like a 'wild, wild person' (p. 489). Second, she detailed how once she has become very angry, she has little control over it. She noted being aware that she is about to lash out in a physically aggressive manner, for example breaking ornaments or a mirror, but that she cannot stop herself from doing so. She also talked about being dissociated from her anger: afterwards she is often unable to recall what she's done until she sees the damage that she has caused. Third, she discussed how she is often not provoked by an outsider. Instead, as she becomes increasingly angry, it is her own internal anger and negative emotions that trigger aggressive behaviour rather than the behaviour of anyone else.

Discussion

This type of qualitative analysis is very useful for gaining an in-depth understanding of the subjective experiences that accompany aggressive behaviour, which quantitative research may be less able to capture. A limitation of this approach, however, is that one would have to interview many individuals to get a broader understanding of how subjective experiences of anger vary from person to person, and what factors explain such variations. Accordingly, many researchers advocate using qualitative and quantitative research side by side in order to gain a fully inclusive understanding of social psychological phenomenan like aggression.

FORMS OF AGGRESSION IN SOCIETY

In this chapter we have discussed the broad reasons why aggression exists, the specific determinants of aggression, and reasons why typically non-aggressive norms are sometimes abandoned. In this last section we focus in on four specific forms of aggression that have received particular attention from social psychologists: *domestic violence*, *sexual harassment*, *sexual aggression*, and *terrorism*.

Domestic Violence

Considerable attention has been devoted to the issue of domestic violence in recent years, in terms of both research and media coverage. Every minute in the UK, the police receive a call for assistance regarding domestic violence. This amounts to over 570,000 calls a year (Stanko, 2000). However, because victims of domestic violence often feel scared or ashamed, these statistics may not be an accurate representation of how widespread the problem is. According to the British Crime Survey, only 40.2 per cent of actual domestic violence crime is reported to the police (Dodd et al., 2004). While traditionally we perceive the term domestic violence to refer to aggression by a male partner towards a female partner, it can be more accurately defined as verbal or physical aggression towards any member of one's family. Indeed, women are actually slightly more likely to engage in physical violence towards their partners than men in heterosexual relationships (Archer, 2000). However, acts of domestic violence committed by men tend to receive more attention because they are more likely to result in serious injury or death.

Shockingly, people are more likely to be killed or physically assaulted by members of their own family than by anyone else (Gelles, 1997). Gelles and Straus (1979) argued that because people spend more time with family members, and engage in a broader range of activities with family members than with anyone else, family members are highly dependent on one another, and have an intimate knowledge of the strengths and weaknesses of other family members. When things are going well, these characteristics are good things, but when things go wrong, they may be used as a means of harming other family members. Moreover, the physical proximity of family members means that they are more likely to become the targets of frustration and stress when it arises. Factors that are associated with domestic violence include stress, for example financial difficulties and illness, and alcohol abuse on the part of the perpetrator. People who themselves have previously been the target of domestic violence are also more likely to aggress against a family member, resulting in a cycle of abuse that passes down from generation to generation.

Sexual Harassment

Sexual harassment is a form of sex discrimination. The legal definition of sexual harassment is 'unwelcome verbal, visual, or physical conduct of a sexual nature that is severe or pervasive and affects working conditions or creates a hostile work environment' (Equality Rights Advocate, 2009). It encompasses a wide range of behaviours of varying severity, from degrading remarks, to unwanted sexual advances, through to sexual assault. Statistics indicate that sexual harassment is, regrettably, very widespread. One survey showed that 40–50% of women in schools, colleges, and workplaces have fallen victim to sexual harassment (Crawford & Unger, 2004). Men are thought to harass women in order to exercise power and control over them (Stark, 2007). In addition to negative emotional and physical consequences for women who are harassed, harassment in the workplace can also damage financial security and limit career advancement (Looby, 2001)

So what factors might predict sexual harassment? Well, a number of social psychologists believe that the media plays an important role. Ferguson and colleagues (2005) presented participants with clips of promiscuous or non-promiscuous women on the *Jerry Springer Show*. They were then presented with a scenario about sexual harassment, and were asked to evaluate the situation. It emerged that participants who observed the promiscuous woman rated the victim of harassment as less traumatized by the harassment and more responsible for what happened to her compared to participants who observed media containing non-promiscuous women. This effect can be explained by stereotype application: participants who observed promiscuous women in the media were more likely to assume that women in general were promiscuous, which in turn, affected their evaluation of a sexual harassment case.

Dill, Brown, and Collins (2008) wondered whether aggressive video games might also increase tolerance for sexual harassment. Although previously research on video games has primarily looked at their effect on generalized aggression rather than harassment of women in particular, Dill and colleagues noted that the majority of male video game characters are violent and hyper-masculine, and videos tend to include scenes that glamorize violence and sexual aggression. There are also highly stereotypical and marginalized perceptions of women in these games: women rarely appear, but those present tend to be beautiful, busty and scantily clad sex objects (Dill & Thill, 2007). Dill and colleagues had male and female participants watch a presentation of sex-typed video game characters, or in a control condition, US senators and congresspersons. To re-enforce the impact of this task, participants were asked to try to remember as many characters as possible for a subsequent recall test. Participants were subsequently asked to read a real-life story of sexual harassment perpetrated by a male college professor against a female college student, and rate how serious it was, how guilty the perpetrator was, and how responsible the female victim was. It emerged that male (but not female) participants who watched the presentation of video game characters subsequently showed more tolerance of sexual harassment than those in the control condition.

Sexual Aggression

The British Crime Survey (2002) estimated that during 2001, there were 190,000 incidences of serious sexual assault and 47,000 female victims of rape or attempted rape (Walby & Allen, 2004). Social-psychological investigations have attempted to uncover why **sexual aggression** occurs.

One factor that may contribute towards sexual aggression is the availability of pornographic material – magazines, films, and internet websites that show material of a sexual nature. Studies have shown that exposure to pornographic material may increase tolerance for sexual aggression, and actual aggression towards others. Zillman and Bryant (1984), for example, exposed participants to either a low, moderate, or large amount of violent pornography. Participants who had viewed a large amount of pornography, and who had also been insulted by a confederate, subsequently viewed rape more tolerantly, recommending lower prison sentences for the crime than those who had had less exposure to the pornography.

To investigate the effect of pornography on *actual* violence, Donnerstein and Berkowitz (1981) had female confederates insult male participants to make them angry. The participants then watched one of two versions of a sexually violent film, in which two men raped a woman. In one version, the victim appeared to be enjoying the experience, whereas in the other film, the victim was clearly distressed by the experience. Participants were then given the opportunity to behave aggressively (by administering electric shocks) towards the confederate who they had previously met. Compared to participants in a control condition who had watched a non-violent film, men who had watched either of the violent films *and* who had previously been angered by the female confederate administered larger shocks to her. When they had not been insulted (and were therefore not angry), however, men only administered larger shocks to the confederate when they had seen the film in which the woman appeared to be enjoying the sexual assault.

One reason why pornography and sexually aggressive films increase tolerance for sexual aggression and actual aggression towards women is that it perpetuates the rape myth. This is the inaccurate belief that women secretly enjoy being sexually assaulted. Malamuth and Check (1981) found that male college students who had watched sexually aggressive movies were later more likely to accept rape myths and interpersonal aggression against women than men who had watched a mainstream romantic movie.

A second explanation offered for sexual aggression, such as the rape of women, particularly *acquaintance rape* where the victim knows or is even dating the perpetrator, concerns the role of women compared to men in society. Traditionally, while men are applauded for sexual promiscuity, women who appear to be too sexually active, particularly outside of a relationship, are seen as 'loose' and immoral in some way. Instead, women are implicitly expected to be chaste and resist the sexual advances of men. Some researchers have argued that this double standard may lead women to engage in token resistance. Muehlenhard and Hollabaugh (1988), for example, found that 39 per cent of a sample of female undergraduate students admitted that they had at times said 'no' to sex when they had actually meant 'yes'. Such behaviour is dangerous as it perpetuates the rape myth and encourages men to ignore women when they say they do not want sex. However, recent studies have placed the estimate of the proportion of women who show token resistance at a much lower level, around 10 per cent (Shotland & Hunter, 1995). Moreover, despite modest evidence for its role, it is important to emphasize that the concept of token resistance cannot in any way be used as an excuse to justify rape.

Terrorism

Since the start of this millennium, we have witnessed a number of catastrophic acts of international terrorism. On 11 September 2001, 3057 people were killed when four planes were hijacked, two of which were crashed into the twin towers of the World Trade Center in New York and one of which was crashed into the Pentagon in Washington DC. On 11 March 2004, a coordinated terrorist attack on the commuter train system in Madrid killed 192 and injured a further 2050 people. On the morning of 7 July 2005, four bombers killed themselves and 52 others when they exploded bombs on three underground trains and a bus in central London. As people learnt about these, and other, terrorist attacks, many undoubtedly wondered what sort of individuals could bring themselves to cause so much harm to others.

Moghaddam (2005) proposed the **staircase to terrorism**, a psychological model which may help to explain how and why certain individuals come to commit such atrocities. He used the metaphor of a narrowing staircase leading to the terrorist act at the top of a building. Potential terrorists go through several stages, as they proceed up to each floor of the building, before a terrorist act will be committed. At each floor the number of options that an individual can pursue reduces until there is no option remaining apart from the destruction of others. Below, the processes that are thought to take place on each floor are outlined.

Ground Floor – Perceptions of Relative Deprivation: Hundreds of millions of people occupy the ground floor. They believe in the importance of fairness and just treatment, but feel that they are not receiving the benefits that they should be. Although poverty and a lack of education may be contributing factors at this level, it is the *relative* rather than the *absolute* level of deprivation that is important here. Terrorists are often not the poorest individuals living in the poorest regions; rather they are people who, regardless of how affluent or educated they are, perceive there to be injustices regarding their groups' position in society relative to other groups.

First Floor – Perceptions of Procedural Justice: A minority of individuals on the ground floor will climb to the first floor in search of solutions for perceived injustices. If individuals perceive there to be opportunities for them to individually move out of their deprived social group to a better position, they are unlikely to continue further up the staircase. Another important factor at this stage is the perception of *procedural justice*, how fair the individual perceives their government to be, and how much of an opportunity they have to take part in the decision-making process or voice dissatisfaction.

Second Floor – Displacement of Aggression: When individuals cannot publicly voice their dissatisfaction, they will climb to the second floor, displacing their aggression by blaming other groups for their perceived problems. An example of this might be the anti-Americanism that exists in many countries in the Middle East. Individuals who *actively* seek out opportunities to aggress against the blamed group will climb to the third floor, searching for ways in which they can take direct action against their perceived enemy.

Third Floor – Adoption of an Alternative Moral Code: On the third floor, individuals are recruited into terrorist organizations. While mainstream society views them as immoral, within terrorist organizations an alternative version of morality is adopted. Here, it is the enemy that is seen as immoral, while the terrorists perceive themselves to be martyring themselves for a just goal. This fits in with *emergent norm theory*, discussed earlier in the chapter – the idea that people behave aggressively because they are adhering to a new set of aggressive social norms that emerge from the formation of a new group, rather than because they are ignoring egalitarian social norms.

Fourth Floor – Categorical Thinking and Perceived Legitimacy: The new recruits to the terrorist organizations become part of small cells. They are encouraged to think categorically and highlight the difference between 'us' (the terrorist group) and 'them' (the enemy), which helps to legitimize the goals of the terrorist (see the above section on dehumanization). At this point, they have little opportunity to escape, as there is often a very short period of time between recruitment and carrying out of the terrorist attack. Prior to any attack, the recruits are encouraged by being lavished with encouragement and attention by the other members of the cell. The cell leader is often a strong authority figure who will not tolerate disobedience or disloyalty. From this point, the actions of the individual are therefore strongly controlled.

Fifth Floor – The Terrorist Act: Two mechanisms operate which finally lead an individual to harm innocent civilians. First, civilians are categorized as part of the outgroup, and second, the psychological distance between the ingroup and the out-group is exaggerated. By seeing civilians as part of an enemy group, the soon-to-be terrorist sidesteps the normal inhibitory mechanisms that stop people from harming others (see the earlier sections on *dehumanization* and *delegitimization*). In addi-tion, because victims are not normally aware of the impending danger, they do not have the opportunity to behave in ways that might trigger inhibitory mechanisms, like pleading, crying, and making eye contact with the perpetrator.

Moghaddam (1998) noted that although some people are probably more likely to become terrorists than others, it is the conditions on the ground floor which ulti-mately lead to terrorism. He argued that only by changing the conditions on the ground floor can terrorism be effectively stopped.

Summary

In this section we have identified three specific forms of aggression that occur all too frequently in society. *Domestic violence* refers to verbal or physical aggression towards a family member. People are more likely to be physically harmed by members of their own family than by anyone else; the physical proximity of family members means that they are most likely to become scapegoats for stress and frustration. There is some evidence that tolerance for sexual harassment is increased by television programmes and video games that portray women as stereotypical and promiscuous, and men as hyper-masculine. *Sexual aggression*, on the other hand, may be exacerbated by the increasing availability of pornographic materials. Research shows that exposure to pornography increases tolerance for sexual violence, perhaps because it perpetuates the *rape myth*. The start of this century has seen an unprecedented number of acts of terrorism against the West. According to the *staircase to terrorism* model, relative deprivation and a perceived lack of procedural justice leads some people to voice their dissatisfaction through acts of terrorism. According to this model, changing societal conditions will be ultimately more effective than fighting individual terrorists.

CHAPTER SUMMARY

In this chapter, we have provided an overview of the social psychological research on aggression. We have explained *why* we have a general tendency to behave aggressively, *when* we are most likely to be aggressive, and some of the ways in which aggression manifests itself in society. There are a number of reasons why we might behave aggressively. *Biological theories* argue that we behave aggressively because it is adaptive for us to do so, enabling us to protect our genes by ensuring the survival of ourselves and our offspring. However, although there may be some biological tendencies towards aggression, these tendencies are undoubtedly shaped by our social environment.

Social psychologists have argued that we may become aggressive because we feel frustrated by concerns in our lives which we cannot resolve and take out our frustrations on an available scapegoat to achieve *catharsis*. Environmental cues that generate frustration lead to physiological arousal which increases the likelihood of aggressive behaviour. According to the *cognitive neoassociationalist model*, if a particular stimulus has been repeatedly associated with an angry response, the mere presence of that stimulus – be it another person or a situation – will result in anger and aggression. Interestingly, even arousal that does not actually arise as a result of frustration or anger, for example physiological arousal from playing sport, can be incorrectly attributed to anger. We also learn aggressive behaviour from the behaviour of those around us. *Social learning theory* has important implications for aggression in society because it implies that merely watching acts of aggression, for example in films or on video games, will increase the likelihood that we will behave aggressively ourselves.

In addition to these overarching theories of why aggression occurs in general, research has revealed a diverse range of factors which influence whether or not specific people will behave aggressively. Some of these factors relate to characteristics of the potential perpetrator of aggression. There are, for example, significant *gender differences* in aggression. Traditionally, men are perceived as being more aggressive, but a closer examination has revealed that men and women *both* show aggression; the key difference lies in the *type* of aggression they show. Men are typically more physically aggressive, but females employ more subtle forms of aggression. These patterns reflect not only hormonal and physical differences between the sexes, but also the fact that women tend to have larger and more intimate social networks where indirect forms of aggression are more likely to be effective. An individual's personality may also make them more or less likely to behave aggressively; people who score high on *agreeableness* are not as likely to be aggressive whereas individuals with a *type A personality* or *high self-esteem* combined with an *ego threat* are more likely to aggress. People who are under the influence of *alcohol*

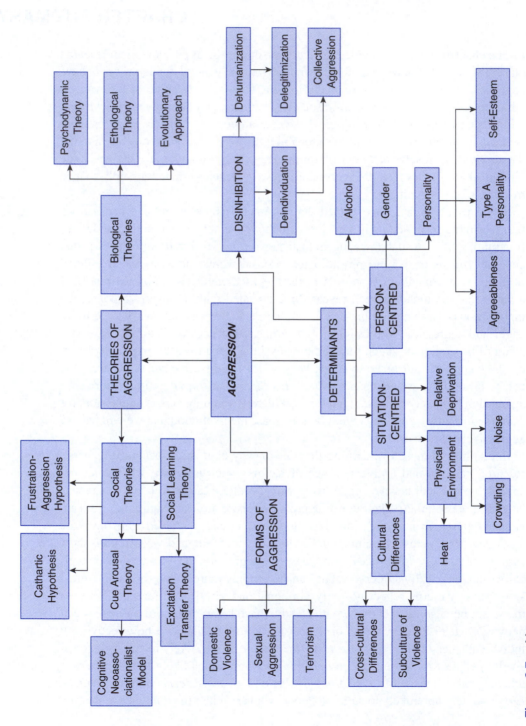

Figure 9.7   Memory map

also behave more aggressively because of impairments in neuropsychological function which decrease their ability to carefully process information about a situation.

These individual differences in aggression are likely to interact with the *situation* in which people find themselves. People are, for example, more likely to be aggressive when the weather is *hot* (but not too hot), when they are part of a large *crowd* and when it is *noisy*, particularly if the noise is too loud or unpredictable. Broader societal factors may also be important; those who feel *deprived* relative to relevant others are more likely to behave aggressively, particularly if they feel they cannot escape their social disadvantage in a more constructive way. Certain cultures may also be generally more aggressive than others, although it is difficult to compare subjectively defined levels of aggression from culture to culture. Nevertheless, there is some evidence that the southern and western states of the United States are generally more aggressive than the northern states because they endorse a *culture of honour*. Moreover, certain minority groups have a *subculture of violence*, where aggression is the norm, something that is actively encouraged and rewarded.

Although most societies have a social norm of pro-social behaviour and non-violence which means we are generally reluctant to behave aggressively, people sometimes choose to violate these norms and behave aggressively anyway, a process known as *disinhibition*. People who are in a crowd or acting as a member of a large social group are more likely to behave aggressively because they feel *anonymous and less responsible* for their individual actions. This process of *deindividuation* helps to explain acts of collective aggression. Disinhibition may, however, also lead to aggression when the *victims* of aggression seem to be anonymous. When people become *dehumanized*, it is easier to behave aggressively towards them without feelings of shame or guilt.

Aggression manifests itself in many different ways. *Domestic violence*, verbal or physical aggression towards any member of one's family, is a form of aggression that has received considerable research and media attention in recent years. Although violent attacks on women by their male partners tend to be the most high profile cases, women can also be the perpetrators of domestic violence. Social psychologists have also studied sexual harassment and *sexual aggression*, such as rape and sexual assault, and attempted to uncover its antecedents. One factor experimentally shown to contribute towards tolerance of sexual aggression and actual aggression towards woman is exposure to pornographic material. Pornography perpetuates the *rape myth*, the erroneous belief that women enjoy being sexually assaulted. Finally, we discussed the role of a particularly catastrophic and far-reaching form of aggression – that of terrorism. Although the acts of terrorists seem understandably senseless to the majority of people, social psychologists have proposed that complex societal conditions interact with personal characteristics to edge individuals ever closer to committing acts of terrorism. The *staircase to terrorism* proposes that broad societal change will ultimately be the most effective way of eradicating terrorism.

Taking it Further

Try This

Think of a time when you have behaved aggressively towards someone else. How well do the predictors of aggression discussed in this chapter explain your aggressive behaviour? Was it a hot day, or had you been drinking alcohol, or were there many aggressive cues around you? Which predictors appear to be most relevant, or can you identify other social psychological causes not covered above?

Debate This

Qualitative research on aggression focuses on an individual's subjective experience of aggression. Quantitative research, on the other hand, identifies broader trends and predictors of aggression. Which approach do you think provides the best answer to understanding aggression, and why?

Something for the Weekend

Based on what you have learnt about aggression in this chapter, design an intervention for reducing aggressive and anti-social behaviour in schools. First, think about where and when aggressive behaviour is most likely to be observed – can you predict this based on the situational determinants of aggression that we have discussed in this chapter (think about crowding, disindividuation, etc.)? As well as making the environment less conducive to aggression, are there other things you could do based more broadly on the topics we have explored in the book so far? For example, could you use persuasion (Chapter 4) or social influence (Chapter 6) to help you change norms that define the situations in which aggressive behaviour is seen as acceptable or unacceptable?

Further Readings

The Essentials

Geen, R.G. (1998) Aggression and antisocial behaviour. In D.T. Gilbert, S.T. Fiske, & G. Lindzey (eds.), *The handbook of social psychology* (4th ed., Vol. 2, pp. 317–356). New York: McGraw-Hill.

This handbook chapter provides a great overview of research on aggression and anti-social behaviour, and expands on many of the topics we have introduced in this chapter.

Next Steps

Anderson, C.A. & Bushman, B.J. (2002) Human aggression. *Annual Review of Psychology*, *53*, 27–51.

Malamuth, N.M. & Addison, T. (2001) Integrating social psychological research on aggression within an evolutionary-based framework. In G.J.O. Fletcher & M.S. Clark (Eds.), *Blackwell handbook of social psychology: Interpersonal processes* (pp. 129–161). Malden, MA: Blackwell.

The first is a comprehensive review article written by Craig Anderson and Brad Bushman, two of the leaders in the field when it comes to aggression, so it's a great next step if you want to get to know more about aggression research. If the evolutionary perspective on aggression has got you interested, this second chapter provides an overview of how evolutionary theory can inform social psychological approaches to understanding aggression.

Delving Deeper

Anderson, C.A., Gentile, D.A., & Buckley, K.E. (2007). *Violent video game effects on children and adolescents: Theory, research, and public policy*. New York: Oxford University Press.

This book by Craig Anderson and colleagues is a must for anyone interested in the debate over the role of media in generating violent behaviour.

Prosocial Behaviour

10

What is Prosocial Behaviour?

Origins of Prosocial Behaviour
Evolutionary Perspective
Social Norms
Modelling

Situation-Centred Determinants of Helping
Latané and Darley's Cognitive Model
The Bystander Apathy Effect
Piliavin's Bystander-Calculus Model

Perceiver-Centred Determinants of Helping
Personality
Competence
Mood
Empathy-Altruism
Gender Differences in Helping

Recipient-Centred Determinants of Helping
Similarity
Group Membership
Attractiveness
Responsibility for Misfortune

Receiving Help

Prosocial Behaviour

After Flight 11 crashed into the north tower of the World Trade Center on 11 September 2001, Frank De Martini and Pablo Ortiz helped rescue people on the 88th floor of the north tower where they worked. They then led a group up towards the crash zone. Using a crowbar and a flashlight, the group prised open doors and cleared rubble on 12 floors along the boundary of the crash zone, where many people were trapped. In their account of events, Dwyer and Flynn (2005: 88) noted, 'It was hardly the job of De Martini and Pablo Ortiz and the others ... to go around prying doors open. Their responsibilities at the trade centre during an emergency were to get themselves out of the building'. Despite this, they saved the lives of at least 70 people. Sadly, they paid the ultimate sacrifice for their actions, losing their own lives when the tower collapsed because, rather than head to safety, they had put the lives of others first.

WHAT IS PROSOCIAL BEHAVIOUR?

The actions of De Martini and Ortiz are examples of prosocial behaviour, actions that are generally valued by other people in a particular society. Many types of behaviour can be classified as prosocial, for example friendship, charity, sacrifice, sharing and cooperation. However, the majority of research on prosocial behaviour focuses on two specific types of prosocial behaviour, helping behaviour and altruism. **Helping behaviour** refers to acts where people voluntarily and intentionally behave in a way that they believe will benefit others, although at the same time the behaviour may benefit them as well. Because helping behaviour has to be intentional, this definition therefore excludes behaviour which incidentally benefits another person but was not intended, for example dropping some money by accident, which someone else happens to find later on. In addition, because help-ing behaviour has to be intentional, this definition also excludes behaviour which appears to be aimed at helping others (for example, a company making a donation to a charity) but that has actually been carried out entirely for selfish purposes (to raise the company profile and therefore increase future profit). This definition does not, however, exclude behaviour that benefits others and oneself. We might, for example, donate money to a charity because we want to help, but also because it makes us feel good about ourselves. **Altruism** is a more specific form of helping behaviour referring to an act of prosocial behaviour which benefits others but is not expected to have any personal benefits. De Martini and Ortiz behaved altruistically on 11 September 2001; their actions had no personal benefits, and in fact clearly put them at risk, but they continued nonetheless.

Much of social psychology focuses on negative aspects of human social behav-iour, for example how people discriminate against and show prejudice towards those who do not belong to the same group as them (see Chapter 7), and people's capacity to behave in an aggressive manner (see Chapter 9). These lines of research seem to suggest that, ultimately, we behave in ways that best serve our own inter-ests. However, the capacity that we have to behave in a prosocial manner, to vol-untarily help others regardless of whether it is in our best interests, gives us reason for optimism. In this chapter, we focus on this positive aspect of social behaviour. We first outline the origins of this tendency to help others. We then examine the factors that affect *when* we help and when we do not. Some of these factors relate to the situation in which help is needed and others relate to characteristics of the potential helper. We will also look at *who* we help. We are more likely to help those who are similar to us, who are ingroup members, who we find attractive, and who we believe our deserving of our help. Finally, we consider what it is like to be a recipient of help.

ORIGINS OF PROSOCIAL BEHAVIOUR

There are three broad accounts of why we help others. Some psychologists argue that we are innately predisposed to help others because of our evolutionary make-up. Two other accounts rely on more social psychological theories. Some psychologists argue that we are socialized to help others, and that our helping behaviour relates to internalized *beliefs* about the social norms of the society in which we live. A third explanation argues that we attend to the helping behaviour of those around us, and that this leads us to copy, or model, such behaviours. These three approaches and the evidence that has been found in support of each are outlined below.

Evolutionary Perspective

The **evolutionary perspective** argues that we are biologically predisposed to help others. Put another way, we are born with an in-built tendency to look after those around us, even if it does not have any obvious benefit for us. But why would this be the case? According to sociobiologists, we engage in helping behaviour to ensure the survival of our genes. By helping our blood relatives, we improve their chances of survival, thus increasing the likelihood that they will survive to pass our genes on to future generations. Accordingly, it has been argued that the genes responsible for prosocial behaviour might be self-selected as, in the long term, they increase the probability that the species will survive.

This approach has generated heated debate between social psychologists and sociobiologists. First, we help not only relatives, but also friends and even complete strangers. It is not clear how this would increase the chances of our *own* genes surviving. Second, social psychologists argue that despite anecdotal evidence, there are, in fact, no empirical studies that clearly support the evolutionary explanation for prosocial behaviour in humans. This is due to an inherent problem with evolutionary explanations: the processes that are assumed to explain behaviour (i.e. evolution of genetic typology) cannot be observed over an appropriate timescale in the laboratory. Third, the approach fails to explain why people help in some circumstances but fail to help in others. Evolutionary theory would predict, quite simply, that we should help blood relatives in every situation – any situation that requires help may be a potential threat to genes being passed on. However, this is clearly not the case, as instances of child abuse by family members vividly illustrate. Any complete explanation of helping behaviour will need to explain not only when helping behaviour will occur, but also explain why in some cases it does not. These three critical limitations mean that whilst it is likely that evolutionary theory has some role to play in explaining helping behaviour, a comprehensive account of prosocial behaviour will need to consider other factors.

Standing in contrast to the evolutionary explanation are two social psychological accounts of why people exhibit helping behaviour. The first account explains helping with reference to social norms. The second account argues that social learning explains helping; we help because we have repeatedly observed other people behaving helpfully, providing a model for our own behaviour. Below, we first discuss how social norms explain why we help others.

Social Norms

Social norms (see Chapter 6 on social influence) reflect what is considered normal and acceptable in a given group, culture or society. They are common-held attitudes, beliefs and behaviours that have a powerful influence on how we behave. Indeed, there is evidence that people are rewarded (e.g. approval, social acceptance) for behaving in accordance with social norms, but punished for violating social norms (e.g. disapproval, rejection), as we saw in Chapter 6. Although social norms differ between different social groups and different cultures, almost every culture holds a norm that we should help others whenever possible. Three normative beliefs may explain why we have a tendency to help others: reciprocity, social responsibility, and social justice.

According to the **reciprocity principle** (Gouldner, 1960) we should help those who help us. This principle is universally held, and plays an important role in interpersonal processes (see Chapter 11). We do not, however, automatically help others who have helped us: we are more likely to reciprocate to another person if they previously made a big, unexpected, sacrifice for us (Tesser, Gatewood, & Driver, 1968).

In contrast, the **social responsibility** norm holds that we should help those in need regardless of whether they have helped us, or are likely to be able to help us in the future. There is evidence that people are often willing to help needy others, even when they remain anonymous and do not expect to be rewarded by approval from others (Berkowitz, 1972). We do not, however, help any needy person. Instead, we are selective. Whether the person is seen as having brought their misfortune on themselves may influence whether we decide to help. The just world hypothesis may explain this tendency.

The **just-world hypothesis** (Lerner & Miller, 1978) is the general belief people have that the world is a just, fair, place where people get what they deserve (an example of a heuristic belief; see Chapter 3). According to this norm people typically believe that 'good things happen to good people, bad things happen to bad people'. However, when we are confronted with a person who appears to be suffering undeservedly, this undermines our belief in a just world. To restore our believe that the world is a fair place, we have a tendency to help others who are in need, but *only* if we believe their suffering is through no fault of their own. According to this principle, we are more likely to donate money to a breast cancer charity (where sufferers are seen as having no role in developing the disease) than to a lung cancer charity (where we may assume smoking is often to blame for the disease).

Although social norms may play a role in explaining helping behaviour, not all social psychologists agree that they are the key to our understanding of the phenomenon. Teger (1970) argued that while we may verbally endorse the idea of helping others, we do not necessarily act on this endorsement (i.e. there is sometimes a mismatch between attitudes and behaviour; see Chapter 4). There is also evidence that external factors influence whether an attitude predisposed towards helping will actually translate into helping behaviour. Warren and Walker (1991) looked at the effect of 'need persistence' (how long help is needed for) on helping behaviour, and found that people were more likely to donate money to a refugee family from the Sudan when the family only needed financial assistance in the short term rather than in the long term (see Figure 10.1). It appeared that the social norm of helping only

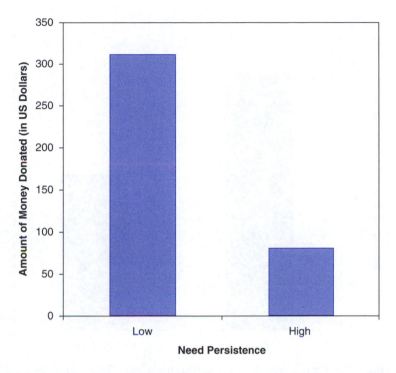

Figure 10.1 The effect of need persistence on size of donation. Data from Warren and Walker (1991)

translated into helping behaviour when the behaviour was perceived as being likely to be effective. This study highlights the possibility that it is not only internally held beliefs – like social norms – that determine whether people help, but that there are *situational* factors that play a role. Observation of what other people are doing in the situations we find ourselves in is the basis for the second social-psychological account of why we help others.

Modelling

The second reason why we have a tendency to engage in helping behaviour is that we have learnt to do so by observing the behaviour of others, a process known as **modelling** or observational learning. The previous social psychological explanation of helping behaviour – social norms – is based on processes that are internal to the perceivers, that is, the attitudes they hold. This final explanation focuses more on external factors; is it the observation of others in the situation that explains why we help others?

Bryan and Test (1967) investigated whether modelling would increase the likelihood of helping behaviour. In a highly realistic experiment, motorists passed a woman whose car had a flat tyre. In the modelling condition, another car had pulled

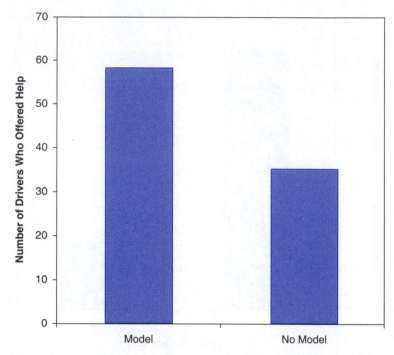

Figure 10.2 The effect of modelling on helping behaviour. Data from Bryan and Test (1967)

over and appeared to be helping her change the tyre. Motorists then came across a second woman whose car had a flat tyre, but who this time was receiving no assistance. In the control condition, the drivers saw no model prior to coming across the car with the flat tyre. Motorists who had observed a model of helping behaviour (another motorist helping the first women) were more likely to stop than if they had not observed such a model (see Figure 10.2).

In a similar experiment, Rushton and Campbell (1977) had female participants interact with a friendly woman, actually a confederate, as part of what they had been told was a study on social interaction (although this was just a cover story). As the women left the laboratory together at the end of the 'study' they were asked if they would make a pledge to give blood. When the confederate was asked first, and signed up to give blood, 67 per cent of participants also agreed to give blood. In contrast, when participants were asked first, only 25 per cent agreed to give blood.

According to Bandura's (1972) *social learning theory*, observing the helping behaviour of others should increase the likelihood of us helping others because it shows us that the behaviour is appropriate and increases perceptions of *self-efficacy*, our belief that we can successfully help another person. Bandura noted, however, that modelling will only produce helping behaviour if it had a positive outcome.

Hornstein (1970) conducted an experiment in which participants observed another person returning a lost wallet. The person returning the wallet either seemed pleased to help or displeased at the bother of having to help. Hornstein found that when participants came across another lost wallet, those who had observed the positive reaction were more likely to help than those who had observed the negative reaction.

The mass media can also be used to increase a prosocial orientation. Greitemeyer (2009) asked participants to listen to a prosocial song ('Love Generation', by Bob Sinclair) or in a control condition, a neutral song ('Rock This Party', by Bob Sinclair). A pre-test established that the lyrics of the first song were significantly more prosocial than the lyrics of the second. In one study, after listening to one of the two songs, participants were asked to read essays, supposedly by other students who had suffered misfortunes such as a broken leg or a painful relationship break-up, and were asked to rate how empathic they felt towards the writer. In a second study, after listening to one of the two songs, participants were asked to consider donating their participant fee to charity. It emerged that participants who had listened to the prosocial song were more empathic towards victims of misfortune, and were more likely to donate money to charity. The long-term effects of listening to a prosocial song were not considered, but the author argued that repeated exposure to prosocial songs may have benefits for prosocial behaviour. Looking at the effects of prosocial video games, Gentile and colleagues (2009) found that children who played prosocial video games were more likely to help, rather than harm, a participant on a subsequent task, and tended to have a more prosocial orientation in general. It seems, therefore, that the media can have a positive effect on behaviour. But unfortunately, as the research discussed in Chapter 9 shows, people are also frequently exposed to violent media, which can increase aggressive behaviours.

Summary

So far in this chapter, we have identified some of the possible origins of helping behaviour. We saw how although there may be some evolutionary basis to the way in which we help others, social psychologists believe that there are other more likely explanations. Specifically, we are influenced by *societal norms*, such as *reciprocity*, *social responsibility* and *fairness*. *Social learning* may also play a role. We may help because we model our helping behaviour on the behaviour of others. In the following sections, we will be talking about some of the specific situations that psychologists have identified where helping is, or is not, offered. In particular, psychologists have been concerned with trying to explain when people do not help, even though it is apparent that the situation is an emergency. We divide this research into three broad sections, reflecting three distinct types of factor that determine helping: situational factors, preceiver factors, and recipient factors.

SITUATION-CENTRED DETERMINANTS OF HELPING

Some of the studies discussed in the previous section on the origins of prosocial behaviour (e.g. Bryan & Test, 1967; Warren & Walker, 1991) illustrate that we do not always offer help. Instead, situational factors appear to play an important role. Although contemporary research on prosocial behaviour has broadened to consider any situation in which help might be needed, much of the research and theory has focused on when people help in an *emergency*, behaviour commonly referred to by social psychologists as **bystander intervention**.

The much cited and discussed case that generated the rapid expansion of research on bystander intervention was the murder of a young woman walking home through Kew Gardens in Queens, New York, in March 1964. Kitty Genovese was on her way home from work late at night when she was attacked by a man with a knife. She fought her attacker, and shouted and cried for help, escaping him on two occasions. However, each time, no one responded to her cries for help. Indeed, in police interviews the following day, 38 residents admitted to hearing the screams but failing to act. Kitty eventually died after being stabbed eight times and sexually molested.

The case of Kitty Genovese received national media attention in America, with reporters asking one question: Why did not one person come to help her? It is perhaps understandable that people did not want to risk their own lives by facing the attacker, but the fact that they did not call the police seemed inexplicable. Psychological research generated by this case led to the development of two models, Latané and Darley's cognitive model and Piliavin's bystander-calculus model. Both models attempted to uncover the processes by which we make the decision to help another person and, in doing so, help us to understand why people help in some situations and not in others.

Latané and Darley's Cognitive Model

Latané and Darley (1968) proposed that a bystander goes through several cognitive stages before making a final decision about whether or not to help a person in an emergency situation. These stages are outlined below.

1. **Attend to the incident:** In the first instance, the bystander needs to actually notice that an incident is taking place. When we pass a potential emergency, there may be many other things going on in the environment, which may lead us to miss the emergency altogether. This 'stimulus overload effect'

is especially likely to occur in densely populated urban areas (Milgram, 1970).

2. **Define the incident:** Having noticed the incident, the bystander needs to define it as an emergency. This may sound straightforward, but because emergency situations are highly unusual and unexpected, even clear-cut emergency situations might be misinterpreted. Moreover, if the situation is ambiguous, there is every chance that we will interpret it as a normal day-to-day event rather than an emergency. If someone was screaming, for example, we might believe it is laughter or someone joking around rather than a sign of someone who is scared or in pain. When situations are ambiguous, we are likely to look to those around us to see how they behave (see discussion of informational social influence in Chapter 6). If others appear to be concerned, we may be more likely to define the situation as an emergency.

3. **Accept personal responsibility:** Whether or not the bystander decides it is their responsibility to help in the emergency may depend on whether there are other people present who might deal with the problem instead, and how competent the bystander feels in the situation. If there is an authority figure nearby, the bystander might decide that the authority figure is better able to deal with the situation appropriately, and absolve her or himself from personal responsibility.

4. **Decide what to do:** Once the bystander has noticed the situation, realized it is an emergency, and decided they are personally responsible for dealing with it, they must then decide whether it is possible for them to help and, if so, what they can actually do in the situation. Emergency situations are unforeseen and highly unusual, outside the bystander's usual repertoire of behaviours. It is therefore likely to be difficult to decide what the best course of action is. The behaviour of others may have a powerful influence on the bystander's behaviour at this stage.

If the bystander has progressed through these four stages – noticing the incident and interpreting it as an emergency, taking responsibility and knowing how to deal with the situation – they will make a final decision regarding whether or not to help. Although Latané and Darley proposed this to be the fifth and final stage of the model, it is probably easier to conceive of the final decision as the *outcome* of the four stages. In Text Box 10.1, we illustrate with an example how the cognitive model might be applied to a real-life emergency, the case of a road traffic accident.

Text Box 10.1

Applying Latané and Darley's Cognitive Model to a Real Emergency: the Case of a Road Traffic Accident

Imagine that you are walking along a street when a car hits a nearby pedestrian who was crossing the road. What factors will determine whether you go and help the injured pedestrian? We apply Latané and Darley's cognitive model to answer this question.

1. **Attention:** Did you happen to be looking at the road when the incident took place? Or were you having an argument with your boyfriend or chatting on your phone to a friend? If you were otherwise occupied and not looking at the road, you may well not notice that an accident has taken place. Are you walking down a nearly-deserted side street, or are you on a busy shopping street? You are much more likely to notice what has happened if you are on a quiet street. If you are somewhere busy, many other things may capture your attention, taking your attention away from the accident.

2. **Interpretation:** You notice the pedestrian lying in the road, but as this is a highly unusual situation that you haven't encountered before, you may not be sure what to make of it. How serious does the situation look? Is the pedestrian lying motionless, or are they trying to get up? If they appear to be unharmed, you may decide that this is not an emergency and continue on your way. What are the people around you doing? Are they walking past unconcerned or do they look alarmed by the event? You are much more likely to help if the people around you behave as if they perceive the situation to be an emergency.

3. **Responsibility:** You decide that you are dealing with an emergency as the pedestrian is not moving and other nearby pedestrians look disturbed by the situation. But should you take responsibility for helping the pedestrian? Are you the only person on the street or are there many other people around? If you are the only other person, you may assume responsibility because the fate of the victim may fall directly on your shoulders – walking away may result in their further deterioration or even their death. If there are others around, are any of them wearing a police or paramedic uniform? If so, you may expect them to take responsibility instead. Are you trained in first-aid? If you believe you are more competent than those around you, you will be more likely to take responsibility.

4. **Deciding on a strategy:** You decide you are responsible for the injured pedestrian. But how can you actually help them? Have you ever been in this situation before? If you have seen a previous incident, you may know how to act in this instance. Do you have first-aid experience? If yes, you may decide that your initial job is to check the victim's breathing and circulation, and put them in the recovery position. Alternatively, you may decide to call the emergency services. But what are the people around you doing? Is another person administering first aid, calling for help, or clearing the area? If so, you may follow their lead. If, however, no-one else is acting and you have no experience in this type of situation, you may worry about behaving inappropriately, feel that you do not have the expertise to intervene, and therefore decide not to help.

The Bystander Apathy Effect

Latané and Darley (1968) experimentally tested their model by investigating when and whether the presence of other bystanders would influence responses to an emergency. Participants completed a questionnaire either on their own or with two other participants. The room was then filled with smoke from a vent in the wall – this was to create an emergency situation. A further experimental manipulation was applied to the condition in which there were two others completing the questionnaire. Here the individuals were either genuine fellow participants or confederates of the experimenter who had been instructed to completely ignore the smoke. As expected, Latané and Darley found that people were highly influenced by those around them. While 75 per cent of participants who were alone raised the alarm by reporting the smoke to the experimenter in the other room, only 38 per cent of those with two other participants took any action, and only 10 per cent of those with a confederate who ignored the smoke reported the problem. Participants later reported thinking that the situation could not be an emergency as the other participants did not behave as if it was the case. These findings show that people are less likely to help in an emergency when they are with others present than when they are alone, a phenomenon known as the **bystander apathy effect**. Note also that this effect is very similar to the idea of modelling discussed earlier in this chapter, except that here the behaviour copied from others is inaction rather than action.

Darley and Latané (1969) found the same effect when the emergency involved *another person* being in trouble, even though other bystanders were not physically present. They conducted an experiment in which participants communicated with one another via microphones while in separate cubicles. Participants were led to believe that they were taking part in a group experiment which consisted of just two people, four people, or six people. One of the participants told the others by microphone that he suffered from epilepsy. Later in the experiment, he was heard to make sounds of distress, as if he was having a seizure, before falling silent. Darley and Latané found that the more bystanders people thought there were, the less likely they were to help. Before the end of the fit, 85 per cent of participants who thought they were the only other participant helped, but only 64 per cent of those who believed that two others were present and 31 per cent of those who thought there were four others present helped. Darley and Latané's study provided a classic illustration of how the presence of others inhibits helping. This bystander effect is incredibly strong. In fact, it has recently been found that even just *imagining* the presence of others can have this inhibitory effect (see Text Box 10.2).

Text Box 10.2

Simply Imagining the Presence of Others Can Cause the Bystander Apathy Effect

Classic research on the bystander apathy effect shows that, because of diffusion of responsibility, and informational and normative social influence, the presence of others reduces helping behaviour. But do other people actually have to be *present* for this effect to occur? Garcia, Weaver, Moskowitz, and Darley (2002) investigated the possibility that even *imagining* the presence of others might lead to bystander apathy.

Method

One hundred and twenty-nine undergraduate students were randomly assigned to one of three conditions. In the *group condition* participants were asked in a questionnaire to 'Imagine you won a dinner for yourself and 10 of your friends at your favorite restaurant'; in the *one person condition*, participants were asked to 'Imagine you won a dinner for yourself and a friend at your favorite restaurant'. In the *control condition*, participants were not asked to imagine any task. To measure *helping behaviour*, participants were then asked on the next page of the questionnaire: 'In addition to this survey, we are conducting a brief experiment in another room. How much time are you willing to spend on this other experiment?' They had the option of offering between 0 minutes and 30 minutes of their time. After completing this measure, participants were told that there was no further experiment, and the true rationale for the experiment they had just taken part in was explained to them.

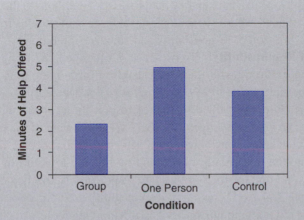

Results

The graph illustrates the results of the experiment. Participants who imagined a group of 10 people offered significantly less of their time than did people who imagined one person. There was no statistical difference between the time offered by people in the *one person condition* and the *control condition*.

Interpreting the Findings

According to Latané and Darley's cognitive model, it is the presence of others in the situation where help is needed that leads to bystander apathy, but in this study, simply imagining others prior to the situation where help is needed caused bystander apathy. Why did this pattern of results emerge? Many studies have shown that subtle cues or *primes* in our environment can activate, or make more accessible, knowledge structures in memory, affecting our behaviour and social perceptions. Garcia and colleagues (2002) argue that thinking about being in a large group triggers concepts that usually come to mind when we are actually in a large group, such as feeling lost in a crowd, and feeling less accountable for our behaviour. When participants were called upon to help in an experiment, they were influenced by this accessible feeling of diminished responsibility, and were less likely to help.

Processes Underlying the Bystander Apathy Effect

The findings above show that the more bystanders that are present, the less likely it is that the victim of an emergency would be offered help by any individual bystander. This trend had been confirmed in more than 50 studies, in both laboratory and field settings (for a review of this work see Latané & Nida, 1981). Going back to the cognitive model, it is clear that the presence of others can influence decision-making at almost every stage of the model. But exactly what processes contribute to the bystander apathy effect? Latané and Darley (1976) suggest two basic explanations for when helping does not occur: diffusion of responsibility and audience inhibition.

Diffusion of Responsibility: The presence of other people during an emergency will lead bystanders to transfer their responsibility for helping onto others. As the study by Darley and Latané (1969) showed, it is not necessary for other bystanders to be physically present for diffusion of responsibility to occur. Instead, there simply needs to be the knowledge that others are also aware of the emergency and could potentially take responsibility for it. This means that people on their own in any situation are the most likely to respond by helping a victim in an emergency because there is no-one for them to pass on responsibility to: they carry the entire responsibility themselves. Diffusion of responsibility offers an explanation for why so many people did not help when they heard Kitty Genovese.

Audience Inhibition: People are often uncomfortable about acting in front of other people, particularly in an emergency situation where there are no clear guidelines on how to behave. As a result, people may be worried about overreacting to a situation or dealing with the situation in an incompetent manner, which might result in other bystanders laughing at them or thinking badly of them. This audience inhibition can be seen as a product of *normative social influence* that we discussed in Chapter 6. In Chapter 6 we saw that in groups, people often go along with the majority attitude even when they privately do not agree with it for fear of being laughed at or ridiculed by the group. The difference here is that rather than promoting action, the fear of getting it wrong and being laughed at leads to inaction.

In Chapter 6 we also discussed how people go along with groups because of *informational social influence* which describes how, when we have not encountered a situation before and so there are no clear guidelines on how to behave, we are especially likely to rely on the behaviour of those around us. If we are concerned that an emergency situation has arisen, but those around us appear to be unconcerned, we may be influenced by other bystanders, and conclude that the situation is not a true emergency.

Latané and Darley (1976) tested the role of all three of these processes in a complex but ingenious experiment. In the original experiment Latané and Darley use the terms audience inhibition and social influence to refer to what we know of as normative social influence and informational social influence respectively. We use these latter terms to describe the experiment below because they allow us to see more clearly how the social influence processes discussed in Chapter 6 have an impact also on helping behaviour.

Participants were asked to observe another person respond to verbal stimuli and rate whether or not that person had received an electric shock. Participants were told that they would observe the person on a television monitor from another room. In all but one condition, participants believed they had been recruited in pairs. In reality, however, the second participant was always a confederate, acting on behalf of the experimenter. Prior to the experiment, the pair of participants were shown the room where the person to be observed would be sitting during the experiment. There was a shock generator in the room, and the experimenter commented that it was old and unreliable. The participants were then sent into separate cubicles, each of which contained two TV monitors and a camera. The first monitor showed the room with the shock generator.

The participants were told that the second monitor (which could show the neighbour in the next cubicle) and the camera (which could show the participant to the neighbour) had been left there by another researcher and were irrelevant to the current study. However, this equipment was actually used to create several experimental conditions. The camera could either be pointed at the participant or not, allowing the manipulation of *normative social influence*, whether or not participants believed they were being observed. The TV monitor, on the other hand, could either be showing the neighbour or not, allowing the manipulation of *informational social influence*, whether or not participants could observe the reactions of their neighbour. To manipulate *diffusion of responsibility*, in one condition participants were recruited alone, whereas in all other conditions the participants worked alongside a confederate. These manipulations created five conditions designed to discover whether and how the three processes all played a role in creating the bystander apathy effect.

In the *alone* condition, the participant worked alone, the camera was pointed at the ceiling, and the monitor showed a shot of the ceiling in the second, empty, cubicle. This provided a baseline against which to compare all the other conditions. In the *diffusion of responsibility* condition, the camera was pointed at the ceiling, and the monitor showed only the ceiling of the second cubicle, but the participant was aware that there was a person in the second cubicle taking part in the same study. In this condition, then, there could be no normative or informational social influence, but the simple awareness of the presence of others in the situation should be enough to lead to a diffusion of responsibility. In the *diffusion of responsibility plus informational social influence* condition, the monitor showed the participant in the second cubicle, but the camera was pointed at the ceiling. The participant could see, but not be seen themselves. As such they could use the other person's behaviour as a guide to their own, but could rest assured that their own behaviour did not run the risk of being evaluated by others. In the *diffusion of responsibility plus normative social influence* condition, this situation was reversed. The monitor only showed the ceiling of the second cubicle, but the camera was pointed at the participant. The participant could therefore not see the confederate, but knew they could be seen – and evaluated – by the other participant. In the *diffusion of responsibility plus information social influence plus normative social influence* condition, the participant could see the other participant on the monitor, and also knew they could be seen by the other participant through the camera. The predicted findings can be found in Figure 10.3.

Condition	Strength of Social Influence	Predicted Probability of Helping
Alone	0	Highest
Diffusion of responsibility	+1	High
Diffusion of responsibility AND Informational Influence OR Normative Influence	+2	Low
Diffusion of responsibility AND Informational Influence AND Normative Influence	+3	Lowest

Figure 10.3 Predicted probability of helping as a function of diffusion of responsibility and informational and/or normative influence in Latané and Darley's (1976) experiment

Once the participants were waiting in their individual cubicle, the experimenter returned to the room with the shock generator. On the first monitor, participants observed first the experimenter pick up some wires on the generator and then appear to have an electric shock, scream, jump in the air, and then fall to the floor. The researchers timed how long participants in each condition took to help the experimenter, and their findings confirm the importance of all three processes in producing the bystander apathy effect. Participants in the *alone* condition, who were not being influenced by diffusion of responsibility, audience inhibition *or* social influence, were the quickest and most likely to help the experimenter. *Diffusion of responsibility* reduced helping behaviour, but helping was even less likely when either informational social influence *or* normative social influence were in effect (the results of these two conditions were combined by the researchers because they did not differ from one another). Finally, when all three processes were in operation, participants were least likely to help the experimenter.

We know that audience inhibition is one of the primary causes of bystander apathy, and recently Van den Bos, Müller, and van Bussel (2009) have used this knowledge to develop an intervention to *reduce* bystander apathy. Audience inhibition is just one form of general behavioural inhibition, which can occur in any circumstances where we don't act as we want to because we fear the reactions of others. van den Bos and colleagues hypothesized that weakening general behavioural inhibition, by reminding participants of times when they have acted *without* inhibition, may reduce bystander apathy. To test this idea, they stopped participants at a railway station in a waiting room where multiple people were present, and asked them to complete a short questionnaire. Half of the participants answered three open-ended questions which primed disinhibition, for example, 'Please briefly describe a situation out of your own life where you acted with no inhibitions'. Participants in the control condition were simply asked to describe a regular day. After this, the experimenter left the waiting room. One minute after this, another passenger in the room (actually a confederate) got up in a hurry to catch a train, but in doing so dropped various pens on the floor. It emerged that participants who had received the disinhibition manipulation were more likely to help the confederate to pick up the pens, and started helping the confederate more quickly than participants in the control condition. In a follow-up study involving a more serious bystander situation – a fellow participant who appeared to be choking on sweets – a similar effect occurred. These findings are interesting, because normally we think of disinhibition as something that causes anti-social and aggressive behaviour (see Chapter 9). Here, however, we can see that sometimes disinhibition can be a good thing, leading to an increase in prosocial behaviour.

Piliavin's Bystander-Calculus Model

Piliavin and colleagues (Piliavin, Piliavin, Dovidio, Gaertner, & Clark, 1981) also proposed a model to explain why people do not always help in an emergency. Like Latané and Darley's (1968) model, their model included the role of diffusion of responsibility in explaining the bystander apathy effect, but they also took into account people's *physiological* response when they witness an emergency situation. The **bystander-calculus model** proposes that bystanders go through three stages when they have observed an emergency situation. First, they experience physiological arousal. Second, they try to understand why they feel arousal and label this emotional response. Third, they calculate the costs of helping and the costs of not helping and come to a decision about whether to act (see social exchange theory, Chapter 12, for a similar approach explaining whether or not we choose to maintain an interpersonal relationship). These three stages are explained below.

Physiological Arousal

According to Piliavin and colleagues, when we first observe an emergency situation, we have an *orienting reaction*, showing a lowered – rather than heightened – physiological response. This allows us to assess the situation and decide how to proceed without panicking. This is quickly followed by a *defence reaction*, a rapid increase in physiological response, which prepares us to act. Gaertner and Dovidio (1977) found that when observing an emergency in which a woman had been hurt by falling chairs, bystanders with an elevated heart rate helped much more quickly than those with a less acute physiological reaction.

Labelling the Arousal

So we know that in an emergency we experience physiological arousal, but what does this arousal mean? We experience physiological arousal in a variety of contexts (see our discussion of the two-factor theory of emotion in Chapter 11); for instance, in the presence of someone we find attractive, when we have had a fight with someone, or when we have been on a rollercoaster ride. Social psychologists believe that the physiological reaction we have is similar in each of these situations, but we differentiate them by giving them different labels – attraction, anger or exhilaration, depending on the external cues in a particular context. In the case of an emergency situation, the bystander-calculus model states that we attribute this arousal to *personal distress* at seeing someone else suffer, and therefore a key motive for helping others is to reduce this unpleasant feeling of arousal. In other words, when we help others, we do so because it serves our self-interests, ridding us of our negative emotional response. Batson and colleagues (e.g. Batson & Coke, 1981) have also proposed a second process – empathic concern – arguing that, as long as we believe we are similar to the person in distress and can identify with them, we experience *empathy*. This emotional response is focused on the person in need of help rather than ourselves. The different consequences of these two types of emotional response are discussed in more detail later in the chapter.

Calculating the Costs

Having identified their experience of arousal as personal distress at the situation, Piliavin argued that bystanders try to work out which course of action is most likely to reduce their personal distress by weighing the costs of different possible options. To do so, they must consider two types of costs, the *costs of helping* and the *costs of not helping*. Helping someone may be costly in several ways. It involves expending time and effort to deal with the situation. There may, for example, be the potential for negative personal consequences such as personal injury. The greater these costs, the less likely it is that the bystander will help. However, *not* helping someone may also be costly. Piliavin noted that not helping can lead to *personal costs*, for example feeling guilty or to blame for the fate of the victim and *empathy costs*; if a bystander feels empathic concern for a person in need but fails to help them, negative emotions at the thought of the victim suffering cannot be dispelled. The cost of not helping is greater when the costs of helping are low (e.g. you are near the emergency and could effectively make a difference) and the probability of a negative outcome if you do not help is high (e.g. the victim might be seriously injured or die). According to Piliavin and colleagues, the *bystander apathy effect* occurs because the presence of others reduces the cost of not helping. If a bystander sees that there are others who might help, they will perceive that if they do not intervene, it is likely that others will.

Piliavin proposed a matrix, shown in Figure 10.4, to illustrate how the cost of helping and the cost of not helping interact with one another to determine whether a bystander will help in an emergency, and what kind of help they will offer. They argue that cost of helping and cost of not helping can be either high or low, creating four types of situation, each with very different outcomes. When the cost of helping is low, but the cost

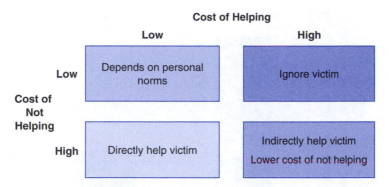

Figure 10.4   Piliavin's reward-cost matrix: How do the costs of helping and the costs of not helping affect how a bystander responds to an emergency?

of not helping is high, a bystander is likely to directly intervene in an emergency. Seeing a teenage boy collapsed in a deserted alleyway would be such a situation. When the cost of helping is low, but the cost of not helping is also low, how the bystander responds is likely to be guided by the personal norms. If, for example, the teenager in the previous example had not collapsed but had only stumbled, a bystander with a strong sense of social responsibility might ask if he was alright. When the cost of helping is high and the cost of not helping is low, the bystander is very unlikely to intervene, and is more likely to ignore the incident. Seeing the teenage boy having an argument with some other boys might be such a situation; the bystander might assume that it is just some friends having a minor disagreement and that the boys might turn on the bystander if they were to try to intervene. Finally, when the cost of helping is high, but the cost of not helping is also high, for example if the teenage boy was being beaten up by a gang of boys, the bystander may engage in a number of possible responses. They might help indirectly by calling the emergency services, but if this is not possible, they may attempt to lower the costs of not helping in a different way, for example by reinterpreting the situation as being not that much of an emergency. Alternatively, the bystander might decide that the victim deserves their fate; the boy might be a gang member having a fight with members of a different gang.

Shotland and Straw (1976) carried out a study that supports the bystander-calculus model. They had participants watch a videotape of a fight between a man and a woman. In one condition, the woman shouted 'Get away from me! I don't know you!', and in a second condition the woman shouted 'Get away from me! I don't know why I ever married you!' Participants believed the woman was in greater danger when fighting with a stranger, and that they would be in more danger intervening in the domestic fight (see Figure 10.5). These findings indicate that participants would be more likely to intervene when they observed a woman fighting a stranger, because the costs of helping were lower and the costs of not helping were higher than for the domestic fight.

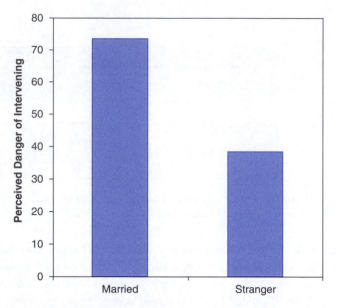

Figure 10.5   Perceived danger of intervening in a domestic fight compared to a fight between two strangers. Data from Shotland and Straw (1976)

The primary goal of the cognitive model (Latané and Darley, 1968) and the bystander-calculus model (Piliavin et al., 1981) was to explain the situational factors that influence helping behaviour. Recently, some social psychologists have argued that there is a third factor that may also be a key situational determinant of helping – that is, cues in our environment that trigger a fear of death. We talk about some of this research in Text Box 10.3.

Text Box 10.3

Can a Fear of Death Increase Prosocial Behaviour?

Most of the situational determinants of helping discussed in this chapter are specific to the situation in which help is needed. Recently, however, Jonas, Schimel, Greenberg, and Pyszczynski (2002) conducted two studies to test the intriguing possibility that making us aware of our eventual and inevitable death will increase prosocial behaviour.

Study 1

Thirty-one pedestrians were stopped in the street and asked to take part in a short survey about charities. To manipulate *mortality salience*, participants were either stopped in front of a funeral home or several blocks away from the funeral home. The dependent measure, *favourability towards charitable organizations*, asked participants to indicate how beneficial, desirable, and necessary they thought the two charities were. Jonas and colleagues found that people were more favourable towards charitable organizations when their mortality was made salient. A second study was conducted to (a) test the effect of mortality salience on actual helping behaviour, and (b) see whether the effect of mortality salience on helping behaviour is limited to certain recipients.

Study 2

Twenty-seven American students took part in a lab-based test in which they were assigned to one of two conditions. In the *mortality salience condition* they were told: 'Please briefly describe the emotions that the thought of your own death arouses in you' and 'Jot down, as specifically as you can, what you think will happen to *you* as you physically die and once you are physically dead'. In the *control condition*, participants were asked similar questions about dental pain. They were then given the opportunity to donate money to two different

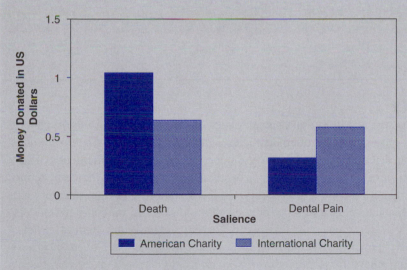

(Continued)

charities, one which helped people in the United States and one which helped people in other countries. The figure illustrates the results. In the control condition people donated an equal amount to the national and the international charity. When people were made aware of their own death, however, they donated significantly more money to the charity that would benefit people from the same culture as them.

Interpreting the Findings

According to Terror Management Theory (Greenberg et al., 1986), human beings have a strong survival instinct. However because, unlike other animals, we also possess the intellectual capacity to realize that one day we will die, we can become paralysed with fear at the prospect of our own mortality. To stop this fear becoming overwhelming, we hold a cultural worldview (a set of values, e.g. religious beliefs and social norms) which provides a sense of meaning to the world and maintains our belief that our lives are important and significant. Our cultural worldview is important because it allows us to transcend death, either through a belief in an afterlife or by culturally making a mark on the world so we will not be forgotten. Given its cultural value, behaving prosocially helps us to manage our fear of death. We therefore behave prosocially when we are made aware of our death as a strategy to manage our fear. Awareness of our own mortality does not, however, increase our helping behaviour towards *any* other people. Instead, we are more likely to want to help causes that promote our own culture. You can read more about terror management theory, and how it exerts effects on intergroup relations, in Chapter 8.

Summary

In this section we have looked at characteristics of the situation that inhibit people from helping others in apparent emergencies. Latané and Darley's *cognitive model* explains what determines whether a bystander will help in an emergency. They argued that to make the decision to help, a bystander must notice the incident, define it as an emergency, accept responsibility for the situation, and then decide what action they should take. In a series of studies, they showed that the more bystanders present during an emergency, the less likely it is that any individual will offer help, a phenomenon known as *bystander apathy*. Three processes have been shown to inhibit helping behaviour: *diffusion of responsibility* (assuming that others present will take responsibility), *normative social influence* (the fear of appearing foolish in front of others) and *informational social influence* (if others seem unconcerned, the bystander may decide there is no need to help). Piliavin proposed the alternative *bystander-calculus model* to explain why people do not always help. People assess the *costs of helping* and the *costs of not helping* when deciding whether to help. According to the model, people are most likely to help when the costs of helping are low and the costs of not helping are high, and least likely to help when the costs of helping are high and the costs of not helping are low.

We have now outlined the situational factors that determine helping. In the next section we consider *perceiver*-centred determinants of helping.

PERCEIVER-CENTRED DETERMINANTS OF HELPING

What aspects of the perceiver influence whether or not they help a person in need? Are some types of people more likely to help than others? High profile and dramatic helping behaviour, for example the heroic actions of De Martini and Ortiz in the World Trade Center on 11 September 2001, may lead us to conclude that some people are simply more likely to help than others because of their personal attributes i.e. have an **altruistic personality**. Do these people have a 'better' *personality*, or do they have greater *competence* in an emergency that leads them to help? Alternatively, does the likelihood of helping depend on a person's general emotional state or *mood* at a particular point in time? Moreover, does the *specific emotional response* of an individual – whether they experience personal distress or empathic concern in response to a situation in which help is needed – influence their motivation for offering help and, subsequently, the nature of the help offered? Finally, are there *gender differences* in helping behaviour? We now discuss each of these possibilities.

Personality

Researchers have been keen to identify whether there is such a thing as an altruistic personality. Although social psychologists generally accept that situational factors can override factors related to the individual, there is some evidence for individual differences in helping behaviour that are stable over time. Eisenberg and colleagues (1999) found, for example, that pre-school children's spontaneous prosocial behaviour predicted their helpfulness in later childhood and early adulthood. Rushton and colleagues (1984) proposed that there might be a genetic basis to differences in helpfulness, finding that generally identical twins are more similar in terms of their tendency to be helpful than fraternal twins, who are not genetically identical.

Although early research by Latané and Darley (1970) found no relationship between a host of personality traits – including authoritarianism, alienation, trustworthiness, and need for approval – and helping behaviour, there is some evidence that people who help have certain characteristics. Earlier, we discussed how we help, in part, because we are guided by the universal *norm of social responsibility*. Although we are probably all influenced by this norm to some degree, the extent to which people feel socially responsible varies. Berkowitz and Daniels (1964) found that helpers scored higher on a social responsibility scale than non-helpers. This is because people who feel socially responsible are likely to feel greater obligation to help in emergency situations, even if they would rather not.

Bierhoff, Klein, and Kramp (1991) investigated the concept of an altruistic personality by comparing the responses on a personality questionnaire of people who had intervened to help the victims of a traffic accident with 'non-helpers' (sex, age and socioeconomic status-matched control participants who had witnessed an accident and had not helped). Like Berkowitz and Daniels (1964), they also found that helpers emphasized social responsibility more than non-helpers. In addition, they found that those who had helped had a higher internal locus of control than non-helpers. An individual's locus of control is a reflection of where they place the responsibility for the outcome of events in their lives. People with an internal locus of control perceive that they can personally exert control over events, in contrast to people with an external locus of control, who are more likely to believe that they are the victims of circumstance. They are therefore more likely to help because they have greater self-efficacy, and believe that their help will make a difference.

Finally, people with greater **dispositional empathy**, who have a general tendency to feel empathy and take the perspective of others, are more likely to help. Bierhoff and colleagues (1991) found that people who had intervened to help the victims of a traffic accident showed greater dispositional empathy than those who did not help. One study sums up the role of personality in producing helping behaviour where it really counts. Oliner and Oliner (1988) interviewed people who helped to rescue Jews in Nazi Europe. They found that compared to a matched control group of people who did not help Jews, these people had a higher degree of social responsibility, a greater internal locus of control, and higher empathy.

One should exercise some caution, however, in concluding that there are people who simply have personalities predisposed to helping. The empirical evidence discussed above is all correlational, and as such we cannot necessarily infer causality. In the Oliner and Oliner (1988) study described above, did the people who helped rescue Jews in Nazi Europe help them only because they had dispositions that inclined them to do so? It might be the case that people helped because of the situation they were in, but subsequently inferred that they were a more helpful person (or even subsequently became a more helpful person) as a result of their actions (see the discussion of how self-perception of one's own behaviour can change attitudes, Chapter 4). Although it is likely that people differ in their predispositions to help others, situational factors are also likely to play an important role.

Competence

If the bystander feels they will be able to competently deal with an emergency, they will be much more likely to help. This idea fits in well with the bystander-calculus model discussed earlier. If the bystander feels competent, the costs of helping are much lower than if they feel incompetent, as the emergency will presumably involve less time and effort, and may be more likely to have a positive outcome. Cramer, McMaster, Bartell, and Dragna (1988) had participants who were either registered nurses (high competence) or non-medical students (low competence) wait in a corridor with a confederate, ostensibly to take part in a study. While the pair was waiting, a rigged accident took place in the adjoining corridor, in which a workman had apparently fallen off a ladder and was then moaning as if in pain. The confederate did not offer to help. Cramer and colleagues found that the nurses were much more likely to help the workman than the students. They later reported that they felt they had helped because they felt they had the necessary skills (but see also the discussion of social norms in Chapter 6). Pantin and Carver (1982) artificially manipulated competence by showing some of the participants a series of films on first aid and dealing with emergencies. They found that participants who had seen the films were much more likely to help a confederate who appeared to be choking than participants who had not seen the films.

These findings seem fairly straightforward. People who are trained to deal with emergencies are more likely to help. Interestingly, however, there is some evidence that even the *perception* of competence is sufficient to produce helping behaviour. Schwartz and David (1976) found that telling a participant that they were good at handling rats increased the probability that they would subsequently help catch a laboratory rat. Perceiving oneself to be competent in one domain can even lead to helping behaviour in an unrelated domain. Kazdin and Bryan (1971) found that participants who had been told that they had done well on a creativity task or a health examination task were later more willing to donate blood.

Allocating participants to a leadership position, thereby increasing their perceptions of competence, also increased the probability of helping behaviour. Baumeister, Chesner, Senders, and Tice (1988) told participants that they would work on a task in a four-person group, in which they had been randomly allocated to be either the leader or one of three followers. Participants worked individually on the task but believed that all the group members could communicate with one another through an intercom system. On hearing a group member over the intercom system apparently choking and asking for help, 80 per cent of leaders but only 35 per cent of followers went to offer assistance. Given that the leaders were randomly allocated to the role, this cannot have been due to their greater competence as a leader. Baumeister proposed that acting as leader increases the bystander's perception of personal responsibility, therefore eliminating the possibility of passing responsibility on to another group member (i.e. preventing diffusion of responsibility).

Mood

The transitory psychological state of a bystander can have a profound influence on whether or not help is offered. In general, good moods increase helping behaviour while bad moods reduce helping behaviour. Below, we discuss the evidence for this claim and note one exception to the rule – the effect of *guilt* on helping behaviour.

Isen (1970) asked participants to complete a task on which they were then told they had either performed very well or very poorly. Other participants were given no feedback about their performance, or did not complete the task at all. Isen found that participants who thought they had done well at the task were more likely to help a woman struggling to carry some books than any of the other participants. Similarly, Holloway, Tucker, and Hornstein (1977) found that people who had received good news showed greater attraction to strangers and greater willingness to help compared to people who had received bad news. However, Isen, Clark, and Schwartz (1976) demonstrated that the effects of mood do not last for long. They delivered a free gift to residents of a town in Pennsylvania. Then, between 1 and 20 minutes after the free gift had been received, the residents received a phone call from a 'wrong number', and were asked if they could help the caller out by making a phone call for them. Isen and colleagues found that if the request was made up to 7 minutes after receipt of the free gift, the majority of participants helped by making the phone call. With a delay of 10 minutes or more, however, only about half of participants helped. By 20 minutes after receipt of the gift, only one-tenth of participants helped (see Figure 10.6).

Despite the limited time span of the effect of being in a good mood on helping, the effect is very reliable. Carlson, Charlin, and Miller (1988) looked at 61 studies which had compared people in a positive mood to people in a neutral mood. Using meta-analysis they found a reliable effect of being in a positive mood on helping behaviour. But why does being in a positive mood increase the probability that help will be offered?

According to the **affect-priming model** (Bower, 1981; Forgas, 1992), when we are in a good mood, mood-congruent information in our memory is more accessible. As a result, positive thoughts and feelings, including a positive orientation to prosocial behaviour, are more likely to be activated. Alternatively, the **affect-as-information model** (Schwarz, 1990) suggests that we use our current mood as a piece of information, to help us understand how we feel about things in our environment. To give an example of this, if we meet a friend while we are in a bad mood, we may view them in a less positive light than if we were in a good mood, because we infer from our negative mood that we are not happy with them. In the context of prosocial behaviour, when a bystander encounters an emergency situation, they may take their positive emotional state to mean that it will be safe and worthwhile to intervene.

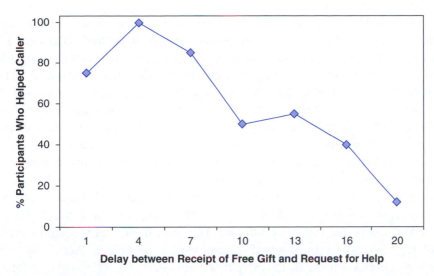

Figure 10.6 Effect of mood on helping behaviour as a function of time between mood induction and opportunity to help. Data from Isen, Clark, and Schwartz (1976)

A number of studies show that people in a negative psychological state are less likely to help others. Berkowitz (1972) found that the more self-concern students felt while awaiting the outcome of an important exam, the less they offered helped to others. However, one negative psychological state does *not* decrease helping behaviour. Regan, Williams, and Sparling (1972) found that when participants had been led to believe that they had broken an expensive camera, they were subsequently more likely to help another person who had dropped some groceries. Two explanations have been offered for this effect. According to the *image-reparation hypothesis*, guilty people want to make up for what they have done. This does not, however, explain why the participants were willing to help someone unrelated to the incident over which they felt guilt. An alternative explanation can account for this. The *negative relief state model* (Cialdini & Kenrick, 1976) argues that because guilt leads to a negative affective state, people help in order to feel good about themselves again (helping behaviour elevates mood).

The research we have been talking about in this section has shown how *general* positive or negative internal mood states influence helping behaviour. We now turn to the empathy-altruism hypothesis, which provides an explanation for helping behaviour that is based on two *specific* internally experienced emotions.

Empathy-Altruism

Batson (1994) argued that sometimes our motive for helping others is *altruistic*, a desire to benefit others without the expectation of anything in return. At other times, our motive for helping others is *egoistic*. In this case, we help someone else because it has personal benefits for us. The **empathy-altruism hypothesis** (Batson, 1991) explains why we sometimes help others for egoistical purposes, and sometimes for altruistic purposes. When we witness someone suffering, we can experience two different types of emotional reaction: personal distress and empathy. *Personal distress* is a self-focused negative state of arousal that we feel when we see someone suffering. Rather than thinking about how the sufferer is feeling, personal distress is a preoccupation with how the suffering makes *us* feel. We have already discussed how personal distress can result in helping behaviour earlier in this chapter, with reference to the bystander-calculus model. According to this model, when people feel arousal as a result of observing someone who is in need of help, they label that arousal as personal distress. Batson argues, however, that we may also feel *empathic concern* when we see someone suffering. This state of arousal is victim-focused, involving feelings of sympathy and compassion for the sufferer. According to the empathy-altruism hypothesis, the more empathic concern we feel the more altruistic will be our response. In contrast, if we primarily feel personal distress, we are more likely to respond egoistically. Batson et al.'s two explanations for helping usefully extend Piliavin and colleagues' (1981) bystander-calculus model. When people feel physiological arousal, they *either* label it as personal distress *or* empathic concern. The emotion they experience subsequently influences whether their motives for helping are egoistic or altruistic.

A number of studies have supported the empathy-altruism hypothesis. Batson and colleagues (1981) asked female students to observe a female confederate appearing to receive electric shocks, ostensibly as part of a study they were taking part in. As the confederate appeared to be in a great deal of pain, the experimenter offered the participant the chance to help by taking the place of the confederate for the rest of the experiment. To manipulate the extent of empathic concern felt by the participant, they were either told that the confederate had very similar attitudes to them, or very different attitudes to them. This manipulation was used because we are more likely to feel empathy towards people who we believe are similar to us. The difficulty of escaping from the situation was also manipulated. In the *difficult to escape* condition, participants were told that they would have to observe the victim until the very end of the experiment if they did not help. In the *easy to escape* condition, participants were told that they would soon be able to leave.

The findings to this study are illustrated in Figure 10.7. If the sufferer was thought to be similar to the participant, a high proportion offered to take the sufferer's place in the experiment, regardless of whether they could easily escape. However, if the sufferer was thought to be dissimilar to the participant, participants only offered to help when they could not easily escape. This pattern of results can be explained by the empathy-altruism hypothesis. People who were motivated by empathy (i.e. who believed they were highly similar to the participant) reacted altruistically; their goal

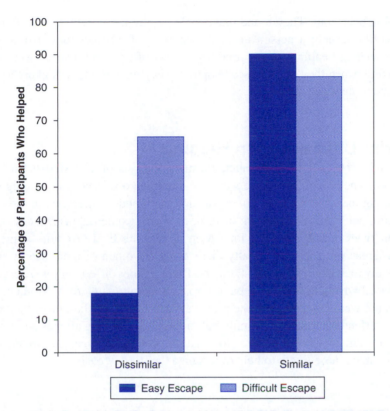

Figure 10.7   The effect of similarity of victim in producing egoistic and altruistic helping. Data from Batson et al. (1981)

was to reduce the suffering of the victim, and this would not be diminished by simply escaping the situation. In contrast, people who were not motivated by empathy (i.e. low similarity) reacted egoistically; their goal was to reduce their own personal suffering. When they had no alternative, they helped the victim, to reduce the negative arousal they were feeling. However, given the option of escaping, this is the behaviour they chose, because this reduced their negative arousal at less of a personal cost.

Although the results of the Batson et al. (1981) experiment are indicative of support for the empathy-altruism hypothesis, they do not provide direct evidence that personal distress or empathy are related to the behaviour observed. To be fully convinced of empirical support for any hypothesis it is necessary to measure the hypothesized psychological process, as well as the predicted outcome (see Baron & Kenny, 1986). Because of this, in a further experiment using the same paradigm, Toi and Batson (1982) did measure the hypothesized empathy and distress variable to provide direct evidence that the type of emotional response could explain the type of helping behaviour. They found that people who reported high levels of empathy were willing to help a person in need regardless of whether they had an escape option, whereas people who reported high levels of personal distress were willing to help only when they had no escape option. They were much less likely to help if an escape route was available.

Gender Differences in Helping

Eagly and Crowley (1986) conducted a meta-analysis of 172 studies on helping behaviour. They found that there were some notable differences in helping behaviour among men and women. There was no clear gender difference in the *amount* of helping behaviour engaged in; instead, men and women appeared to engage in different *types* of helping behaviour. Men were more likely to help women than men, whereas women were equally likely to help women or men. Men were also more likely than women to help strangers. These gender differences were especially pronounced when the helping situation was potentially dangerous. Women, on the other hand, were more likely to help in everyday situations than men, for example helping a friend out, providing emotional support, and looking after children and the elderly. In sum, men behave more prosocially in unusual, dangerous circumstances, but women are more likely to help others on a day-to-day basis.

RECIPIENT-CENTRED DETERMINANTS OF HELPING

So far, our discussion of helping behaviour has focused on the potential helper and the situation in which they find themselves. Whether or not help is offered may, however, also depend upon characteristics of the potential *recipient* of the help. Here we outline four factors which may influence whether or not help is offered: how similar the recipient is to us, whether or not they are a member of the same social group as us, how attractive we find them, and whether we believe they are responsible for their misfortune.

Similarity

Several studies show that we are more likely to help those who we believe are similar to us (see Chapter 11 for a discussion of the relationship between similarity and attraction). Krebs (1975) found that when people see someone being given electric shocks, the more similar they are to the victim, they greater physiological arousal they experience and the more altruistic they are towards the victim. Being similar to us in terms of personal attributes or simply by virtue of being a member

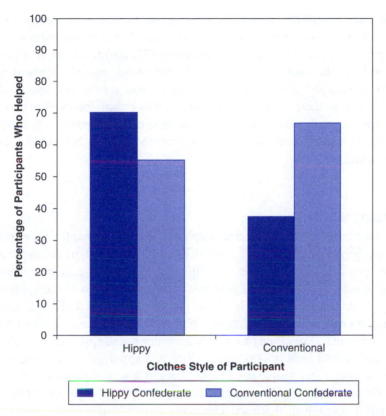

Figure 10.8 Effect of similarity on helping behaviour. Data from Emswiller et al. (1971)

of the same group as us may increase the likelihood of us helping someone in need. But what determines whether we see someone as similar to us? Emswiller, Deaux, and Willits (1971) investigated whether students in the 1970s would be more likely to help someone who dressed the same as them. Confederates who were dressed either conventionally or in an alternative style (as a hippie) asked passers-by for a coin to make a phone call. Students were more likely to help the confederate who was dressed in a similar way than those who were dressed differently (see Figure 10.8). It appeared that assumptions had been made, based on the appearance of the confederate, about their similarity to the participants in other areas, for example personality and beliefs.

Group Membership
We appear to be more willing to help ingroup members than outgroup members (i.e. people who share our social group membership compared to people who do

not). Ellis and Fox (2001) found that heterosexual bystanders were more likely to help a person who was identified as heterosexual than a person who was identified as gay or lesbian. Gaertner and Dovidio (1977) also found an effect of group membership in the context of ethnicity. If they were the only bystander, white participants were just as likely to help a black woman in need as a white woman in need. If, however, there were other bystanders, white participants were more likely to help a white woman than a black woman. In sum, participants only treated outgroup members in the same way as ingroup members when they could not diffuse responsibility.

Attractiveness

The bias we have towards attractive people, described in Chapter 11, also applies to helping behaviour. Benson, Karabenick, and Lerner (1976) demonstrated the effect of physical attractiveness on helping behaviour. A researcher left completed graduate school application forms, including a photo of the applicant and a stamped addressed envelope, in phone booths at an airport. The photo accompanying the application was either of a physically attractive or a relatively unattractive individual. They then observed whether or not people making a phone call at the booth would send the materials which had apparently been forgotten. The researchers found that people were more likely to send the materials of the attractive applicants than the materials of the unattractive applicants. The effect is not only restricted to physical attractiveness; the attractiveness of the *personality* of the person in need of help can also affect whether or not help is offered. Lynn and Mynier (1993) found that friendly individuals are more likely to be helped than less friendly individuals.

Responsibility for Misfortune

We are more likely to help people who are in need through no fault of their own than those who are responsible for their misfortune. Barnes and colleagues (1979) had confederates who were pretending to be students call other students and ask to borrow their notes to help prepare for an exam. In the low responsibility condition, the confederate claimed that they needed help because they weren't very good at taking notes, even though they tried really hard. In the high responsibility condition, the confederate claimed that they needed help because although they could take good notes, they couldn't be bothered to attend class. Participants were much more likely to offer help to the confederate if they were perceived to be less responsible for their need of help. Similarly, DePalma and colleagues (1999) found that students were more likely to offer help to a medical patient if the individual was portrayed as not being responsible for the onset of the illness they suffered from.

Summary

There are a number of person-centred determinants of helping, which can be to do with the helper, or the person receiving help. The personality and transient mood state of the helper are influential; happy or guilty people who have a *dispositional inclination* towards empathy and social responsibility are most likely to help others. People who have the skills to deal with emergencies or who believe they are *competent* are also more likely to help. Although there is no *gender difference* in the amount of help women and men give, they differ in the *type* of help they offer. Finally, with respect to recipient qualities, we are more likely to help people who are *similar* to us, who belong to the *same group* as us, who we find *attractive*, and who we believe are *deserving* of our help.

RECEIVING HELP

So far we have focused on the point of view of the bystander, discussing the situations and characteristics of the perceiver that influence whether or not people help others. Helping others makes us feel good about ourselves (Millar, Tesser, & Millar, 1988), but how does being helped affect the *recipient* of the help? Understandably, if we offer to help someone, we expect them to be happy and grateful to us. Sometimes, this is the case. Cook and Pelfry (1985) found that participants who were struggling with their work load during a group task evaluated a confederate who offered to help them more positively than a confederate who failed to help them, and confederates who offered help voluntarily were liked more than those who only offered help after being instructed to.

It is, however, by no means certain that the help-recipient will always respond with relief and gratitude. Just as a bystander has a range of thoughts and feelings as they decide whether or not to help, the help-recipient also has a range of emotional reactions to being helped. Being helped may make the recipient feel embarrassed and inferior, resulting in them reacting negatively. This is especially the case in individualistic societies, such as the UK and the USA, where self-reliance is a highly regarded attribute. The negative reactions of recipients of help might be explained by the concept of reciprocity and equity (see equity theory, Chapter 12). We prefer our relationships with others to be well balanced, with those involved making equal contributions to the relationship. If a help-recipient cannot reciprocate they may feel distressed.

Nadler and Fisher (1986) proposed the threat-to-self-esteem model to explain why people have different reactions to being helped. They argued that donor characteristics (e.g. donor's motive for helping – self-interest, empathy), recipient characteristics (e.g. self-esteem, feeling threatened), aid characteristics (e.g. amount of help given), and context characteristics (e.g. opportunity to reciprocate help) interact with one another to influence whether the recipient feels self-threat or self-support. If the help given conveys caring for the recipient and provides real benefits, it will be seen as self-supporting, and should result in the recipient of help feeling positive about themselves and expressing gratitude to the help-giver. If, however, the help given implies that the recipient is inferior to the helper and conflicts with values of self-reliance and independence, it will be seen as self-threatening. In this context, the recipient is likely to have negative feelings about themselves and be highly motivated to improve themselves in the future so they no longer need to rely on help. They are also likely to negatively evaluate the helper and the aid they received. This was succinctly demonstrated by Blaine, Crocker, and Major (1995) who had participants imagine that they were a stigmatized person who received a job either because of their qualifications or because the employer felt sympathy for their stigmatized condition. Participants reported lower self-esteem, more negative affect and lowered work motivation when the job was offered out of sympathy than when it was offered based on qualifications.

CHAPTER SUMMARY

In this chapter, we have provided an overview of the social psychological research on prosocial behaviour. We have explained *why* we have a general tendency to help others in the first place, *when* we are most likely to offer help, and how prosocial behaviour affects the recipients of help. Although there are negative aspects of human social behaviour, for example prejudice and aggression, our propensity to help others gives us reason for optimism. There are a number of reasons why we help others. Sociobiologists argue that our tendency to help others has been passed down from generation to generation, in order for us to protect those who are related to us to ensure the survival of our genes. However, this does not explain why we help friends and even strangers. Social psychologists argue, alternatively, that helping behaviour is learned by observing and copying the helping behaviour of others, or by adhering to social norms of helping that are held in high regard in most

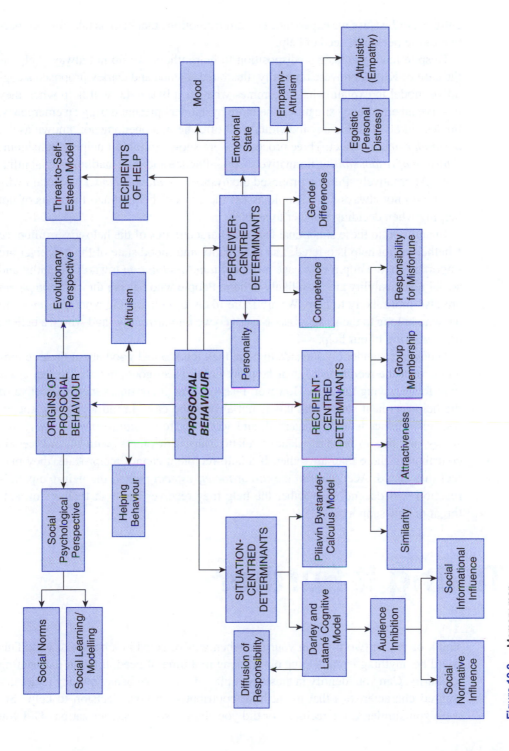

Figure 10.9 Memory map

cultures, or because we experience empathic emotions that help us take the perspective of the person in need of help.

Despite having a basic predisposition to help others, we do not always help, as the case of Kitty Genovese tragically illustrated. Latané and Darley proposed a cognitive model to explain what determines whether a bystander will help when they observe an emergency situation. The more bystanders present during an emergency, the less likely it is that any individual will offer help, a phenomenon known as the *bystander apathy* effect. Three processes were shown to inhibit helping behaviour: *diffusion of responsibility*, normative social influence and informational social influence. Alternatively, Piliavin proposed the *bystander-calculus model* to explain why people do not always help. People assess the costs of helping and the costs of not helping when deciding whether to help.

In addition to these situational factors, characteristics of the help-giver influence whether or not help is offered. The personality and mood state of the perceiver are important here. People who have a *dispositional inclination* towards empathy and social responsibility are most likely to help. People who believe they are *competent* are also more likely to help. We are more likely to help people who are *similar* to us, who belong to the *same group* as us, who we find *attractive*, and who we believe are *deserving* of our help.

When a bystander does decide to help, they tend to feel good about their actions and expect the recipients of their help not only to feel good, but also to feel gratitude for receiving the help. However, research which considers the perspective of the help-recipient shows that this is not always the case. In individualistic societies, self-reliance is highly regarded, and according to the *norms of reciprocity and equity*, we like to have a balanced relationship with others, with no one person contributing more than any other. If a help-recipient cannot reciprocate, they may feel threatened. According to the *threat-to-self-esteem model*, the help-recipient's reaction will depend on whether the help they receive results in feelings of self-threat or self-support.

Taking it Further

Try This

Think of one or two times in your life when you've acted in a prosocial way. This could be anything from helping out a friend in a time of need, through to donating to charity. Can you identify in these examples of your own behaviour any recipient-centred characteristics that might have contributed to your decision to help? So, were you similar to the recipient or did you share a social categorization? Did you find them attractive or did you perceive them to have no responsibility for their misfortune?

Debate This

There is now a large body of research focusing on the role of observed behaviour, and in particular the mass media, in affecting whether we behave in a positive, prosocial manner or a negative, antisocial manner. Do the mass media really have that powerful an effect on how we behave? Do we really have such little control over our own actions? And which side of the media is winning the war to influence our behaviour: the positive, prosocial side, or the aggressive, violent side? Based on what the psychological research is showing us (not only about media and pro-social behaviour, but also about the media and aggression) what advice would you offer a Government committee investigating this issue.

Something for the Weekend

Following the incident involving Kitty Genovese, who infamously received no help from bystanders as she was being murdered, there was much recrimination about the less-than-positive behaviour that people, in general, seem to show towards one another. But on the other hand, we often read about people who *do* step in to protect others, sometimes even at the expense of their own safety (think about Frank De Martini and Pablo Ortiz who you read about at the start of this chapter). Try finding one or two recent newspaper reports featuring people helping others in need. Can you identify, from these stories, the factors outlined in Latané and Darley's (1968) cognitive model that would make helping behaviour more likely?

Further Reading

The Essentials

Latané, B. & Darley, J.M. (1968). Group inhibition of bystander intervention in emergencies. *Journal of Personality and Social Psychology*, *10*, 215–221.
This is one of the classics of social psychology – a must.

Next Steps

Batson, C.D. (1998). Altruism and prosocial behaviour. In D.T. Gilbert, S.T. Fiske, & G. Lindzey (Eds.), *The handbook of social psychology* (4th edn, Vol. 2, pp. 282–316).
Penner, L.A., Dovidio, J.F., Piliavin, J.A., & Schroeder, D.A. (2005). Prosocial behaviour: Multilevel perspectives. *Annual Review of Psychology*, 56, 365–392.

If you want to know about prosocial behaviour in more depth, here are a couple of more detailed review articles on the topic, written by leaders in the field.

Delving Deeper

Dovidio, J.F., Piliavin, J.A., Schroeder, D.A., & Penner, L.A. (2006). *The social psychology of prosocial behaviour.* New York: Psychology Press.

In this recent book on the topic of prosocial behaviour you will learn about the most recent and cutting-edge developments in the field, as well as a clear, lively account of the classic approaches to helping. Whether you're interested in studying more on prosocial behaviour later on, or whether you think what you've read about in this chapter will be useful to you in your future career, this will be a great book to cement your understanding.

Affiliation and Attraction

11

Affiliation and Attraction

In this chapter and the next we focus on the most specific forms of human social interaction: affiliation, friendship, attraction and love. Where do we start in trying to understand such interpersonal relations? The essential starting point in any discussion of friendship and love (which we get to in Chapter 12) is why we should want to spend time with someone in the first place. We are social creatures, we spend considerable time in the company of others, and we appear to enjoy and benefit from these **affiliations**. In this chapter we will discuss when and why we choose to spend time in the company of others, and what happens when we are isolated or excluded from others. We will then look in detail at what determines interpersonal attraction, factors that range from physical characteristics through to psychological characteristics such as similarity, familiarity, and complementarity. Finally, we will talk about the recent phenomenon of online dating, considering how we attract others online, and what we ourselves find attractive in an online setting. These processes set the scene for the last chapter in this book where we see how attraction to others turns into long-term friendship and love. But, we're getting ahead of ourselves. The starting point is affiliation; why are we social creatures in the first place?

AFFILIATION

The tendency to affiliate is something people have from early on in their lives. Larson, Csikszentmihalyi and Graef (1982) found that adolescents spent about 75 per cent of their waking time with other people. Such sociability appears to yield benefits. Teenagers were happier, more alert, and more excited when in the company of others than when alone. In contrast, a lack of affiliation may have a lasting negative impact. In research among children raised in orphanages a lack of social and physical contact adversely affected the ability of the brain and the hormonal system to cope with stress (Gunnar, 2000). At first glance then, affiliation seems to be a good thing. These statistics give us clues, but not an understanding of why this might be the case. In an effort to uncover exactly why people choose to affiliate with others, and why this has benefits for individuals, psychologists have proposed a number of theories. We discuss these theories in the next section.

When and Why Do We Affiliate?

According to evolutionary psychologists, our tendency to seek out others and form close relationships is an inherited trait that helps us to survive and repro-duce by providing us with a network of support that will help us when we are in need. On the one hand, there are some basic principles that apply to everyone that can explain why people's desire for affiliation varies from time to time. There are, however, also chronic differences in people's desire to affiliate with others, that is, some people, in general, are more inclined than others to seek out affiliation. We discuss below first these basic processes, and then individual dif-ferences in our desire to affiliate.

Psychological Determinants of Affiliation

The **privacy regulation theory** (Altman, 1975) argues that our ideal level of pri-vacy (as opposed to sociability) fluctuates over time, influenced by two principles. According to the *dialectic principle*, our desire for privacy (versus affiliation) can vary from being open to others or closed off to others, even in the space of a few hours. We also operate by an *optimization principle*, where we try to align our desired level of contact with our actual level of contact with others. If we have too little contact, we feel isolated, but if we have too much contact, we feel crowded. This theory is useful in explaining why our feelings of isolation or being over-crowded are entirely subjective and relative. Rather than being constant, they vary depending on the desired level of contact at a given time.

   A second explanation for differences in people's desire to affiliate over time is offered by the **social affiliation model** (O'Connor & Rosenblood, 1996). This model proposes that rather than showing wide variations in our need to affiliate, we operate according to the principle of **homeostasis**. This is the idea that people control their level of contact with others to keep it stable and as close as possible to a desired level. To demonstrate their theory, O'Connor and Rosenblood had students carry pagers, which went off intermittently over a period of four days. The pager sounded roughly once an hour and when it did, participants were required to write down the extent of their current contact and their desired level of contact. They found that most participants interacted with others at their preferred level, demon-strating that they could effectively regulate their need for affiliation.

Individual Differences in Affiliation

The *privacy regulation theory* and *social affiliation model* described above both assume no differences between people in typical needs for affiliation. There are, however, also differences *between* people in the extent to which they typically, or chronically, have a need to affiliate with others. Both biological and cultural explanations have been offered to explain these individual differences. Differences in affiliative desires may be reflected in the central nervous system. Brain imaging studies conducted by Johnson and colleagues (1999) show that *introverts* are higher in arousability, the degree to which stimulation typically produces arousal of the central nervous system, than *extroverts*. The authors of this research argue that introverts are likely to steer clear of social interaction to avoid their arousal from reaching uncomfortable levels. In contrast, extroverts, who have low levels of arousal, have to seek out social situations to stimulate a desirable level of arousal. Affiliation can, however, also be shaped by *culture*. In a study of 22 countries, Hofstede (1980) found that the more individualistic a country was, the more its members desired affiliation. He argued that in individualistic cultures people develop social relationships in many and varied settings, but these relationships tend not to be particularly close. In collectivist cultures, on the other hand, people develop relatively few, but deep and long-lasting, relationships. To summarize, the studies discussed above suggest that in individualistic cultures, people may develop friendships in a fairly self-serving manner, whereas in collectivist cultures, friendships might be more likely to be characterized by selflessness and obligation.

Problems with Affiliation and Affiliating

So far, we have largely focused on the positive aspects of affiliation. We have a general tendency to seek out the company of others but there is always the possibility that we will not meet the criteria for attraction, and that we will therefore be rejected. As a result, seeking affiliation can be fraught by discomfort and anxiety. Conversely, if we cannot satisfy our affiliation needs, this *absence* of social interaction can also have a detrimental effect on people.

Here we discuss two problems that can arise in interpersonal interactions. First, people may experience the negative emotion of social anxiety, which can lead to negative behaviours that elicit negative reactions from others and lead to the avoidance of social situations. Second, if people fail to form relationships that fulfil their social needs, they may suffer from loneliness. All of us may feel socially anxious or lonely from time to time, but for some people these are chronic problems.

Social Anxiety

Social anxiety is the negative emotion we experience due to our concern with interpersonal evaluation. Social anxiety can occur during interpersonal interactions, or even when merely anticipating an interaction with another person. It has a number of negative consequences for our interactions; we talk less, stammer or stutter when we speak and disclose less about ourselves. We may even avoid social interactions altogether. Although most of us feel social anxiety at some point, some people are victims of chronic social anxiety, known as social anxiousness. People who are highly socially anxious expect rejection and have quicker and stronger reactions to rejection when they perceive it to have occurred. Pishyar and colleagues (2004) found that socially anxious individuals are more attentive to faces with negative expressions than those with positive or neutral expressions. As they are more attuned to noticing negative feedback during interactions, the socially anxious are likely to behave in a nervous and uncomfortable manner, resulting in them actually receiving negative feedback – in other words, leading to a self-fulfilling prophecy.

Social anxiety can be understood in terms of Schachter's (1964) **two-factor theory of emotion**, which proposes that emotional experience is based on two factors, *physiological arousal* and a *search for cues* in the social environment which might explain that arousal. If people are anxious, they are likely to attribute that anxiety to the behaviour of others, assuming that others do not evaluate them highly. A study by Olson (1988) clearly illustrates how this can occur. Participants were asked to read a speech while being videoed, while simultaneously listening to noise through headphones. Some were told that the noise contained a subliminal sound that would make them feel anxious, whilst others were told that the noise would make them feel relaxed and calm and others, in a control condition, were told that the noise would have no effect. Olson found that those who believed that they would feel anxious due to the sound gave smoother and more fluent speeches than those who expected to feel calm, or were in a control condition (see Figure 11.1). These findings are likely to be due to a misattribution of arousal. In other words, participants attributed the anxiety to the noise, and so did not feel anxious as a result of the speech.

Loneliness

A different problem that can arise in the domain of social interaction is the absence of contact, or loneliness. According to Perlman and Peplau (1998), 25 per cent of Americans reported that they had felt lonely or remote from others in the two weeks prior to sampling.

A number of studies have investigated why people feel lonely. In a study of first-year university students, Williams and Solano (1983) found that although lonely students did not differ from non-lonely students in terms of how many best friends they had, they perceived a lack of intimacy with their friends. These findings indicate that it is poor *quality* rather than a low *quantity* of relationships which contributes towards feeling lonely. Maxwell and Coebergh (1986) found that how close people were to the closest person in their life, how many close friends they had, how

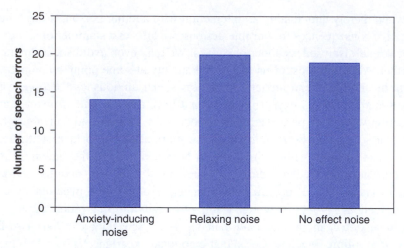

Figure 11.1 Illustration of Olson's (1988) misattribution of anxiety. Data from Olson (1988)

satisfied people were with their relationships, and whether they had daily contact with others were the four strongest predictors of loneliness.

Berscheid and Reis (1998) reviewed the existing literature and identified three main factors that related to loneliness. First, lonely people are more likely to have certain personality traits, such as shyness, depression, introversion, self-conscious-ness and low self-esteem. Second, social circumstances play a role. Lonely people spend less time with women (regardless of gender), and experience less intimacy and disclosure. Third, lonely people have certain social-cognitive tendencies, for example judging others harshly.

Whether loneliness is a temporary state or whether it becomes chronic depends on how we interpret it and how we react to its perceived causes. Cutrona (1982) investigated the duration of loneliness experienced by first-year college students. She found that those who blamed themselves for their loneliness, by making more internal, stable, attributions, for example, 'I'm too shy', were more likely to suffer from chronic loneliness than those who made situational attributions such as 'I'm new here' (see the discussion of internal versus external attributions in Chapter 2).

Summary

From early on in our lives, we have a desire to affiliate. Psychologists have proposed a number of theories which may explain why this is the case. According to *evolutionary* psychologists, affiliation is an inherited trait that helps us to survive and reproduce, but this cannot explain the temporary and chronic differences in our desire to affiliate. According to the *privacy regulation theory*, our desire for privacy versus affiliation varies over time and we try to align the desired level of contact we have at any given time with our actual level of contact with others. Alternatively, the *social affiliation model* proposes that we operate according to the principle of *homeostasis*, keeping our level of contact as stable, and as close to our desired level, as possible. There are also chronic differences in our desire to affiliate. These differences may be explained by our biology; brain imaging studies show that stimulation produces greater arousal of the central nervous system in introverts than in extroverts. *Introverts* may therefore steer clear of social interaction in order to avoid uncomfortable levels of arousal. *Culture* may also help to explain these chronic differences; the more individualistic a culture, the more people desire affiliation, although their relations tend not to be as deep or long lasting as in collectivist cultures.

Although there are many positive aspects of affiliation, it also has a downside. People may experience the negative emotion of *social anxiety*, which can lead to negative behaviours that elicit negative reactions from others and lead to the avoidance of social situations. Although we may all feel anxious in social situations from time to time, some people suffer from chronic social anxiousness. The *two-factor theory of emotion* explains why social anxiety might occur. It proposes that emotional experience is based on physiological arousal and a search for environmental cues which might explain that arousal. If people are anxious, they are likely to attribute that anxiety to the behaviour of others, assuming that others do not evaluate them highly. Although social interaction can lead to anxiousness, a lack of good quality contact with others can also be problematic. Research indicates that *loneliness* is related to three main factors: *personality* (e.g. shyness, introversion), *social circumstances* (lack of intimacy and disclosure), and *social-cognitive tendencies* (tendency to judge others harshly). People who blame themselves for their loneliness are most likely to suffer from chronic, rather than temporary, loneliness.

Text Box 11.1

Ostracism

We've all been there. Lined up in the playground … gradually each person being picked for either team … and you realize with that sinking feeling in your stomach that *you* are going to be last (and if you're really unlucky, there will be the wrong number for equal sides and you won't get to play at all!). That feeling of being excluded is excruciating for most of us, and illustrates just how strong our need for affiliation is.

(Continued)

Some inspiring work by Kip Williams has explored social exclusion in its most acute form – ostracism – and shows us the incredible power of social affiliation (or rather, the power of it being withheld). In this work Williams and colleagues have demonstrated the visceral power of being excluded. No-one likes being left out, but did you know that it doesn't matter who ostracizes you? Williams and Jarvis (2006) came up with an ingenious computer program called 'Cyberball'. In Cyberball the three 'stick people' on a screen throw a ball to each other (check it out at: http://www1.psych.purdue.edu/~willia55/Announce/cyberball. htm). The participant is one of the stick people and can press a button to throw the ball to one of the other players – who they think are both fellow students in adjoining cubicles (in fact they are not real participants but pre-programmed by the experimenters to follow a specific set of behaviours). After a few trials throwing the ball to each other and the participant, the two other stick players just throw the ball to each other and totally ignore the participant!

Now you might think that participants won't worry about this – it's only a psychology experiment after all. In fact, they are incredibly bothered, even if they don't know who the other players are supposed to be, even if they clock that the other players are just computer AI (i.e. not even human! See Williams, 2001; 2007). And it gets worse … Gonsalkorale and Williams (2007) showed that ostracism by despised groups still upsets us: even if they are a group like the Ku Klux Klan.

So ostracism has an incredibly powerful effect on us, regardless of who is doing the ostracizing (and regardless of whether we would even want to be a member of their group). There are a number of potential reasons for this, but one intriguing fMRI study by Eisenberger, Lieberman, and Williams (2003) suggests that some basic biological hard-wiring may help explain the wide generality of ostracism effects. They found, using Cyberball, that ostracism led to the same areas of the brain being activated as when we are physically hurt. Perhaps we have evolved to see social ostracism as just as physically threatening as actual physical pain. This may be because throughout history, time and time again, we have seen how we are much stronger together than when we are apart. In other words, our need for social affiliation may have become so important to us that it has become hard-wired.

INTERPERSONAL ATTRACTION

In the previous section we discussed how humans are social animals who, to a greater or lesser extent, have a desire to affiliate with others. This is the starting point on the road to any more developed form of interpersonal relationship; we have to be inclined to place ourselves in situations where we might meet people before anything more intimate can develop. As we saw, this inclination to be sociable can vary from person to person. Some people have a stronger desire to affiliate than others. Moreover, the desire to affiliate varies across time and situations. It is clear, however, that not *anyone* will always do to satisfy our desire to be around people. Why do we choose to affiliate more closely with some people than others? What makes particular people *attractive* to us?

Interpersonal attraction describes the desire to approach another individual, to seek them out for interaction. The issue of attraction is the critical next step in helping us to understand how friendships and romantic relationships develop. Of particular interest to social psychologists are the issues of *why* and *when* we approach, and conversely, why we sometimes avoid, other people. These questions are answered in the next section. The determinants of attraction can be divided up into those that are target-centred or perceiver-centred. That is, whether the determinants have something to do with the person who we may or may not end up finding attractive, or something to do with our own subjective experiences or feelings. Below we deal with each of these in turn.

Target-Centred Determinants of Attraction

What is it about other people that makes them attractive to us? Psychologists have identified four key factors: physical appearance, perceived similarity, complementarity and reciprocity. These four key sources of attraction are discussed below.

Physical Characteristics

When we meet someone for the first time, one of the first things we notice is their physical appearance. But what makes a personal physically attractive? Moreover, do the characteristics of physical attractiveness vary from culture to culture, or are there universal features of attractiveness? Well, there do appear to be variations in what is considered to be physically attractive. Cogan and her colleagues (1996) found that college students in Ghana, West Africa, showed a preference for larger women than did college students in the United States. Anderson and colleagues (1992) also found that while slim women were preferred in cultures where there is a reliable food supply, larger women were preferred in cultures where the availability of food was unpredictable, presumably – from an evolutionary perspective – because they carry a built-in food-supply that increases the likelihood that they will be fertile and produce offspring even during times of food shortages.

There are, however, commonalities across cultures. Cross-culturally, women are defined more in terms of physical attractiveness than are men (Ford & Beach, 1951). Concerning body shape, there is evidence that men worldwide prefer women with a small *waist-to-hip ratio*, a ratio of 0.7 being the most desirable, the classic 'hourglass' figure (Streeter & McBurney, 2003). This may be particularly attractive because it signifies youthfulness, good health, and fertility. It is also an indicator that a woman is not currently pregnant and therefore sexually available. From an evolutionary point of view, they are therefore more likely to successfully produce offspring (Furnham et al., 2002).

There is also evidence that certain aspects of facial attractiveness are universal. We tend to prefer people with **facial symmetry**, where the left and right hand side of the face are well matched, because according to evolutionary psychologists this indicates physical health and the lack of genetic defects, important in producing healthy offspring. Accordingly, many studies have shown that facial symmetry is positively related to genetic, physical and mental health, and negatively related to genetic mutations. In Text Box 11.2 you can read about a fascinating study about the effects of facial symmetry on attraction.

Text Box 11.2

The Scent of Symmetry

Asymmetry results from genetic mutations and inbreeding, and has been shown to negatively predict growth rate, longevity and health status, whereas symmetry is associated with increased genetic, physical, and mental health and – among men – larger body size and a more muscular physique. Based on these findings, it is not that surprising that more symmetrical people are considered more attractive than asymmetrical people. Thornhill and Gangestad (1999) tested the intriguing possibility that there is a human sex pheromone that signals symmetry. Specifically, they examined whether we prefer the *smell* of people who are symmetrical to the smell of those who are not.

Method

Eighty male participants had their degree of symmetry measured by researchers. They were then given a clean, unworn, cotton t-shirt to wear for two nights while sleeping. During this time they were asked to refrain from using scented soaps, deodorants and cologne, eating strongly flavoured foods, drinking alcohol and smoking tobacco, to ensure that their natural odour was not contaminated by other smells. On the same morning when the men had dropped off their shirts, 82 female participants smelled each shirt and rated its pleasantness, sexiness and intensity. They also completed a questionnaire about their menstrual cycle and when they last had a period, allowing the researchers to work out whether each participant was currently ovulating.

Results

There was a positive relationship between male participants' facial symmetry and female participants' preference for their t-shirt odour; in other words, women preferred the smell of men who had a symmetrical face. This effect occurred despite the fact that women did not know who had worn each shirt. Interestingly, however, the relationship between facial symmetry and odour preference only emerged for women who were about to ovulate. Women who were not at their most fertile when the experiment took place were just as likely to favour the smell of men with asymmetrical faces as men with symmetrical faces. This pattern of results is illustrated in the graph below.

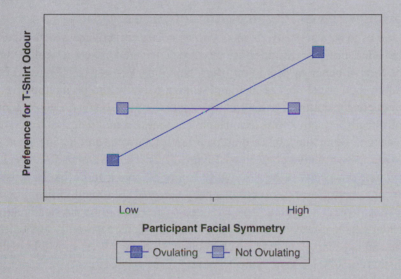

Interpreting the Findings

Thornhill and Gangestad suggest that there may be a chemical scent emitted by men that differs depending on a man's genetic health, and therefore the symmetry of his face. According to the evolutionary perspective, this difference should only matter for ovulating women who may potentially be about to conceive and need to ensure they produce healthy offspring.

We also tend to prefer faces that represent the average face in a given population. Rhodes and Tremewan (1996) asked participants to judge caricatures of faces which were systematically varied from average to distinctive. They found that the more average a face was, the more attractive it was considered to be. Similarly, Langlois, Roggman, and Musselman (1994) found that people preferred 'average' composite faces generated by a computer, created by combining a series of individual faces, to those individual faces that made up the composites. This may be because we prefer people and objects that are familiar to us (see a discussion of the familiarity and mere exposure effects in attitude formation in Chapter 4).

Facial maturity influences attractiveness differently for men and women. Many studies show that females are considered more attractive if their features are somewhat immature (for example small nose, full lips, small chin and delicate jaw) whereas men are considered more attractive if their features are mature (for example a broad fore-head, thick eyebrows and large jaw). There preferences parallel gender stereotypes in society, because immature features are associated with dependence and helplessness, whereas mature features are considered to be dominant and powerful.

Consequences of Physical Attractiveness

There seems to be a pervasive tendency to associate attractiveness with other positive characteristics. As a result, those who are considered to be physically attractive may be treated better in life. Dion, Berscheid, and Walster (1972) asked college students to look at pictures of men and women perceived to be unattractive, averagely attractive and attractive and then evaluate their personality. People perceived to be physically attractive were assumed to have more socially desirable personality traits, such as being successful, dominant, and intelligent and having good social skills, than less attractive people (see Figure 11.2). They were also seen as having better future prospects: to be less likely to get divorced, more likely to be good parents, and more likely to experience deep personal fulfilment in their social and professional lives. The finding that individuals perceived to be physically attractive have better personalities and lead happier lives has been consistently replicated over the years and appears to hold true across cultures, having been shown in both individualistic (e.g. US, UK) and collectivist (e.g. Korea) countries.

Given that people perceived to be physically attractive are considered to have superior personality traits, it is not surprising that this has a powerful influence on how people are treated by others and how successful they are. Dion (1972) had student teachers read a negative evaluation of a child who had allegedly been caught throwing stones at a cat. She found that when the evaluation was accompanied by a picture of an attractive child, the student excused the behaviour as being atypical of the child, did not recommend punishment, and considered the child unlikely to misbehave again. When the accompanying picture was of an unattractive child, however, the behaviour was attributed to her personality, was looked upon more severely, and the child was considered likely to misbehave again (see Figure 11.3).

There is also evidence that attractiveness can affect success as an adult. Landy and Sigall (1974) had male students grade either a good or poor essay, to which a photograph of the supposed writer, a female student, was attached. Participants either saw a photo of an attractive or an unattractive woman. After reading the essay, male students gave better grades to the attractive student. Frieze and co-workers (1991) obtained pictures

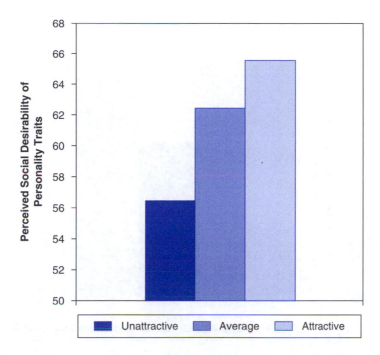

Figure 11.2 'What is Beautiful is Good'. Data from Dion, Berscheid, and Walster (1972)

of a representative sample of 700 MBA graduates, and information on their career success. They found a $2200 difference between the starting salaries of good-looking men and those who were judged as being below average in attractiveness. Although this difference did not emerge for women, attractiveness instead had an impact on their later salaries. Once hired, women of above-average attractiveness had an average annual salary that was $4200 more than those who were below average in attractiveness.

It is clear from these findings that attractiveness influences perceptions of intelligence and success, which in turn affects actual career success. But is the attractiveness stereotype accurate? Feingold (1992) conducted a meta-analysis looking at more than 90 studies that investigated the relationship between attractiveness and personality. He found no significant relationship between physical attractiveness and intelligence, dominance, self-esteem and mental health. He did, however, find that attractive people were less socially anxious, more socially skilled and less lonely than less attractive people. The reasons why this might be were demonstrated by Snyder, Tanke, and Berscheid (1977). Male students were given either a photo of an attractive woman or an unattractive woman who they were led to believe they would talk to on the telephone. The woman they actually spoke to was, however, not in either photo. The conversations were rated by independent judges, who rated the men who thought they were talking to an attractive woman as more outgoing and sociable than those who believed they were talking to an unattractive woman. Moreover, the woman they spoke to was rated by the judges as being more warm, confident,

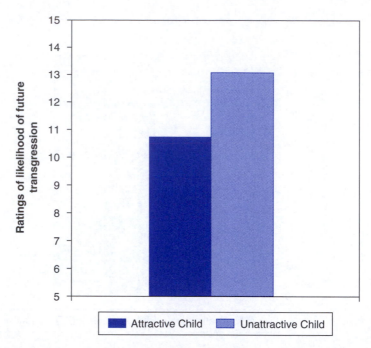

Figure 11.3 Mean ratings for perceived likelihood of future transgressions by attractive versus unattractive children (0 = very unlikely, 17 = very likely). Data from Dion (1972)

animated and attractive when the man to whom they spoke believed they were attractive rather than unattractive. These findings show evidence for a **self-fulfilling prophecy**, whereby someone's beliefs about another person can cause that person to behave in a manner that confirms those expectations. In this context, attractive people may be more confident and have better social skills because the people they interact with treat them as such.

Similarity to the Self

Although physical attractiveness is a powerful determinant of whether we will want to affiliate with a particular person, people also attend to other characteristics in making such decisions. Social psychological research shows that we are generally attracted to those who are *similar* to us. Kandel (1978), for instance, found that high school students' best friends were those with similar demographics to them; they were similar to their best friends in terms of sex, race, age and school year. It is not, however, only physical or obvious characteristics that form the basis for similarity. *Similarity of attitudes* is also an important determinant of how much people like one another. Newcomb (1961) had participants fill in questionnaires about their attitudes and values before they arrived at university. Although in their first few weeks of university participants preferred those who lived close to them, over time attraction was more closely related to similarity in their initial attitudes. Interestingly, this implies that physical or obvious bases for similarity are important early on in relationships, but that as time goes on it is similarity on the basis of psychological characteristics that becomes more important.

Byrne and Nelson (1965) went on to experimentally investigate how attitude similarity leads to attraction. They had participants complete attitude questionnaires and later introduced them to another person by having them read a similar questionnaire, ostensibly completed by that person but actually completed by the researcher to be either similar or dissimilar to the responses of the participant. The greater the proportion of similar attitudes they thought they shared with the other individual, the more participants liked them (see Figure 11.4).

Evidence for the importance of similarity has also been found in romantic relationships. Couples who are evenly matched in their appearance, social background, personality, interests, and leisure activities are more likely to be attracted to one another. Moreover, people tend to become more evenly matched over time. In a longitudinal study of married couples over 21 years, Gruber-Baldini, Schaie, and Willis (1995) found that although spouses were similar in a number of ways at the start of the study, they become increasingly matched over time in terms of their mental abilities and attitudes. This implies a reciprocal relationship between similarity and attraction: similarity can make someone more attractive to us, but attraction may also lead us to bring our attitudes and opinions more in line with the target of our affections.

Gruber-Baldini et al.'s findings suggest that similarity is not something that people are unaware of in interpersonal relationships. Rather, people seem quite attuned to the fact that similarity leads to attraction, and may use this fact strategically in targeting others with whom they would like to develop closer ties. Some further research supports this idea. Although, as we discussed above, we are all generally drawn towards those who are physically attractive, people also have a tendency to prefer those who are *similar* in physical attractiveness to them. In other words, regardless of any objective or consensual indications of physical attractiveness, people tend to seek out affiliation with those who they believe to have a similar level of physical attractiveness as themselves. Why should this be?

Social psychologists have suggested that we may be particularly attracted to those who are of similar attractiveness to us because we estimate they will also have a similar opinion about us. This reduces the risk of dealing with the unpleasant potential for a rejection of our advances. This tendency, known as the **matching hypothesis** (e.g. Garcia & Khersonsky, 1997), is a socially shared belief. People believe that similarly matched couples in terms of attractiveness will be happier in their relationship and, indeed, there is evidence for this. Murstein (1972) found that physically similar couples are more intimate and report greater love than dissimilar couples. The same patterns emerge for friendships. Carli and colleagues (1991) found that similarly attractive roommates were more satisfied, felt their roommates were more satisfied, and were more likely to want the same roommate for next year than those who were dissimilar in terms of attractiveness.

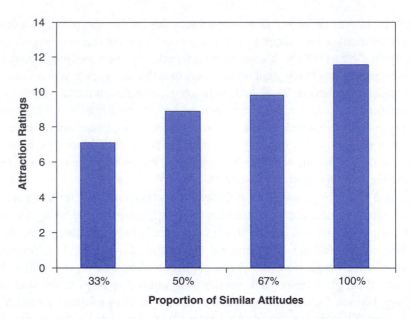

Figure 11.4 Attraction as a function of the proportion of similar attitudes. Data from Byrne and Nelson (1965)

There is mixed support for the matching hypothesis. Berscheid, Dion, Walster, and Walster (1971) found that although perceiver attractiveness was correlated with target attractiveness, there is still an overriding tendency for even less attractive people to report a preference for attractive others. But Van Straaten, Engels, Finkenauer, and Holland (2009) argued that while less attractive people might *prefer* to have a highly attractive partner, they are more likely to *pursue* a partner of similar attractiveness in order to avoid rejection. In order to test this idea, they had single undergraduate students (who had been rated by independent observers for attractiveness) interact with either an attractive or an unattractive confederate of the opposite sex whom they believed to be single. These interactions were recorded on hidden cameras, and were rated for approach behaviours, which refer to the extent to which the participant engaged in behaviours reflecting warmth, interpersonal interest, and responsiveness, all of which communicate a desire to make a positive impression on another person. Participants also rated their interest in dating their interaction partner. It emerged that participants were more interested in dating attractive interaction partners, regardless of their own level of attractiveness. However, male participants showed more approach behaviours when interacting with women of a similar level of attractiveness to themselves (see Figure 11.5). Women, on the other hand, showed relatively low levels of approach behaviour, and no differences were observed on the basis of similarity of attractiveness.

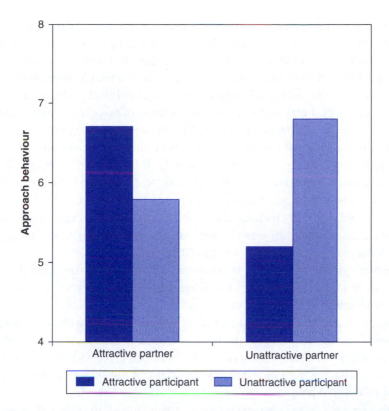

Figure 11.5 Approach behaviour among male participants as a function of participant and interaction partner attractiveness. Data from Van Straaten et al. (2009)

So it seems that although people prefer attractive mates in principle, men are more willing to indicate their attraction to those of similar attractiveness to them, presumably because it reduces the chance of facing rejection. But why does this same trend not apply to women? According to the **parental investment theory** (Trivers, 1972), men and women differ considerably in their strategies to attract a mate for evolutionary reasons. Reproduction has more serious and long lasting consequences for women than for men: women must go through pregnancy and childbirth, and are primarily responsible for childcare. They therefore need to be sure that they are attracting the right mate. Moreover, showing interest to a man who is not interested may damage her reputation and value as a potential mate to others. Accordingly, women are more reserved about communicating attraction (e.g. Baumeister & Vohs, 2004), regardless of how attractive the potential mate is.

Clearly, similarity is an important predictor of attraction, but why? There are a number of possible explanations. Fritz Heider's (1958) **balance theory** proposed that people try to maintain a sense of balance, or cognitive consistency, in their thoughts, feelings and social relationships. A relationship between two people will be balanced when they value the same thing. If, for example, two friends both have liberal political views, their relationship will be balanced. Their similar liberal beliefs are compatible with their liking for one another. If two people who encounter one another have very different political beliefs – if one is politically liberal and the other is conservative – they may dislike each other because of this discrepancy. Again, this relationship is balanced; the two people dislike one another because they do *not* share the same values. Balanced relationships have been shown to be not only more pleasant and rewarding, but also arise more frequently. If two people are friends but have opposing political views, however, they are likely to experience imbalance. This will produce negative tension and arousal, leading to attempts to restore the balance. This can be achieved by either changing their attitude towards each other, or by changing their attitudes so that they are more in line with one another (see the discussion of the related concept of cognitive dissonance in Chapter 4).

A further explanation for the relationship between similarity and attraction is our desire for *social comparison*. One of the main reasons why we like to compare ourselves to others is because it offers social validity to important aspects of our self-concept. Clore (1976) argued that when someone agrees with our perceptions, our point of view is reinforced, which leads to greater liking. As a result, it makes sense that we prefer those who agree, rather than disagree, with our point of view. People who disagree with us may cause us to doubt our beliefs and therefore our sense of self. These people should, accordingly, be avoided.

Finally, there may also be an *evolutionary explanation* for the effect of similarity on attraction. There is evidence that friends have a tendency to be similar to one another on certain genetically determined characteristics (Rushton, 1989). It may be that humans are unconsciously attracted to similar others because they share similar genes. By looking out for our friends, we may be increasing the probability that genes similar to our own will be passed on to future generations.

Complementary Characteristics

Despite this preference for similar others, there is also evidence that on certain criteria we are attracted to those with characteristics that *complement*, rather than mirror, our own. Put another way, we find others attractive when they hold a trait that we value, but do not possess ourselves. It is important to note that this is distinct from the idea that 'opposites attract', i.e. that we are sometimes attracted to dissimilar others. Instead, an attraction to complementary characteristics reflects the fact that we like people who have traits that we do not have, but would like to. Buss (1989) found, across 37 countries, that men prefer women who are younger whereas women generally prefer men who are slightly older than themselves. There is also evidence that beauty is a more important factor in attractiveness for men, while social status is an important component of attractiveness for women. Townsend and Levy (1990) asked students to evaluate strangers who varied in physical attractiveness and social status. Men showed a preference for highly attractive but low-status women. In contrast, women found that high-status men who were only moderately attractive were as appealing to women as highly attractive but only moderate-status men. Thus, women can trade looks for status, and men can trade status for looks, but the reverse is not true. These results can be explained in terms of a **looks-for-status exchange**. Men are attracted to young women because female youth signifies beauty, whilst women are attracted to older men because age is likely to be accompanied by higher social status.

There are two competing explanations for these gender differences. According to the evolutionary perspective, attraction is associated with maximizing the probability of producing offspring and therefore passing on genes to the next generation. Accordingly, men are predisposed to prefer young women because they are more likely to reproduce and women are predisposed to prefer older, high-status men because they are able to protect them, and provide resources to support them and their offspring. This viewpoint has, however, been criticized as a justification of the 'status quo' with regard to gender inequality in society. The alternative socio-cultural perspective proposes that because historically men hold more power than women in society, men view women as objects of exchange, with the quality, or beauty, of this object of principal importance. Women, because of their historical lack of power and therefore inability to advance based on their own skills, have traditionally been forced to find a man who is socially dominant and has high status if they are to achieve that status themselves.

These two explanations are not mutually exclusive. Although there is likely to be a strong evolutionary role in gender differences in attraction, as women have become more financially independent and successful, preferences are changing. Gil-Burmann and colleagues (2002), based on a content analysis of personal ads in a Spanish newspaper, found that although the looks-for-status exchange predictions still applied overall, women under the age of 40 sought physical attractiveness rather than socio-economic status in men. Strassberg and Holty (2003) found a similar change among men. They posted several versions of a 'female seeking male' personal ad on internet bulletin boards and found that an ad in which the women was described as successful and ambitious generated 50 per cent more responses than the next most popular ad, which described the woman as attractive and slim.

Reciprocity

We may find someone else attractive, but what if they do not feel the same way? What happens to interpersonal attraction when it is, and when it is not, reciprocated? Whether our attentions are returned or not does appear to have an impact on our level of attraction. According to the *reciprocity principle*, we have a tendency to like those who like us, and dislike those who dislike us. Dittes and Kelley (1956) had participants take part in small group discussions. Prior to this, anonymous written evaluations (actually written by the experimenters) led participants to believe that other group members either liked them or disliked them. Results showed that students who believed they were liked were more attracted to the group than those who believed that they were disliked.

Reciprocity may be more or less predictive of attraction depending on personal characteristics. Dittes (1959) investigated the effect of *self-esteem* on the importance of reciprocity. Participants with high or low self-esteem interacted with a group of other people, who either behaved in a positive, accepting way, or in a negative, rejecting way towards the participant. Dittes found that participants with low self-esteem reported liking the group when it behaved positively, but disliked the group when it behaved negatively. In contrast, participants with high self-esteem were not affected by the group behaviour, showing no difference in their ratings of the two groups. It appears that reciprocity is more important for participants with low rather than high self-esteem, presumably because they rely on assurances from others to bolster their sense of self-worth.

The role of reciprocity in attraction may be explained by *balance theory* (Heider, 1958). As we discussed earlier, this theory proposed that we like people who value the same things as us. We are therefore likely to be attracted to a person who values us as much as we value ourselves. Knowing that another person likes us might also increase mutual attraction via a *self-fulfilling prophecy*. If we think a person with whom we are interacting likes us, we are likely to behave in a friendly manner, and therefore further increase the likelihood that the person likes us.

Summary

In this section we have discussed the target-centred factors that determine attraction: physical attractiveness, similarity, complementarity, and reciprocity. *Physical attractiveness* is important because of societal beliefs or stereotypes as to the relationship between physical attractiveness and other positive characteristics. However, this general tendency to prefer more physically attractive people is qualified by *similarity*: We prefer to seek affiliation with people who are closer to our own perceived level of physical attractiveness. We also attend to other characteristics and prefer others who share similar attitudes, opinions, and beliefs as us, and there is some evidence that whilst similarity in terms of physical characteristics is important for initial attraction, over time psychological characteristics become more important. We also seek *complementarity* in our interpersonal affiliations. Sometimes we want to affiliate with particular people because they can offer us something we don't have. Evidence for this can be found in the tendency for older men to prefer younger women, and vice-versa, in romantic relationships. Finally, we are attracted to people who *reciprocate* our attentions – we like those who like us. Reciprocity is less important for certain types of people, for example those who have high self-esteem and are therefore not reliant on the assurances of others.

Perceiver-Centred Determinants of Attraction

Above we have discussed the four target-centred factors that can determine whether we feel interpersonal attraction. In this section, we discuss two *perceiver*-based factors. In contrast to the type of determinants of attraction that we discussed above (physical attractiveness, similarity to self, complementarity and reciprocity), all of which depend upon the potential target of our attraction, here we discuss two determinants of attraction that depend on the thoughts, feelings and experiences of the *perceiver*. These are how *familiar* we perceive other people to be, and how *anxious* we feel in social settings.

Familiarity

A powerful determinant of friendships, and even romantic relationships, is proximity. This was demonstrated in an investigation of friendships among graduate students living in a series of housing units at the Massachusetts Institute of Technology, conducted by Festinger, Schachter, and Back (1950). Despite the fact that they had been randomly assigned to the housing units and so did not know one another prior to moving in, two-thirds of the residents' closest friends resided not only in the same building but also on the same floor as them. Moreover, residents were nearly twice as likely to name next-door neighbours as close friends than those living two doors away.

The reason why proximity may have an impact on attraction is that we see people who live or work close to us more frequently than other people. In other words, they become more familiar to us. Zajonc (1968)'s *mere exposure hypothesis* (see Chapter 4) proposed that being exposed to someone or something repeatedly increases attraction, even if no information is provided about the object or person. Saegert, Swap, and Zajonc (1973) tested the mere exposure effect by conducting a study in which undergraduate women were asked to evaluate a number of pleasant (different flavours of soft drink) and unpleasant (vinegar, citric acid) tasting liquids. During the course of the experiment, participants were required to move from room to room, to visit different tasting stations, during which time they were differentially exposed to a number of other individuals who were also participating. When, at the end of the study, they were asked to rate how much they liked each individual they had encountered, participants liked the people they had seen more often than those they had seen less frequently, regardless of the quality of liquids they were tasting at those times (see Figure 11.6). Grush and colleagues (1978) have also demonstrated the powerful effects of familiarity. They found that in 83 per cent of cases, the successful candidate in the 1972 congressional primaries in the United States could be predicted by the amount of media exposure they received.

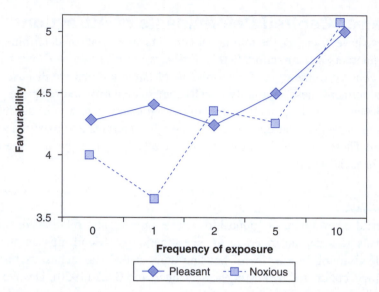

Figure 11.6 Favourability as a function of number of exposures and pleasantness of taste. Data from Saegert, Swap, and Zajonc (1973)

Anxiety

Experiencing anxiety and stress has been shown to increase affiliation with others. Here we are talking about general anxiety, as distinct from *social anxiety*, discussed earlier, where people are likely to avoid rather than seek out affiliation. Schachter (1959) conducted an experiment in which female college students were told that they would receive a series of electric shocks as part of a physiology experiment. Although no shocks were ever delivered, in the 'high anxiety' condition, participants were told that the shocks would be quite painful, while in the 'low anxiety' condition, participants were told that the shocks would be not at all painful. The participants were then told that there would be a 10-minute delay while the equipment was set up and asked whether they would prefer to wait alone or with another participant in the study. Schachter found that 63 per cent of those in the high anxiety but only 33 per cent of those in the low anxiety condition opted to wait with another participant.

Anxiety may have caused people to seek out others to take their mind off the anxiety they were experiencing. In a follow-up study, however, Schachter found that participants in the high anxiety condition showed an overwhelming preference to spend time with a fellow participant rather than other students who were not taking part in the experiment. Anxious people want to spend time not just with any other people, but specifically with those who are going through the *same experience as them*. Schachter proposed that anxious people are attracted to others who are going through a similar experience for the purpose of *social comparison* (see also Chapter 1), to better understand their reaction to the situation. If, for example, an anxious person can see that others also feel anxious in the situation, this will validate their emotional response, confirming that it is a normal, understandable reaction.

The events of 11 September 2001 provide a real-life example of the consequences of stress and anxiety. In the aftermath of the terrorist attacks on New York and Washington, DC, Mehl and Pennebaker (2003) attached small digital voice recorders to the clothing of participants and randomly recorded their conversations in the 10 days following the attacks. They found that although people did not change in their amount of interaction with others, these interactions shifted from group-based and telephone conversations to face-to-face conversations with just one other person. Moreover, those who shifted from group to one-on-one encounters dealt with the stress they were experiencing the best. These findings are compelling evidence of the role of anxiety in drawing people together on an interpersonal level in real life situations.

Summary

In this section we have discussed perceiver-centred determinants of attraction: *familiarity* and *anxiety*. We tend to prefer affiliation with those who are close to us: we like people who we see frequently. This makes sense; if we can predict how people will behave towards us, this makes the world more stable for us (see the discussion of people's preference for a *coherent and predictable world* in Chapter 2). Finally, we seek affiliation in times of anxiety because others provide a source of social support (see the discussion of the benefits of social support in social influence research, Chapter 6), especially if they are going through the same experience.

Text Box 11.3

Does Interacting with Attractive Women make men Stupid?

Most of us can think of a time when we have been having a conversation with someone of the opposite sex whom we find rather attractive. Sometimes in this situation it is hard to act normally: we might find it hard to think clearly and embarrass ourselves by forgetting what we are talking about, or saying

(Continued)

something stupid. Karremans, Verwijmeren, Pronk, and Reitsma (2009) looked at the effect of interacting with the opposite sex on cognitive functioning in order to shed some light on this intriguing phenomenon.

Method

Fifty-three male and fifty-eight female participants were randomly paired with either a participant of the same sex as them, or a partner of the opposite sex. These pairs were then instructed to have a five minute conversation with one another. Participants completed a measure of cognitive functioning, known as the modified Simon task, before and after the interaction. This task involved presenting participants with a series of words in blue, green, or white. If the word was in white, participants had to indicate as fast as possible whether it was a positive or negative word, but if the word was blue or green, they had to indicate what colour it was instead. This is known to be a very cognitively demanding task, as it requires the ability to switch between tasks and inhibit

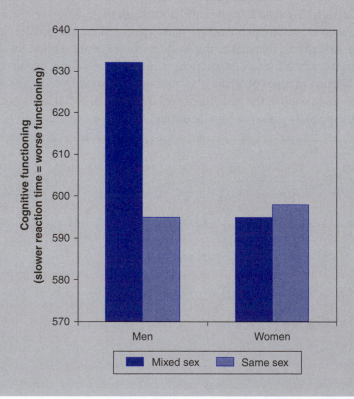

incorrect responses. Impression management – participants' desire to make a good impression on their interaction partner – was also assessed.

Results

Male participants performed worse on the cognitive functioning task following a mixed-sex interaction than following a same-sex interaction, but intriguingly, female participants' performance was not affected by the sex of their interaction partner. Among all participants, the higher the desire to make a good impression on the interaction partner, the worse the cognitive performance. But only male participants reported a greater desire to make a good impression when interacting with a woman than when interacting with a man.

Interpreting the Findings

Karremans and colleagues suggest that when people meet someone of the opposite sex, compared to someone of the same sex, leaving a favourable impression is important. But there is evidence that mixed-sex interactions are more likely to activate mating goals in men than in women (e.g. Baumeister, Catanese, & Vohs, 2001). Accordingly, men are more prone to engage in effortful and cognitively demanding attempts to impress an opposite sex partner. As we illustrated in Chapter 1 on the self, we have limited cognitive resources at our disposal to regulate our behaviour. So, because men have used up their cognitive resources on effortful impression management, they find subsequent cognitive tasks more difficult.

Online Attraction

Once upon a time, people met their partners for the first time through friends and family, or through chance meetings at social events. In recent years, however, following the advent of the internet, many people go about meeting friends and partners online, through chat rooms, social networking sites, and internet dating. Illustrating the scale of this phenomenon, the popular dating website match.com has 6.5 million members. Recently, social psychologists have sought to understand how people go about attracting partners online, and how this process differs from what happens when we first meet a potential partner face-to-face, or 'offline'. Below we summarize two factors that are important when developing an online relationship: portraying one's true self, and self-presentation.

Portraying One's True Self

McKenna, Green, and Gleason (2002) argued that two aspects of the self are important when considering online dating. The true self refers to traits that individuals possess but find difficult to express openly when interacting with others. In contrast, the actual self refers to the traits people possess that they are able to express to others in social settings. Note that these aspects of the self are similar to those suggested by Higgins (1987) in his work on self-regulation and self-discrepancy, which we talk about in Chapter 1. The true self is more accessible in memory after interacting with a stranger online when compared to a face-to-face interaction, suggesting that people are better able to disclose their true self online than in person (Bargh, McKenna, & Fitzsimmons, 2002). McKenna and colleagues asked users of online forums to complete a questionnaire. They found that people who conveyed their true self online developed stronger internet relationships, and were more likely to bring those relationships into their 'real' lives. Moreover, a follow-up study two years later showed that these relationships were more likely to last in the long term. People who were socially anxious and lonely were also more likely to believe that they could better express their true selves online than offline. The researchers concluded that the internet may therefore be an especially useful tool for forming relationships among those who have difficulty developing relationships face-to-face.

Self-Presentation Online

Whitty (2008) carried out structured, open-ended interviews with 60 online daters in order to identify how people present themselves when trying to attract a potential partner, and what they find attractive in the profiles of other users. The data were analysed using grounded theory methodology (Glaser & Strauss, 1967). This involves allowing categories of meaning, or themes, to emerge from the data, rather than testing a specific theory or idea. Three themes emerged through these interviews: *constructing an attractive online profile, misrepresentation, and evaluating the profiles of potential partners*.

Constructing an attractive profile. In creating an attractive profile, physical attractiveness emerged as being of utmost importance. Participants typically included the most attractive photo they could find of themselves, even opting for a professional photo shoot to ensure the best photo possible. There were, however, gender differences: more women than men included a photo, and more had a professional photo taken. These findings suggest that, just like in face-to-face encounters, physical characteristics play an important role in attracting a partner, particularly for women looking to attract a man. They also contradict assumptions that physical attractiveness is less important online. The next most important considerations were describing one's favourite interests, making the profile *humorous*, and making one's profile *unique* and *distinct* from others' profiles.

Misrepresentation. Participants frequently reported feeling the need to 'sell themselves' online. Accordingly, it is unsurprising that many admitted misrepresenting themselves in order to appear more attractive. The most common misrepresentations were using a photo that was over a year out of date, missing out information about previous relationships and children, and lying about their age, weight, and socio-economic status. However, most. participants were at pains to point out that rather than telling outright lies, they were simply exaggerating slightly in order to attract a greater number of potential partners.

Evaluation of potential partners. Participants indicated that looks were the most important factor when searching for a partner online, followed by similar interests and values, socio-economic status, and personality. Unlike previous studies on offline attraction, however, there was no evidence of a *looks-for-status* exchange: men did not state significantly more than women that they were looking for physical attraction, and women were not more likely to want someone with a high socio-economic status. Whitty argued that because there are many online daters, the degree of perceived choice is higher than when meeting people face-to-face, for example in a pub or club. Accordingly, online daters have a more stringent 'wish-list' and (regardless of gender) desire someone with good looks and prospects. Finally, despite misrepresenting themselves, participants were often outraged at how other online daters also engaged in misrepresentation, particularly by exaggerating how attractive they were.

Summary

In this section we have discussed how people go about attracting others through online dating. There are some differences between online and offline attraction: it seems easier to show your '*true self*' online, and this is associated with more successful and longer lasting relationships. There also seem to be *fewer gender differences* in the importance of looks versus status as determinants of attraction online. However, there are also similarities between online and offline dating. Even online, physical attractiveness remains the most important factor when representing ourselves to others, and in choosing a potential mate ourselves. It is, however, easier to misrepresent how attractive one is online, by using old or particularly flattering but unrepresentative photos, and by lying about height, age, and weight.

CHAPTER SUMMARY

In this chapter, we have covered a wide range of topics essential to our understanding of interpersonal affiliation and attraction. Humans have a basic desire to affiliate with others and psychologically benefit from such affiliations. We differ, however, in how much we desire affiliation. Some people have a stronger desire to affiliate than others, and our desire can also vary depending on the situation. Although affiliation has many positive consequences for interpersonal relations, social interactions are not always so pleasant. At certain times, interacting with others may be fraught with discomfort. People may experience *social anxiety* during interpersonal interactions, resulting in negative behaviours that elicit negative reactions from others and lead to the avoid-ance of social situations. Second, if people fail to form relationships that fulfil their social needs, they may suffer from *loneliness*. All of us may feel socially anxious or lonely from time to time, but for some people, these are chronic problems.

As well as differing in our *general* desire to affiliate, we also differ in terms of with *whom* we want to affiliate. A consideration of *interpersonal attraction* helps us to understand why our desire to affiliate leads to friendships and romantic relationships with specific others. There is evidence that attraction is in part determined by target-centred factors. A major target-centred factor is *physical attractiveness*. We have a tendency to prefer individuals who have symmetrical, average faces with mature fea-tures for males and immature features for females. Moreover, research shows that we believe physically attractive people have more positive personality characteristics and are more likely to be happy and successful. We are also attracted to those who are *similar* to us, hold characteristics that *complement* our own, and who *reciprocate* our liking of them. We are also influenced by perceiver-centred factors. We are more

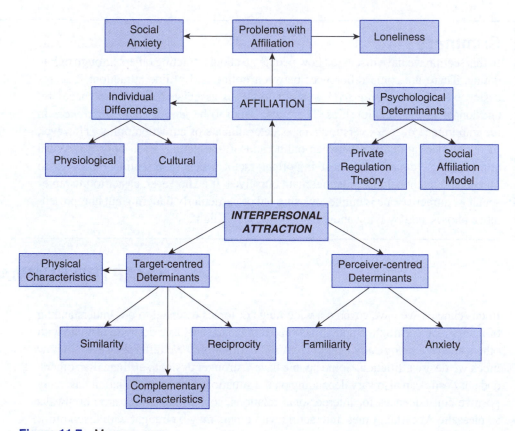

Figure 11.7   Memory map

likely to be attracted to those we are *familiar* with. If we are *anxious*, we also have a preference for affiliating with people who are going through the same experience as us. Finally, recent research has considered how we go about attracting friends and partners *online*. It seems that despite some differences, physical attractiveness is as important online as offline, and people go to some length, including misrepresenting themselves at times, to ensure they are perceived as attractive by potential partners.

Taking it Further

Try This

Try creating your own dating website profile, and drawing on all the research we've discussed in this chapter, design it to be as effective as possible in attracting your ideal partner. As well as key characteristics like humour and distinctiveness, think about how to present the material so that you make your profile utterly irresistible to your target mate – for instance, you might want to give enough information to ensure they perceive high similarity between themselves and you, complementarity, and pre-emptive reciprocity.

Debate This

Much of this chapter has focused on physical attractiveness. Not only do physical characteristics seem to be vital in attracting a potential partner, whether face-to-face or online, but physically attractive people are also treated better by others and seem often to be more successful in life. It is perhaps unsurprising then that today's media, particularly lifestyle and gossip magazines, are so focused on beauty. Is the apparent importance of physical attractiveness a good or a bad thing, or simply a psychological reality? Should we just accept the evolutionary perspective, that we are hardwired to appreciate physical attractiveness over all other forms, or should we attempt to change individuals' and societies' pre-occupation with physical attractiveness. If so, how might we go about this?

Something for the Weekend

People have a general desire to affiliate, and most can manage this affiliation effectively, spending enough time – but not too much time – with others. But some people suffer from difficulties in affiliation, such as loneliness and social anxiety. Imagine that you have been asked to write a self-help book for people who suffer from one of these difficulties. Based on what you have learned about affiliation and attraction in this chapter, what advice would you give them in order to eliminate the loneliness or the social anxiety they experience?

Further Reading

The Essentials

Berscheid, E. & Reis, H.T. (1998). Attraction and close relationships. In D.T. Gilbert, S.T. Fiske, & G. Lindzey (Eds.), *The handbook of social psychology* (4th Edn, Vol. 2, pp. 193–281). New York: McGraw-Hill.

A clear, readable overview of research on attraction and close relationships that builds incrementally on the topics we've discussed in this chapter.

Next Steps

Bargh, J.A. & McKenna, K.Y.A.(2004). The internet and social life. *Annual Review of Psychology*, 55, 573–590.

Elliot, A.J. & Niesta, D. (2008). Romantic red: Red enhances men's attraction to women. *Journal of Personality and Social Psychology*, 95, 1150–1164.

Here are a couple of papers that you might find interesting. The first reviews what we currently know about how the psychology of affiliation and attraction has been affected by the internet age. The second is a fabulous piece of research that shows how even something as simple as a colour can affect who we are attracted to.

Delving Deeper

Berscheid, E. & Hatfield, E. (1978). *Interpersonal attraction* (2nd ed.) Reading, MA: Addison Wesley.

If interpersonal attraction is what fascinates you, find yourself a copy of this classic book, written by Elaine Hatfield and leading pioneers of research on love and interpersonal attraction.

Friendship and Love

12

Friendship and Love

'Love looks not with the eyes but with the mind.'
William Shakespeare (1564–1616)
A Midsummer Night's Dream (I, i, 234)

The last port of call in our voyage of social psychological discovery is friendship and love. In this chapter we'll discuss research on the thoughts, feelings and behaviours we experience in relation to close others. We will look at what makes us become friends with others, what makes other people want to be friends with us, how physical, physiological, and psychological characteristics interact, what makes us fall in love, and what makes us fall out of love. William Shakespeare appears to have got it exactly right: social psychologists have discovered that there is far more to love than meets the eye … and what meets the eye is only a fraction of what determines whether we fall in love.

FRIENDSHIP

Having discussed in Chapter 11 the reasons why people seek affiliation, and the factors that determine why we select particular people as those we would like to get close to, in this chapter we look at what happens after initial attraction, when people move from superficial interactions with one another to close friendships. We will first talk about how friendships develop and how they sometimes break down. We will discuss the gender differences that exist in same-sex friendships, in terms of emotion and physical expression, and why these gender differences exist.

Social Penetration Theory
Social penetration theory (Altman & Taylor, 1973) offers an explanation for why and how friendships develop, focusing on the crucial role of self-disclosure, the

imparting of personal information about oneself to another person. At the early stages of a relationship, two people may exchange superficial information. If they are comfortable with this level of interaction, they may then exchange a more personal and broad range of information. Laurenceau and colleagues (1998) found that as the level of self-disclosure increases during the early stages of friendship, so too does the intimacy level in the relationship. A developing friendship is guided by a norm of self-disclosure reciprocity. Individuals match one another's level of disclosure, only revealing information of greater intimacy when the other person does so. This allows a relationship to develop at a comfortable pace, avoiding rejection as a result of too small a disclosure, or personal invasion and threat as a result of too large or too sudden a disclosure. Once the relationship has reached a high level of intimacy, the level of self-disclosure levels off and is replaced by an exchange of support and understanding.

Self-disclosure is also central to the dissolution of a relationship. When a relationship is in trouble, depenetration occurs, a reverse of the escalating self-disclosure process that occurs in the development of friendship. People may emotionally

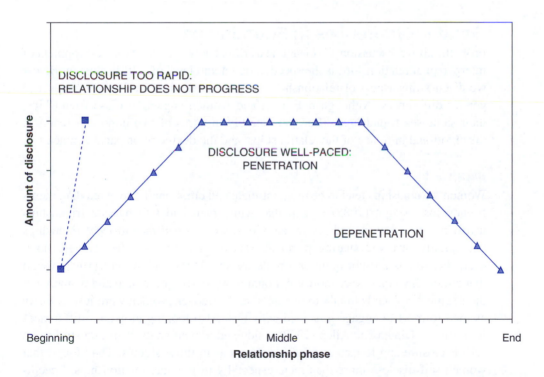

Figure 12.1 An illustration of the processes involved in social penetration theory (Altman & Taylor, 1973)

withdraw from a relationship by reducing the quantity and intimacy of information they disclose. Alternatively, they may increase the intimacy of information disclosed, but direct negative and personally hurtful information at their former friend. In either case, self-disclosure can be instrumental in the destruction of a close relationship. The processes of penetration and depenetration are illustrated in Figure 12.1.

Although self-penetration theory is an adequate description of most relationships, it does not always hold true. Berg (1984) found that some friends or dating partners 'click' straight away and immediately begin disclosing highly intimate information to one another, without the need for a process of reciprocal escalation of self-disclosure. There are also cross-cultural differences. People from individualistic cultures (e.g. North America) disclose more about themselves in a wider variety of settings than people from collectivist cultures (e.g. China, Japan). This is thought to reflect differences in communication styles between the cultures rather than differences in intimacy levels. While social expressiveness is a sign of social competence in Western societies, not such great value is placed on it in Eastern societies. Instead, being socially non-expressive is interpreted as an indication of emotional strength and trustworthiness.

Gender Differences in Friendships

From the above discussion it is clear that a critical determinant of the development of interpersonal relationships is the speed, amount and level of self-disclosure. Below we discuss this aspect of relationships in more detail, specifically with respect to gender differences. Although both men and women engage in close friendships, their same-sex friendships differ considerably in terms of two important features: the emotional intimacy of the relationships, and the degree of physical contact.

Intimacy

Women's friendships tend to be more intimate and emotionally involved than men's friendships. Wright (1982) argued that while men had side-by-side friendships involving shared work and leisure activities, women had face-to-face friendships that largely involved sharing personal issues. Later research has argued, however, that things are not quite as simple as this. Duck and Wright (1993) found that although women were more emotionally expressive, both men and women met their same-sex friends to talk to one another. Moreover, women were just as likely as men to meet to engage in shared activities. Also looking at gender differences in intimacy, Dindia and Allen (1992) conducted a meta-analysis of 205 studies on self-disclosure and looked at gender differences in those studies. They found that women self-disclose more than men, especially in intimate relationships. Specifically, they showed that women disclose more than men to same-sex friends, but there was no gender difference in disclosure to male friends. This may be because men in Western societies are restricted by cultural norms which dictate that they should not act in a vulnerable or dependent manner. This was clearly illustrated in a study conducted by Derlega and Chaikin (1976). Male and female participants read a story about a man or woman who was upset while on a flight because their mother had just suffered an emotional breakdown. Noticing this emotional state, the person in the neighbouring seat asked the person whether he or she was afraid of flying. In one condition, the individual in the story concealed the problem, and said that they were indeed scared of flying, while in a second condition, the individual disclosed the problem. When asked to judge the character, men and women responded in the same way: a male character was seen as better psychologically adjusted if they did not disclose the problem, whereas a female character was seen as better adjusted if they did (see Figure 12.2). Men may therefore avoid self-disclosure to avoid negative evaluations from both men and women.

Physical Contact

Men engage in less physical contact with same-sex friends than do women. In North America and the UK, heterosexual men and women view hugging and other forms

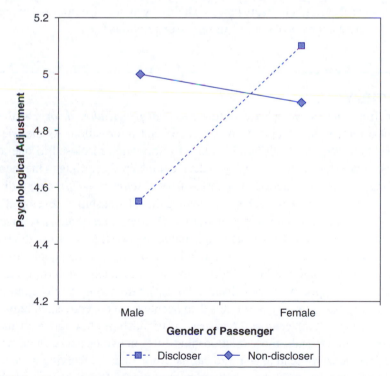

Figure 12.2 Ratings of psychological adjustment as a function of disclosure and gender. Data from Derlega and Chaikin (1976)

of physical intimacy among men as less appropriate than among mixed-sex friendships or same-sex female friendships, although this is not the cultural norm in many European, Latin, African and Middle-Eastern cultures. Derlega and colleagues (1989) asked friends to act out an imaginary scene in which one person was greeting the other at the airport after returning from a trip. The greetings were photographed and evaluated by independent judges for the intimacy of physical contact. They found that male friends employed significantly less touching than did female friends or mixed-sex friends. Moreover, male participants were more likely than female participants to interpret touching as an indication of sexual desire.

Why Do These Gender Differences Exist?

Social scientists have argued that men are socialized to conform to a norm of **heterosexual masculinity**, valuing masculine traits related to power and control, while devaluing feminine traits of tenderness and vulnerability (Brendan, 2002). They are especially likely to conform to this norm while in the company of other men, where their identity as a man is particularly salient. Men who conform to heterosexual masculinity have a tendency to denigrate male homosexuality because they perceive it to be the antithesis of masculinity. Heterosexual men therefore avoid acting in ways that might indicate homosexuality by avoiding emotional expression, self-disclosure and physical contact in same-sex relationships.

Summary

How do friendships develop? According to *social penetration theory*, at the early stages of a relationship people exchange superficial information. As the friendship advances, however, the depth and breadth of information disclosed to one another escalates, as does the level of intimacy in the relationship. According to the theory, the developing friendship is guided by a norm of *self-disclosure reciprocity*; individuals match one another's level of disclosure, allowing the relationship to develop at a comfortable pace. When a relationship is in trouble, *depenetration* occurs, a reverse of the escalating self-disclosure process as people emotionally withdraw from the relationship. The theory cannot, however, explain all relationships; some people 'click' and start disclosing at a high level of intimacy almost immediately. Moreover, the theory is more likely to apply to individualistic cultures, where people disclose more about themselves in a wider variety of settings than people from collectivist cultures.

There are significant *gender differences* in friendship; although both men and women have close friends, those relationships differ in two respects. First, women's same-sex relationships tend to be more intimate than men's, involving greater levels of self-disclosure. Research has shown that men disclose less, at least in Western societies, because cultural norms dictate that they should not appear to be vulnerable. British and American men also engage in less physical contact with same-sex friends than do women, although this is not the case in many other cultures. This is sometimes explained in terms of the norm of *heterosexual masculinity* in North America and the UK, whereby masculine traits like power are valued while feminine traits like vulnerability are devalued.

ROMANTIC RELATIONSHIPS

So far we have looked at how friendships develop from interpersonal attraction. But the most developed and intense type of interpersonal relationship is romantic love. Love is a popular focus of research on interpersonal processes, but we are only just beginning to understand it from a scientific standpoint. This is because it has typically been regarded as something mysterious and unfathomable. Psychologists generally argue that love is qualitatively different from liking. Lamm and Wiesmann (1997), for example, described 'liking' as the desire to interact with another person, but 'love' as also involving trust and being excited by another person.

Types of Love

Lee (1977) created a *typology of love* designed to capture the different ways in which love might manifest itself. He argued that there were three primary types of love: eros (passionate love), ludus (game-playing love), and storge (friendship love). These types of love can be combined to form three secondary types of love: pragma (pragmatic love), which combined friendship and game-playing elements, mania (possessive love), which combined passionate and game-playing love, and agape (altruistic love), which combined passion and friendship. Lee argued that the type of love experienced was not influenced by individual differences and could arise for any person. Sternberg (1986)'s **triangular theory of love** also argued that love could be classified in several different ways depending on the degree of passion, intimacy and commitment. These detailed classifications are very complex, but there *is* strong evidence for at least two clear types of love: *passionate* love and *companionate* love.

Passionate Love

Passionate love is a state of intense longing for another person that is experienced during the early stages of a romantic relationship. This is typically thought to involve very intense emotions, constantly thinking about the lover, and wanting to spend as much time as possible with them, even to the exclusion of other friends.

Neuropsychologists have found that the subjective experience of passionate love is associated with changes in brain chemistry, in particular an increase in the powerful stimulant dopamine, which leads to a sense of physiological arousal. There is also evidence that people in love who are given brain scans show increased activity in the caudate nucleus area near the centre of the brain when they are shown photos of their partners, but not when they are shown pictures of their friends (Fisher, 2004). This primitive brain area directs bodily movements and is also associated with reward and pleasure. Aron, Paris, and Aron (1995) found that people in love report a range of positive experiences, including an increase in self-efficacy and self-esteem. Passionate love therefore is associated with some qualitatively distinct neurophysiological and psychological states. Can we then predict when we might be about to experience passionate love?

Hatfield and Walster (1981) argued that passionate love will arise when three conditions are met. First, it is necessary for an individual to understand what love is and have the expectation that at some point they will fall in love. In other words, whether a person falls in love depends on whether they are from a culture that believes in the concept of love. This is the case in Western cultures, like the UK and USA, but love is considered to be less important in some Eastern cultures, where arranged marriages are the norm. Second, it is necessary to meet someone who fits expectations of what makes an appropriate partner, for example, someone attractive and of the preferred sex. Third, when thinking about or in the presence of this potential partner, the individual must experience a state of physiological arousal, which they then attribute to the lover.

To understand why physiological arousal may lead to feelings of being in love, Hatfield and Walster draw from Schachter and Singer's (1962) two-factor theory of emotions and suggest a **three-factor theory of love**. This theory argues that three conditions must be met to fall in love: (1) meeting a suitable potential lover, (2) attributing physiological arousal to the presence of the potential lover, and (3) understanding and accepting the concept of love. This extends Schachter and Singer's theory by focusing specifically on the role of arousal in romantic love, and highlighting the need to recognize the concept of love. We experience physiological arousal in a variety of contexts, for example when having an argument with someone, when walking in an unsafe area of town, or when receiving the highest grade in an exam. The physiological reaction we have is similar in each of these situations, but we differentiate them by giving them different labels: anger during an argument, fear or anxiety when we feel unsafe, and elation when we achieve something important.

Schachter and Singer proposed that when events elicit internal physiological arousal, we look for external cues to determine the reason for this arousal. When arousal occurs during an interaction with an attractive member of the appropriate sex, this may be interpreted as romantic and sexual attraction. If this theory is correct, arousal from another source might be incorrectly interpreted as romantic attraction in the presence of an attractive person. Zillman (1984) described this psychological process by which arousal caused by one stimulus is transferred and added to arousal elicited by a second stimulus *excitation transfer*. In Text Box 12.1 you can read about an ingenious experiment that illustrates how excitation transfer works.

Text Box 12.1

Mistaking Arousal for Attraction

According to the three-factor theory of love, when we experience physiological arousal we look for external cues to explain it. In the presence of an attractive member of the opposite sex, arousal might be interpreted as romantic attraction. If this theory is correct, arousal from another source, for example anxiety, might be incorrectly attributed to romantic attraction in the presence of an attractive person. To test this idea, Dutton and Aron (1974) conducted an ingenious study in a beauty spot in Vancouver, Canada.

Method
Male or female research assistants waited by two different bridges. One bridge was solidly built and only 10 feet high, crossing a stream, while the other, the Capilano Canyon Suspension Bridge, was only 5 feet wide, 450 feet long and 230 feet high. This bridge wobbled when people walked across it and swayed in the wind. The authors predicted that people would feel relaxed crossing the former bridge, but anxious crossing the latter bridge. When unaccompanied males began to cross either bridge, they were asked if they would write a story in response to a picture while standing on the bridge. Research assistants also gave out their phone number so that the participant could request further information about the study.

Results
Men who were approached by a female research assistant on the suspension bridge told stories with the highest sexual imagery of all the experimental groups and were also more likely to call the assistant afterwards for 'further details' of the study.

(Continued)

Interpreting the Findings

It appeared that participants had misattributed arousal caused by the swaying bridge to the female assistant rather than to the correct source of arousal – anxiety. An alternative explanation for these results might be that the men who chose to walk across the suspension bridge were more adventurous than those who chose the safe bridge. In a further study, however, Dutton and Aron ruled out this possibility by repeating the experiment on the suspension bridge and having all participants either complete the study on the bridge or after they had crossed the bridge and calmed down. Men only used greater sexual imagery and called the assistant more when the study had been completed on the actual bridge. Thus, it was the excitation transfer, rather than adventurous personalities, that explained the behaviour of participants towards female assistants on the suspension bridge.

Despite the evidence for excitation transfer, the three-factor theory cannot fully explain why we fall in love. If all it took to fall in love was understanding the concept, being in the presence of an appropriate other, and arousal, true love could be 'produced' in laboratory settings, but this is not the case. It is clear from our early discussion of the conditions of attraction that many additional factors are necessary, for example being well matched in terms of beliefs and physical appearance, and the potential lover holding characteristics that complement one's own characteristics (as discussed above in the section on the determinants of attraction).

Companionate Love

The early stages of a romantic relationship are defined by passionate love, when there is uncertainty, thrill, excitement, and a tendency to see one another through rose-tinted glasses, as being 'perfect'. This stage is, however, relatively short-lived. If a relationship lasts beyond the passionate love stage, it is replaced by a less passionate but more enduring love, defined by Hatfield (1988) as **companionate love**. This is the affection we feel for someone with whom our lives are deeply entwined and can be applied to friends as well as romantic partners. The level of shared experiences that characterize long-term relationships and companionate love gives rise to some interesting psychological effects, described in Text Box 12.2.

Text Box 12.2

When two become one

When people are in a close relationship they increasingly 'overlap' with their partner, becoming less self-centred and having the ability to take their partner's perspective. A number of studies have shown that the greater our satisfaction, commitment and investment in the relationship, the more our self-concept overlaps with the self-concept of our partner. Smith, Coats, and Walling (1999) used reaction times to investigate the effect of self–partner overlap on mental representations.

Method

Eighty-seven undergraduate students who had been in a romantic relationship for at least three months were given a list of 90 personal traits and were asked to indicate how descriptive each trait was of them, from *not at all* to *extremely*. They then repeated the task with their romantic partner in mind, indicating how much each trait was descriptive of their partner. After completing these questionnaire items, participants completed a task on the computer. The same 90 traits from the questionnaire were displayed one at a time on the computer screen in a random order, and participants were required to respond to each trait by pressing a 'yes' key if the trait was descriptive of their romantic partner or a 'no' key if the trait was not descriptive of their romantic partner.

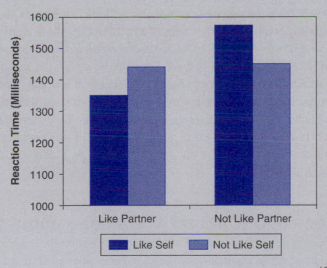

(Continued)

Results

The patterns of results are presented below. Participants were significantly faster to make a judgement about whether their partner was characterized by a trait if it matched their perception of themselves. Put another way, if the trait on the screen characterized the participant and their partner, participants responded very quickly, but if the trait on the screen characterized the partner but *not* the participant, participants appeared to be confused and took longer to come up with the correct response. Smith and colleagues found that this pattern of results was stronger for participants who were in a close romantic relationship.

Interpreting the Findings

When we are in a close romantic relationship with another person, our mental representation overlaps with the mental representation of our partner. As a result, the traits we hold and those held by our partner may be confused, or interfere with one another. When there is a mismatch between participants and their partners on a trait, they are being asked to rate a trait as false for them, but true for someone who is part of them. These findings suggest that in close relationships partners actually begin to see themselves as a collected entity, with less individuated characteristics, and more shared attributes.

This pathway from passionate *to* companionate love has been explained by evolutionary psychologists. In the early stages of a relationship, the sexual mating system, the goal of which is to sexually reproduce and pass on genes to the next generation, is dominant. In the later stages of a relationship, however, the attachment system, the goal of which is to establish and maintain a strong emotional bond between two people, is more important. Attachment to offspring increases their chances of survival, and attachment between parents in companionate love should have the same benefit. Parents who love each other are more likely to stay together to raise their children, and this will ensure the offspring are better provided for and more likely to survive childhood.

Development of Cultural Knowledge about Love

So we know that people understand and experience romantic love, initially as passionate love and later as companionate love, but how does cultural knowledge about romantic love develop, and what norms dictate romantic love among adolescents, who are just beginning to learn what love is all about? Simon, Eder, and Evans

(1992) conducted in-depth interviews with adolescent females attending the sixth–eighth grade (aged 11 to 14 years) in a middle school in the US, in order to investigate the social norms that exist underlying romantic love at this age. They found that romantic love was a highly frequent topic of conversation by the age of 13, with many female students beginning to form relationships with boys. They also identified four key norms:

1. *Moderation in love*: There was the general perception among girls that although boys were important, other concerns such as academic and athletic performance were also important, and that boys should not dominate everything. Girls were openly critical towards friends who were perceived as 'boy crazy', who did not have any interests other than attracting the opposite sex.
2. *Suppression of feelings towards attached others*: While it was acceptable for two or more girls to express feelings towards the same boy, and discuss those feelings, once a group member had acted openly on her feelings towards a particular boy, it was no longer deemed acceptable for other girls to express feelings for him. This norm was conveyed through negative gossip about those who violated the norm.
3. *Monogamy*: There were strong norms expressed against having romantic feelings for more than one person at a time. Girls who violated this norm, and expressed interest for more than one boy, were the subject of gossip and confrontation by other girls.
4. *Continuous love*: Finally, participants expected that they should be in a continuous state of being in love, after the onset of their first romantic relationship. Thus, as soon as one boyfriend was seen as losing interest, girls simply redirected their romantic interests elsewhere. At times it seemed that the target of love itself was not that important, but in order to maintain popularity and status, it was important to be in love at all times.

Summary

Social psychologists have defined love in a number of different ways. According to Lee's *typology of love*, there are three primary types of love (passionate, game-playing, and friendship love) which can be combined in different ways to form three secondary types of love (pragmatic, possessive, and altruistic love), which combined passionate and game-playing love, and agape (altruistic love), which combines passion and friendship. Lee argued that the type of love experienced was not influenced by individual differences and could arise for any person. Alternatively,

(Continued)

Sternberg proposed the *triangular theory of love*, arguing that love could be classified differently depending on the degree of passion, intimacy and commitment. Research into this theory has found clear evidence for two types of love: passionate love and companionate love. *Passionate love* is a state of intense longing for another person experienced early in a romantic relationship and is associated with changes in brain chemistry and increased activity in the caudate nucleus area of the brain, an area also associated with reward and pleasure. According to the *three-factor theory of love*, passionate love will arise when (1) an individual believes in the concept of love, (2) meets someone who fits their expectations of an appropriate partner, and (3) experiences a state of physiological arousal when in the presence of that person, which is then attributed to the presence of that person and labelled romantic attraction. On occasion, physiological arousal from a different source can inadvertently be interpreted as romantic attraction in the presence of an attractive person, a process described as *excitation transfer*.

Passionate love is relatively short-lived. If a relationship lasts beyond this stage, the feelings are replaced by a less passionate but more enduring love, *companionate love*. According to evolutionary psychologists, the sexual mating system explains the early stages of a relationship, but in later stages, the attachment system is more important; parents who are attached to one another are more likely to stay together to raise their children, increasing the offspring's chances of surviving until adulthood.

Finally, love can be defined by cultural norms. In Western societies four norms have been identified that develop around the ages of 11 to 14: *moderation in love*, *suppression of feelings towards attached others*, *monogamy*, and *continuous love*.

RELATIONSHIP SATISFACTION AND COMMITMENT

We now know why and how different types of interpersonal relationships develop. In this final section we discuss the different theories about how relationships progress and change, and how and why they sometimes end. Once people are in an established romantic relationship, what determines whether the relationship will be happy and satisfying? Moreover, what factors determine whether a relationship will last over time or whether it will soon end? Finally, what emotional consequences are there when a relationship breaks down?

Relationship Satisfaction

Relationships are extremely complex. As a consequence, many factors contribute towards whether or not a relationship is satisfying. Important factors that influence relationship satisfaction include whether both partners make an equal contribution to the relationship, the degree of intimacy in a relationship, expression versus concealment of secrets, the interpretation of one another's behaviour, the outcomes of social comparison, the extent to which there is an overlap in partners' social network, and attachment style. Here, we outline some of the most important factors that contribute towards relationship satisfaction.

Social Exchange and Equity

One factor that may contribute towards satisfaction is what each partner contributes to the relationship and whether these contributions are perceived as equal. Some social psychologists argue that social relationships are like economic bargains in which people place a value on the material (e.g. money, food) or non-material (e.g. affection, information) 'goods' that they exchange with one another. According to **social exchange theory**, on some level people keep track of the goods they exchange and make a judgement about whether what they receive is balanced with what they give. According to this premise, people participate in relationships that are personally rewarding, and where the rewards exceed the costs of the relationship. People therefore seek out relationships in which benefits outweigh the costs and where the relationship has overall positive outcomes, but end relationships in which costs outweigh the benefits, where the relationship has overall negative outcomes. According to Thibaut and Kelley (1959), when people are deciding whether to stay in a relationship, they conduct not only a cost-benefit analysis, but also compare their relationship to the possible rewards and costs in alternative relationships. If no more rewarding alternatives are available, they will remain in their current relationship. This may explain why people sometimes stay in destructive relationships.

Equity theory is based on social exchange theory, but is specifically concerned with an individual's expectations of exchange in close relationships, and how they respond to equality and inequality in those exchanges. According to the theory, people in close relationships expect an equal exchange in terms of love, emotional and financial support, and household tasks. The degree of inequity, and the direction of that inequity, may have a profound influence on the relationship. A person in a relationship may feel guilty because they receive more from the relationship than they give, or they may feel resentful because they give more to the relationship than they get in return.

Both these situations of inequity have negative consequences for interpersonal relations. Buunk and VanYperen (1991) found that those who perceived equality in a relationship were most satisfied, followed by those who felt advantaged. Those who felt deprived relative to their partner were the least satisfied in their relationship. Inequity has severe negative implications for a relationship. Prins, Buunk, and VanYperen (1992) found that women in inequitable relationships had a stronger desire to engage in extramarital relationships and had been involved in more extramarital relationships than women in equitable relationships, although a similar relationship did not emerge for men. The role of inequity should, however, be accepted with caution; Cate, Lloyd, and Long (1988) found the receipt of love, information and sexual satisfaction to be more important in predicting relationship satisfaction than equality.

Intimacy

Reis and Patrick (1996) argued that intimate relations are those that are caring, understanding and involve validation. *Caring* is the feeling that our partner loves us and cares about us, and is mentioned by most people as a central component of intimacy. *Understanding* in a relationship is when the partner is perceived to have an accurate perception of how we see ourselves. Specifically, it is important that they understand our feelings, needs, beliefs and life circumstances. Swann, De la Ronde, and Hixon (1994) found that married people were most satisfied with their relationship when their partner perceived them in line with their self-perceptions. *Validation* reflects whether our partner is able to communicate their acknowledgement and support for our point of view. There is evidence that the more partners let one another know that they empathize with one another, the happier they are. Unhappy couples, on the other hand, have a tendency to avoid problematic issues by glossing over them or changing the subject.

Perceived Concealment

Finkenauer, Kerkhof, Righetti, and Branje (2009) argue that the degree to which a couple keep secrets from one another is a major factor predicting relationship satisfaction and wellbeing. They asked 199 newly married couples to complete a questionnaire approximately one month after they got married, and again nine months later, in which they answered questions about how much they believed their partner was keeping secrets from them and several measures of relationship satisfaction. It emerged that participants who felt that their partner was concealing personal information from them early in the marriage reported poorer adjustment to married life, greater frequency of conflict with their partner, and less trust towards their partner nine months later. So why does concealment lead to relationship problems? As we discussed earlier, when someone discloses personal information to us, this conveys intimacy and closeness. Essentially, it shows us that the person likes and trusts us (Altman & Taylor, 1973). Conversely, the concealment of information conveys powerful signals of social distance and separation, leading people to believe that their partner does not like or trust them as much as they should. In line with this explanation, Finkenauer and colleagues showed that perceived exclusion mediated the negative association between concealment and relationship wellbeing.

Interpretation

People in happy and unhappy relationships interpret their partner's characteristics and behaviour very differently. In a happy relationship, problems that arise are likely to be blamed on the self, and the partner is given credit for solving problems (Thompson & Kelley, 1981). In an unhappy relationship, however, people show maladaptive attribution patterns (Fincham & Bradbury, 1991). Specifically, they blame relationship problems on their partner, and see their own and their partner's problematic behaviour as global, affecting other aspects of their relationship, and stable, unlikely to get better in the future. Rather than dealing with problems that arise one at a time, as independent issues, problems are seen as issues typical of the problems that exist in the relationship.

Social Comparison

When happy couples compare themselves to other couples, they tend to feel better about their own relationship (think back to our discussion of social comparison processes in Chapter 1). Buunk and Van den Eijnden (1997) showed that individuals who felt their own relationship was better than most others showed higher levels of relationship satisfaction, and Murray and Holmes (1997) found that romantic couples with high levels of satisfaction perceived their partner more positively than the typical partner and were optimistic about the future of the relationship. Unhappy couples, on the other hand, focus on the negative implications of social comparison. Buunk, Collins, VanYperen, Taylor, and Dakoff (1990) found that those in unhappy marriages felt envious when they saw other couples in a better marriage and worried when they encountered couples with worse marital problems than themselves that their fate might be the same.

Social Networks

Cotton, Cunningham, and Antill (1993) found that husbands and wives both reported greater satisfaction in their relationship when members of their own and their spouse's social networks were connected to one another and when they were friends with some of the people in their spouse's social network. Satisfaction is higher when people's support networks are highly integrated.

Attachment

Attachment describes the emotional bond that forms between a young child and their caregiver (usually the mother). Psychologists have been keenly interested in the idea that the type of attachment formed between a mother and child might explain psychological development. More recently, this research has been extended to consider the effects of attachment experienced as a child on attachment *style* in adulthood, and its subsequent impact on satisfaction in interpersonal relationships. Below, we describe attachment theory, show how attachment to one's primary care giver as a child can influence attachment style in later life, and illustrate the effects of adult attachment on how people deal with interpersonal relationships.

Bowlby (1969) proposed that human infants and their caregivers have a genetic disposition to form a close attachment with one another. In evolutionary terms, infants remain close to their caregivers to protect themselves from predators, while caregivers protect their infant to ensure the child survives to adulthood to pass on their genes to the next generation. Ainsworth (1982) later proposed a qualification to this basic idea: that the *nature* of the relationship with the caregiver can lead to the child holding one of three different *attachment styles*. According to Ainsworth children will develop a *secure attachment* style if their caregiver was caring and responded sensitively to their needs. They are likely to believe they are worthy of love, and that other people can be trusted. In contrast, children who cannot rely on their parents to respond appropriately when they are needed will develop one of two insecure attachment styles. If the caregiver is insensitive to the needs of the child and does not respond consistently, children will develop an *avoidant attachment* style, finding it difficult to trust others. Finally, having a caregiver who shows a lack of interest in interacting with their infant can lead to an *anxious/ambivalent attachment* style. Such children are eager to form close relationships, but struggle to believe that they are worthy of love. In sum, children who are securely attached are more socially competent and have higher self-esteem than children who are insecurely attached.

While initial research on attachment focused on children and adolescents, recent research has considered the effect of the attachment style on the ability to form successful romantic relationships in adulthood. Although there is little direct evidence to show that attachment as a child predicts attachment style as an adult, research has shown that attachment styles held by adults are *similar* to those held by children. While classic attachment research considered there to be three categories of attachment, Bartholomew (1990) proposed that there are two *dimensions* of attachment, depending on (1) whether people believe others to be trustworthy or not and (2) whether people have high self-esteem, and believe they are worthy of love or not. The two dimensions are attachment-avoidance (discomfort with intimacy and dependency) and attachment-anxiety (fear of separation and abandonment).

People high in attachment-*avoidance* try to maintain distance from others to preserve their independence and self-esteem. They tend to be less involved, engaged and support-seeking in relationships, and are uncomfortable with self-disclosure. These individuals show discomfort with closeness and strive for self-dependence. People high in attachment-*anxiety* seek support, acceptance, and closeness to others in response to their fear of rejection. Such individuals use intense efforts to ensure support and maintain proximity to others, showing excessive rumination about abandonment fears and threats to their relationship or self (Shaver & Mikulincer, 2002). People can be high or low on both attachment-avoidance and attachment-anxiety dimensions, resulting in four possible attachment styles in adulthood. In turn, these attachment styles predict how people behave in interpersonal relationships. Below we discuss each type of attachment and its consequences for relationship success.

People who are low on both dimensions have a **secure attachment** style. They have a high self-esteem and generally trust other people. As a result, they handle relationships with ease. Brennan and Shaver (1995) found that securely attached adults found it easy to get close to others and enjoyed more affectionate and long-lasting relationships than those who did not have a secure attachment style. Doherty, Hatfield, Thompson, and Choo (1994) also found that people with a secure attachment style were more likely to experience *companionate love* than people with avoidance or anxious attachments (see our discussion of companionate love earlier in this chapter). Securely attached people are, unsurprisingly, the most desired partners. Chappell and Davis (1998) found that regardless of their own attachment style, the majority of participants would rather date someone with a secure attachment style.

People who are low on attachment-avoidance but high on attachment-anxiety have a **preoccupied attachment** style. Although they have a positive view of others, they have low self-esteem and worry that people will not love them because they are not good enough. As a result, they tend to be preoccupied with their close interpersonal relationship partners and have a fear that the people they like or love will not return their feelings. They often consider their self-worth in terms of their physical appearance rather than their personal character traits. Brennan and Shaver (1995) found that anxious adults fell in love easily, but their relationships were emotionally unstable, and they were more likely to be perceived as unhappy.

People who are high on attachment-avoidance but low on attachment-anxiety have a **dismissing-avoidant attachment** style. Although these people have a high self-esteem, they find it difficult to trust others and are uncomfortable with intimacy. They struggle to recognize when others are expressing warmth towards them, and have a tendency to withdraw from relationships when there are conflicts rather than try to deal with problems (Mikulincer, 1998; Mikulincer & Arad, 1999). In sum, although they tend to be confident, they are compulsively self-reliant. Finally, people who are high on both anxiety and avoidance have a **fearful-avoidant attachment** style. They have low self-esteem and do not trust others. They are also more likely to notice negativity in others, strengthening their belief that others cannot be trusted. Niedenthal et al. (2002) found that fearful-avoidants were more attentive to angry and sad facial expressions. As a result, they are more likely to suffer from negative interpersonal experiences (McNally et al., 2003). Both high-avoidance attachment styles are associated with negative consequences for interpersonal relationships. Klohnen and Bera (1998) looked at female participants who were either avoidant or secure at the age of 27, and then at 43 and 52. They found that avoidant women experienced less interpersonal closeness, were less socially confident, were more emotionally distant, and less trusting than securely attached adults. Campbell, Simpson, Boldry, and Kashy (2005) conducted a diary study with dating partners over 14 days. They found that anxiously attached individuals perceived greater relationship conflict, less satisfaction and closeness in their relationships, and less optimistic views about the future of the relationship on days where they perceived there to be conflict than those who were not anxiously attached. Unsurprisingly, dismissing-avoidants and fearful-avoidants are generally seen as the least desirable partners (Pietromonaco & Carnelly, 1994).

Interdependence Theory

All of the theories we have discussed in this section provide explanations for relationship satisfaction. To fully understand how people act and react in close relationships it is likely that all of the factors discussed above will apply, to a greater or lesser extent. Rusbult and Van Lange (2003) argue just this; that to understand the nature of relationships, we need to consider the effect of situational factors on *both* individual factors (e.g. attachment style) and interpersonal processes (how partners interact with one another). They provide a broad, overarching framework that explains how people interact with one another in relationships, and the outcomes of these interactions, based on the collected contributions of the theories we have outlined above.

Summary

Many factors contribute towards whether or not a relationship is satisfying. First, what each partner contributes to the relationship and whether these contributions are perceived as equal plays a part in determining relationship satisfaction. According to *social exchange theory*, people keep track of what they have contributed (materially and psychologically) and received in a relationship and conduct a cost-benefit analysis. People only stay in a relationship if the rewards outweigh the cost, and if there are no better alternatives available. According to *equity theory*, a person in an unequal relationship may feel guilty because they receive more from the relationship than they give, or they may feel resentful because they give more to the relationship than they get in return. Both these situations of inequity have negative consequences for interpersonal relations.

Intimacy also contributes to relationship satisfaction. Reis and Patrick (1996) argued that intimate relationships are those in which we feel loved and cared for by our partner, where we feel our partner understands our feelings, needs and beliefs, and where we feel our partner supports and validates our point of view. People who are satisfied with their relationship interpret things very differently from people who are unsatisfied; satisfied people take personal responsibility for problems but unsatisfied individuals blame problems on their partner. People also decide whether they are happy in their relationship through a process of *social comparison*; individuals who feel their relationship is better than most others show the greatest levels of relationship satisfaction. Couples who have highly interconnected *social networks* also tend to be more satisfied with their relationship.

Attachment style in adulthood has a significant impact on the success of relationships. Avoidant people do not display enough intimacy because they do not trust relationship partners, whereas anxious people have a tendency to display too much intimacy because they trust relationship partners but do not believe they are worthy of affection in return. Securely attached people, however, display the appropriate level of intimacy, because they neither distrust their partners nor fear rejection. Finally, *interdependence theory* proposes that to understand the nature of relationships, we need to consider the effect of situational factors on *both* individual factors and interpersonal processes.

What Determines Whether a Relationship Will Last?

Commitment is the desire or intention to continue an interpersonal relationship. One might expect satisfaction in a relationship to strongly co-occur with relationship commitment but, counterintuitive though it may seem, this is not always the case. Happy relationships are not always stable and long-lasting. On the other hand, people frequently fail to end a relationship, even if they are unhappy. A number of social psychologists have tried to identify when people are likely to be committed to relationships.

The Investment Model

Rusbult's (1983) **investment model** argued that commitment is dependent on three factors. First, *high satisfaction* in a relationship has an impact on commitment, but this cannot alone explain relationship satisfaction. Second, *investment size* also plays a role in relationship commitment. Two people in a relationship become increasingly intertwined. They invest time and effort in each other, make sacrifices, develop mutual friends and shared memories, and have shared activities and possessions. The greater the investment, the more committed people tend to be in a relationship. Third, the low *perceived quality of alternatives* predicts relationship commitment. This refers to the best alternative to the present relationship, be that the best imagined alternative relationship, the actual presence of an alternative partner, the appeal of living alone, having an enjoyable job and good friends, and so on. Clearly, the presence of an attractive alternative may seriously threaten the stability of an existing romantic relationship. Fortunately, when we are in a successful, committed relationship, we tend to engage in relationship maintenance strategies to ward off the lure of these alternatives. Lydon, Fitzsimons, and Naidoo (2003) found that people highly committed to a relationship derogated attractive individuals from the opposite sex as a means of closing themselves off from alternatives.

We also behave differently when interacting with a potential alternative partner, depending on whether we are in a relationship, and how satisfying our relationship is. Karremans and Verwijmeren (2008) experimentally demonstrated the effect

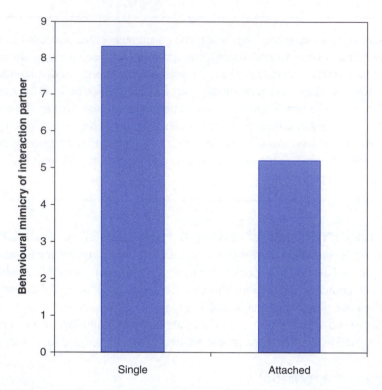

Figure 12.3 The effect of relationship status on mimicry of an attractive interaction partner. Data from Karremans and Verwijmeren (2008)

of relationship status and satisfaction on behaviour. Male and female heterosexual participants, half of whom were in a romantic relationship, were asked to complete a task with an attractive confederate of the opposite sex. These interactions were videotaped, and were rated for how much the participant mimicked the behaviour of the confederate. Following this task, participants who were in a relationship were asked to indicate how close they felt to their partner at the moment, and how attractive they found their interaction partner. It emerged that participants who were in a relationship mimicked the behaviour of their interaction partner to a lesser extent than participants who were currently single (see Figure 12.3). Moreover, among participants who were in a relationship, the closer they were to their partner, the less they mimicked the behaviour of their interaction partner. Although mimicry seems to be unconscious, it serves an important social function, creating a smoother, more pleasant interaction, and induces liking from one's interaction partner. By mimicking less, people who were happy in their relationship reduced their chance of a successful interaction, and thus protected their current relationship from the risk posed by an attractive alternative.

Other Models of Commitment

Adams and Jones (1997) proposed three factors that contribute to whether a relationship will last. These are: (1) *personal dedication*, a positive attraction to the relationship, (2) *moral commitment*, a sense of obligation, religious duty or social responsibility, based on a person's values and principles, and (3) *constraint commitment*, factors that make it costly to leave, such as lack of attractive alternatives, and personal, social, financial or legal investments in the relationship. Johnson (1991) put this succinctly: whether a relationship will be maintained depends on whether a person wants to continue it, ought to continue it, or must continue it.

Consequences of Commitment

Commitment, like satisfaction, has important consequences for a relationship. Some of these consequences are positive: highly committed individuals are more willing to make sacrifices for their relationship, giving up valued aspects of their life to maintain their relationship. Wieselquist, Rusbult, Foster, and Agnew (1999) found that commitment inspired accommodation and willingness to sacrifice, both of which were good predictors of someone's pro-relationship motives. Commitment can, however, also have negative consequences. Rusbult and Martz (1995) found that women suffering from violence at the hands of their husband were more likely to return to their partner after departure from a refuge shelter if they had been highly committed to the relationship before entering the shelter.

The Breakdown of a Relationship

Rusbult and Zembrodt (1983) argued that once deterioration has been identified, a partner's response may be positive or negative, active or passive. If a partner wants to save the relationship, they may react with *loyalty*, passively waiting for the relationship to improve, or *voice behaviour*, by actively working at the relationship. If, on the other hand, a partner thinks the relationship is truly over, they may respond with *neglect*, passively letting the relationship deteriorate, or *exit behaviour*, choosing to end the relationship.

To explain the final stages of a relationship, Duck (1992) proposed the **relationship dissolution model**. According to this model, partners pass through four phases on the way to a break-up.

1. **The Intrapsychic Phase:** The partner thinks in detail about the sources of the relationship problems, conducting an internal cost-benefit analysis, and may either repress the problem or discuss it with friends.
2. **The Dyadic Phase:** The difficult decision is made that something must be done, so the couple actively discuss the situation. At this stage, there may be negotiation and attempts at reconciliation, or arguments that further highlight the problems faced.

3. **The Social Phase:** When it is accepted that the relationship is ending, both partners turn to friends as a means of social support and find ways of presenting themselves to save face.
4. **The Grave Dressing Phase:** This may involve the division of property and access to children, and a further working towards an assurance for one's reputation. It is also a phase of accepting and getting over the end of the relationship and letting others know one's version of events.

So what happens following the end of a relationship? And how long does it take to recover? Sbarra and Emery (2005) found that following a break-up, feelings of anger dissipate very quickly, typically within a week to 18 days of a break-up. In contrast, sadness declines relatively slowly, taking at least a month to dissipate.

There are three key factors that predict how badly someone is affected by a break-up. First, *attachment style* is a predictor. Sbarra and Emery (2005) found that participants who had a secure or fearful-avoidant attachment style showed the fastest rates of decline in sadness, whereas individuals with a dismissing-avoidant attachment style felt both sad and angry for the longest period of time. Second, a *partner-initiated break-up* causes more suffering. Individuals who are left by their partner tend to feel more depressed and anxious, report more emotional distress, and greater pre-occupation with their former partner, and are less well adjusted five years later, than those who initiated a break-up (e.g. Kitson & Holmes, 1992; Wang & Amato, 2000). This may be explained by a perceived lack of control over the situation, and the unexpectedness of the break-up. Those who have been rejected are often left with a sense of emotional and cognitive disorganization, as they attempt to understand what went wrong (Sbarra, 2006). They may also suffer from feelings of unrequited love (Baumeister, Wotman, & Stillwell, 1993). Third, *rejection sensitivity*, the degree to which people anxiously expect rejection, and overreact to rejection, can have an impact. Ayduk, Downey, and Kim (2001) conducted a six-month longitudinal study with female college students, and found that those high in rejection sensitivity were more likely to become depressed following a break up, although only if the break-up was initiated by their partner.

Lucas (2005) examined data from an 18-year-long panel study of 30,000 Germans in order to examine how life satisfaction was affected in the years prior to, and following, a divorce. An illustration of the findings can be seen in Figure 12.4. He found that life satisfaction dropped considerably as people moved closer to the point at which they got divorced. However, on a positive note, their life satisfaction began to increase again following the divorce. People did not, however, return to as high a level of life satisfaction as they had pre-divorce. These findings suggest that people *can* recover from a painful break-up, but following a divorce, they may never be quite as happy as they were before.

There is little clear evidence regarding the 'best way' to deal with a break-up. The pain will inevitably be worse for those who have invested a great deal in the

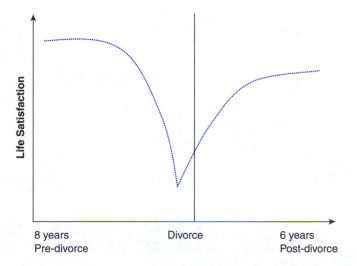

Figure 12.4 Life satisfaction following divorce. Data from Lucas (2005)

relationship. Having a good level of social contact and support from friends and family should, however, be particularly beneficial. If loneliness can be avoided, pain will be minimized.

Summary

Social psychologists have tried to identify when people are likely to show commitment to a relationship. The investment model proposes that commitment depends upon *satisfaction*, the *perceived quality of alternatives*, and how much has been *invested* in the relationship. Commitment has important consequences for a relationship; committed individuals make greater sacrifices and are more accommodating. On the downside, however, commitment can stop people leaving a relationship even when it is in their best interests. People who are unhappy with a relationship may respond positively (with *loyalty*, or by *voicing* their concerns) or negatively (by *neglecting* or *exiting* the relationship). According to the *relationship dissolution model*, partners pass through four phases as they gradually move from initial *identification* of relationship problems, to attempts at *reconciliation* and discussion, to gaining *social support* from family and friends, and finally, *extricating* themselves from the relationship and moving on. A number of factors, including *attachment style*, *rejection sensitivity*, and *who initiated* the break-up, can affect how much pain a break-up causes.

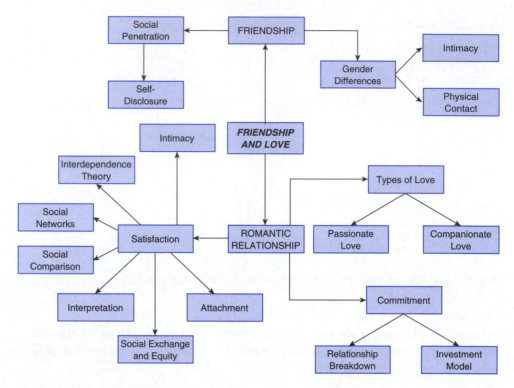

Figure 12.5 Memory map

CHAPTER SUMMARY

In this chapter, we have covered a wide range of topics essential to our under-standing of friendship and love, from how our relationships with others develop, to what determines whether those relationships last. Where people are attracted to one another, and positive social interactions ensue, friendships may develop. According to *social penetration theory*, friendships develop as a result of a grad-ual increase in the intimacy and breadth of personal information disclosed to one another. The level of *disclosure* must be carefully monitored for a relationship to develop successfully, as too much or too little disclosure may disrupt the develop-ment of the friendship. Disclosure of negative, hurtful information can also lead to the breakdown of a relationship. There are also *gender differences* in the devel-opment of friendships; in Western cultures, women tend to show greater levels of intimacy and self-disclosure and more physical contact than do men, in part as a consequence of societal expectations.

The most developed and intense type of interpersonal relationship is *romantic love*. A number of classifications of different types of love have been offered by social psychologists, but strong evidence exists for two types: *passionate love*, an intense state of longing for another person experienced in the early stages of a romance relationship, and *companionate love*, the deep bond of friendship we feel for someone in a long-term relationship. The *three-factor theory of love* proposes that passionate love arises when we understand what love is, are in the presence of a suitable potential lover, and feel emotional arousal which we attribute to that person. There is evidence that norms about romantic relationships develop during early adolescence. When we reach the companionate love stage, whether a relationship will last is determined by our *satisfaction*, *quality of alternatives*, and *investment*. If we lack satisfaction and commitment, the relationship can break down. According to the *relationship dissolution model*, break-ups pass through four phases from *identification* of problems, attempts at *reconciliation*, gaining *social support*, and finally, *extrication*. How long it takes people to recover from break-ups is dependent upon *attachment style*, *rejection sensitivity*, and *who initiated* the break-up.

Taking it Further

Try This
Pick a close friend of yours, and think about how you met, and how that friendship developed. To what extent does the story of your friendship match up with the theories of friendship discussed in this chapter? Are there gaps in the theory that cannot explain how your friendship developed? And if so, what do you think needs to be added to create an optimal theory of friendship development?

Debate This
Passionate love is an important aspect of social relationships in Western societies. There are, however, cultural differences in how love is experienced and expressed. In many cultures, arranged marriages are common, and less emphasis is put on passionate love. Is love real? Or is it something that we have invented to fulfil certain needs? And is the Western approach to love best, or would the perhaps more pragmatic approach favoured in other cultures be more realistic and sustainable?

Something for the Weekend
Imagine that you are a marriage guidance counsellor. Based on social psychological theory and research, what advice would you give to a couple who are experiencing

problems in their relationship? Think about what advice you could give based on equity theory, or the investment model, and what insights the couple could be given with a greater understanding of different attachment styles.

Further Reading

The Essentials

Hatfield, E. & Rapson, R.L. (1993). *Love, sex, and intimacy: Their psychology, biology, and history*. New York: HarperCollins.

Elaine Hatfield is a pioneer of research on love and sex. This article provides an interesting overview of research in this area. You could also check out Dr Hatfield's website: www.elainehatfield.com

Next Steps

Baumeister, R.F. & Bratslavsky, E. (1999). How is friendship different from love? Passion, intimacy, and time: Passionate love as a function of change in intimacy. *Personality and Social Psychology Review*, 3, 49–67.

If you are interested in learning more about friendship, love, and how they compare to one another, you'll find this review article very useful.

Delving Deeper

Duck, S. (1992). *Human relationships* (2nd ed.). London: Sage.

Fehr, B. (1996). *Friendship processes*. Thousand Oaks, CA: Sage.

If after reading this chapter you feel like getting deeper into love and friendship, together these two books will give you quite a detailed and inclusive account of theory and research.

Glossary

Affect-as-Information Model: The idea that we use our mood as a piece of information, to help us understand how we feel about something.

Affect-Priming Model: Model proposing that information and memories congruent with our mood are more easily accessible than incongruent information.

Affective Aggression: An act of aggression where the purpose is to cause harm.

Affiliation: The term that describes a social link formed between two or more individuals.

Aggression: A verbal or physical act intended to cause harm to someone or something.

Alcohol Expectancy Theory: The argument that drunken people behave aggressively because of their expectations about how alcohol will affect their behaviour.

Alternation Model: An individual may successfully take part in two different cultures by understanding the cultural assumptions that guide attitudes and behaviour in both, and switching smoothly between the two depending on the social context.

Altruism: An action intended to benefit others, without any expectation of personal gain.

Altruistic Personality: While accepting that there are situational differences in helping behaviour, this is the idea that some people might be innately more helpful across situations than others.

Anchoring Heuristic: The tendency to be biased towards the starting value, or anchor, in making quantitative judgements.

Archival Research: The reanalysis and interpretation of information collected by others for a different purpose.

Attachment: The emotional bond formed between a young child and their primary care giver, which has a powerful impact on the child's future relationships.

Attachment Theory: Developmental theory which proposes that depending on the relationship with their primary care giver, human infants form one of three attachment styles: secure, anxious/ambivalent, or avoidant.

Attitude: A set of beliefs that we hold in relation to an attitude object, where an attitude object can be a person, thing, event or issue.

Attribution Theory: Heider proposed that we have a basic need to attribute causality as this ascribes meaning to our social world, making it more clear, definable and predictable.

Audience Inhibition: The failure to act in an emergency because of (a) a fear of being ridiculed, and (b) assuming, based on the inaction of others, that the situation is not critical enough to be acted upon.

Authoritarian Personality: The theory that people who have overly strict parents during childhood have a tendency to derogate and show hostility towards minority groups.

Autocratic Leadership: Hierarchical style of leadership in which the leader gives orders to group members in order to achieve the goals of the group.

Availability Heuristic: The tendency to judge the frequency of an event in terms of how easy it is to bring to mind examples of that particular event. We use availability as a cognitive short-cut; the easier it is for something to come to mind, the more likely it is that it will affect our behaviour.

Aversive Racism: People often have a conflict between modern egalitarian values and negative emotions towards outgroup members, resulting in negative emotions such as uneasiness, fear, and discomfort. Aversive racists may feel shame and guilt, publicly avoiding expressing their feelings or interacting with outgroup members.

Balance Theory: Heider's (1958) proposal that we prefer the various aspects of our lives to be consistent, or in balance, with one another.

Basking in Reflected Glory: People often derive a positive self-concept from the achievements of other group members even if they were not personally instrumental in those achievements.

Behavioural Assimilation: The phenomenon whereby when people think about a particular category, they can unconsciously begin to act in line with the stereotype associated with that category.

Behavioural Intention: A person's attitude, subjective norms, and perceived control over the behaviour combine in an interactive way to determine behavioural intention, which in turn determines whether or not the behaviour will be carried out.

Belief Similarity: Criticism of the original minimal group paradigm experiment that people may show a preference for their ingroup because they inferred that, because they liked the same painting style, for example, they might share other beliefs with ingroup members. Subsequent studies have discounted this criticism.

Bystander Apathy Effect: The more bystanders present during an emergency, the lower the likelihood that a bystander will demonstrate helping behaviour.

Bystander-Calculus Model: The idea that we respond to an emergency by feeling physiological arousal, labelling that arousal as personal distress or empathic concern, and then calculate the costs of helping versus not helping before making a decision on how to act.

Bystander Intervention: When an individual who has observed someone in an emergency situation makes the decision to actively help that person.

Category Differentiation Model: A model outlining the cognitive effects of categorization on perceived similarities and differences.

Cathartic Hypothesis: The theory that frustration leads to aggression because 'letting off steam' helps to restore emotional balance.

Central Route: When people are motivated to think carefully about the content of a message, they are influenced by the strength and quality of the arguments.

Classical Conditioning: A type of associative learning, whereby two things (e.g. outgroup and negative attitude) become strongly connected because we are repeatedly exposed to them. Subsequently, when we see an outgroup member, the negative attitude may be automatically activated.

Cognitive Dissonance Theory: When people behave in a way that is inconsistent with their existing attitude, they experience discomfort. To eliminate this discomfort, it is necessary to adjust one's attitude in line with one's behaviour.

Cognitive Miser: The theory that, far from being naïve scientists, we are reluctant to expend cognitive resources and look for any opportunity to avoid engaging in effortful thought.

Cognitive Neoassociationalist Model: Berkowitz argued that frustration generates anger, which in turn prepares people to behave aggressively. This state will only lead to aggressive behaviour if an appropriate environmental cue is present.

Cohesiveness: The extent to which group members are attracted to the group.

Collectivist Culture: Cultures that promote conformity, and actions that promote the best interests of the group rather than its individual members, placing high value on cooperation, social support and respect for others, for example China and India.

Common Ingroup Identity Model: Theory that cooperation between members of different groups reduces intergroup bias because it creates a common ingroup identity, whereby former outgroup members are now seen as ingroup members.

Companionate Love: This is the less intense but more enduring type of love that characterizes long-term relationships, once passionate love has waned, and close friendships. It is characterized by trust, respect, and mutual understanding.

Compliance: A change in public but *not* private attitude.

Confederate: An individual who is ostensibly a participant in the experiment but who is actually following a script designed by the experimenter.

Conformity: Attitude or behaviour change in response to an implicit social norm.

Confounding: This is when a variable that is extraneous to the aims of the study co-varies with the independent variable, making it impossible to distinguish which of these variables is affecting the dependent variable.

Contact Hypothesis: The premise that under conditions of cooperation, common goals, equal status and institutional support, contact between members of two different groups should lead to an increase in mutual liking and respect towards the other group.

Contingency Theory: Fiedler (1965) proposed that whether a socio-emotional or task-oriented leadership style is effective depends upon how much situational control the leader has over their group.

Control Theory of Self-Regulation: Theory proposing that we use our self-awareness to assess whether or not we are meeting our goals and, if not, make efforts to improve the self in line with these goals.

Conversion: A change of both private *and* public attitude.

Correlation: An index of the strength of the relationship between two variables. Two variables are positively correlated if an increase in one is associated with an increase in the other, or negatively correlated if an increase in one is associated with a decrease in the other. A correlation does not, however, provide any information about the direction of the relationship.

Correspondent Inference Theory: Theory proposing that people prefer internal attributions over external attributions because they are perceived as being more useful when making predictions about behaviour.

Co-Variation Model: Kelley's (1967) model, which accounts for multiple behaviours, detailing the processes that result in external as well as internal attributions.

Co-Variation Principle: For something to be the cause of particular behaviour, it must be present when the behaviour is present, and absent when the behaviour is absent. In other words, it must co-vary.

Crossed Categorization: The idea that intergroup bias can be reduced by getting people to categorize others in many different ways. Rather than seeing people in terms of just one categorization (e.g. race), they can be seen in terms of race, gender, age *and* occupation at the same time.

Cutting Off Reflected Failure: When a group is unsuccessful, group members may limit damage to their own self-concept by distancing themselves from the group. However, this strategy is only used by individuals for whom the group is not highly important.

Decategorization: The process by which people switch from forming impressions based on categories to forming impressions based on individual characteristics.

Dehumanization: A form of disinhibition in which the targets of aggression are seen as anonymous or less than human, and therefore excluded from the usual norms of non-violence.

Deindividuation: The process by which people lose their identity as an idiosyncratic individual and come to perceive themselves as an anonymous – and therefore less accountable – group member.

Delegitimization: When a group is seen as threatening the norms and values of the ingroup, it may be placed in an extremely negative social category, allowing aggression against that group to be justified.

Demand Characteristics: Environmental cues that make participants aware of what the experimenter expects to find or how participants are expected to behave.

Democratic Leadership: Interactive style of leadership in which the leader discusses their plans with group members and makes them part of the decision-making process.

Depersonalized: The process by which, when group membership is salient, individuals come to see themselves in terms of the shared features that define group membership, thinking and behaving as a group member rather than as a unique individual.

Diffusion of Responsibility: The tendency perceivers have to assume that if others are present, they will take personal responsibility for a situation, absolving the perceiver of personal responsibility.

Disinhibition: A reduction in the constraints which usually stop us from behaving in an anti-social manner.

Dismissing-Avoidant Attachment: Dismissing avoidants have high self-esteem but they do not trust other people. They therefore rely on themselves while avoiding close relationships with others.

Dispositional Empathy: Some people have a general tendency to show more empathy than others, regardless of the situation.

Distraction-Conflict Theory: Theory proposing that social facilitation and inhibition are a consequence of conflict experienced by the participant between the task at hand and attending to others in the immediate surroundings.

Divergent Thinking: Thinking creatively and going beyond the information given.

Double-Blind: Procedure in which the experimenter does not know the hypothesis or is unaware of what experimental condition the participant has been assigned to.

Drive Theory: Zajonc (1965) proposed that the mere presence of others increases physiological arousal which, in turn, enhances the performance of well-learned and automatic response tendencies.

Dual Process Theory: Brewer argues that when forming impressions of others, people take either a heuristic (category) or a systematic (individuated) approach.

Egalitarianism: A belief in the equal treatment of all people.

Elaboration-Likelihood Model: Petty and Cacioppo (1986a) argued that attitudes could change via two routes depending on how much an individual *elaborates* on the message, that is, thinks carefully about issue-relevant arguments contained in a persuasive communication.

Emergent Norm Theory: Theory that criticizes deindividuation, arguing that members of a group may be more aggressive not because they ignore the existing group norm but rather because they are conforming to a new group norm, one of aggression.

Empathy-Altruism Hypothesis: The idea that if we empathize with someone in need, we are more likely to help them for altruistic – rather than egoistic – reasons.

Entitativity: The extent to which a collection of individuals are perceived as 'group-like'. A group has entitativity if it is cohesive, interconnected and similar, shares common goals and involves physical interaction.

Equity Theory: Based on social exchange theory, this theory proposes that a relationship is most likely to be successful when each partner believes their ratio of inputs to outputs is equal.

Evaluation Apprehension: Concern about being evaluated by others. People who are publicly self-aware tend to be more nervous at the prospect of a negative evaluation from those around them.

Evolutionary Perspective: The idea that social behaviours, such as aggression, helping, and altruism, have developed – and been passed down from generation to generation – to help us and our offspring survive.

Exchange Relationship: A relationship in which material (power, status) and psychological (e.g. trust, liking) resources are exchanged between two individuals.

Excitation-Transfer Model: Theory which proposes that aggression is a result of arousal, and an interpretation of that arousal as a situation that warrants aggressive behaviour.

Experimenter Effects: Subtle cues or signals from an experimenter that affect the performance or response of participants in the experiment.

Extended Contact: A form of indirect contact in which *just the knowledge* that other people in your group have friends in the outgroup can reduce prejudice, even when you yourself have no direct contact with the outgroup.

External Attribution: An explanation that locates the cause as being external to the person, such as the actions of others, the nature of the situation, social pressures, or luck.

Facial Feedback Hypothesis: People's own facial expression provides a cue to their attitudes. Thus, people who are made to smile form a more positive attitude than people who are made to frown.

Facial Symmetry: The degree to which the two halves of a person's face are well matched, which is associated with good genetic health.

False Consensus Effect: The robust bias we have to overestimate how common one's own opinion is in the general population.

Fearful-Avoidant Attachment: Fearful avoidants have low self-esteem and cannot trust others. They tend to have particularly poor interpersonal relations.

Frustration-Aggression Hypothesis: The idea that aggression is a direct consequence of feelings of frustration that people experience. The theory has been used to explain hate crimes during times of economic difficulty.

Functional Approach: Attitudes are sometimes *actively* rather than *passively* formed, based on the degree to which they satisfy an individual's psychological needs.

Fundamental Attribution Error: People have an overall tendency to make internal rather than external attributions, even when there are clear potential situational causes.

Group Polarization: A shift in attitude towards an extreme version of the initial group norm.

Groupthink: An extreme form of polarization that can lead to groups making poorly judged decisions.

Helping Behaviour: An intentional action that benefits another person.

Heterosexual Masculinity: Men are socialized to value masculine traits and devalue feminine traits. They are particularly likely to conform to this norm when in the company of other men.

Heuristic-Systematic Model: Chaiken (1980) argued that when people hear a persuasive communication, they either process it systematically, considering its strengths or weaknesses, or use heuristic 'short-cuts'.

Heuristics: Timesaving mental shortcuts that reduce complex judgements to simple rules of thumb.

Homeostasis Principle: The principle that people control their level of contact with others, so that it is stable and as close to their desired level of contact as possible.

Hypotheses: Tentative predictions or explanations for an observation or phenomenon that can be empirically tested.

Illusory Correlation: The belief that two variables are associated with one another when there is little or no actual association.

Imagined contact: A form of indirect contact in which people are encouraged to imagine a positive social interaction with a member or members of an outgroup.

Implicit Attitudes: Attitudes that are unintentionally activated by the mere presence of an attitude object, whether actual or symbolic.

Implicit Association Test (IAT): A measure of implicit attitudes that identifies the speed with which participants can categorize positive or negative stimuli (e.g. positive or negative words) alongside ingroup or outgroup stimuli (e.g. names or faces).

Individualist Culture: Cultures that promote individual goals, initiative and achievements, encouraging people to view themselves as unique and independent individuals, for example the United States and Europe.

Individuation: Seeing a person as an idiosyncratic individual with unique characteristics rather than as an interchangeable group member.

Informational Influence: We are especially reliant on the attitudes of others around us when we have not encountered a situation before, and therefore have no clear guidelines on how to behave. This can contribute to audience inhibition; if no-one else acts in an emergency, we may take this to mean the situation is not serious enough to warrant help being offered.

Ingroup Bias: The higher positive evaluation of ingroup members compared to outgroup members.

Instrumental Aggression: An act of aggression which serves a purpose other than to cause harm.

Internal Attribution: An explanation that locates the cause as being internal to the person, such as personality, mood, abilities, attitudes, and effort.

Internal Validity: The extent to which an association between an independent variable and a dependent variable reflects a causal relationship between the two.

Interpersonal Attraction: Our desire to get to know and spend time with another person.

Investment Model: A theory that proposes that people will be committed to a relationship to the extent that they have high satisfaction, low perceived quality of alternatives and a high level of investment.

Just-World Hypothesis: The belief people have that the world is a fair place, where good things happen to good people, but where bad people are punished for their actions.

Laissez-Faire Leadership: Distant style of leadership in which the leader rarely intervenes in the activities of the group.

Leader-Member Exchange Theory: Theory which proposes that effective leaders will be those that have a high quality exchange relationship with their group members.

Looks-for-Status Exchange: Youth and beauty tend to be more important determinants of attractiveness in women than status, whereas status and power are more important than physical attributes in men.

Matching Hypothesis: A socially shared belief that couples of a similar level of attractiveness will be better suited to one another.

Mere Exposure Effect: The more exposure we have to a stimulus, whether it is an object or a person, the more positive is our attitude towards it.

Meta-Contrast Principle: Group members exaggerate similarities within the group ('we are all the same') and differences with other groups ('we are very different from them').

Minimal Group Paradigm: Classic experimental context in which groups are formed on an ad hoc basis, with no obvious reason to compete with one another.

Modelling: The tendency people have to observe, and then reproduce, the actions of another person.

Motivated Tacticians: This is the idea that people are neither cognitive misers nor naïve scientists. Instead, they are strategic in their allocation of cognitive resources, deciding whether to be a cognitive miser or a naïve scientist depending on the situation.

naïve Scientists: People rationally and logically test out hypotheses about the behaviour of others because of a desire for consistency and stability.

Narcissism: A personality trait held by individuals who are characterized by extremely high but unstable self-esteem.

Normative Influence: Our tendency to go along with the majority attitude, even if we privately disagree with it, for fear of being laughed at or ridiculed by the group. This plays a key role in audience inhibition.

Obedience: Attitude or behaviour change in response to an explicit order.

Operant Conditioning: A type of associative learning, whereby an association forms between a behaviour and a consequence. Also called response-stimulus conditioning.

Optimal Distinctiveness Theory: Theory stating that people seek out groups that provide a balance in satisfying two conflicting motives, the need for assimilation and the need for differentiation.

Outgroup Homogeneity Effect: The general tendency that people have to perceive outgroup members to be more homogeneous than ingroup members.

Parental Investment Theory: The theory that men and women differ in their strategies to attract mates for evolutionary reasons, specifically because reproduction has more serious and long lasting consequences for women than for men (Trivers, 1972).

Passionate Love: The state of intense longing for another person experienced during the early stages of a relationship.

Perceived Control: A person's perception of how easy or difficult it is to perform the behaviour.

Peripheral Route: When people are unwilling or unable to analyse message content, they instead pay attention to cues that are irrelevant to the content or quality of the communication to make a decision more quickly and with less effort.

Persuasion: When attitudes change as a result of being influenced by an external message.

Preoccupied Attachment: People who are able to trust others but who have low self-esteem and do not believe they are worthy of love. They tend to be obsessed with their relationship partners and fear their feelings will not be reciprocated.

Priming: Activating a specific attitude, for example a stereotype, can exert an influence on people's subsequent behaviour.

Privacy Regulation Theory: The theory that the need for affiliation, which varies over time, is satisfied by aligning our desire for privacy with our actual level of contact.

Private Self-Awareness: People who are privately self-aware (e.g. on their own and thus aware of only their own personal attitude on a topic) are likely to behave in correspondence with their attitude.

Private Self-Consciousness: Individuals with chronically heightened private self-awareness experience more intense emotions, have more accurate self-perceptions, and adhere to personal standards of behaviour.

Prosocial Behaviour: Behaviour that is valued by others in a particular culture.

Prototype: The most representative or typical object, person, or characteristic in a particular category.

Public Self-Awareness: Temporary awareness of aspects of oneself that can be seen and evaluated by others. People who are publicly self-aware (e.g. with a group of peers who are voicing their own opinions) are less likely to behave in line with their private attitudes, as they may be influenced by the group norm.

Public Self-Consciousness: Individuals with chronically heightened public self-awareness are more likely to suffer from evaluation apprehension, adhere to social standards of behaviour, and avoid potentially embarrassing situations.

Realistic Group Conflict Theory: The theory, derived from Sherif's summer camp studies, that conflict between groups results from competition for scarce resources.

Reciprocity Principle: The universally held belief that we should treat others as they treat us. According to this principle, if we believe another person would help us, we should help them. On the other hand, people are more likely to behave aggressively if they are provoked by the aggressive behaviour of another person.

Relationship Dissolution Model: Duck's (1992) proposed sequence of events which characterize the end of a long-term relationship.

Relative Deprivation: Distinct from a person's absolute level of deprivation, relative deprivation refers to a person's perception that they are being unfairly disadvantaged when compared to other people or groups.

Representativeness Heuristic: The tendency to allocate a set of attributes to someone if they match the prototype of a given category.

Secure Attachment: People who have a high self-esteem and are able to trust relationship partners. They tend to have the most successful relationships and are also seen as the most desirable partners.

Self-Affirmation Theory: The idea that people respond to threats to self by affirming positive aspects of themselves, allowing them to maintain a positive self-concept.

Self-Anchoring Theory: The idea that for novel groups, we project our own positive attributes to create a positive norm, but we don't do this for outgroups. This creates ingroup favouritism.

Self-Assessment: People are motivated to hold an accurate self-perception and seek out information which will help them to do so.

Self-Categorization Theory: An extension of social identity theory, which proposes that when an individual's social identity is salient they come to see themselves as a depersonalized group member rather than an idiosyncratic individual. They depersonalize, assimilate to group norms, and take on the characteristics associated with a typical group member, a process referred to as self-stereotyping.

Self-Discrepancy Theory: According to this theory, we compare the self to two points of reference, the ideal self (how we would ideally like to be) and the ought self (how we believe we should be, based on a sense of obligation or duty). Discrepancies between actual and ideal self can lead to dejection-related emotions, while discrepancies between actual and ought self lead to agitation-related emotions.

Self-Enhancement: People are motivated to hold a positive self-image and are selectively biased towards information that helps them to see themselves in a positive light.

Self-Esteem: An individual's personal evaluation of their own self-concept.

Self-Evaluation Maintenance Model: Tesser proposed that comparison with someone who is successful results in self-reflection or social-comparison, depending on whether that success is in a *relevant* domain, and on whether we are *certain* of our own performance in that domain.

Self-Fulfilling Prophecy: When an initially false belief about a person causes that person to behave in ways that objectively confirm that belief.

Self-Perception Theory: Theory proposing that we form attitudes through the observation of our *own* behaviour.

Self-Regulation: A deliberate process through which people monitor prejudice-related thoughts and consistently inhibit them, replacing them with a low-prejudiced response.

Self-Schema: A schema or knowledge structure that reflects our perception of the self on a particular dimension.

Self-Schematic: We are self-schematic on a particular self-schema if it is highly embedded in our self-concept. This is likely to be the case for a self-schema that we are extreme on, that is particularly important to us, and for which we are certain that the opposite is not true.

Self-Serving Attribution Bias: We have a pervasive tendency to attribute successes to internal, personal attributes, and failure to external factors outside of our control.

Self-Verification: People are motivated to confirm their existing self-perceptions and so often seek out similar others who are most likely to do so.

Sexual Aggression: Verbal or physical aggression towards another person that has a sexual component.

Social Affiliation Model: A psychological model that specifies that we have the ability to keep our desired and actual level of contact very close to one another, enabling us to keep our need to affiliate stable over time.

Social Anxiety: The negative emotion we experience due to our concern with interpersonal evaluation. This can be either an occasional experience or a chronic problem.

Social Behaviour: Behaviour that takes place in a social context and results from interaction between individuals.

Social Categorization: The way in which we organize things, such as objects, people, attitudes and attributes, into categories in order to simplify our social world.

Social Cognition: The way in which perceivers encode, process, remember, and use information in social contexts in order to make sense of other people's behaviour.

Social Comparison Theory: Theory which proposes that we form a definition of the self by comparing ourselves with those around us.

Social Dominance Orientation: People who favour intergroup hierarchies, believing that high status groups deserve their dominance over low status groups.

Social Exchange Theory: According to this theory, a key characteristic of social relationships is the exchange of valuable 'goods', whether material or emotional.

Social Facilitation: The tendency for people to perform better when in front of an audience.

Social Identity Complexity: An individual's subjective representation of the inter-relationships among his or her multiple group identities.

Social Identity Theory: Theory which proposes that when our membership in a particular group is salient, it is our social self rather than our personal self that guides our self-concept, attitudes and behaviour. The theory explains how affiliation to groups influences group behaviour.

Social Impact Theory: A unifying theory that accounts for conformity and obedience findings.

Social Influence: Any effect that another person or group has on your own attitudes or behaviour.

Social Inhibition: In certain situations, the presence of an audience can have a detrimental effect on performance.

Social Learning Theory: Bandura (1977) proposed that people learn how to behave by observing the behaviour of others.

Social Loafing: The tendency for individuals to reduce the amount of effort they put in as group size increases.

Social Norms: Attitudes and behaviours that are commonly held in a particular group, and exert a powerful influence over the attitudes and behaviours of group members.

Social Penetration Theory: The proposal that the way in which friendships initially develop – and break down – is dependent upon reciprocal self-disclosure.

Social Reflection: Associating ourselves with the success of close others.

Social Responsibility: The idea that we should help people who are dependent on us and in need of our help, regardless of whether they can help us in return.

Socio-Emotional Leadership: Style of leadership in which the leader concentrates on ensuring positive interpersonal dynamics within the group.

Staircase to Terrorism: Psychological model which proposes five stages or 'floors' past which disaffected individuals climb before committing a terrorist act.

Stereotype: The prototype of a *social* category.

Stereotype Threat: When a negative stereotype about the group to which we belong is made salient, we tend to show impaired performance on dimensions related to that stereotype.

Stigmatization: When a person is ascribed negative characteristics because they belong to what is considered by dominant group members as a low status social category.

Subjective Norms: The perceived expectations of significant others who may approve or disapprove of the planned behaviour.

Subjective Uncertainty Reduction Hypothesis: People are motivated to maintain the distinctiveness of their group to reduce subjective uncertainty.

Subtype: Even if stereotype inconsistent information is remembered, it may often be discounted as an 'exception to the rule' where the stereotype is concerned. Subtyping often therefore preserves and perpetuates the overall stereotype as it negates the impact of disconfirming information.

Survey: A procedure for gathering information which involves asking participants questions, either by interview or questionnaire.

Task-Focused Leadership: Style of leadership in which the leader concentrates on achieving the goals of the group by effectively carrying out tasks.

Terror Management Theory: The theory that humans, unlike other animals, possess the intellectual capacity to realize that one day we will die – a fact that can paralyse us with fear at the prospect of our own mortality, with considerable implications for behaviour.

Theory of Planned Behaviour: Theory developed to explain the processes by which people deliberately decide to engage in a specific action.

Threat-to-Self-Esteem Model: Model which proposes that characteristics of the help-giver, helping situation and help-recipient interact to determine whether recipients feel self-threat or self-support. Recipients will feel good and react positively if they feel supported, but they will feel bad and react negatively to the help-giver if they feel threatened.

Three-Factor Theory of Love: This theory argues that three conditions must be met to fall in love: (1) understanding and accepting the concept of love, (2) meeting a suitable potential lover, and (3) attributing physiological arousal to the presence of the potential lover.

Transformational Leader: An exceptional leader who motivates group members to abandon self-interest in order to work for group goals, often transforming the attitudes, behaviour, direction and goals of a group.

Triangular Theory of Love: Theory that there are seven different types of love, which differ depending on the degree of passion, intimacy, and commitment.

Two-Factor Theory of Emotion: The theory that emotional experience is based on two factors: physiological arousal and a search for cues which might explain that arousal.

Type A Personality: People with this type of personality tend to be competitive high achievers, perfectionists who are obsessed with completing tasks quickly and on time. They also have an elevated risk of coronary heart disease.

Uncertainty: In Sherif's social norm study, the more participants felt uncertain about the task, the quicker they converged on the group norm.

Vascular Theory of Emotion: Alternative explanation offered for the facial feedback hypothesis: Smiling increases the flow of blood to the brain and lowers brain temperature, creating a positive mood, whereas frowning constricts blood flow to the brain, increasing brain temperature and creating a negative mood.

References

Abrams, D. & Hogg, M.A. (1990). *Social identity theory: Constructive and critical advances.* London: Harvester Wheatsheaf.

Abrams, D. & Hogg, M.A. (2001). Collective identity: Group membership and self-conception. In M.A. Hogg & R.S. Tindale (Eds.), *Blackwell handbook of social psychology: Group processes* (pp. 425–460). Oxford: Blackwell.

Adams, J. & Jones, W.H. (1997). The conceptualization of marital commitment: An integrative analysis. *Journal of Social and Personal Relationships, 11,* 1177–1196.

Adorno, T.W., Frenkel-Brunswick, E., Levinson, D.J., & Stanford, R.N. (1950). *The authoritarian personality.* New York: Harper & Row.

Agnew, C.R., Van Lange, P.A.M., Rusbult, C.E., & Langston, C.A. (1998). Cognitive interdependence: Commitment and the mental representation of close relationships. *Journal of Personality and Social Psychology, 74,* 939–954.

Ainsworth, M.D.S. (1982). Attachments beyond infancy. *American Psychologist, 44,* 709–716.

Ajzen, I. (1989). Attitude structure and behaviour. In A.R. Pratkanis, S.J. Breckler & A.G. Greenwald (Eds.), *Attitude structure and function* (pp. 241–274). Hillsdale, NJ: Erlbaum.

Ajzen, I. (1996). The social psychology of decision making. In E.T. Higgins & R.M. Sorrentino (Eds.), *Handbook of motivation and cognition: Foundations of social behaviour* (Vol. 2, pp. 297–325). New York: Guilford.

Ajzen, I. & Fishbein, M. (1980). *Understanding attitudes and predicting social behaviour.* Englewood Cliffs, NJ: Prentice Hall.

Allen, V.L. (1975). Social support for nonconformity. In L. Berkowitz (Ed.), *Advances in experimental social psychology* (Vol. 18, pp. 2–43). New York: Academic Press.

Allen, V.L. & Levine, J.M. (1971). Social support and conformity: The role of independent assessment of reality. *Journal of Experimental Social Psychology, 7,* 48–58.

Allman, J.M. & Hasenstaub, A. (1999). Brains, maturation times, and parenting. *Neurobiology of Aging, 20,* 447–454.

Allport, F.H. (1920). The influence of the group upon association and thought. *Journal of Experimental Psychology, 3,* 159–182.

Allport, G.W. (1954). *The nature of prejudice.* Reading, MA: Addison-Wesley.

Allport, G.W. (1985). The historical background of social psychology. In G. Lindzey & E. Aronson (Eds.), *Handbook of social psychology* (Vol. 1, pp. 1–46). New York: Random House.

Alper, A., Buckhout, R., Chern, S., Harwood, R., & Slomovic, M. (1976). Eyewitness identification: Accuracy of individual vs. composite recollection of a crime. *Bulletin of the Psychonomic Society, 8,* 147-149.

Altman, I. (1975). *The environment and social behaviour.* Monterey, CA: Brooks/Cole.

Altman, I. & Taylor, D.A. (1973). *Social penetration: The development of interpersonal relationships.* New York: Holt, Rinehart, & Winston.

Amir, Y. (1969). Contact hypothesis in ethnic relations. *Psychological Bulletin, 71,* 319–342.

Anderson, C.A. & Anderson, D.C. (1984). Ambient temperature and violent crime: Tests of the linear and curvilinear hypothesis. *Journal of Personality and Social Psychology, 46,* 91–97.

Anderson, C.A. & Bushman, B.J. (2001). Effects of violent video games on aggressive behaviour, aggressive cognition, aggressive affect, physiological arousal, and prosocial behaviour: A meta-analytic review of the scientific literature. *Psychological Science, 12*, 353–359.

Anderson, C.A. & Bushman, B.J. (2002). Human aggression. *Annual Review of Psychology, 53*, 27–51.

Anderson, C.A., Bushman, B.J., & Groom, R.W. (1997). Hot years and serious deadly assault: Empirical tests of the heat hypothesis. *Journal of Personality and Social Psychology, 73*, 1213–1223.

Anderson, C.A., Carnagey, N.L., & Eubanks, J. (2003). Exposure to violent media: The effects of songs with violent lyrics on aggressive thoughts and feelings. *Journal of Personality and Social Psychology, 84*, 960–971.

Anderson, C.A., Gentile, D.A., & Buckley, K.E. (2007). *Violent video game effects on children and adolescents: Theory, research, and public policy.* New York: Oxford University Press.

Anderson, E. (1994). The code of the streets. *Atlantic Monthly, 5*, 81–94.

Anderson, J.L., Crawford, C.B., Nadeau, J., & Lindberg, T. (1992). Was the Duchess of Windsor right? A cross-cultural review of the socioecology of ideals of the female body shape. *Ethology and Sociology, 13*, 197–227.

Archer, J. (2000). Sex differences in aggression between heterosexual partners: A meta-analytic review. *Psychological Bulletin, 126*, 651–680.

Aron, A., Aron, E.N., & Smollan, D. (1992). Inclusion of the other in the self scale and the structure of interpersonal closeness. *Journal of Personality and Social Psychology, 63*, 596–612.

Aron, A., Melinat, E., Aron, E.N., Vallone, R.D., & Bator, R.J. (1997). The experimental generation of interpersonal closeness: A procedure and some preliminary findings. *Personality and Social Psychology Bulletin, 23*, 363–377.

Aron, A., Paris, M., & Aron, E.N. (1995). Falling in love: Prospective studies of self-concept change. *Journal of Personality and Social Psychology, 69*, 1102–1112.

Aronson, E. (1969). The theory of cognitive dissonance: A current perspective. In L. Berkowitz (Ed.), *Advances in experimental social psychology* (Vol. 4, pp. 1–34). New York: Academic Press.

Asch, S.E. (1951). Effects of group pressure upon the modification and distortion of judgments. In H. Guetzkow (Ed.), *Groups, leadership and men: Research in human relations* (pp. 177–190). Pittsburgh, PA: Carnegie Press.

Asch, S.E. (1952). *Social psychology.* Englewood Cliffs, NJ: Prentice Hall.

Asch, S.E. (1955). Studies of independence and conformity: A minority of one against a unanimous majority. *Psychology Monographs, 70*, 1–70.

Asch, S.E. (1956). Opinions and social pressure. *Scientific American, 193*, 31–35.

Asch, S.E. (1959). A perspective on social psychology. In S. Koch (Ed.), *Psychology: A study of science* (Vol. 3, pp. 363–383). New York: McGraw-Hill.

Ayduk, O., Downey, G., & Kim, M. (2001). Rejection sensitivity and depressive symptoms in women. *Personality and Social Psychology Bulletin, 27*, 868–877.

Ayman, R. & Chemers, M.M. (1983). The relationship of supervisory behaviour ratings to work group effectiveness and subordinate satisfaction among Iranian managers. *Journal of Applied Psychology, 68*, 338–341.

Bachman, R. & Peralta, R. (2002). The relationship between drinking and violence in an adolescent population: Does gender matter? *Deviant Behaviour, 23*, 1–19.

Bales, R.F. (1950). *Interaction process analysis: A method for the study of small groups.* Reading, MA: Addison Wesley.

Bandura, A. (1972). *Social learning theory.* New York: General Learning Press.

Bandura, A. (1977). *Social learning theory* (2nd ed.). Englewood Cliffs, NJ: Prentice Hall.

Bandura, A., Ross, D., & Ross, S.A. (1961). Transmission of aggression through imitation of aggressive models. *Journal of Abnormal and Social Psychology*, *63*, 575–582.

Bargh, J.A. (1984). Automatic and conscious processing of social information. In R.S. Wyer & T.K. Srull (Eds.), *Handbook of social cognition.* Hillsdale, NJ: Lawrence Erlbaum.

Bargh, J.A., Chen, M., & Burrows, L. (1996). The automaticity of social behaviour: Direct effects of trait concept and stereotype activation on action. *Journal of Personality and Social Psychology*, *71*, 230–244.

Bargh, J.A. & McKenna, K.Y.A. (2004). The internet and social life. *Annual Review of Psychology*, 55, 573–590.

Bargh, J.A., McKenna, K.Y.A., & Fitzsimmons, G.M. (2002). Can you see the real me? Activation and expression of the 'true self' on the internet. *Journal of Social Issues*, *58*, 33–48.

Bargh, J.A. & Pratto, F. (1986). Individual construct accessibility and perceptual selection. *Journal of Experimental Social Psychology*, *22*, 293–311.

Barnes, R.D., Ickes, W., & Kidd, R.F. (1979). Effects of the perceived intentionality and stability of another's dependency on helping behavior. *Personality and Social Psychology Bulletin*, *5*, 367–372.

Baron, L. & Straus, M.A. (1989). *Four theories of rape in American society: A state-level analysis.* New Haven, CT: Yale University Press.

Baron, R.A. (1986). Self-presentation in job interviews: When there can be 'too much of a good thing'. *Journal of Applied Social Psychology*, *16*, 16–28.

Baron, R.M. & Kenny, D.A. (1986). The moderator-mediator variable distinction in social psychological research: Conceptual, strategic, and statistical considerations. *Journal of Personality and Social Psychology*, *51*, 1173–1182.

Baron, R.S., Vandello, J., & Brunsman, B. (1996). The forgotten variable in conformity research: Impact of task importance on social influence. *Journal of Personality and Social Psychology*, *71*, 915–927.

Barsalou, L.W. (1991). Deriving categories to achieve goals. In M.I. Posner (Ed.), *The psychology of learning and motivation* (Vol. 27, pp. 1–64). New York: Academic Press.

Bar-Tal, D. (1990). Causes and consequences of delegitimization: Models of conflict and ethnocentrism. *Journal of Social Issues*, *46*, 65–81.

Bartholomew, K. (1990). Avoidance of intimacy: An attachment perspective. *Journal of Personality and Social Psychology*, *7*, 147–178.

Bass, B.M. (1985). *Leadership and performance beyond expectations.* New York: Free Press.

Bass, B.M. (1990). From transactional to transformational leadership: Learning to share the vision. *Organizational Dynamics*, *18*, 19–31.

Bass, B.M., Avolio, B.J., & Goodheim, L. (1987). Biography and the assessment of transformational leadership at the world-class level. *Journal of Management*, *3*, 7–19.

Batson, C.D. (1991). *The altruism question: Toward a social-psychological answer.* Hillsdale, NJ: Erlbaum.

Batson, C.D. (1994). Why act for the public good? Four answers. *Personality and Social Psychology Bulletin*, *20*, 603–610.

Batson, C.D. (1998). Altruism and prosocial behavior. In D.T. Gilbert, S.T. Fiske, & G. Lindzey (Eds.), *The handbook of social psychology* (4th edn, Vol. 2, pp. 282–316). New York: McGraw-Hill.

Batson, C.D. & Coke, J.S. (1981). Empathy: A source of altruistic motivation for helping? In J.P. Rushton & R.M. Sorrentino (Eds.), *Altruism and helping behavior: Social, personality, and development perspectives* (pp. 167–183). Hillsdale, NJ: Erlbaum.

Batson, C.D., Duncan, B.D., Ackerman, P., Buckley, T., & Birch, K. (1981). Is empathic emotion a source of altruistic motivation? *Journal of Personality and Social Psychology*, *40*, 290–302.

Baumeister, R.F. (1998). The self. In D.T. Gilbert, S.T. Fiske, & G. Lindzey (Eds.), *The handbook of social psychology* (Vol. 1, 4th edn, pp. 680–740). New York: McGraw-Hill.

Baumeister, R.F. & Bratslavsky, E. (1999). How is friendship different from love? Passion, intimacy, and time: Passionate love as a function of change in intimacy. *Personality and Social Psychology Review*, *3*, 49–67.

Baumeister, R.F., Bratslavsky, E., Muraven, M. & Tice, D.M. (1998). Ego depletion: Is the active self a limited resource? *Journal of Personality and Social Psychology*, *74*, 1252–1265.

Baumeister, R.F., Catanese, K.R., & Vohs, K.D. (2001). Is there a gender difference in strength of sex drive? Theoretical views, conceptual distinctions, and a review of relevant evidence. *Personality and Social Psychology Review*, *5*, 242–273.

Baumeister, R.F., Chesner, S.P., Senders, P.S., & Tice, D.M. (1988). Who's in charge here? Group leaders to lend help in emergencies. *Personality and Social Psychology Bulletin*, *14*, 17–22.

Baumeister, R.F., Smart, L., & Boden, J.M. (1996). Relation of threatened egotism to violence and aggression: The dark side of high self-esteem. *Psychological Review*, *103*, 5–33.

Baumeister, R.F., Tice, D.M. & Hutton, D.G. (1989). Self-presentational motivations and personality differences in self-esteem. *Journal of Personality*, *57*, 647–679.

Baumeister, R.F. & Vohs, K.D. (2004). Sexual economics: Sex as female resource for exchange in heterosexual interactions. *Personality and Social Psychology Review*, *8*, 339–363.

Baumeister, R.F., Wotman, S.R., & Stillwell, A.M. (1993). Unrequited love: On heartbreak, anger, guilt, scriptlessness, and humiliation. *Journal of Personality & Social Psychology*, *64*, 377–394.

Baumrind, D. (1991). The influence of parenting style on adolescent competence and substance use. *Journal of Early Adolescence*, *11*, 56–95.

Bem, D.J. (1965). An experimental analysis of self-persuasion. *Journal of Experimental Social Psychology*, *1*, 199–218.

Benet-Martínez, V., Leu, J., Lee, F., & Morris, M. (2002). Negotiating biculturalism: Cultural frame-switching in biculturals with 'oppositional' vs. 'compatible' cultural identities. *Journal of Cross-Cultural Psychology*, *33*, 492–516.

Bengry-Howell, A. & Griffin, C. (2007). Self-made motormen: The material construction of working-class masculine identities through car modification. *Journal of Youth Studies*, *10*, 439–458.

Benson, P.L., Karabenick, S.A., & Lerner, R.M. (1976). Pretty pleases: The effects of physical attractiveness, race, and sex on receiving help. *Journal of Experimental Social Psychology*, *12*, 409–415.

Berg, J.H. (1984). The development of friendships between roommates. *Journal of Personality and Social Psychology*, *46*, 346–356.

Berkowitz, L. (1969). The frustration-aggression hypothesis revisited. In L. Berkowitz (Ed.), *Roots of aggression* (pp. 1–28). New York: Atherton Press.

Berkowitz, L. (1972). Social norms, feelings, and other factors affecting helping and altruism. In L. Berkowitz (Ed.), *Advances in experimental social psychology* (Vol. 6). New York: Academic Press.

Berkowitz, L. (1974). Some determinants of impulsive aggression: Role of mediated associations with reinforcements of aggression. *Psychological Review*, *81*, 165–176.

Berkowitz, L. (1978). Decreased helpfulness with increased group size through lessening the effects of the needy individual's dependency. *Journal of Personality*, *46*, 299–310.

Berkowitz, L. (1989). The frustration-aggression hypothesis: An examination and reformulation. *Psychological Bulletin*, *106*, 59–73.

Berkowitz, L. & Daniels, L.R. (1964). Affecting the salience of the social responsibility norm: Effects of past help on the response to dependency relationships. *Journal of Abnormal and Social Psychology*, *68*, 275–281.

Berkowitz, L. & LePage, A. (1967). Weapons as aggression-eliciting stimuli. *Journal of Personality and Social Psychology*, *7*, 202–207.

Berman, M., Gladue, B., & Taylor, S. (1993). The effects of hormones, type A behaviour pattern, and provocation on aggression in men. *Motivation and Emotion*, *17*, 125–138.

Berry, J.W. & Annis, R.C. (1974). Acculturative stress: The role of ecology, culture and differentiation. *Journal of Cross-Cultural Psychology*, *5*, 382–406.

Berscheid, E.H. (1990). Contemporary vocabularies of emotion. In B.S. Moore & A. Isen (Eds.), *Affect and social behavior* (pp. 22–28). New York: Cambridge University Press.

Berscheid, E., Dion, K., Walster, E., & Walster, G.W. (1971). Physical attractiveness and dating choice: A test of the matching hypothesis. *Journal of Experimental Social Psychology*, *7*, 173–189.

Berscheid, E. & Hatfield, E. (1978). *Interpersonal attraction* (2nd ed.). Reading, MA: Addison Wesley.

Berscheid, E.H. & Reis, H.T. (1998). Attraction and close relationships. In D.T. Gilbert, S.T. Fiske, & G. Lindzey (Eds.), *The handbook of social psychology* (4th ed., Vol. 2, pp. 193–281). New York: McGraw-Hill.

Bettencourt, B.A. & Miller, N. (1996). Gender differences in aggression as a function of provocation: A meta-analysis. *Psychological Bulletin*, *119*, 422–447.

Bierhoff, H.W., Klein, R., & Kramp, P. (1991). Evidence for the altruistic personality from data on accident research. *Journal of Personality*, *59*, 263–280.

Bigler, R.S. & Liben, L.S. (1992). Cognitive mechanisms in children's gender stereotyping: Theoretical and educational implications of a cognitive-based mechanism. *Child Development*, *63*, 1351–1363.

Billig, M. & Tajfel, H. (1973). Social categorization and similarity in intergroup behavior. *European Journal of Social Psychology*, *3*, 27–52.

Björkqvist, K., Lagerspetz, K.M.J., & Kaukiainen, A. (1992). Do girls manipulate and boys fight? Development trends regarding direct and indirect aggression. *Aggressive Behavior*, *18*, 117–127.

Björkqvist, K., Österman, K., & Kaukiainen, A. (2002). Sosiaalinen älykkyys – empatia = epäsuora aggressio? [Social intelligence – empathy = indirect aggression?] *Psykologia*, *37*, 163–170.

Blaine, B., Crocker, J., & Major, B. (1995). The unintended negative consequences of sympathy for the stigmatized. *Journal of Applied Social Psychology*, *25*, 889–905.

Blair, I.V., Ma, J.E., & Lenton, A.P. (2001). Imagining stereotypes away: The moderation of implicit stereotypes through mental imagery. *Journal of Personality and Social Psychology*, *81*, 828–841.

Blanchard, F.A., Adelman, L., & Cook, S.W. (1975). Effect of group success and failure upon interpersonal attraction in cooperating interracial groups. *Journal of Personality and Social Psychology*, *31*, 1020–1030.

Bohner, G., Crow, K., Erb, H., & Schwartz, N. (1992). Affect and persuasion: Mood effects on the processing of message content and context cues and on subsequent behaviour. *European Journal of Social Psychology*, *22*, 511–530.

Bond, R. & Smith, P.B. (1996). Culture and conformity: A meta-analysis of the Asch line judgment task. *Psychological Bulletin*, *119*, 111–137.

Bond, R. & Titus, L.J. (1983). Social facilitation: A meta-analysis of 241 studies. *Psychological Bulletin*, *94*, 265–292.

Book, A.S., Starzyk, K.B., & Quinsey, V.L. (2001). The relationship between testosterone and aggression: A meta-analysis. *Aggression and Violent Behavior*, *6*, 579–599.

Bornstein, R.F. (1989). Exposure and affect: Overview and meta-analysis of research, 1968–1987. *Psychological Bulletin*, *106*, 265–289.

Bornstein, R.F., Leone, D.R. & Galley, D.J. (1987). The generalizability of subliminal mere exposure effects: Influence of stimuli perceived without awareness on social behaviour. *Journal of Personality and Social Psychology*, *53*, 1070–1079.

Bower, G.H. (1981). Emotional mood and memory. *American Psychologist*, *36*, 129–148.

Bowlby, J. (1969). *Attachment and loss (Vol. 1): Attachment.* London: Hogarth Press.

Brendan, G. (2002). 'I've always tolerated it but…': Heterosexual masculinity and its discursive reproduction of homophobia. In A. Coyle & C. Kitzinger (Eds.), *Lesbian and gay psychology: New perspectives* (pp. 219–238). Oxford: Wiley-Blackwell.

Brennan, K.A. & Shaver, P.R. (1995). Dimensions of adult attachment, affect regulation, and romantic relationship functioning. *Personality and Social Psychology Bulletin*, *21*, 267–283.

Brewer, M.B. (1979). Ingroup bias and the minimal group paradigm: A cognitive-motivational analysis. *Psychological Bulletin*, *86*, 307–324.

Brewer, M.B. (1988). A dual process model of impression formation. In T.K. Srull and R.S. Wyer (Eds.), *Advances in social cognition* (Vol. 1, pp. 1–36). Hillsdale, NJ: Erlbaum.

Brewer, M.B. (1991). The social self: On being similar and different at the same time. *Personality and Social Psychology Bulletin*, *17*, 475–482.

Brewer, M.B. (1998). A dual process model of impression formation. In T.K. Srull, & R.S. Wyer, Jr. (Eds.), *Advances in social cognition* (pp. 1–36). Hillsdale, NJ: Erlbaum.

Brewer, M.B. & Gaertner, S.L. (2001). Towards reduction of prejudice: Intergroup contact and social categorization. In R. Brown & S.L. Gaertner (Eds.), *Intergroup processes: Blackwell handbook of social psychology* (pp. 451–472). Malden, MA: Blackwell.

Brewer, M.B. & Gardner, W. (1996). Who is this 'we'? Levels of collective identity and self-representation. *Journal of Personality and Social Psychology*, *71*, 83–93.

Brewer, M.B. & Miller, N. (1984). Beyond the contact hypothesis: Theoretical perspectives on desegregation. In N. Miller and M.B. Brewer (Eds.), *Groups in contact: The psychology of desegregation*. New York: Academic Press.

Brewer, M.B. & Pierce, K.P. (2005). Social identity complexity and outgroup tolerance. *Personality and Social Psychology Bulletin*, *31*, 428–437.

Brickman, P., Redfield, J., Harrison, A.A., & Crandall, R. (1972). Drive and predisposition as factors in the attitudinal effects of mere exposure. *Journal of Experimental Social Psychology* *8*, 31–44.

British Crime Survey (2002). Retrieved 30 May 2006 from http://www.homeoffice.gov.uk/rds/bcs2.html.

Brown, J.D. & Dutton, K.A. (1995). The thrill of victory, the complexity of defeat: Self-esteem and people's emotional reactions to success and failure. *Journal of Personality and Social Psychology*, *68*, 712–722.

Brown, R. & Gaertner, S. (Eds.) (2001). *Blackwell handbook of social psychology: Intergroup processes*. Malden, MA: Blackwell.

Brown, R. & Hewstone, H. (2005). An integrative theory of intergroup contact. In M.P. Zanna (Ed.), *Advances in experimental social psychology* (Vol. 37, pp. 255–343). San Diego, CA: Academic Press.

Brown, R.J. (1995). *Prejudice: Its social psychology* (Chp. 8). Oxford: Blackwell.

Brown, R.J. (2000). *Group processes* (2nd edn). Oxford: Blackwell.

Brown, R.J. & Wootton-Millward, L. (1993). Perceptions of group homogeneity during group formation and change. *Social Cognition*, *11*, 126–149.

Bruner, J.S., Goodnow, J.J., & Austin, G.A. (1956). *A study of thinking.* New York: Wiley.

Bryan, J. & Test, M.A. (1967). Models and helping: Naturalistic studies in aiding behavior. *Journal of Personality and Social Psychology, 6*, 400–407.

Buccino, G., Binkofski, F., Fink, G.R., Fadiga, L., Fogassi, L., Gallese, V., Seitz, R.J., Zilles, K., Rizzolatti, G. & Freund, H.J. (2001). Action observation activates premotor and parietal areas in a somatotopic manner: An fMRI study. *European Journal of Neuroscience, 13*, 400–404.

Buriel, R.W., Perez, W., DeMent, T., Chavez, D., & Moran, V. (1998). The relationship of language brokering to academic performance, biculturalism, and self-efficacy among Latino adolescents. *Hispanic Journal of Behavioral Sciences, 20*, 283–297.

Bushman, B.J. & Baumeister, R.F. (1998). Threatened egotism, narcissism, self-esteem, and direct and displaced aggression: Does self-love or self-hate lead to violence? *Journal of Personality and Social Psychology, 75*, 219–229.

Bushman, B.J., Baumeister, R.F., & Stack, A.D. (1999). Catharsis, aggression, and persuasive influence: Self-fulfilling or self-defeating prophecies? *Journal of Personality and Social Psychology, 76*, 367–376.

Bushman, B.J. & Cooper, H.M. (1990). Effects of alcohol on human aggression: An integrative research review. *Psychological Bulletin, 107*, 341–354.

Buss, D.M. (1989). Sex differences in human mate preferences: Evolutionary hypotheses tested in 37 cultures. *Behavioural and Brain Sciences, 12*, 1–49.

Buunk, B.P. (2001). Affiliation, attraction and close relationships. In M. Hewstone & W. Strocbe (Eds.), *Introduction to social psychology* (3rd edn, pp. 371–400). Oxford: Blackwell.

Buunk, B.P., Collins, R., VanYperen, N.W., Taylor, S.E., & Dakoff, G. (1990). Upward and downward comparisons: Either direction has its ups and downs. *Journal of Personality and Social Psychology, 59*, 1238–1249.

Buunk, B.P. & Van den Eijnden, R.J.J.M. (1997). Perceived prevalence, perceived superiority, and relationship satisfaction: Most relationships are good, but ours is the best. *Personality and Social Psychology Bulletin, 23*, 219–228.

Buunk, B.P. & VanYperen, N.W. (1991). Referential comparisons, relational comparisons and exchange orientation: Their relation to marital satisfaction. *Personality and Social Psychology Bulletin, 17*, 710–718.

Byrne, D. & Nelson, D. (1965). Attraction as a linear function of proportion of positive reinforcements. *Journal of Personality and Social Psychology, 1*, 659–663.

Cacioppo, J.T., Marshall-Goodell, B.S., Tassinary, L.G., & Petty, R.E. (1992). Rudimentary determinants of attitudes: Classical conditioning is more effective when prior knowledge about the attitude stimulus is low than high. *Journal of Experimental Social Psychology, 28*, 207–233.

Cadinu, M.R. & Rothbart, M. (1996). Self-anchoring and differentiation process in the minimal group setting. *Journal of Personality and Social Psychology, 70*, 661–677.

Calkin, B. (1985). 'Joe Lunch Box': Punishment and resistance in prisons. *Race Gender Class, 1*, 5–16.

Cameron, L. & Rutland, A. (2006). Extended contact through story reading in school: Reducing children's prejudice toward the disabled. *Journal of Social Issues, 62*, 469–488.

Campbell, A., Muncer, S., Guy, A., & Banim, M. (1996). Social representations of aggression: Crossing the sex barrier. *European Journal of Social Psychology, 26*, 135–147.

Campbell, A., Sapochnik, M., & Muncer, S. (1997). Sex differences in aggression: Does social representation mediate form of aggression? *British Journal of Social Psychology, 36*, 161–171.

Campbell, L., Simpson, J.A., Boldry, J.G., & Kashy, D. (2005). Perceptions of conflict and support in romantic relationships: The role of attachment anxiety. *Journal of Personality and Social Psychology, 88*, 510–531.

Caprara, G.V., Barbaranelli, C., & Zimbardo, P.G. (1996). Understanding the complexity of human aggression: Affective, cognitive, and social dimensions of individual differences in propensity towards aggression. *European Journal of Personality*, *10*, 133–155.

Caprara, G.V., Perugini, M., & Barbaranelli, C. (1994). Studies of individual differences in aggression. In M. Potegal & J.F. Knutson (Eds.), *The dynamics of aggression: Biological and social processes in dyads and groups* (pp. 123–153). Hillsdale, NJ: Erlbaum.

Carli, L.L., Ganley, R., & Pierce-Otay, A. (1991). Similarity and satisfaction in roommate relationships. *Personality and Social Psychology Bulletin*, *17*, 419–426.

Carlsmith, J.M. & Anderson, C.A. (1979). Ambient temperature and the occurrence of collective violence: A new analysis. *Journal of Personality and Social Psychology*, *37*, 337–344.

Carlson, M., Charlin, V., & Miller, N. (1988). Positive mood and helping behavior: A test of six hypotheses. *Journal of Personality and Social Psychology*, *55*, 211–229.

Carter, L. & Nixon, M. (1949). Ability, perceptual, personality, and interest factors associated with different criteria of leadership. *Journal of Psychology*, *27*, 377–388.

Carver, C.S. & Glass, D.C. (1978). Coronary-prone behaviour pattern and interpersonal aggression. *Journal of Personality and Social Psychology*, *36*, 361–366.

Carver, C.S. & Scheier, M.F. (1981). *Attention and self-regulation: A control theory approach to human behaviour*. New York: Springer.

Carver, C.S. & Scheier, M.F. (1998). *On the self-regulation of behaviour*. Cambridge: Cambridge University Press.

Cate, R.M., Lloyd, S.A., & Long, E. (1988). The role of rewards and fairness in developing premarital relationships. *Journal of Marriage and the Family*, *50*, 443–452.

Chaiken, S. (1979). Communicator physical attractiveness and persuasion. *Journal of Personality and Social Psychology*, *37*, 1387–1397.

Chaiken, S. (1980). Heuristic versus systematic information processing and the use of source versus message cues in persuasion. *Journal of Personality and Social Psychology*, *39*, 752–766.

Chaiken, S. & Baldwin, M.W. (1981). Affective-cognitive consistency and effect of salient behavioural information on the self-perception of attitudes. *Journal of Personality and Social Psychology*, *41*, 1–12.

Chaiken, S., Pomerantz, E.M., & Giner-Sorolla, R. (1995). Structural consistency and attitude strength. In R.E. Petty & J.A. Krosnick (Eds.), *Attitude strength: Antecedents and consequences* (pp. 387–412). Mahwah, NJ: Erlbaum.

Chappell, K.D. & Davis, K.E. (1998). Attachment partner choice, and partner perception: An experimental test of the attachment-security hypothesis. *Personal Relationships*, *5*, 327–342.

Chartrand, T.L. & Bargh, J.A. (1999). The chameleon effect: The perception-behaviour link and social interaction. *Journal of Personality and Social Psychology*, *76*, 893–910.

Chemers, M.M. (2001). Leadership effectiveness: An integrative review. In M.A. Hogg & S. Tindale (Eds.), *Blackwell handbook of social psychology: Group processes*. Malden, MA: Blackwell.

Chemers, M.M., Watson, C.B., & May, S. (2000). Dispositional affect and leadership effectiveness: A comparison of self-esteem, optimism and efficacy. *Personality and Social Psychology Bulletin*, *26*, 267–277.

Chen, H., Yates, B.T., & McGinnies, E. (1988). Effects of involvement on observers' estimates of consensus, distinctiveness, and consistency. *Personality and Social Psychology Bulletin*, *14*, 468–478.

Chen, S.C. (1937). Social modification of the activity of ants in nest-building. *Physiological Zoology*, *10*, 420–436.

Cialdini, R.B., Borden, R.J., Thorne, A., Walker, M.R., Freeman, S., & Sloan, L.R. (1976). Basking in reflected glory: Three football field studies. *Journal of Personality and Social Psychology*, *34*, 366–375.

Cialdini, R.B. & Kenrick, D.T. (1976). Altruism as hedonism: A social development perspective on the relationship of negative mood state and helping. *Journal of Personality and Social Psychology*, *34*, 907–914.

Clement, R.W. & Krueger, J. (2000). The primacy of self-referent information in perceptions of social consensus. *British Journal of Social Psychology*, *39*, 279–299.

Clore, G.L. (1976). Interpersonal attraction: An overview. In J.W. Thibaut, J.T. Spence, & R.T. Carson (Eds.), *Contemporary topics in social psychology* (pp. 135–175). Morristown, NJ: General Learning Press.

Cogan, J.C., Bhalla, S.K., Sefa-Dedeh, A., & Rothblum, E.D. (1996). A comparison study of United States and African students on perceptions of obesity and thinness. *Journal of Cross-Cultural Psychology*, *27*, 98–113.

Cohen, C.E. (1981). Person categories and social perception: Testing some boundary conditions of the processing effects of prior knowledge. *Journal of Personality and Social Psychology*, *40*, 441–452.

Cohen, D., Nisbett, R.E., Bowdle, B.F., & Schwarz, N. (1996). Insult, aggression, and the southern culture of honor: An 'experimental ethnography'. *Journal of Personality and Social Psychology*, *70*, 945–960.

Cohn, E.G. (1993). The prediction of police calls for service: The influence of weather and temporal variables on rape and domestic violence. *Journal of Environmental Psychology*, *13*, 71–83.

Cohn, E.G. & Rotton, J. (1997). Assault as a function of time and temperature: A moderator-variable time-series analysis. *Journal of Personality and Social Psychology*, *72*, 1322–1334.

Comer, D.R. (1995). A model of social loafing in real work groups. *Human Relations*, *48*, 647–667.

Condor, S., Figgou, L., Gibson, S., & Stevenson, C. (2006). 'They're not racist. . .': Prejudice denial, mitigation and suppression in dialogue. *British Journal of Social Psychology*, *45*, 441–462.

Cook, S.W. (1978). Interpersonal and attitudinal outcomes in cooperating interracial groups. *Journal of Research and Development in Education*, *12*, 97–113.

Cook, S.W. & Pelfry, M. (1985). Reactions to being helped in cooperating interracial groups: A context effect. *Journal of Personality and Social Psychology*, *49*, 1231–1245.

Cotton, S., Cunningham, J.D., & Antill, J. (1993). Network structure, network support and the marital satisfaction of husbands and wives. *Australian Journal of Psychology*, *45*, 176–181.

Cottrell, N.B. (1972). Social facilitation. In C.G. McClintock (Ed.), *Experimental social psychology* (pp. 185–236). New York: Holt.

Cottrell, N.B., Wack, D.L., Sekerak, G.J., & Rittle, R.H. (1968). Social facilitation of dominant responses by the presence of an audience and the mere presence of others. *Journal of Personality and Social Psychology*, *9*, 245–250.

Coyne, S.M., Nelson, D.A., Lawton, F., Haslam, S., Rooney, L., Titterington, L., Trainor, H., Remnant, J., & Ogunlaja, L. (2008). The effect of viewing physical and relational aggression in the media: Evidence for a cross-over effect. *Journal of Experimental Social Psychology*, *44*, 1551–1554.

Cramer, R.E., McMaster, M.R., Bartell, P.A., & Dragna, M. (1988). Subject competence and minimization of the bystander effect. *Journal of Applied Social Psychology*, *18*, 1133–1148.

Crandall, J.E. (1970). Preference and expectancy arousal: Further evidence. *Journal of General Psychology*, *83*, 267–268.

Crano, W.D. & Prislin, R. (2006). Attitudes and persuasion. *Annual Review of Psychology*, *57*, 345–374.

Crawford, M. & Unger, R. (2004). *Women and gender: A feminist psychology*. Boston: McGraw-Hill.

Crisp, R.J. & Abrams, D. (2008). Improving intergroup attitudes and reducing stereotype threat: An integrated contact model. In W. Stroebe & M. Hewstone (Eds.), *European Review of Social Psychology* (Vol. 19, pp. 242–284). Hove: Psychology Press (Taylor & Francis).

Crisp, R.J. & Beck, S.R. (2005). Reducing intergroup bias: The moderating role of ingroup identification. *Group Processes and Intergroup Relations*, *8*, 173–185.

Crisp, R.J., Heuston, S., Farr, M.J., & Turner, R.N. (2007). Seeing red or feeling blue: Differentiated intergroup emotions and ingroup identification in soccer fans. *Group Processes and Intergroup Relations*, *10*, 9–26.

Crisp, R.J. & Hewstone, M. (1999). Subcategorization of physical stimuli: Category differentiation and decategorization processes. *European Journal of Social Psychology*, *29*, 665–671.

Crisp, R.J. & Hewstone, M. (2001). Multiple categorization and implicit intergroup bias: Differential category dominance and the positive-negative asymmetry effect. *European Journal of Social Psychology*, *31*, 45–62.

Crisp, R.J. & Hewstone, M. (2007). Multiple social categorization. In M.P. Zanna (Ed.), *Advances in experimental social psychology* (Vol. 39, pp. 163–254). Orlando, FL: Academic Press.

Crisp, R.J., Hewstone, M., & Rubin, M. (2001). Does multiple categorization reduce intergroup bias? *Personality and Social Psychology Bulletin*, *27*, 76–89.

Crisp, R.J., Stone, C.H., & Hall, N.R. (2006). Recategorization and subgroup identification: Predicting and preventing threats from common ingroups. *Personality and Social Psychology Bulletin*, *32*, 230–243.

Crisp, R.J. & Turner, R.N. (2009). Can imagined interactions produce positive perceptions? Reducing prejudice through simulated social contact. *American Psychologist*, *64*, 231–240.

Crocker, J., Major, B., & Steele, C. (1998). Social stigma. In F. Fiske, D. Gilbert, & G. Lindzey (Eds.) *Handbook of social psychology* (Vol. 2, pp. 504–553). Boston, MA: McGraw-Hill.

Cunningham, W.A., Johnson, M.K., Raye, C.L., Gatenby, J.C., Gore, J.C., & Banaji, M.R. (2004). Separable neural components in the processing of black and white faces. *Psychological Science*, *15*, 806–813.

Cutrona, C. (1982). Transition to college: Loneliness and the process of social adjustment. In L.A. Peplau & D. Perlman (Eds.), *Loneliness: A sourcebook of current theory, research and therapy* (pp. 291–309). New York: John Wiley.

Darley, J.M. & Latané, B. (1969). Bystander intervention in emergencies: Diffusion of responsibility. *Journal of Personality and Social Psychology*, *8*, 100–108.

Das, E., Bushman, B.J., Bezemer, M.D., Kerkhof, P., & Vermeulen, I.E. (2009). How terrorism news reports increase prejudice against outgroups: A terror management account. *Journal of Experimental Social Psychology*, *45*, 453–459.

DePalma, M.T., Madey, S.F., Tillman, T.C., & Wheeler, J. (1999). Perceived patient responsibility and belief in a just world affect helping. *Basic and Applied Social Psychology*, *21*, 131–137.

Derlega, V. & Chaikin, A.L. (1976). Norms affecting self-disclosure in men and women. *Journal of Consulting and Clinical Psychology*, *44*, 376–380.

Derlega, V., Lewis, R.J., Harrison, S., Winstead, B.A. & Costanza, R. (1989). Gender differences in the initiation and attribution of tactile intimacy. *Journal of Nonverbal Behaviour*, *13*, 83–96.

Deschamps, J.-C. & Doise, W. (1978). Crossed category memberships in intergroup relations. In H. Tajfel (Ed.), *Differentiation between social groups* (pp. 141–158). Cambridge: Cambridge University Press.

Deutsch, M. & Gerard, H.B. (1955). A study of normative and informational influences upon individual judgment. *Journal of Abnormal and Social Psychology*, *51*, 629–636.

Devine, P.G. (1989). Stereotypes and prejudice: Their automatic and controlled components. *Journal of Personality and Social Psychology*, *56*, 5–18.

Devine, P.G., & Monteith, M.J. (1999). Automaticity and control in stereotyping. In S. Chaiken & Y. Trope (Eds.), *Dual-process theories in social psychology* (pp. 339–360). New York: Guilford Press.

DeWall, C.N. & Bushman, B.J. (2009). Hot under the collar in a lukewarm environment: Words associated with hot temperature increase aggressive thoughts and hostile perceptions. *Journal of Experimental Social Psychology.* DOI: 10.1016/j.jesp.2009.05.003

Dijksterhuis, A. & Van Knippenberg, A. (1998). The relation between perception and behavior, or how to win a game of trivial pursuit. *Journal of Personality and Social Psychology, 74*, 865–877.

Dill, K.E., Brown, B.P., & Collins, M.A. (2008). Effects of exposure to sex-stereotyped video game characters on tolerance of sexual harassment. *Journal of Experimental Social Psychology, 44*, 1402–1408.

Dill, K.E. & Thill, K.P. (2007). Video game characters and the socialization of gender roles: Young people's perceptions mirror sexist media depictions. *Sex Roles, 57*, 851–865.

Dindia, K. & Allen, M. (1992). Sex differences in self-disclosure: A meta-analysis. *Psychological Bulletin, 112*, 106–124.

Dion, K. (1972). Physical attractiveness and evaluation of children's transgressions. *Journal of Personality and Social Psychology, 24*, 207–213.

Dion, K., Berscheid, E., & Walster, E. (1972). What is beautiful is good. *Journal of Personality and Social Psychology, 24*, 285–290.

Dittes, J.E. (1959). Attractiveness of a group as function of self-esteem and acceptance by group. *Journal of Abnormal and Social Psychology, 59*, 77–82.

Dittes, J.E. & Kelley, H.H. (1956). Effects of different conditions of acceptance upon conformity to group norms. *Journal of Abnormal and Social Psychology, 53*, 100–107.

Dodd, T., Nicholas, S., Povey, D., & Walker, A. (2004). *Crime in England and Wales 2003/04.* London: Home Office.

Doherty, R.W., Hatfield, E., Thompson, K., & Choo, P. (1994). Cultural and ethical influences on love and attachment. *Personal Relationships, 1*, 391–398.

Doise, W. (1976). *L'articulation psychosociologique et les relations entre groupes.* Brussels: De Boeck.

Doise, W. (1978). *Groups and individuals: Explanations in social psychology.* Cambridge: Cambridge University Press.

Dollard, J., Doob, L.W., Miller, N.E., Mowrer, O.H., & Sears, R.R. (1939). *Frustration and aggression.* New Haven, CT: Yale University Press.

Donnerstein, E. & Berkowitz, L. (1981). Victim reactions in aggressive erotic films as a factor in violence against women. *Journal of Personality and Social Psychology, 41*, 710–724.

Dovidio, J.F., Evans, N.E., & Tyler, R.B. (1986). Racial stereotypes: The contents of their cognitive representations. *Journal of Experimental Social Psychology, 22*, 22–37.

Dovidio, J.F. & Gaertner, S.L. (Eds.) *Prejudice, discrimination and racism.* New York: Academic Press.

Dovidio, J.F., Gaertner, S.L., Isen, A.M., & Lowrance, R. (1995). Group representations and intergroup bias: Positive affect, similarity, and group size. *Personality and Social Psychology Bulletin, 21*, 856–865.

Dovidio, J.F., Piliavin, J.A., Schroeder, D.A., & Penner, L.A. (2006). *The social psychology of prosocial behavior.* New York: Psychology Press.

Duck, S. (1992). *Human relationships* (2nd ed.). London: Sage.

Duck, S. & Wright, P.H. (1993). Reexamining gender differences in same-gender relationships: A close look at two kinds of data. *Sex Roles, 28*, 709–727.

Dutton, D.G. & Aron, A.P. (1974). Some evidence for heightened sexual attraction under conditions of high anxiety. *Journal of Personality and Social Psychology, 28*, 510–517.

Dwyer, J. & Flynn, K. (2005). *102 minutes: The untold story of the fight to survive inside the twin towers*. New York: Holt.

Eagly, A.H. & Chaiken, S. (1993). *The psychology of attitudes.* Fort Worth: Harcourt, Brace, Jovanovich.

Eagly, A.H. & Crowley, M. (1986). Gender and helping behavior: A meta-analytic review of the social psychological literature. *Psychological Bulletin, 117*, 125–145.

Eagly, A.H. & Steffen, V.J. (1986). Gender and aggressive behaviour: A meta-analytic review of social psychological literature. *Psychological Bulletin, 100*, 309–330.

Eatough, V. & Smith, J. (2006). 'I was like a wild, wild person': Understanding feelings of anger using interpretative phenomenological analysis. *British Journal of Psychology, 97*, 483–498.

Echabe, A.E. & Garate, J.F.V. (1994). Private self-consciousness as moderator of the importance of attitude and subjective norm: The prediction of voting. *European Journal of Social Psychology, 24*, 285–293.

Eisenberg, N., Guthrie, I.K., Murphy, B.C., Shepard, S.A., Cumberland, A., & Carlo, G. (1999). Consistency and development of prosocial dispositions: A longitudinal study. *Child Development, 70*, 1360–1372.

Eisenberger, N.I., Lieberman, M.D., & Williams, K.D. (2003). Does rejection hurt? An fMRI study of social exclusion. *Science, 302*, 290–292.

Eiser, J.R., Van der Pligt, J., & Gossop, M.R. (1979). Categorization, attitude, and memory for the source of attitude statements. *European Journal of Social Psychology, 9*, 243–251.

Elliot, J.A. & Niesta, D. (2008). Romantic red: Red enhances men's attraction to women. *Journal of Personality and Social Psychology, 95*, 1150–1164.

Ellis, J. & Fox, P. (2001). The effect of self-identified sexual orientation on helping behavior in a British sample: Are lesbians and gay men treated differently? *Journal of Applied Social Psychology, 31*, 1238–1247.

Emswiller, T., Deaux, K., & Willits, J.E. (1971). Similarity, sex, and requests for small favors. *Journal of Applied Social Psychology, 1*, 284–291.

Ensari, N. & Miller, N. (2001). Decategorization and the reduction of bias in the crossed categorization paradigm. *European Journal of Social Psychology, 31*, 193–216.

Equality Rights Advocate (2009). *Know your rights: Sexual harassment at work.* Retrieved 20 July 2009 from http://www.equalrights.org/publications/kyr/shwork.asp

Fazio, R. (1990). Multiple processes by which attitudes guide behavior: The MODE model as an interpretative framework. In M.P. Zanna (Ed.), *Advances in Experimental Social Psychology* (Vol. 23, pp. 75–109). San Diego, CA: Academic Press.

Fazio, R.H. (1995). Attitudes as object-evaluation associations: Determinants, consequences, and correlates of attitude accessibility. In R.E. Petty and J.A. Krosnick (Eds.), *Attitude strength: Antecedents and consequences* (pp. 247–282). Mahwah, NJ: Erlbaum.

Fazio, R.H., Jackson, J.R., Dunton, B.C., & Williams, C.J. (1995). Variability in automatic activation as an unobtrusive measure of racial attitudes: A bona fide pipeline? *Journal of Personality and Social Psychology, 69*, 1013–1027.

Fazio, R.H., Powell, M.C., & Herr, P.M. (1983). Toward a process model of the attitude-behavior relation: Accessing one's attitude upon mere observation of the attitude object. *Journal of Personality and Social Psychology, 44*, 723–735.

Fazio, R.H., Sanbonmatsu, D.M., Powell, M.C., & Kardes, F.R. (1986). On the automatic activation of attitudes. *Journal of Personality and Social Psychology, 50*, 229–238.

Fazio, R.H. & Williams, C.J. (1986). Attitude accessibility as a moderator of the attitude-perception and attitude-behaviour relationship: An investigation of the 1984 presidential election. *Journal of Personality and Social Psychology, 51*, 505–514.

Fehr, B. (1996). *Friendship process*. Thousand Oaks, CA: Sage.

Feingold, A. (1992). Good-looking people are not what we think. *Psychological Bulletin, 111*, 304–341.

Ferguson, T., Berlin, J., Noles, E., Johnson, J., Reed, W., & Spicer, C.V. (2005). Variation in the application of the 'promiscuous female' stereotype and the nature of the application domain: Influences on sexual harassment judgments after exposure to the Jerry Springer Show. *Sex Roles, 52*, 477–487.

Feshbach, S. and Singer, R. (1971). *Television and aggression*. San Francisco, CA: Jossey-Bass.

Festinger, L. (1954). A theory of social comparison processes. *Human Relations, 7*, 117–140.

Festinger, L. (1957). *A theory of cognitive dissonance*. Stanford, CA: Stanford University Press.

Festinger, L. & Carlsmith, J.M. (1959). Cognitive consequences of forced compliance. *Journal of Abnormal and Social Psychology, 58*, 203–210.

Festinger, L., Schachter, S., & Back, K. (1950). *Social pressures in informal groups: A study of human factors in housing*. New York: Harper.

Fiedler, F.E. (1965). The contingency model: A theory of leadership effectiveness. In H. Proshansky & B. Seidenberg (Eds.), *Basic studies in social psychology*. New York: Holt.

Fielding, K.S. & Hogg, M.A. (1997). Social identity, self categorization, and leadership: A field study of small interactive groups. *Group Dynamics: Theory, Research, and Practice, 1*, 39–51.

Fincham, F.D. & Bradbury, T.N. (1991). Cognition in marriage: A program of research on attributions. In W.H. Jones and D. Perlman (Eds.), *Advances in personal relationships* (Vol. 2, pp. 159–204). London: Jessica Kingsley.

Fine, G.A. & Holyfield, L. (1996). Secrecy, trust, and dangerous leisure: Generating group cohesion in voluntary organisations. *Social Psychology Quarterly, 59*, 22–38.

Finkenauer, C., Kerkhof, P., Righetti, F., & Branje, S. (2009). Living together apart: Perceived concealment as a signal of exclusion in marital relationships. *Personality and Social Psychology Bulletin*. DOI: 10.1177/0146167209339629

Fishbein, M. & Ajzen, I. (1974). Attitudes toward objects as predictors of single and multiple behavioral criteria. *Psychological Review, 81*, 59–75.

Fishbein, M. & Ajzen, I. (1975). *Belief, attitude, intention and behaviour: An introduction to theory and research*. Reading, MA: Addison-Wesley.

Fishbein, M. & Coombs, F.S. (1974). Basis for decision: An attitudinal analysis of voting behaviour. *Journal of Applied Social Psychology, 4*, 95–124.

Fisher, H. (2004). *Why we love: The nature and chemistry of romantic love*. New York: Holt.

Fiske, S.T., Lin, M., & Neuberg, S.L. (1999). The continuum model: Ten years later. In S. Chaiken & Y. Trope (Eds.), *Dual-process theories in social psychology* (pp. 231–254). New York: Guilford Press.

Fiske, S.T. & Neuberg, S.L. (1989). Category-based and individuating processes as a function of information and motivation: Evidence from our laboratory. In D. Bar-Tal, C.F. Graumann, A.W. Kruglanski, & W. Stroebe (Eds.), *Stereotypes and prejudices: Changing conceptions* (pp. 83–104). New York: Springer-Verlag.

Fiske, S.T. & Neuberg, S.L. (1990). A continuum of impression formation, from category-based to individuating processes: Influences of information and motivation on attention and interpretation. In L. Berkowitz (Ed.), *Advances in experimental social psychology* (Vol. 23, pp. 1–74). New York: Academic Press.

Fiske, S.T. & Taylor, S.E. (1991). *Social cognition* (2nd ed.). New York: McGraw-Hill.

Ford, C.S. & Beach, F.A. (1951). *Patterns of sexual behavior*. New York: Harper.

Forgas, J.P. (1992). Affect and social perception: Research evidence and an integrative theory. In W. Stroebe & M. Hewstone (Eds.), *European Review of Social Psychology* (Vol. 3, pp. 183–223). Chichester: Wiley.

Freud, S. (1921). Group psychology and the analysis of the ego. In J. Strachey (Ed.), *Standard edition of the complete psychological works* (Vol. 18, pp. 1953–1964). London: Hogarth Press.

Freud, S. (1930). *Civilization and its discontents.* London: Hogarth Press.

Frieze, I.H., Olson, J.E., & Russell, J. (1991). Attractiveness and income for men and women in management. *Journal of Applied Social Psychology, 21*, 1039–1057.

Froming, W.J., Corley, E.B., & Rinker, L. (1990). The influence of public self-consciousness and the audience's characteristics on withdrawal from embarrassing situations. *Journal of Personality, 58*, 603–622.

Furnham, A., Moutafi, J., & Baguma, P. (2002). A cross-cultural study of the role of weight and waist-to-hip ratio on female attractiveness. *Personality and Individual Differences, 32*, 729–745.

Gaertner, S. & Bickman, L. (1971). Effects of race on the elicitation of helping behavior: The wrong number technique. *Journal of Personality and Social Psychology, 20*, 218–222.

Gaertner, S.L. & Dovidio, J.F. (1977). The subtlety of white racism, arousal, and helping behaviour. *Journal of Personality and Social Psychology, 35*, 691–707.

Gaertner, S.L. & Dovidio, J.F. (1986). The aversive form of racism. In J.F. Dovidio & S.L. Gaertner (Eds.) *Prejudice, discrimination and racism: Theory and research* (pp. 61–89). Orlando, FL: Academic Press.

Gaertner, S.L. & Dovidio, J.F. (2000). *Reducing intergroup bias: The common ingroup identity model.* New York: Psychology Press.

Gaertner, S.L., Mann, J.A., Murrell, A.J., & Dovidio, J.F. (1989). Reducing intergroup bias: The benefits of recategorization. *Journal of Personality and Social Psychology, 57*, 239–249.

Gaertner, S.L. & McLaughlin, J.P. (1983). Racial stereotypes: Associations and ascriptions of positive and negative characteristics. *Social Psychology Quarterly, 46*, 23–40.

Garcia, S.D. & Khersonsky, D. (1997). 'They are a lovely couple': Further examination of perceptions of couple attractiveness. *Journal of Social Behaviour and Personality, 12*, 367–380.

Garcia, S.M., Weaver, K., Moskowitz, G.B., & Darley, J.M. (2002). Crowded minds: The implicit bystander effect. *Journal of Personality and Social Psychology, 83*, 843–853.

Gardner, W.L., Gabriel, S., & Lee, A.Y. (1999). 'I' value freedom but 'we' value relationships: Self-construal priming mirrors cultural differences in judgment. *Psychological Science, 10*, 321–326.

Gates, M.F. & Allee, W.C. (1933). Conditioned behaviour of isolated and grouped cockroaches on a simple maze. *Journal of Comparative Psychology, 15*, 331–358.

Gelles, R.J. (1997). *Intimate violence in families* (3rd ed.). Thousand Oaks, CA: Sage.

Gelles, R.J. & Straus, M.A. (1979). Determinants of violence in the family: Toward a theoretical integration. In W.R. Burr, R. Hill, F.I. Nye, & I.L. Reiss (Eds.), *Contemporary theories about the family* (Vol. 1, pp. 549–581). New York: Free Press.

Gelles. R.J. & Straus, M.A. (1988). *Intimate violence.* New York: Simon & Schuster.

Gentile, D.A., Anderson, C.A., Yukawa, S., Nobuko, I., Saleem, M., Ming, L.K., Shibuya, A., Liau, A.K., Khoo, A., Bushman, B.J., Huesmann, L.R., & Sakamoto, A. (2009). The effects of prosocial video games on prosocial behaviors: International evidence from correlational, longitudinal, and experimental studies. *Personality and Social Psychology Bulletin, 35*, 752–763.

Giancola, P.R. & Zeichner, A. (1997). The biphasic effects of alcohol on human physical aggression. *Journal of Abnormal Psychology, 106*, 598–607.

Gibbons, F.X., Carver, C.S., Scheier, M.F., & Hormuth, S.E. (1979). Self-focussed attention and the placebo effect: Fooling some of the people some of the time. *Journal of Experimental Social Psychology, 15*, 263–274.

Gilbert, D.T. (1989). Thinking lightly about others: Automatic components of the social inference process. In J. Uleman & J. Bargh (Eds.), *Unwanted thought: Limits of awareness, intention, and control* (pp. 189–211). New York: Guilford Press.

Gilbert, D.T. & Hixon, J.G. (1991). The trouble of thinking: Activation and application of stereotypic beliefs. *Journal of Experimental Social Psychology, 60,* 509–517.

Gil-Burmann, C., Peláez, F., & Sánchez, S. (2002). Mate choice differences according to sex and age: An analysis of personal advertisements in Spanish newspapers. *Human Nature, 13,* 493–508.

Glaser, B.G., & Strauss, A. (1967). *The discovery of grounded theory: Strategies for qualitative research.* Chicago: Aldine Publishing Co.

Glass, D.C. & Singer, J.E. (1973). Experimental studies of uncontrollable and unpredictable noise. *Representative Research in Social Psychology, 4,* 165–183.

Gleason, K.A., Jensen-Campbell, L.A., & Richardson, D.S. (2004). Agreeableness as a predictor of aggression in adolescence. *Aggressive Behavior, 30,* 43–61.

Glick, P., Diebold, J., Bailey-Werner, B., & Zhu, L. (1997). The two faces of Adam: Ambivalent sexism and polarized attitudes towards women. *Personality and Social Psychology Bulletin, 23,* 1323–1334.

Gonsalkorale, K. & Williams, K.D. (2007). The KKK won't let me play: Ostracism even by a despised outgroup hurts. *European Journal of Social Psychology, 37,* 1176–1186.

Gorer, G. (1968). Man has no 'killer' instinct. In M.F.A. Montagu (Ed.), *Man and aggression* (pp. 27–36). New York: Oxford University Press.

Gouldner, A.W. (1960). The norm of reciprocity: A preliminary statement. *American Sociological Review, 25,* 161–178.

Green, R.G. (1998). Aggression and antisocial behavior. In D.T. Gilbert, S.T. Fiske, & G. Lindzey (Eds.), *The handbook of social psychology* (4th ed., Vol. 2, pp. 317–356). New York: McGraw-Hill.

Green, D.P., Glaser, J., & Rich, A. (1998). From lynching to gay bashing: The elusive connection between economic conditions and hate crime. *Journal of Personality and Social Psychology, 75,* 82–92.

Greenberg, J., Pyszczynski, T., & Solomon, S. (1986). The causes and consequences of self-esteem: A terror management theory. In R. Baumeister (Ed.), *Public self and private self* (pp. 189–212). New York: Springer.

Greenberg, J., Pyszczynski, T., Solomon, S., Rosenblatt, A., Veeder, M., Kirkland, S., et al. (1990). Evidence for terror management II: The effects of mortality salience on reactions to those who threaten or bolster the cultural worldview. *Journal of Personality and Social Psychology, 58,* 308–318.

Greenwald, A.G., McGhee, D.E., & Schwartz, J.L.K. (1998). Measuring individual differences in implicit cognition: The implicit association test. *Journal of Personality and Social Psychology, 74,* 1464–1480.

Greitemeyer, T. (2009). Effects of songs with prosocial lyrics on prosocial thoughts, affect, and behavior. *Journal of Experimental Social Psychology, 45,* 186–190.

Greitemeyer, T. & Osswald, S. (2009). Prosocial video games reduce aggressive cognitions. *Journal of Experimental Social Psychology.* DOI: 10.1016/j.jesp.2009.04.005.

Gross, S.R. & Miller, N. (1997). The 'golden section' and bias in perceptions of social consensus. *Personality and Social Psychology Review, 1,* 241–271.

Gruber-Baldini, A.L., Schaie, K.W., & Willis, S.L. (1995). Similarity in married couples: A longitudinal study of mental abilities and rigidity-flexibility. *Journal of Personality and Social Psychology, 69,* 191–203.

Grush, J.E., McKeough, K.L., & Ahlering, R.F. (1978). Extrapolating laboratory exposure to actual political elections. *Journal of Personality and Social Psychology, 36,* 257–270.

Gunnar, M.R. (2000). Early adversity and the development of stress reactivity and regulation. In C.A. Nelson (Ed.), *The effects of adversity on neurobehavioral development: Minnesota symposia on child psychology* (Vol. 31, pp. 163–200). Mahwah, NJ: Erlbaum.

Gustavo, C. (1999). Consistency and development of prosocial dispositions: A longitudinal study. *Child Development, 70,* 1360–1372.

Hall, N.R. & Crisp, R.J. (2005). Considering multiple criteria for social categorization can reduce intergroup bias. *Personality and Social Psychology Bulletin, 31,* 1435–1444.

Hamilton, D.L. (2004). *Social cognition: Essential readings.* Philadelphia, PA: Psychology Press.

Hamilton, D.L. & Gifford, R.K. (1976). Illusory correlation in interpersonal personal perception: A cognitive basis of stereotypic judgements. *Journal of Experimental Social Psychology, 12,* 392–407.

Harding, J., Kutner, B.M., Proshansky, H., & Chein, I. (1954). Prejudice and ethnic relations. In G. Lindzey (Ed.), *Handbook of social psychology* (pp. 1021–1061). Cambridge, MA: Addison-Wesley.

Harmon-Jones, E., Greenberg, J., Solomon, S., & Simon, L. (1996). The effects of mortality salience on intergroup bias between minimal groups. *European Journal of Social Psychology, 25,* 781–785.

Harries, K.D. & Stadler, S.J. (1983). Determinism revisited: Assault and heat stress in Dallas, 1980. *Environment and Behaviour, 15,* 235–256.

Hastie, R. & Kumar, P.A. (1979). Person memory: The processing of consistent and inconsistent person information. *Journal of Personality and Social Psychology, 37,* 25–38.

Hatfield, E. (1988). Passionate and compassionate love. In R.J. Sternberg & M.L. Barnes (Eds.), *The psychology of love* (pp. 191–217). New Haven, CT: Yale University Press.

Hatfield, E. & Rapson, R.L. (1993). *Love, sex, and intimacy: Their psychology, biology, and history.* New York: HarperCollins.

Hatfield, E. & Walster, G.W. (1981). *A new look at love.* Reading, MA: Addison Wesley.

Hau, K.T. & Salili, F. (1991). Structure and semantic differential placement of specific causes: Academic causal attributions by Chinese students in Hong Kong. *Journal of Personality and Social Psychology, 63,* 308–319.

Haugtvedt, C.P. & Petty, R.E. (1992). Personality and persuasion: need for cognition moderates the persistence and resistance of attitude changes. *Journal of Personality and Social Psychology, 63,* 308–319.

Hayes, J., Schimel, J., & Williams, T. J. (2008). Fighting death with death: The buffering effects of learning that worldview violators have died. *Psychological Science, 19,* 501–507.

Heider, F. (1958). *The psychology of interpersonal relations.* New York: Wiley.

Heider, F. & Simmel, M. (1944). An experimental study of apparent behavior. *American Journal of Psychology, 57,* 243–259.

Heimpel, S.A., Wood, J.V., Marshall, M.A., & Brown, J.D. (2002). Do people with low self-esteem really want to feel better? Self-esteem differences in motivation to repair negative moods. *Journal of Personality and Social Psychology, 82,* 128–147.

Heingartner, A. & Hall, J.V. (1974). Affective consequences in adults and children of repeated exposure to auditory stimuli. *Journal of Personality and Social Psychology, 29,* 719–723.

Heuer, L. & Penrod, S. (1994). Trial complexity: A field investigation of its meaning and its effect. *Law and Human Behaviour, 18,* 29–51.

Hewstone, M. (1989). *Casual attribution: From cognitive processes to collective beliefs.* Oxford: Blackwell.

Hewstone, M. (1990). The 'ultimate attribution error': A review of the literature on intergroup causal attribution. *European Journal of Social Psychology, 20,* 311–335.

Hewstone, M. (1996). Contact and categorization: Social psychological interventions to change intergroup relations. In C.N. Macrae, C. Stangor, & M. Hewstone (Eds.), *Stereotypes and stereotyping* (pp. 323–368). New York: Guilford Press.

Hewstone, M. & Brown, R. (1986). Contact is not enough: An intergroup perspective on the 'contact hypothesis'. In M. Hewstone and R. Brown (Eds.), *Contact and conflict in intergroup encounters* (pp. 1–44). Oxford: Blackwell.

Hewstone, M. & Jaspars, J.M.F. (1982). Intergroup relations and attribution processes. In H. Tajfel (Ed.), *Social identity and intergroup relations* (pp. 99–133). Cambridge: Cambridge University Press.

Hewstone, M., Macrae, C.N., Griffiths, R.J., Milne, A.B., & Brown, R. (1994). Cognitive models of stereotype change: Measurement, development and consequences of subtyping. *Journal of Experimental Social Psychology, 30*, 505–526.

Hewstone, M., Rubin, M., & Willis, H. (2002). Intergroup bias. *Annual Review of Psychology, 53*, 575–604.

Higgins, E.T. (1987). Self-discrepancy: A theory relating self and affect. *Psychological Review, 94*, 319–340.

Higgins, E.T., Bond, R.N., Klein, R., & Strauman, T. (1986). Self-discrepancies and emotional vulnerability: How magnitude, accessibility, and type of discrepancy influence affect. *Journal of Personality and Social Psychology, 51*, 5–15.

Hofstede, G. (1980). *Culture's consequences: International differences in work-related values*. Beverly Hills, CA: Sage.

Hogg, M.A. (1992). The social psychology of group cohesiveness: From attraction to social identity. London: Harvester Wheatsheaf.

Hogg, M.A. (2000). Subjective uncertainty reduction through self-categorization: A motivational theory of social identity processes. *European Review of Social Psychology, 11*, 223–255.

Hogg, M.A. (2001). Social categorization, depersonalization, and group behavior. In M.A. Hogg & R.S. Tindale (Eds.), *Blackwell handbook of social psychology: Group processes* (pp. 56–85). Oxford: Blackwell.

Hogg, M.A. (2002). Social identity. In M.R. Leary & J.P. Tangney (Eds.), *Handbook of self and identity* (pp. 462–479). New York: Guilford Press.

Hogg, M.A. & Abrams, D. (1988). *Social identifications: A social psychology of intergroup relations and group processes*. London: Routledge.

Hogg, M.A. & Abrams, D. (1993). Towards a single-process uncertainty-reduction model of social motivation. In M.A. Hogg & D. Abrams (Eds.), *Group motivation* (pp. 173–190). New York: Harvester Wheatsheaf.

Hogg, M.A., & Mullin, B.A. (1999). Joining groups to reduce uncertainty: Subjective uncertainty reduction and group identification. In D. Abrams & M.A. Hogg (Eds.), *Social identity and social cognition* (pp. 249–279). Malden, MA: Blackwell.

Hogg, M.A. & Van Knippenberg, D. (2003). Social identity and leadership processes in groups. *Advances in Experimental Social Psychology, 35*, 1–52.

Holloway, S., Tucker, L., & Hornstein, H.A. (1977). The effects of social and nonsocial information on interpersonal behavior of males: The news makes news. *Journal of Personality and Social Psychology, 35*, 514–522.

Hong, Y., Morris, M.W., Chiu, C., & Benet-Martinez, V. (2000). Multicultural minds: A dynamic constructivist approach to culture and cognition. *American Psychologist, 55*, 709–720.

Hornstein, H.A. (1970). The influence of social models on helping. In J. Macaulay & L. Berkowitz (Eds.), *Altruism and helping behaviour* (pp. 29–42). New York: Academic Press.

Horowitz, I.A. & Bordens, K.S. (1990). An experimental investigation of procedural issues in complex tort trials. *Law and Human Behavior, 14*, 269–285.

Hovland, C.I. & Sears, R.R. (1940). Minor studies in aggression: VI. Correlation of lynchings with economic indices. *Journal of Psychology, 9*, 301–310.

Hovland, C.I. & Weiss, W. (1951). The influence of source credibility on communication effectiveness. *Public Opinion Quarterly*, *15*, 635–650.

Howard, J.W. & Rothbart, M. (1980). Social categorization and memory for ingroup and outgroup behaviour. *Journal of Personality and Social Psychology*, *38*, 301–310.

Hull, C.L. (1943). *Principles of behaviour: An introduction to behaviour therapy*. New York: Appleton-Century-Crofts.

Hull, J.G. (1981). A self-awareness model of the causes and effects of alcohol consumption. *Journal of Abnormal Psychology*, *90*, 586–600.

Hymowitz, C. & Schellhardt, T.D. (1986). The glass ceiling: Special report on the corporate woman. *The Wall Street Journal*, 24 March.

Ingram, R.E. & Kendall, P.C. (1987). The cognitive side of anxiety. *Cognitive Therapy and Research*, *11*, 523–536.

Isen, A.M. (1970). Success, failure, attention, and reaction to others: The warm glow of success. *Journal of Personality and Social Psychology*, *15*, 294–301.

Isen, A.M., Clark, M., & Schwartz, M. (1976). Duration of the effect of good mood on helping: 'Footprints on the sand of time'. *Journal of Personality and Social Psychology*, *34*, 385–393.

Jackson, J.M. & Williams, K.D. (1985). Social loafing on difficult tasks: Working collectively can improve performance. *Journal of Personality and Social Psychology*, *49*, 937–942.

Jackson, S.E., Brett, J.F., Sessa, V.I., Cooper, D.M., Julin, J.A., & Peyronnin, K. (1991). Some differences make a difference: Individual dissimilarity and group heterogeneity as correlates of recruitment, promotions, and turnover. *Journal of Applied Psychology*, *76*, 675–689.

Janis, I. (1982). *Groupthink* (2nd ed.). Boston, MA: Houghton Mifflin.

Jankowski, M.S. (1991). *Islands in the streets: Gangs and American urban society*. Berkeley, CA: University of California Press.

Jarvis, W.B.G. & Petty, R.E. (1995). The need to evaluate. *Journal of Personality and Social Psychology*, *70*, 172–192.

Jetten J., Spears R., & Manstead, A.S.R. (1996). Intergroup norms and intergroup discrimination: Distinctive self-categorization and social identity effects. *Journal of Personality and Social Psychology*, *71*, 1222–1233.

Jetten, J., Spears, R., & Postmes, T. (2004). Intergroup distinctiveness and differentiation: A meta-analytic integration. *Journal of Personality and Social Psychology*, *86*, 862–879.

Johnson, D.J. & Rusbult, C.E. (1989). Resisting temptation: Devaluation of alternative partners as a means of maintaining commitment in close relationships. *Journal of Personality and Social Psychology*, *57*, 967–980.

Johnson, D.L., Wiebe, J.S., Gold, S.M., Andreasen, N.C., Hichwa, R.D., Watkins, G.L., et al. (1999). Cerebral blood flow and personality: A positron emission tomography study. *American Journal of Psychiatry*, *156*, 252–257.

Johnson, M.P. (1991). Commitment to personal relationship. In W.H. Jones & D. Perlman (Eds.), *Advances in personal relationships* (Vol. 3, pp. 117–143). London: Jessica Kingsley.

Johnston, L. & Hewstone, M. (1992). Cognitive models of stereotype change (3): Subtyping and the perceived typicality of disconfirming group members. *Journal of Experimental Social Psychology*, *28*, 360–386.

Jonas, E., Schimel, J., Greenberg, J., & Pyszczynski, T. (2002). The Scrooge effect: Evidence that mortality salience increases prosocial attitudes and behavior. *Personality and Social Psychology Bulletin*, *28*, 1342–1353.

Jones, E.E. & Davis, K.E. (1965). From acts to dispositions: The attribution process in person perception. In L. Berkowitz (Ed.), *Advances in experimental social psychology* (Vol. 2, pp. 219–266). New York: Academic Press.

Jones, E.E. & Goethals, G.R. (1972). Order effects in impression formation: Attribution context and the nature of the entity. In E.E. Jones, D.E. Kanouse, H.H. Kelley, R.E. Nisbett, S. Valins & B. Weiner (Eds.), *Attribution: Perceiving the causes of behaviour* (pp. 27–46). Morristown, NJ: General Learning Press.

Jones, E.E. & Harris, V.A. (1967). The attribution of attitudes. *Journal of Experimental Social Psychology*, *3*, 1–24.

Jones, E.E. & Nisbett, R.E. (1972). The actor and the observer: Divergent perceptions of the causes of behaviour. In E.E. Jones, D.E. Kanouse, H.H. Kelley, R.E. Nisbett, S. Valins & B. Weiner (Eds.), *Attribution: Perceiving the causes of behaviour* (pp. 79–94). Morristown, NJ: General Learning Press.

Jones, E.E., Wood, G.C., & Quattrone, G.A. (1981). Perceived variability of personal characteristics in ingroups and outgroups: The role of knowledge and evaluation. *Personality and Social Psychology Bulletin*, *7*, 523–528.

Judge, T.A., Bono, J.E., Ilies, R., & Gerhardt, M. (2002). Personality and leadership: A qualitative and quantitative review. *Journal of Applied Psychology*, *87*, 765–780.

Judge, T.A. & Cable, D.M. (2004). The effect of physical height on workplace success and income: Preliminary test of a theoretical model. *Journal of Applied Psychology*, *89*, 428–441.

Kacmar, K.M., Witt, L.A., Zivnuska, S., & Gully, S.M. (2003). The interactive effect of leader-member exchange and communication frequency on performance ratings. *Journal of Applied Psychology*, *88*, 764–772.

Kahneman, D. (1973). *Attention and effort*. Englewood Cliffs, NJ: Prentice Hall.

Kahneman, D. & Tversky, A. (1973). On the psychology of prediction. *Psychological Review*, *80*, 237–51.

Kandel, D.B. (1978). Similarity in real-life adolescent friendship pairs. *Journal of Personality and Social Psychology*, *36*, 306–312.

Karau, S.J. & Williams, K.D. (1995). Social loafing: Research findings, implications, and future directions. *Current Directions in Psychological Science*, *4*, 134–140.

Karpinski, A. & Hilton, J.L. (2001). Attitudes and the implicit association test. *Journal of Personality and Social Psychology*, *81*, 774–788.

Karremans, J. C. & Verwijmeren, T. (2008). Mimicking attractive opposite-sex others: The role of romantic relationship status. *Personality and Social Psychology Bulletin*, *34*, 939–950.

Karremans, K.C., Verwijmeren, T., Pronk, T.M., & Reitsma, M. (2009). Interacting with women can impair men's cognitive function. *Journal of Experimental Social Psychology*. DOI: 10.1016/j.jesp.2009.05.004

Kassin, S.M. (1979). Consensus information, prediction, and causal attribution: A review of the literature and issues. *Journal of Personality and Social Psychology*, *37*, 1966–1981.

Katz, D. (1960). The functional approach to the study of attitudes. *Public Opinion Quarterly*, *24*, 163–204.

Katz, J. (1988). *Seductions of crime: Moral and sensual attractions in doing evil*. New York: Basic Books.

Kazdin, A.E. & Bryan, J. (1971). Competence and volunteering. *Journal of Experimental Social Psychology*, *7*, 87–97.

Kelley, H.H. (1967). Attribution theory in social psychology. In D. Levine (Ed.), *Nebraska symposium on motivation* (pp. 192–238). Lincoln, NE: University of Nebraska Press.

Kelley, H.H. & Michela, J. L. (1980). Attribution theory and research. *Annual Review of Psychology*, *31*, 457–501.

Kelman, H.C. & Hovland, C.I. (1953). 'Reinstatement' of the communicator in delayed measurement of opinion change. *Journal of Abnormal and Social Psychology*, *48*, 327–335.

Kennedy, J.K. (1982). Middle LPC leaders and the contingency model of leadership effectiveness. *Organizational Behavior and Human Performance, 30,* 1–14.

Kernis, M.H. & Paradise, A.W. (2002). Distinguishing between fragile and secure forms of high self-esteem. In E.L. Deci and R.M. Ryan (Eds.), *Handbook of self-determination research* (pp. 339–360). Rochester, NY: University of Rochester Press.

Kerr, N.L. (1992). Norms in social dilemmas. In D. Schroeder (Ed.), *Social dilemmas: Psychological perspectives.* New York: Praeger.

Kirschner, D. (1992). Understanding adoptees who kill: Dissociation, patricide, and the psychodynamics of adoption. *International Journal of Offender Therapy and Comparative Criminology, 36,* 323–333.

Kitson, G.C. & Holmes, W.M. (1992). *Portrait of divorce: Adjustment to marital breakdown.* New York: Guilford Press.

Kjaer, T., Nowak, M., & Lou, H. (2002). Reflective self-awareness and conscious states: PET evidence for a common midline parietofrontal core. *NeuroImage, 17,* 1080–1086.

Kleinpenning, G. & Hagendoorn, L. (1993). Forms of racism and the cumulative dimension of ethnic attitudes. *Social Psychology Quarterly, 56,* 21–36.

Klohnen, E.C. & Bera, S. (1998). Behavioural and experiential patterns of avoidantly and securely attached women across adulthood: A 31-year longitudinal perspective. *Journal of Personality and Social Psychology, 74,* 211–223.

Krebs, D.L. (1975). Empathy and altruism. *Journal of Personality and Social Psychology, 32,* 1134–1146.

Krueger, J. & Clement, R.W. (1996). Inferring category characteristics from sample characteristics: Inductive reasoning and social projection. *Journal of Experimental Psychology – General, 125,* 52–68.

Krueger, J. & Rothbart, M. (1988). Use of categorical and individuating information in making inferences about personality. *Journal of Personality and Social Psychology, 55,* 187–195.

Kruglanski, A.W. (1996). Motivated social cognition: Principles of the interface. In E.T. Higgins & A.W. Kruglanski (Eds.), *Social psychology: Handbook of basic principles* (pp. 493–520). New York: Guilford Press.

Kruglanski, A.W., Webster, D.W. & Klem, A. (1993). Motivated resistance and openness to persuasion in the presence or absence of prior information. *Journal of Personality and Social Psychology, 65,* 861–876.

Labov, W. (1973). The boundaries of words and their meanings. In C-J.N. Bailey & R.W. Shuy (Eds.), *New ways of analyzing variation in English* (Vol. 1, pp. 340–373). Washington, DC: Georgetown University Press.

LaFromboise, T., Coleman, H.L., & Gerton, J. (1993). Psychological impact of biculturalism: Evidence and theory. *Psychological Bulletin, 114,* 395–412.

Lamm, H. & Weismann, U. (1997). Subjective attributes of attraction: How people categorize their liking, their love, and their being in love. *Personal Relationships, 4,* 271–284.

Landy, D. & Sigall, H. (1974). Beauty is talent: Task evaluation as a function of the performer's physical attractiveness. *Journal of Personality and Social Psychology, 29,* 299–304.

Lang, A.R., Goeckner, D.J., Adesso, V.J., & Marlatt, G.A. (1975). Effects of alcohol on aggression in male social drinkers. *Journal of Abnormal Psychology, 84,* 508–518.

Langlois, J.H., Roggman, L.A., & Musselman, L. (1994). What is average and what is not average about attractive faces? *Psychological Science, 5,* 214–220.

LaPierre, R.T. (1934). Attitudes vs actions. *Social Forces, 13,* 230–237.

Larson, R., Csikszentmihalyi, M., & Graef, R. (1982). Time alone in daily experience: Loneliness or renewal? In L.A. Peplau & D. Perlman (Eds.), *Loneliness: A sourcebook of current theory, research and therapy* (pp. 40–53). New York: Wiley-Interscience.

Latané, B. (1981). The psychology of social impact. *American Psychologist*, *36*, 343–356.

Latané, B. & Darley, J.M. (1968). Group inhibition of bystander intervention in emergencies. *Journal of Personality and Social Psychology*, *10*, 215–221.

Latané, B. & Darley, J.M. (1970). *The unresponsive bystander: Why doesn't he help?* Englewood Cliffs, NJ: Prentice Hall.

Latané, B. & Darley, J.M. (1976). Help in a crisis: Bystander response to an emergency. In J.W. Thibaut & J.T. Spence (Eds.), *Contemporary topics in social psychology* (pp. 309–332). Morristown, NJ: General Learning Press.

Latané, B. & Nida, S. (1981). Social impact theory and group influence: A social engineering perspective. In P.B. Paulus (Ed.), *Psychology of group influence*. Hillsdale, NJ: Erlbaum.

Latané, B., Williams, K., & Harkins, S. (1979). Many hands make light work: The causes and consequences of social loafing. *Journal of Personality and Social Psychology*, *37*, 822–832.

Laurenceau, J.P., Barrett, L.F., & Pietromonaco, P.R. (1998). Intimacy as an interpersonal process: The importance of self-disclosure, partner disclosure, and perceived partner responsiveness in interpersonal exchanges. *Journal of Personality and Social Psychology*, *74*, 1238–1251.

Lawrence, C. & Andrews, K. (2004). The influence of perceived prison crowding on male inmates' perception of aggressive events. *Aggressive Behavior*, *30*, 273–283.

Lee, J.A. (1977). A typology of styles of loving. *Personality and Social Psychology Bulletin*, *3*, 173–182.

Lerner, M.J. & Miller, D.T. (1978). Just world research and the attribution process. Looking back and ahead. *Psychological Bulletin*, *85*, 1030–1051.

Levine, J.M. & Moreland, R.L. (Eds.) (2006). *Small groups: Key readings*. Philadelphia, PA: Psychology Press.

Levine, R.A. & Campbell, D.T. (1972). *Ethnocentrism: Theories of conflict, attitudes and group behavior*. New York: Wiley.

Lewis, M. & Brooks, J. (1978). Self-knowledge in emotional development. In M. Lewis & L. Rosenblum (Eds.), *The development of affect* (pp. 205–226). New York: Plenum.

Lickel, B., Hamilton, D.L., Lewis, A., Sherman, S.J., Wierczorkowska, G., & Uhles, A.N. (2000). Varieties of groups and the perception of group entitativity. *Journal of Personality and Social Psychology*, *78*, 223–246.

Liden, R.C., Sparrowe, R.T., & Wayne, S.J. (1997). Leader-member exchange theory: The past and potential for the future. *Research in Personnel and Human Resources Management*, *15*, 47–119.

Lieberman, A. & Chaiken, S. (1996). The direct effect of personal relevance on attitudes. *Personality and Social Psychology Bulletin*, *22*, 269–280.

Linville, P.W., Fischer, G.W., & Salovey, P. (1989). Perceived distributions of the characteristics of the ingroup and outgroup members: Empirical evidence and a computer simulation. *Journal of Personality and Social Psychology*, *57*, 165–188.

Lippitt, R. & White, R. (1943). The 'social climate' of children's groups. In R.G. Barker, J. Kounin, & H. Wright (Eds.), *Child behavior and development* (pp. 485–508). New York: McGraw-Hill.

Long, D. (1990). *The anatomy of terrorism*. New York: Free Press.

Looby, E.J. (2001). The violence of sexual harassment: Physical, emotional, and economic victimization. In D.S. Sandhu (Ed.), *Faces of violence: Psychological correlates, concepts, and intervention strategies*. Hauppauge, NY: Nova Science

Lorenzo-Hernandez, J. (1998). How social categorization may inform the study of Hispanic immigration. *Hispanic Journal of Behavioral Sciences*, *20*, 39–60.

Lucas, R.E. (2005). Time does not heal all wounds: A longitudinal study of reaction and adaptation to divorce. *Psychological Science*, *16*, 945–950.

Lydon, J.E., Fitzsimons, G.M., & Naidoo, L. (2003). Devaluation versus enhancement of attractive alternatives. A critical test using the calibration paradigm. *Personality and Social Psychology Bulletin, 29*, 349–359.

Lynn, M. & Mynier, K. (1993). Effect of server posture on restaurant tipping. *Journal of Applied Social Psychology, 23*, 678–685.

Maass, A. & Clark, R.D. III. (1984). Hidden impact of minorities: Fifteen years of minority influence research. *Psychological Bulletin, 95*, 428–450.

MacDonald, J.M. (1975). *Armed robbery: Offenders and their victims.* Springfield, IL: Charles C. Thomas.

Macrae, C.N., Bodenhausen, G.V., Milne, A.B., & Jetten, J. (1994). Out of mind but back in sight: Stereotypes on the rebound. *Journal of Personality & Social Psychology, 67*, 808–817.

Macrae, C.N., Hewstone, M., & Griffiths, R.J. (1993). Processing load and memory for stereotype-based information. *European Journal of Social Psychology, 23*, 77–87.

Macrae, C.N., Milne, A.B. & Bodenhausen, G.V. (1994). Stereotypes as energy-saving devices: A peek inside the cognitive toolbox. *Journal of Personality and Social Psychology, 66*, 37–47.

Malamuth, N.M. & Addison, T. (2001). Integrating social psychological research on aggression within an evolutionary-based framework. In G.J.O. Fletcher & M.S. Clark (Eds.), *Blackwell handbook of social psychology: Interpersonal processes* (pp. 129–161). Malden, MA: Blackwell.

Malamuth, N.M. & Check, J.V.P. (1981). The effects of mass media exposure on acceptance of violence against women: A field experiment. *Journal of Research in Personality, 15*, 436–446.

Mandler, G. (1975). Consciousness: Respectable, useful, and probably necessary. In R. Solso (Ed.), *Information processing and cognition: The Loyola Symposium.* Hillsdale, NJ: Erlbaum.

Mann, L. (1981). The baiting crowd in episodes of threatened suicide. *Journal of Personality and Social Psychology, 41*, 703–709.

Mann, L., Newton, J.W., & Innes, J.M. (1982). A test between deindividuation and emergent norm theories of crowd aggression. *Journal of Personality and Social Psychology, 42*, 260–272.

Mann, R.D. (1959). A review of the relationship between personality and performance in small groups. *Psychological Bulletin, 56*, 241–270.

Marks, G. & Miller, N. (1987). Ten years of research on the false-consensus effect: An empirical and theoretical review. *Psychological Bulletin, 2*, 165–177.

Markus, H. (1977). Self-schemata and processing information about the self. *Journal of Personality and Social Psychology, 35*, 63–78.

Markus, H. & Sentis, K.P. (1982). The self in social information processing. In J. Suls (Ed.), *Psychological perspectives of the self* (Vol. 1, pp. 41–70). Hillsdale, NJ: Erlbaum.

Martin, R. & Hewstone, M. (2003a). Majority versus minority influence: When, not whether, source status instigates heuristic or systematic processing. *European Journal of Social Psychology, 33*, 313–330.

Martin, R. & Hewstone, M. (2003b). Social influence processes of control and change: Conformity, obedience to authority, and innovation. In M.A. Hogg & J. Cooper (Eds.), *The Sage handbook of social psychology* (pp. 347–366). London: Sage.

Martinez, A.R. (1987). The effects of acculturation and racial identity on self-esteem and psychological well-being among young Puerto Ricans. *Dissertation Abstracts International, 49*, 9163.

Mausner, B. (1954). The effect of one partner's success in a relevant task on the interaction of observer pairs. *Journal of Abnormal and Social Psychology, 49*, 557–560.

Maxwell, G.M. & Coebergh, B. (1986). Patterns of loneliness in a New Zealand population. *Community Mental Health in New Zealand, 2*, 48–61.

McArthur, L.A. (1972). The how and what of why: Some determinants of consequences of causal attributions. *Journal of Personality and Social Psychology, 22,* 171–193.

McConnell, A.R. & Leibold, J.M. (2001). Relations among the implicit association test, discriminatory behaviour, and explicit measures of racial attitude. *Journal of Experimental Social Psychology, 37,* 435–442.

McDougall, W. (1908). *An introduction to social psychology.* London: Cambridge University Press.

McGarty, C. (1999). *Categorization in social psychology.* London: Sage.

McKenna, K.Y.A., Green, A.S., & Gleason, M.E.J. (2002). Relationship formation on the internet: What's the big attraction? *Journal of Social Issues, 58,* 9–31.

McNally, A.M., Palfai, T.P., Levine, R.V., & Moore, B.M. (2003). Attachment dimensions and drinking-related problems among young adults: The mediational role of coping motives. *Addictive Behaviors, 28,* 1115–1127.

Mehl, M.R. & Pennebaker, J.W. (2003). The sounds of social life: A psychometric analysis of students' daily social environments and natural conversations. *Journal of Personality and Social Psychology, 84,* 857–870.

Meyer, J.P. & Koebl, S.L.M. (1982). Dimensionality of students' causal attributions for test performance. *Personality and Social Psychology Bulletin, 8,* 31–36.

Michaels, J.W., Blommel, J.M., Brocato, R.M., Linkous, R.A., & Rowe, J.S. (1982). Social facilitation and inhibition in a natural setting. *Replications in Social Psychology, 2,* 21–24.

Milgram, S. (1963). Behavioral study of obedience. *Journal of Abnormal and Social Psychology, 67,* 371–378.

Milgram, S. (1970). The experience of living in cities. *Science, 167,* 1461–1468.

Milgram, S. (1974). *Obedience to authority: An experimental view.* London: Tavistock Publications.

Millar, K.U., Tesser, A., & Millar, M.G. (1988). The effects of a threatening life event on behavior sequences and intrusive thought: A self–disruption explanation. *Cognitive Therapy and Research, 12,* 441–457.

Miller, J.G. (1984). Culture and the development of everyday social explanation. *Journal of Personality and Social Psychology, 46,* 961–978.

Mikulincer, M. (1998). Adult attachment style and individual differences in functional versus dysfunctional experiences of anger. *Journal of Personality and Social Psychology, 74,* 513–524.

Mikulincer, M. & Arad, D. (1999). Attachment, working models, and cognitive openness in close relationships: A test of chronic and temporary accessibility effects. *Journal of Personality and Social Psychology, 77,* 710–725.

Mischel, W., Ebbesen, E.B., & Zeiss, A.R. (1976). Determinants of selective memory about the self. *Journal of Consulting and Clinical Psychology, 44,* 92–103.

Mita, T.H., Dermer, M., & Knight, J. (1977). Reversed facial images and the mere exposure hypothesis. *Journal of Personality and Social Psychology, 35,* 597–601.

Mitchell, J.P., Banaji, M.R., & Macrae, C.N. (2005). General and specific contributions of the medial prefrontal cortex to knowledge about mental states. *NeuroImage, 28,* 757–762.

Moghaddam, F.M. (1998). *Social psychology: Exploring universals across cultures.* New York: Freeman.

Moghaddam, F.M. (2005). The staircase to terrorism: A psychological exploration. *American Psychologist, 60,* 161–169.

Monteith, M.J. (1993). Self-regulation of prejudiced responses: Implications for progress in prejudice-reduction efforts. *Journal of Personality and Social Psychology, 65,* 469–485.

Morling, B. & Epstein, S. (1997). Compromises produced by the dialectic between self-verification and self-enhancement. *Journal of Personality and Social Psychology, 73,* 1268–1283.

Morris, M.W. & Peng, K.P. (1994). Culture and cause: American and Chinese attributions for social and physical events. *Journal of Personality and Social Psychology, 67*, 949–971.

Moscovici, S. (1961). *La psychanalyse, son image et son public*. Paris: Presses Universitaires de France.

Moscovici, S. (1980). Toward a theory of conversion behavior. In L. Berkowitz (Ed.), *Advances in experimental social psychology* (Vol. 13, pp. 209–239). New York: Academic Press.

Moscovici, S., Lage, E., & Naffrechoux, M. (1969). Influence of a consistent minority on the responses of a majority in a color perception task. *Sociometry, 32*, 365–379.

Moskowitz, G.B., Gollwitzer, P.M., Wasel, W., & Schaal, B. (1999). Preconscious control of stereotype activation through chronic egalitarian goals. *Journal of Personality and Social Psychology, 77*, 167–184.

Muehlenhard, C.L. & Hollabaugh, L.C. (1988). Do women sometimes say no when they mean yes? The prevalence and correlates of women's token resistance to sex. *Journal of Personality and Social Psychology, 54*, 872–879.

Mueller, J.H. & Thompson, W.B. (1984). Test anxiety and distinctiveness of personal information. In H.M. Ploeg, R. Schwarzer, & C.D. Spielberger (Eds.), *Advances in test anxiety research* (Vol. 3, pp. 21–37). Hillsdale, NJ: Erlbaum.

Mullen, B. & Suls, J. (1982). Know thyself: Stressful life changes and the ameliorative effect of private self-consciousness. *Journal of Experimental Social Psychology, 18*, 43–55.

Mullen, B., Brown, R., & Smith, C. (1992). Ingroup bias as a function of salience, relevance, and status: An integration. *European Journal of Social Psychology, 22*, 103–122.

Mullen, B., Salas, E., & Driskell, J.E. (1989). Salience, motivation, and artefact as contributions to the relation between participation rate and leadership. *Journal of Experimental Social Psychology, 25*, 545–559.

Murray, S.L. & Holmes, J.G. (1997). A leap of faith? Positive illusions in romantic relationships. *Personality and Social Psychology Bulletin, 23*, 586–604.

Murstein, B.I. (1972). Physical attractiveness and marital choice. *Journal of Personality and Social Psychology, 22*, 8–12.

Nadler, A. & Fisher, J.D. (1986). The role of threat to self-esteem and perceived control in recipient reactions to aid: Theory development and empirical validation. In L. Berkowitz (Ed.), *Advances in experimental social psychology* (Vol. 19). New York: Academic Press.

Nemeth, C. (1977). Interactions between jurors as a function of majority vs. unanimity decision rules. *Journal of Applied Social Psychology, 7*, 38–56.

Nemeth, C. (1986). Differential contributions of majority and minority influence processes. *Psychological Review, 93*, 10–20.

Nemeth, C.J. & Wachtler, J. (1983). Creative problem solving as a result of majority vs. minority influence. *European Journal of Social Psychology, 13*, 45–55.

Neumann, R. (2000). The causal influences of attributions on emotions: A procedural priming approach. *Psychological Science, 11*, 179–182.

Newcomb, T.M. (1961). *The acquaintance process*. New York: Holt, Rinehart & Winston.

Ng, B., Kumar, S., Ranclaud, M., & Robinson, E. (2001). Ward crowding and incidents of violence on an acute psychiatric inpatient unit. *Psychiatric Services, 52*, 521–525.

Nieburg, H. (1969). *Political violence: The behavioral process*. New York: St. Martin's Press.

Niedenthal, P.M., Brauer, M., Robin, L., & Innes–Ker, A.H. (2002). Adult attachment and the perception of facial expression of emotion. *Journal of Personality & Social Psychology, 82*, 419–433.

Nisbett, R.E. & Cohen, D. (1996). *Culture of honor: The psychology of violence in the south*. Boulder, CO: Westview Press.

Northouse, P.G. (2001). *Leadership: Theory and practice* (2nd ed.). Thousand Oaks, CA: Sage.

Nosek, B.A., Banaji, M.R., & Greenwald, A.G. (2002). Math = male, me = female, therefore math ≠ me. *Journal of Personality and Social Psychology, 83*, 44–59.

Oakes, P.J. & Turner, J.C. (1990). Is limited information processing capacity the cause of social stereotyping? In W. Stroebe & M. Hewstone (Eds.), *European review of social psychology* (Vol. 1, pp. 111–137). New York: Wiley.

O'Connor, S. & Rosenblood, L. (1996). Affiliation motivation in everyday experience: A theoretical perspective. *Journal of Personality and Social Psychology, 70*, 513–522.

Oliner, S.P. & Oliner, P.M. (1988). *The altruistic personality: Rescuers of Jews in Nazi Europe.* New York: Free Press.

Olson, J.M. (1988). Misattribution, preparatory information, and speech anxiety. *Journal of Personality and Social Psychology, 54*, 758–767.

Olson, J.M. & Ross, M. (1988). False feedback about placebo effectiveness: Consequences for the misattribution of speech anxiety. *Journal of Experimental Social Psychology, 24*, 275–291.

Orne, M.T. (1962). On the social psychology of the psychology experiment: With particular reference to demand characteristics and their implications. *American Psychologist, 17*, 776–783.

Oskamp, S. & Jones, J. M. (2000). Promising practice in reducing prejudice: A report from the President's Initiative on Race. In S. Oskamp (Ed.), *Reducing prejudice and discrimination* (pp. 319–334). Mahwah, NJ: Erlbaum.

Otten, S. & Wentura, D. (1999). About the impact of automaticity in the minimal group paradigm: Evidence from affective priming tasks. *European Journal of Social Psychology, 29*, 1049–1071.

Pantin, H.M. & Carver, C.S. (1982) Induced competence and the bystander effect. *Journal of Applied Social Psychology, 12*, 100–111.

Paolini, S., Hewstone, M., Cairns, E., & Voci, A. (2004). Effects of direct and indirect cross-group friendships on judgements of Catholics and Protestants in Northern Ireland: The mediating role of an anxiety-reduction mechanism. *Personality and Social Psychology Bulletin, 30*, 770–786.

Park, A., Curtice, J., Thomson, K., Jarvis, L., & Bromley, C. (Eds.) (2003). *British social attitudes: The 20th report.* London: Sage.

Park, B. & Judd, C.M. (1990). Measures and models of perceived group variability. *Journal of Personality and Social Psychology, 59*, 173–191.

Park, B. & Rothbart, M. (1982). Perception of outgroup homogeneity and levels of social categorization: Memory for the subordinate attributes of ingroup and outgroup members. *Journal of Personality and Social Psychology, 42*, 1051–1068.

Pavlov, I.P. (1906). The scientific investigation of the psychical faculties or processes in the higher animals. *Science, 24*, 613–619.

Payne, B.K. (2001). Prejudice and perception: The role of automatic and controlled processes in misperceiving a weapon. *Journal of Personality and Social Psychology, 81*, 1–12.

Pendry, L. & Carrick, R. (2001). Doing what the mob do: Priming effects on conformity. *European Journal of Social Psychology, 31*, 83–92.

Penner, L.A., Dovidio, J.F., Piliavin, J.A., & Schroeder, D.A. (2005). Prosocial behaviour: Multilevel perspectives. *Annual Review of Psychology, 56*, 365–392.

Perdue, C.W., Dovidio, J.F., Gurtman, M.B., & Tyler, R.B. (1990). 'Us' and 'them': Social categorization and the process of intergroup bias. *Journal of Personality and Social Psychology, 59*, 475–486.

Perlman, D. & Peplau, L.A. (1998). Loneliness. *Encyclopaedia of mental health* (Vol. 2, pp. 571–581). New York: Academic Press.

Pettigrew, T.F. (1958). Personality and socio-cultural factors in intergroup attitudes: a cross-national comparison. *Journal of Conflict Resolution*, *2*, 29–42.

Pettigrew, T.F. (1997). Generalised intergroup contact effects on prejudice. *Personality and Social Psychology Bulletin*, *23*, 173–185.

Pettigrew, T.F. & Tropp, L.R. (2006). A meta-analytic test of intergroup contact theory. *Journal of Personality and Social Psychology*.

Petty, R.E. & Cacioppo, J.T. (1986a). The elaboration likelihood model of persuasion. In L. Berkowitz (Ed.), *Advances in experimental social psychology* (Vol. 19, pp. 123–205). New York: Academic Press.

Petty, R.E. & Cacioppo, J.T. (1986b). *Communication and persuasion: Central and peripheral routes to attitude change*. New York: Springer.

Petty, R.E., Haugtvedt, C.P., & Smith, S.M. (1995). Elaboration as a determinant of attitude strength: Creating attitudes that are persistent, resistant, and predictive of behaviour. In R. E. Petty & J. A. Krosnick (Eds.), *Attitude strength: Antecedents and consequences*. Hillsdale, NJ: Erlbaum.

Phinney, J.S., Lochner, B., & Murphy, R. (1990). Ethnic identity development and psychological adjustment in adolescence. In A. Stiffman & L. Davis (Eds.), *Ethnic issues in adolescent mental health* (pp. 53–72). Newbury Park, CA: Sage.

Piaget, J. (1965). *The child's conception of number*. New York: Norton.

Pietromonaco, P.R. & Carnelley, K.B. (1994). Gender and working models of attachment: Consequences for perception of self and romantic relationships. *Personal Relationships*, *1*, 3–26.

Piliavin, I.M., Piliavin, J.A., & Rodin, J. (1975). Costs, diffusion and the stigmatized victim. *Journal of Personality and Social Psychology*, *32*, 429–438.

Piliavin, J.A., Piliavin, I.M., Dovidio, J.F., Gaertner, S.L., & Clark, R.D. III (1981). *Emergency intervention*. New York: Academic Press.

Pilner, P. (1982). The effects of mere exposure on liking for edible substances. *Appetite*, *3*, 283–290.

Pishyar, R., Harris, L.M., & Menzies, R.G. (2004). Attentional bias for words and faces in social anxiety. *Anxiety, Stress, and Coping*, *17*, 23–36.

Plant, E.A. & Devine, P.G. (1998). Internal and external motivation to respond without prejudice. *Journal of Personality and Social Psychology*, *75*, 811–832.

Plant, E.A., Devine, P.G., Cox, W.T.L., Columb, C., & Miller, S.L. (2009). The Obama effect: Decreasing implicit prejudice and stereotyping. *Journal of Experimental Social Psychology*. DOI:10.1016/j.jesp.2009.04.018

Plous, S. (1989). Thinking the unthinkable: The effects of anchoring on likelihood estimates of nuclear war. *Journal of Applied Social Psychology*, *19*, 67–91.

Postmes, T., Spears, R., & Lea, M. (2002). Intergroup differentiation in computer- mediated communication: Effects of depersonalization. *Group Dynamics: Theory, Research and Practice*, *6*, 3–16.

Pratto, F., Sidanius, J., Stallworth, L.M., & Malle, B.F. (1994). Social dominance orientation: A personality variable predicting social and political attitudes. *Journal of Personality and Social Psychology*, *67*, 741-763.

Prins, K.S., Buunk, A.P., & VanYperen, N.W. (1992). Equity, normative disapproval and extra-marital sex. *Journal of Social and Personal Relationships*, *10*, 39–53.

Ramirez, M. (1983). *Psychology of the Americas: Mestizo perspectives on personality and mental health* (pp. 93–107). New York: Pergamon Press.

Regan, D.T., Williams, M., & Sparling, S. (1972). Voluntary expiation of guilt: A field experiment. *Journal of Personality and Social Psychology*, *18*, 124–132.

Reicher, S.D., Spears, R., & Postmes, T. (1995). A social identity model of deindividuation phenomena. *European Review of Social Psychology*, *6*, 161–198.

Reis, H.T. & Patrick, B.C. (1996). Attachment and intimacy: Component processes. In E.T. Higgins & A.W. Kruglanski (Eds.), *Social psychology: Handbook of basic principles* (pp. 523–563). New York: Guilford Press.

Renzetti, C.M. (1992). *Violent betrayal: Partner abuse in lesbian relationships*. Newbury Park, CA: Sage.

Rhodes, G. & Tremewan, T. (1996). Averageness, exaggeration, and facial attractiveness. *Psychological Science*, *2*, 105–110.

Robins, R.W., Trzesniewski, K.H., Tracy, J.L., Gosling, S.D., & Potter, J. (2002). Global self-esteem across the lifespan. *Psychology and Aging*, 17, 423–434.

Roccas, S. & Brewer, M. (2002). Social identity complexity. *Personality and Social Psychology Review*, *6*, 88–106.

Rogler, L.H., Cortes, D.E., & Malgady, R.G. (1991). Acculturation and mental health status among Hispanics: Convergence and new directions for research. *American Psychologist*, *46*, 585–597.

Rosch, E. (1978). Principles of categorization. In E. Rosch and B.B. Lloyd (Eds.), *Cognition and categorization* (pp. 27–48). Hillsdale, NJ: Erlbaum.

Ross, E.A. (1908). *Social psychology*. New York: Macmillan.

Ross, L. (1977). The intuitive psychologist and his shortcomings. In L. Berkowitz (Ed.), *Advances in experimental social psychology* (Vol. 10, pp. 174–220). New York: Academic Press.

Ross, L., Greene, D., & House, P. (1977). The 'false consensus effect': An egocentric bias in social perception and attribution processes. *Journal of Experimental Social Psychology*, *13*, 279–301.

Rubin, M. & Hewstone, M. (1998). Social identity theory's self-esteem hypothesis: A review and some suggestions for clarification. *Personality and Social Psychology Review*, *2*, 40–62.

Rusbult, C.E. (1983). A longitudinal test of the investment model: The development (and deterioration) of satisfaction and commitment in heterosexual involvements. *Journal of Personality and Social Psychology*, *45*, 101–117.

Rusbult, C.E. & Martz, J.M. (1995). Remaining in an abusive relationship: An investment model analysis of nonvoluntary dependence. *Personality and Social Psychology Bulletin*, *21*, 558–571.

Rusbult, C.E. & Van Lange, P.A.M. (2003). Interdependence, interaction, and relationships. *Annual Review of Psychology*, *54*, 351–375.

Rusbult, C.E. & Zembrodt, I.M. (1983). Responses to dissatisfaction in romantic involvements: A multi-dimensional scaling analysis. *Journal of Experimental Social Psychology*, *19*, 274–293.

Rushton, J.P. (1989). Genetic similarity in male friendships. *Ethology and Sociobiology*, *10*, 361–373.

Rushton, J.P. & Campbell, A. (1977). Modeling, vicarious reinforcement and extraversion on blood donating in adults: Immediate and long term effects. *European Journal of Social Psychology*, *7*, 297–306.

Rushton, J.P., Russell, R.J., & Wells, P.A. (1984). Genetic similarity theory: Beyond kin selection. *Behavior Genetics*, *14*, 179–193.

Saegert, S., Swap, W., & Zajonc, R. (1973). Exposure, context and interpersonal attraction. *Journal of Personality and Social Psychology*, *25*, 234–242.

Sanchez-Burks, J., Nisbett, R.E., & Ybarra, O. (2000). Cultural styles, relational schemas and prejudice against outgroups. *Journal of Personality and Social Psychology*, *79*, 174–189.

Sanders, G.S. & Baron, R.S. (1975). The motivating effects of distraction on task performance. *Journal of Personality and Social Psychology*, *32*, 956–963.

Sawyer, A.G. (1981). Repetition, cognitive response, and persuasion. In R.E. Petty, T.M. Ostrom, and T.C. Brock (Eds.), *Cognitive responses in persuasion*. Hillsdale, NJ: Erlbaum.

Sbarra, D.A. (2006). Predicting the onset of emotional recovery following nonmarital relationship dissolution: Survival analysis of sadness and anger. *Personality and Social Psychology Bulletin*, *32*, 298–312.

Sbarra, D.A., & Emery, R.E. (2005). The emotional sequelae of non-marital relationship dissolution: Analysis of change and intraindividual variability over time. *Personal Relationships*, *12*, 213–232.

Schachter, S. (1959). *The psychology of affiliation*. Stanford, CA: Stanford University Press.

Schachter, S. (1964). The interaction of cognitive and physiological determinants of emotional state. In L. Berkowitz (Ed.), *Advances in experimental social psychology* (Vol. 1). New York: Academic Press.

Schachter, S. & Singer, J.E. (1962). Cognitive, social and physiological determinants of emotional state. *Psychological Review*, *69*, 379–399.

Scheier, M.F. & Carver, C.S. (1977). Self-focussed attention and the experience of emotion: Attraction, repulsion, elation & depression. *Journal of Personality and Social Psychology*, *35*, 625–636.

Scheier, M.F. & Carver, C.S. (1980). Private and public self-attention, resistance to change, and dissonance reduction. *Journal of Personality and Social Psychology*, *39*, 390–405.

Schmader, T. (2002). Gender identification moderates stereotype threat effects on women's math performance. *Journal of Experimental Social Psychology*, *38*, 194–201.

Schriesheim, C.A., Tepper, B.J., & Tetrault, L.A. (1994). Least preferred coworker score, situational control, and leadership effectiveness: A meta-analysis of contingency model performance predictions. *Journal of Applied Psychology*, *79*, 561–573.

Schwartz, S.H. & David, T.B. (1976). Responsibility and helping in an emergency: Effects of blame, ability and denial of responsibility. *Sociometry*, *39*, 406–415.

Schwarz, N. (1990). Feeling as information: Informational and motivational functions of affective states. In E.T. Higgins & R. Sorrentino (Eds.), *Handbook of motivation and cognition* (Vol. 2, pp. 527–561). New York: Guilford Press.

Schwarz, N., Bless, H., Strack, F., Klumpp, G., Rittenauer-Schatka, H., & Simons, A. (1991). Ease of retrieval as information: Another look at the availability heuristic. *Journal of Personality and Social Psychology*, *61*, 195–202.

Schwarzer, R., Bowler, R., & Rauch, S. (1985). Psychological indicators of acculturation: Self-esteem, racial tension and inter-ethnic contact. In L. Ekstrand (Ed.), *Ethnic minorities and immigrants in a cross-cultural perspective* (pp. 211–229). Lisse: Swets & Zeitlinger.

Sears, D.O. (1983). The person-positivity bias. *Journal of Personality and Social Psychology*, *44*, 233–250.

Sedikides, C. (1993). Assessment, enhancement, and verification determinants of the self-evaluation process. *Journal of Personality and Social Psychology*, *65*, 317–338.

Sedikides, C. & Gregg, A.P. (2002). Internal mechanisms that implicate the self enlighten the egoism-altruism debate. *Behavioral and Brain Sciences*, *25*, 274–275.

Sedikides, C. & Gregg, A.P. (2003). Portraits of the self. In M.A. Hogg & J. Copper (Eds.), *The Sage handbook of social psychology* (pp. 110–138). London: Sage.

Sedikides, C., Olsen, N., & Reis, H.T. (1993). Relationships as natural categories. *Journal of Personality and Social Psychology*, *64*, 71–82.

Shapiro, P.N. & Penrod, S. (1986). Meta-analysis of facial identification studies. *Psychological Bulletin*, *100*, 139–156.

Shaver, P.R. & Mikulincer, M. (2002). Attachment-related psychodynamics. *Attachment and Human Development*, *4*, 133–161.

Sherif, M. (1935). A study of some social factors in perception. *Archives of Psychology*, *27*, 1–60.

Sherif, M. (1966). *In common predicament: Social psychology of intergroup conflict and cooperation*. Boston, MA: Houghton-Mifflin.

Sherif, M. & Sherif, C.W. (1953). *Groups in harmony and tension: An integration of studies of intergroup relations*. Oxford: Harper & Brothers.

Sherif, M., White, B.J., & Harvey, O.J. (1955). Status in experimentally produced groups. *American Journal of Sociology*, *60*, 370–379.

Shotland, R.L. & Hunter, B.A. (1995). Women's 'token resistant' and compliant sexual behaviours are related to uncertain sexual intentions and rape. *Personality and Social Psychology Bulletin*, *21*, 226–236.

Shotland, R.L. & Straw, M.K. (1976). Bystander response to an assault: When a man attacks a woman. *Journal of Personality and Social Psychology*, *34*, 990–999.

Sidanius, J. (1993). The psychology of group conflict and the dynamics of oppression: A social dominance perspective. In S. Iyengar & W. McGuire (Eds.), *Explorations in political psychology* (pp. 183–219). Durham, NC: Duke University Press.

Sidanius, J. & Pratto, F. (1999). *Social dominance: An intergroup theory of social hierarchy and oppression*. New York: Cambridge University Press.

Sidanius, J., Pratto, F., & Brief, D. (1995). Group dominance and the political psychology of gender: A cross-cultural comparison. *Political Psychology*, *16*, 381–396.

Simon, B., Aufderheide, B., & Kampmeier, C. (2001). The social psychology of minority-majority relations. In R. Brown & S. Gaertner (Eds.), *Blackwell handbook of social psychology: Intergroup processes* (pp. 303–323). Oxford: Blackwell.

Simon, R.W., Eder, D., & Evans, C. (1992). The development of feeling norms underlying romantic love among adolescent females. *Social Psychology Quarterly*, *55*, 29–46.

Simons, H.W., Berkowitz, N.N., & Moyer, R.J. (1970). Similarity, credibility, and attitude change: A review and a theory. *Psychological Bulletin*, *73*, 1–16.

Simonton, D.K. (1980). Techno-scientific activity and war: A yearly time-series analysis, 1500–1903 A.D. *Scientometrics*, *2*, 251–255.

Simpson, J.A. & Kenrick, D. (1997). *Evolutionary social psychology*. Mahwah, NJ: Erlbaum.

Singer, H.A. (1948). The veteran and race relations. *Journal of Eductional Sociology*, *21*, 397–408.

Skinner, B.F. (1938). *The behaviour of organisms: An experimental analysis*. New York: Appleton-Century.

Skinner, B.F. (1953). *Science and human behavior*. New York: Macmillan.

Smith, E.R., Coats, S., & Walling, D. (1999). Overlapping mental representations of self, ingroup, and partner: Further response time evidence and a connectionist model. *Personality and Social Psychology Bulletin*, *25*, 873–882.

Smith, E.R. & Henry, S. (1996). An ingroup becomes part of the self: Response time evidence. *Personality and Social Psychology Bulletin*, *22*, 635–642.

Smith, E.E. & Medin, D.L. (1981). *Categories and concepts*. Cambridge, MA: Harvard University Press.

Smith, J.A. & Osborn, M. (2003). Interpretative phenomenological analysis. In J.A. Smith (Ed.), *Qualitative psychology: A practical guide to research methods* (pp. 51–80). London: Sage.

Smith, M.B. (1956). *Opinions and personality*. New York: Wiley.

Smith, S.M., Haugtvedt, C.P., & Petty, R.E. (1994). Humor can either enhance or disrupt message processing: The moderating role of humour relevance. Unpublished manuscript.

Snyder, C.R., Lassegard, M., & Ford, C.E. (1986). Distancing after group success and failure: Basking in reflected glory and cutting off reflected failure. *Journal of Personality and Social Psychology*, *51*, 382–388.

Snyder, M. & DeBono, K.G. (1985). Appeals to image and claims about quality: Understanding the psychology of advertising. *Journal of Personality and Social Psychology, 49,* 586–597.

Snyder, M., Tanke, E.D. & Berscheid, E. (1977). Social perception and interpersonal behaviour: On the self-fulfilling nature of the social stereotype. *Journal of Personality and Social Psychology, 35,* 656–666.

Sorrentino, R.M. & Field, N. (1986). Emergent leadership over time: The functional value of positive motivation. *Journal of Personality and Social Psychology, 50,* 1091–1099.

Srull, T.K. (1981). Person memory: Some tests of associative storage and retrieval models. *Journal of Experimental Psychology: Human Learning and Memory, 7,* 440–463.

Staats, C.K. & Staats, A.W. (1958). Attitudes established by classical conditioning. *Journal of Abnormal and Social Psychology, 57,* 37–40.

Stangor, C., Sullivan, L.A., & Ford, T.E. (1991). Affective and cognitive determinants of prejudice. *Social Cognition, 9,* 359–380.

Stanko, E.A. (2000). *The day to count: A snapshot of domestic violence in the UK.* http://www.domesticviolencedata.org.

Stark, E. (2007). *Coercive control.* New York: Oxford University Press.

Stathi, S. & Crisp, R.J. (2008). Imagining intergroup contact promotes projection to outgroups. *Journal of Experimental Social Psychology, 44,* 943-957.

Staub, E. (1996). Cultural-societal roots of violence: The example of genocidal violence and contemporary youth violence in the United States. *American Psychologist, 51,* 117–132.

Steele, C.M. (1975). Name-calling and compliance. *Journal of Personality and Social Psychology, 31,* 361–369.

Steele, C.M. (1997). A threat in the air: How stereotypes shape intellectual identity and performance. *American Psychologist, 52,* 613–629.

Steele, C.M. & Aronson, J. (1995). Stereotype threat and the intellectual test performance of African Americans. *Journal of Personality and Social Psychology, 69,* 797–811.

Stephan, W.G. & Stephan, C.W. (1985). Intergroup anxiety. *Journal of Social Issues, 41,* 157–176.

Sternberg, R.J. (1986). A triangular theory of love. *Psychological Review, 93,* 119–135.

Stewart, J. E. (1980). Defendant's attractiveness as a factor in the outcome of criminal trials: An observational study. *Journal of Applied Social Psychology, 10,* 348–361.

Stogdill, R.M. (1974) *Handbook of leadership: A survey of theory and research.* New York: Free Press.

Storms, M.D. (1973). Videotape and the attribution process: Reversing actor's and observer's points of view. *Journal of Personality and Social Psychology, 27,* 165–175.

Stouffer, S.A., Suchman, E.A., Devinney, L.C., Star, S.A., & Williams, R.M., Jr. (1949). *The American soldier: Adjustment during army life. (Studies in social psychology in World War II, Vol. 1.).* Princeton, NJ: Princeton University Press.

Strack, F., Martin, S., & Stepper, L.L. (1988). Inhibiting and facilitating conditions of facial expressions: A non-obtrusive test of the facial feedback hypothesis. *Journal of Personality and Social Psychology, 54,* 768–777.

Strack, F., Schwarz, N., & Wanke, M. (1991). Semantic and pragmatic aspects of context effects in social and psychological research. *Social Cognition, 9,* 111–125.

Strassberg, D.S. & Holty, S. (2003). An experimental study of women's internet personal ads. *Archives of Sexual Behavior, 32,* 253–260.

Streeter, S.A. & McBurney, D.H. (2003). Waist-hip ratio and attractiveness: New evidence and a critique of a critical test. *Evolution and Human Behavior, 24,* 88–98.

Sumner, W.G. (1906). *Folkways.* Boston, MA: Ginn.

Sutton, R.M. and McClure, J.L. (2001). Covariational influences on goal-based explanation: An integrative model. *Journal of Personality and Social Psychology, 80,* 222–236.

Swann, W.B. Jr. (1997). The trouble with change: Self-verification and allegiance to the self. *Psychological Science, 8,* 177–183.

Swann, W.B. Jr., De La Ronde, C., & Hixon, J.G. (1994). Authenticity and positive strivings in marriage and courtship. *Journal of Personality and Social Psychology, 66,* 857–869.

Swann, W.B. Jr., Stein-Seroussi, A., & Giesler, R.B. (1992). Why people self-verify. *Journal of Personality and Social Psychology, 62,* 392–401.

Tajfel, H. (1978). *Differentiation between social groups: Studies in the social psychology of intergroup relations.* London: Academic Press.

Tajfel, H., Billig, M., Bundy, R., & Flament, C. (1971). Social categorization and intergroup behaviour. *European Journal of Social Psychology, 1,* 149–178.

Tajfel, H. & Turner, J.C. (1979). An integrative theory of intergroup conflict. The social identity theory of intergroup behaviour. In W.G. Austin & S. Worchel (Eds.), *The social psychology of intergroup relations* (pp. 33–47). Monterey, CA: Brooks/Cole.

Tajfel, H. & Wilkes, A.L. (1963). Classification and quantitative judgement. *British Journal of Social Psychology, 54,* 101–114.

Taylor, S.E. & Fiske, S.T. (1975). Point-of-view and perceptions of causality. *Journal of Personality and Social Psychology, 32,* 439–445.

Taylor, S.E., Fiske, S.T., Close, N.M., Anderson, C.E., & Ruderman, A.J. (1977). Solo status as a psychological variable: The power of being distinctive. Unpublished manuscript, Harvard University, Cambridge, MA.

Teger, A.I. (1970). The effect of early cooperation on the escalation of conflict. *Journal of Experimental Social Psychology, 6,* 187–204.

Terry, D.J., Hogg, M.A., & White, K.M. (1999). The theory of planned behavior: Self-identity, social identity, and group norms. *British Journal of Social Psychology, 38,* 225–244.

Tesser, A. (1988). Toward a self-evaluation maintenance model of social behaviour. In L. Berkowitz (Ed.), *Advances in experimental social psychology* (Vol. 21, pp. 181–227). San Diego, CA: Academic Press.

Tesser, A., Gatewood, R., & Driver, M. (1968). Some determinants of gratitude. *Journal of Personality and Social Psychology, 9,* 233–236.

Thibaut, J.W. & Kelley, H.H. (1959). *The social psychology of groups.* New York: Wiley.

Thompson, S.C. & Kelley, H.H. (1981). Judgements of responsibility for activities in close relationships. *Journal of Personality and Social Psychology, 41,* 469–477.

Thorndike, E.L. (1911). *Animal intelligence: Experimental studies.* New York: Macmillan.

Thornhill, R. & Gangestad, S.W. (1999). The scent of symmetry: A human pheromone that signals fitness? *Evolution and Human Behavior, 20,* 175–201.

Toch, H. (1969). *Violent men.* Chicago: Aldine.

Toi, M. & Batson, C.D. (1982). More evidence that empathy is a source of altruistic motivation. *Journal of Personality and Social Psychology, 43,* 281–292.

Townsend, J.M. & Levy, G.D. (1990). Effects of potential partners' physical attractiveness and socio-economic status on sexuality and partner selection. *Archives of Sexual Behaviour, 19,* 149–164.

Trafimow, D., Triandis, H.C., & Goto, S.G. (1991). Some tests of the distinction between the private self and the collective self. *Journal of Personality and Social Psychology, 60,* 649–655.

Travis, L.E. (1925). The effect of a small audience upon eye–hand coordination. *Journal of Abnormal and Social Psychology, 20,* 142–146.

Triandis, H.C. (1989). The self and social behaviour in differing cultural contexts. *Psychological Review, 96,* 506–520.

Triplett, N. (1897). The dynamogenic factors in pacemaking and competition. *American Journal of Psychology*, *9*, 507–533.

Trivers, R.L. (1972). Parental investment and sexual selection. In B. Campbell (Ed.), *Sexual selection and the descent of man* (pp. 137–179). New York: Aldine de Gruyter.

Trope, Y. (1983). Self-assessment in achievement behavior. In J.M. Suls & A.G. Greenwald (Eds.), *Psychological perspectives on the self* (Vol. 2, pp. 93–121). Hillsdale, NJ: Erlbaum.

Turner, J.C. (1991). *Social influence.* Milton Keynes: Open University Press.

Turner, J.C., Hogg, M.A., Oakes, P.J., Reicher, S.D., & Wetherell, M.S. (1987). *Rediscovering the social group: A self-categorization theory.* Oxford: Basil Blackwell.

Turner, R.N. & Crisp, R.J. (2009). Imagining intergroup contact reduces implicit prejudice. *British Journal of Social Psychology.* DOI: 10.1348/014466609X419901

Turner, R.N., Crisp, R.J., & Lambert, E. (2007). Imagining intergroup contact can improve intergroup attitudes. *Group Processes and Intergroup Relations*, *10*, 427–441.

Turner, R.N., Hewstone, M., & Voci, A. (2007). Reducing explicit and implicit prejudice via direct and extended contact: The mediating role of self-disclosure and intergroup anxiety. *Journal of Personality and Social Psychology*, *93*, 369–388

Turner, R.N., Hewstone, M., Voci, A., Paolini, S. & Christ, O. (2007). Reducing prejudice via direct and extended cross-group friendship. *European Review of Social Psychology*, *18*, 212–255.

Turner, R.N., Hewstone, M., Voci, A., & Vonofakou, C. (2008). A test of the extended intergroup contact hypothesis: The mediating role of intergroup anxiety, perceived ingroup and outgroup norms, and inclusion of the outgroup in the self. *Journal of Personality and Social Psychology*, *95*, 843–860.

Tversky, A. & Kahneman, D. (1973). Availability: A heuristic for judging frequency and probability. *Cognitive Psychology*, *5*, 207–232.

Tversky, A. & Kahneman, D. (1974). Judgement under uncertainty: Heuristics and biases. *Science*, *185*, 1124–1131.

Van den Bos, K., Müller, P.A., & Van Bussel, A.A.L. (2009). Helping to overcome inertia in bystander's dilemmas: Behavioral disinhibition can improve the greater good. *Journal of Experimental Social Psychology.* DOI:10.1016/j.jesp.2009.03.014.

Van den Bos, K., Poortvliet, P.M., Maas, M., Miedema, J., & van den Ham, E-J. (2005). An enquiry concerning the principles of cultural norms and values: The impact of uncertainty and mortality salience on reactions to violations and bolstering of cultural worldviews. *Journal of Experimental Social Psychology*, *41*, 91–113.

Van Straaten, M.A., Engels, R.C.M.E., Finkenauer, C., & Holland, R.W. (2009). Meeting your match: How attractiveness similarity affects approach behaviour in mixed-sex dyads. *Personality and Social Psychology Bulletin*, *35*, 685–697.

Vargas, J.A. (2007). Shadow player. *Washington Post* [online edition]. Retrieved 5 July 2007 from http://www.washingtonpost.com/wp-dyn/content/article/2006/05/10/AR2006051002449.html

Wagner, U. & Machleit, U. (1986). 'Gastarbeiter' in the Federal Republic of Germany: Contact between Germans and migrant populations. In R. Brown & M. Hewstone (Eds.), *Contact and conflict in intergroup encounters* (pp. 59–78). Cambridge, MA: Blackwell.

Walby, S. & Allen, J. (2004) *Domestic violence, sexual assault and stalking: Findings from the British Crime Survey, Home Office Research Study 276.* London: Home Office.

Wang, H. & Amato, P.R. (2000). Predictors of divorce adjustment: Stressors, resources, and definitions. *Journal of Marriage and the Family*, *62*, 655–668.

Warren, P.E. & Walker, I. (1991). Empathy, effectiveness, and donations to charity: Social psychology's contribution. *British Journal of Social Psychology*, *30*, 325–337.

Watt, S.E. & Maio, G.R. (2007). Functions of attitudes toward ethnic groups: Effects of level of abstraction. *Journal of Experimental Social Psychology*, *43*, 441–449.

Webb, T.L. & Sheeran, P. (2008). Mechanisms of implementation intention effects: The role of goal intentions, self-efficacy, and accessibility of plan components. *British Journal of Social Psychology*, *47*, 373–395.

Wegner, D.M. (1994). Ironic processes of mental control. *Psychological Review*, *101*, 34–52.

Weiner, B. (1982). The emotional consequences of causal attributions. In M.S. Clark & S.T. Fiske (Eds.), *Affect and cognition: The 17th Annual Carnegie Symposium on Cognition* (pp. 185–210). Hillsdale, NJ: Erlbaum.

Weiner, B. (1986). 'Spontaneous' causal thinking. *Psychological Bulletin*, *97*, 74–84.

Weisfeld, G.E., Bloch, S.A., & Ivers, J.W. (1984). Possible determinants of social dominance among adolescent girls. *Journal of Genetic Psychology*, *144*, 115–129.

Whitty, M.T. (2008). Revealing the 'real' me, searching for the 'actual' you: Presentation of self on an internet dating site. *Computers in Human Behavior*, *24*, 1707–1723.

Wieselquist, J., Rusbult, C.E., Foster, C.A., & Agnew, C.R. (1999). Commitment, pro-relationship behavior, and trust in close relationships. *Journal of Personality and Social Psychology*, *77*, 942–966.

Wilder, D.A. (1984). Intergroup contact: The typical member and the exception to the rule. *Journal of Experimental Social Psychology*, *20*, 177–194.

Williams, J.G. & Solano, C.H. (1983). The social reality of feeling lonely: Friendship and reciprocation. *Personality and Social Psychology Bulletin*, *9*, 237–242.

Williams, K.D. (2001). *Ostracism: The power of silence*. New York: Guilford Press.

Williams, K.D. (2007). Ostracism: The kiss of social death. *Social and Personality Psychology Compass*, *1*, 236–247.

Williams, K.D. & Jarvis, B. (2006). Cyberball: A program for use in research on interpersonal ostracism and acceptance. *Behavior Research Methods, Instruments, and Computers*, *38*, 174–180.

Wilson, T.D., Lindsey, S., & Schooler, T.Y. (2000). A model of dual attitudes. *Psychological Review*, *107*, 101–126.

Windschild, P.D. & Wells, G.L. (1997). Behavioural consensus information affects people's inferences about population traits. *Personality and Social Psychology Bulletin*, *23*, 148–156.

Wood, J.V., Heimpel, S.A., & Michela, J.L. (2003). Savoring versus dampening: Self-esteem differences in regulating positive affect. *Journal of Personality and Social Psychology*, *85*, 566–580.

Wood, W. (2000). Attitude change: Persuasion and social influence. *Annual Review of Psychology*, *51*, 539–570.

Worchel, S., Axsom, D., Ferris, S., Samaha, C., & Schweitzer, S. (1978). Determinants of the effect of intergroup cooperation on intergroup attraction. *Journal of Conflict Resolution*, *22*, 429–439.

Wright, P.H. (1982). Men's friendships, women's friendships and the alleged inferiority of the latter. *Sex Roles*, *8*, 1–20

Wright, S.C., Aron, A., McLaughlin-Volpe, T., & Ropp, S.A. (1997). The extended contact effect: Knowledge of cross-group friendships and prejudice. *Journal of Personality and Social Psychology*, *73*, 73–90.

Wyer, R.S. Jr. (1976). An investigation of relations among the probability estimates. *Organisational Behaviour and Human Performance*, *15*, 1–18.

Wyer, R.S. (1988). Social memory and social judgment. In P.R. Solomon et al. (Eds.), *Perspectives on memory research*. New York: Springer-Verlag.

Wyer, R.S. Jr. & Frey, D. (1983). The effects of feedback about self and others on the recall and judgments of feedback-relevant information. *Journal of Experimental Social Psychology*, *19*, 540–559.

Yamada, A.M. & Singelis, T.M. (1999). Biculturalism and self-construal. *International Journal of Intercultural Relations*, *23*, 697–709.

Yammarino, F.J. & Bass, B.M. (1990) Transformational leadership and multiple levels of analysis. *Human Relations*, *43*, 975–995.

Yukl, G. (2002). *Leadership in organizations* (5th ed.). Upper Saddle River, NJ: Prentice Hall.

Zajonc, R.B. (1965). Social facilitation. *Science*, *149*, 269–274.

Zajonc, R.B. (1968). Attitudinal effects of mere exposure. *Journal of Personality and Social Psychology*, *9*, 1–27.

Zajonc, R.B. (1993). Brain temperature and subjective emotional experience. In M. Lewis & J.M. Haviland (Eds.), *Handbook of emotions* (pp. 209–220). New York: Guilford Press.

Zajonc, R.B., Murphy, S.T., & Inglehart, M. (1989). Feeling and facial efference: Implications of the vascular theory of emotion. *Psychological Review*, *96*, 395–416.

Zanna, M.P., Kiesler, C.A., & Pilkonis, P.A. (1970). Positive and negative attitudinal affect established by classical conditioning. *Journal of Personality and Social Psychology*, *14*, 321–328.

Zillman, D. (1984). *Connections between sex and aggression.* Hillsdale, NJ: Erlbaum.

Zillman, D. & Bryant, J. (1984). Effects of massive exposure to pornography. In N.M. Malamuth and E. Donnerstein (Eds.), *Pornography and sexual aggression* (pp. 115–138). New York: Academic Press.

Author Index

Indexed by Caroline Eley.

Subject Index

Indexed by Caroline Eley.